Critical Approaches to Comics

Critical Approaches to Comics offers students a deeper understanding of the artistic and cultural significance of comic books and graphic novels by introducing key theories and critical methods for analyzing comics. Each chapter explains and then demonstrates a critical method or approach, which students can then apply to interrogate and critique the meanings and forms of comic books, graphic novels, and other sequential art. Contributors introduce a wide range of critical perspectives on comics, including fandom, genre, intertextuality, adaptation, gender, narrative, formalism, visual culture, and much more.

As the first comprehensive introduction to critical methods for studying comics, *Critical Approaches to Comics* is the ideal textbook for a variety of courses in comics studies.

Contributors include:

David Beronä; Jeffrey A. Brown, Stanford W. Carpenter, Peter Coogan, Randy Duncan, Mel Gibson, Ian Gordon, Pascal Lefèvre, Jeff McLaughlin, Ana Merino, Andrei Molotiu, Christopher Murray, Amy Kiste Nyberg, Brad J. Ricca, Leonard Rifas, Mark Rogers, Marc Singer, Matthew J. Smith, Jennifer K. Stuller, Brian Swafford, Joseph Witek.

Featuring an introduction by Henry Jenkins.

Matthew J. Smith is Professor of Communication at Wittenberg University. He regularly teaches "Graphic Storytelling" and leads an annual field study at Comic-Con International. Recent books include *The Power of Comics: History, Form and Culture* (with Randy Duncan) and *Online Communication: Linking Technology, Culture, and Identity* (with Andrew F. Wood).

Randy Duncan is Professor of Communication at Henderson State University. He is co-author of *The Power of Comics: History, Form and Culture* (with Matthew J. Smith). Duncan is a co-founder (with Peter Coogan) of the Comics Arts Conference, and serves on the Editorial Board of the *International Journal of Comic Art* and the Board of Directors of the Institute for Comics Studies.

Critical Approaches to Comics

Theories and Methods

Edited by Matthew J. Smith and Randy Duncan

Routledge
Taylor & Francis Group

NEW YORK AND LONDON

First published 2012
by Routledge
711 Third Avenue, New York, NY 10017

Simultaneously published in the UK
by Routledge
2 Park Square, Milton Park, Abingdon, Oxon OX14 4RN

Routledge is an imprint of the Taylor & Francis Group, an informa business

Library of Congress Cataloging in Publication Data
Critical approaches to comics : theories and methods / edited by Matthew J. Smith and Randy Duncan.
  p. cm.
  Includes bibliographical references and index.
  1. Comic books, strips, etc.–History and criticism. I. Smith, Matthew J., 1971– II. Duncan, Randy, 1958–
PN6710.C75 2011
741.59–dc23
2011034441

ISBN: 978-0-415-88554-6 (hbk)
ISBN: 978-0-415-88555-3 (pbk)
ISBN: 978-0-203-83945-4 (ebk)

Typeset in Minion
by Wearset Ltd, Boldon, Tyne and Wear

To our contributors
for their willingness
to share their
insight and passion
for comics.

CONTENTS

FIGURES

PREFACE

This is going to be more fun than you think. Engaging in critical analysis is a lot like an episode of *Law and Order*. First, you must be a detective, examining the evidence of how the object of your study was created, how it communicates, or how it functions within the culture. Then you are a lawyer, using the evidence you have gathered to argue for a particular interpretation of the nature, function, or value of the artifact or phenomenon you have studied. There probably will not be any gunfire or fist fights, but conducting a critical analysis and presenting your case can still be challenging and thrilling.

Critical Approaches to Comics: Theories and Methods explores how comics scholarship is produced. With increasing attention devoted to comic books and graphic novels from scholars in all manner of academic disciplines, an overview of the tools through which conference presentations, journal articles, and scholarly books are being generated seems like a timely contribution to the conversation about the development of Comics Studies. This edited volume offers readers an introduction to how each of several methods of comics criticism is performed, complemented by a brief essay practicing the method on a significant comic book, graphic novel, person, place, or phenomenon. The contributors to this volume have been selected for their expertise with these methods and record of previous scholarship.

The entries in this text are written with the proverbial student of the medium in mind, so it is accessible for undergraduates enrolled in a college course on comics or methodology, but also useful as a resource for scholars already in the field. We've attempted to include a range of methods that are widely representative—but by no means exhaustive—of the possible ways to study comics and the culture stemming from them. This means considering methods that examine the formal techniques of comics storytelling, the content of their messages, the industrial practices that produce them, the social contexts that inform their meanings, and the ways audiences receive, interpret, and respond to them. Astute readers will note that three chapters build on ethnographic approaches. Though each of these is related, each is also very different in terms of its approach and application, and we include all three as testimony for just how rich variations on a single methodological tool can be, especially when adapted by scholars from different backgrounds and with diverse objectives.

Each chapter provides readers with the tools they need to develop a deeper understanding of the communicative power and cultural significance of comic books and graphic novels by applying a perspective or critical method towards analyzing the comics they find intriguing. Of course, methodology books of this kind are already commonplace in the analogous fields of Literary, Film, and even Television Studies. We believe it is time for Comics Studies to follow suit. The purpose of each chapter is to explain and demonstrate the application of a method or approach that students will be able to follow in their own critical analysis of a comic book or graphic novel. We asked each contributor to provide some of the assumptions that underlie their perspective, the process to follow in applying the critical method, and a sample analysis that demonstrates the application of the method. Beyond that, we let each chapter take its own shape.

When you conduct your own critical analysis it is likely to take a shape unlike any of the sample analyses in the chapters that follow. Each combination of critic, object of study, and methodology produces a unique result. The strength of your work will lie not in getting "the right answer," but in how well you argue for your interpretation of the data. So conduct your investigation and marshal your evidence to make your best case. Chung CHUNG.

Program Change
April 1, 2015

9:00 – 10:15 AM: Panel Session Four
4A: The Politics of Pop Comics
Moderator: Brannon Costello, Louisiana State University
Location: Carolina Room A

- **It Takes a Superhero: Luke Cage and the Stigma of Black Criminality,** Tracy L. Bealer, Borough of Manhattan Community College
- **Flags of Our Bastards:** *Southern Bastards* **and the Race Politics of the Weird South,** Joshua Plencner, Drexel University
- **Shades of Narrative Subjectivity,** Rachel Graf, University of Washington

10:15 – 10:25AM: Break

Post-Doc : independent short term commitment

Expect to teach something else, smuggle comics in

Academic Paradigm changing

Read the language of job postings

legibility — termal notes

April 14, 2016
Program Change

1:45 – 3:10 PM: Concurrent Panel Session Two

2A: Comics Form, Comics History
Moderator: David Allan Duncan, Savannah College of Art and Design
Location: Carolina Room A

- **Comics and Objecthood: The Matter of Comics of David Mazzucchelli's *Asterios Polyp*,** William Orchard, Queens College/CUNY

- **Honoré Daumier: Caricature and the Conception/Reception of "Fine Art,"** Jasmin W. Cyril, Benedict College

2B: Superheroes Across the Globe
Moderator: Brian Cremins, Harper College
Location: Carolina Room B

- **"The Stereotype is a Fact of Life": Race, Iconography, and Stereotypes in American Comics,** Jeremy Carnes, University of Wisconsin – Milwaukee

- **Fighting in the Streets, Fighting for Place: Superheroes in Yang and Liew's *The Shadow Hero* and Okupe's *E.X.O.*** Matthew L. Miller, University of South Carolina – Aiken

VanDore

ACKNOWLEDGMENTS

The authors wish to thank the editorial team at Taylor and Francis for their enthusiasm in bringing this project to fruition, especially Linda Bathgate, Matt Byrnie, Carolann Madden, and Erica Wetter. Matt would like to thank his wife, Susan, and his sons, Trevor and Kent, for their continued support. He would also like to thank his colleagues at Wittenberg University for their help, most especially that of his academic assistant, Laura Harrison. Randy would like to thank his colleagues and friends at Henderson State University (especially Michael Taylor, Lea-Ann Alexander, and Tommy Cash) for providing support, encouragement, and the occasional much-needed diversion from work. He would also like to thank the students in the HSU Comics Arts Club for reminding him that comic books are not merely artifacts to analyze, but sources of wonder and delight.

CONTRIBUTORS

David A. Beronä is a woodcut novel and wordless comics historian, author of *Wordless Books: The Original Graphic Novels* (Abrams, 2008) and a 2009 Harvey Awards nominee. He is the dean of the Library and Academic Support Services at Plymouth State University, New Hampshire, and a member of the visiting faculty at the Center for Cartoon Studies.

Jeffrey A. Brown is a professor of Popular Culture at Bowling Green State University. He is the author of two books, *Black Superheroes: Milestone Comics and Their Fans* (2001) and *Dangerous Curves: Gender, Fetishism and the Modern Action Heroine* (2011) (both with the University Press of Mississippi), as well as numerous academic articles about gender, ethnicity, and sexuality in contemporary media and culture.

Stanford W. Carpenter is a cultural anthropologist and assistant professor in the Department of Critical and Visual Studies at the School of the Art Institute of Chicago. He uses ethnographic research among artists and media-makers for scholarly manuscripts and arts-based projects. He is currently finishing a book for Duke University Press on identity in comic books from the perspective of comic book creators.

Peter Coogan is director of the Institute for Comics Studies and teaches at Washington University in St. Louis and Webster University. He is the co-editor of *What Is a Superhero?* (Oxford University Press, 2011) and co-founder of the Comics Arts Conference.

Randy Duncan is a professor of communication at Henderson State University. He is co-author of *The Power of Comics: History, Form and Culture* (Continuum, 2009) and co-founder of the Comics Arts Conference. Duncan serves on the boards of the *International Journal of Comic Art* and the Institute for Comics Studies.

Mel Gibson is a senior lecturer at Northumbria University, UK, and is a National Teaching Fellow and winner of the Inge Award for Comics Scholarship. She has encouraged the growth of Comics Studies in Britain through her research on audiences and her work with libraries, schools, universities, and other organizations. Her website (www.dr-mel-comics.co.uk) gives more information.

Ian Gordon is a professor of History and American Studies at the National University of Singapore. He is the author of *Comic Strips and Consumer Culture* (Smithsonian Institution Press, 1998, 2002) and co-editor of *Comics & Ideology* (Lang, 2001) and *Film and Comic Books* (University Press of Mississippi, 2007).

Henry Jenkins is the provost's professor of Communication, Journalism and Cinematic Art at the University of Southern California and the former co-director of the Comparative Media Studies Program at MIT. His 13 published books include *Convergence Culture: Where Old and New Media Collide* (New York University Press, 2006), *Fans, Bloggers, and Gamers: Exploring Participatory Culture* (New York University Press, 2006), and the forthcoming *Spreadable Media: Tracing Value in a Networked Culture*.

Pascal Lefèvre teaches at two Belgian Schools of Art (Sint-Lukas Brussels and MAD-Faculty) and is an affiliated researcher at K.U. Leuven. For a list of his publications and papers, see http://sites.google.com/site/lefevrepascal.

Jeff McLaughlin is an associate professor of Philosophy at Thompson Rivers University. He is editor of *Comics as Philosophy* and *Conversations: Stan Lee* (University Press of Mississippi 2005 and 2007, respectively), as well as *An Introduction to Philosophy in Black and White and Color* (Prentice Hall, 2011).

Ana Merino is an associate professor of Spanish Creative Writing and Cultural Studies at the University of Iowa. She has published a book on Hispanic comics and a monograph on Chris Ware. She serves on the Board of Directors for the Center for Cartoon Studies and is a member of the executive committee of International Comic Art Forum.

Andrei Molotiu teaches in the Department of History of Art at Indiana University, Bloomington. He is the author of *Fragonard's Allegories of Love* (J. Paul Getty Museum, 2007), *Abstract Comics: The Anthology* (Fantagraphics Books, 2009), and *Nautilus* (Fahrenheit, 2009), a collection of his own abstract comics. He is currently writing a monograph on Lee and Ditko's *Amazing Spider-Man*.

Christopher Murray lectures at the University of Dundee, Scotland. He organizes two annual conferences, the Scottish Word and Image Group conference and Dundee Comics Day. His is author of *Champions of the Oppressed: Superheroes and Propaganda* (Hampton Press, 2011) and is editor of the journal *Studies in Comics*.

Amy Kiste Nyberg, Ph.D., University of Wisconsin-Madison, is an associate professor of media studies at Seton Hall University. Her book, *Seal of Approval: The History of the Comics Code* (University Press of Mississippi, 1998), is a study of comic book censorship. She has also written many book chapters and articles on comics.

Brad J. Ricca is a SAGES Fellow at Case Western Reserve University. He is the author of the upcoming *Super Boys: Jerry Siegel, Joe Shuster, and the Creation of Superman* (St. Martin's Press) and was the winner of the St. Lawrence Books Award in 2009.

Leonard Rifas teaches about comics at Seattle Central Community College and the University of Washington, Bothell. He founded EduComics, an educational comic book company, in 1976.

Mark Rogers is a professor of Communication and chair of the Division of Humanities at Walsh University. His previous work on political economy has appeared in the *International Journal of Comic Art* and in book chapters about *The X-Files*, *The Sopranos* and other television programs.

Marc Singer is an assistant professor of English at Howard University in Washington, D.C. He is the co-editor, with Nels Pearson, of *Detective Fiction in a Postcolonial and Transnational World* (Ashgate, 2009) and the author of a monograph on Grant Morrison, forthcoming from the University Press of Mississippi.

Matthew J. Smith is a professor of Communication at Wittenberg University. He is co-author of *The Power of Comics: History, Form and Culture* (Continuum, 2009) and former president of the Ohio Communication Association. In 2009 Wittenberg's Alumni Association recognized him with its Distinguished Teaching Award.

Jennifer K. Stuller is a professional writer, critic, scholar, and pop culture historian, with a special interest in gender, sexuality, and diversity. She authored *Ink-Stained Amazons and Cinematic Warriors: Superwomen in Modern Mythology* (I.B. Tauris, 2010) and is a charter associate member of the Whedon Studies Association.

Brian Swafford is the interim director of Forensics and visiting professor at Boise State University. His research interests center around fan cultures, particularly sports and comics fans. He is concerned with the ways fans form their communities and how rituals and traditions are enacted and maintained within the fan culture.

Joseph Witek is professor of English and Kathleen A. Johnson chair in Humanities at Stetson University. He is the author of *Comic Books as History* (University Press of Mississippi, 1989), editor of the interview collection *Art Spiegelman: Conversations*, and has published a number of articles on comics in journals and edited collections.

INTRODUCTION

Should We Discipline the Reading of Comics?

Henry Jenkins

Even as a child, I knew that reading comics demonstrated a thorough lack of discipline—it was something I did in the summer or at home, sick in bed. In a world before specialized comics shops pulled (reserved) your comics for you, my generation would grab whatever was available to us on the spin-racks at the local drug store—there was not yet a canon (fan or academic) to tell us what we were supposed to read. We read for no purpose other than pleasure—there was no method to tell us how we were supposed to read. Indeed, many adults were there to remind us what a monumental waste of time all of this was—there was nothing like Publish or Perish pushing us to read more comics. We read in secret—under the covers by flashlight, hidden in a textbook in class—with the knowledge that there was something vaguely oppositional about our practices. You didn't stand up in front of a classroom and do a book report on what you'd read, let alone frame a scholarly lecture or essay.

Or at least this is the myth of what it meant to read comics as it has been constructed nostalgically by several generations of fans-turned-critics and intellectuals. Of course, like all of the other aging "boy wonders" constructing that mythical golden age, I should know because I was there.

Given this collective history, why should we discipline the reading of comics?

The book you hold in your hands is arguing for—and performing the work of—creating a discipline called Comics Studies. The authors here each hold forth for their favorite methodology, demonstrating approaches that have emerged from a range of existing disciplines (Art History, Literature, Media and Cultural Studies, Gender and Ethnic Studies, Sociology, Anthropology, Economics, Philosophy) and that are being mobilized to shed some light on what are variously called comics or comix, *Bande Dessinée*, sequential art, or graphic storytelling.

There are several ways to read these chapters. Each acts as an example of Comics Studies in the microcosm (representing a somewhat different—and not necessarily compatible—conception of what the academic study of comics might look like) and each offers a discrete contribution to a larger whole (a broader field which somehow includes all of these approaches). The first represents where we have been: studying comics in isolation, across many different conferences and journals, within larger and more traditional disciplines. The second represents the direction the editors and contributors think we should be going—toward a common ground, a shared space which supports the study of comics—through any means necessary.

Animating this collection is the desire for a place where comics can be taken seriously, on their own terms, read in relation to their own traditions, understood through their own vocabularies, and engaged with by people who already know how comics are produced and consumed. We don't want to have to continuously explain to our colleagues (let alone our parents) what it is we study and why. We want a homeland where comics geeks of all disciplines can come together—perhaps a return to the treehouse where we used to talk about the latest comics with our buddies, or perhaps something which is one part local comics shop and one part university bookstore, where our conversations can go up a notch from the usual debate about whether the Hulk can beat up the Thing. We look over at our colleagues in other fields and, like the patrons in *When Harry Met Sally*, we want what they are having.

COMICS STUDIES: AN ALTERNATIVE HISTORY

Of course, the sad reality is that we could have had something called Comics Studies at many moments in the past. After all, comics have a history at least as long as cinema and we've had decades of academic film studies. In each case, it would have looked different from the contemporary academic field of Comics Studies imagined by this book. For a moment, let's engage in the old fan practice of constructing alternative histories.

Imagine what Comics Studies might have looked like if it had emerged from the writings of Gilbert Seldes in the 1920s and 1930s.[1] Seldes, a leading intellectual, was one of the first people to write passionately, knowingly, and critically about what his contemporaries would have called "the funny pages."[2] A field established by Seldes would have been deeply concerned with aesthetic and cultural issues. Seldes read comics in relation to a larger category of the "lively arts," which included jazz, slapstick film comedy, the Broadway musical, the night club and revue performance, and the comic newspaper column. Seldes wanted to understand what gave comics and the other lively arts their energy, which he connected to the American national character and the urban experience, but not their formal structures. Seldes was not interested in systematic theories or close readings. The core participants in this field would have been his fellow men and women of letters who published their ideas in popular and small press magazines. Given when Seldes was writing, his version of Comics Studies would have included the comic strip but not the comic book (which did not yet exist in the American context). Seldes had no fear of reading *Krazy Kat* against Picasso: His version of Comics Studies would have been conscious of aesthetic hierarchies but not constrained by them. Unlike some contemporary academics, Seldes could embrace comics' pulp roots without feeling the need to turn them into middlebrow literature.

Or let's imagine what would have happened if Comics Studies had taken root in the 1950s, under the leadership of Frederic Wertham.[3] Unlike Seldes, Wertham has an academic pedigree—in psychology and the social sciences. Far from a "lively art," comics (and their influence on American youth) for Wertham were a social problem which urgently needed to be investigated. Wertham's methodologies were surprisingly diverse: he is best known for his "media effects" research into how reading superhero and crime comics influenced his patients, though later a chastened Wertham investigated the fanzine culture, including the emergence of underground comics. Wertham was also involved, though, with symbolic and ideological analysis, trying to understand how the superhero promoted a fascist worldview or how representations of "Bruce and Dick" (a.k.a. Batman and Robin) might encode traces of homosexuality. Wertham was also deeply interested in the relations between texts and images and how our minds processed this "subliterate" form of cultural expression. Wertham's version of Comics Studies would have embraced the concept of the public intellectual. For him, scholarship was not designed to remain within an academic enclosure, but rather to be deployed in shaping public policy and popular opinion. The Wertham version of Comics Studies might look like the field of Communication Studies, which begin in part in response to concerns about propaganda in World War II and advertising in the post-war era, but gradually expanded its methodologies and perspectives to include many other ways of thinking about the communication process.

The comics industry brought forth several academics in defense of their medium, including Josette Frank and Lauretta Bender, but none of them had the impact that Wetham had on the debate.[4] Instead, the industry received support from fans and journalists, best represented by Robert Warshow or Jules Feiffer, often hearkening back to the Seldes legacy.[5]

Let's imagine two other incarnations of Comics Studies which emerged in the 1980s and 1990s, both shaped by the work of expert practitioners, but motivated by somewhat different goals. The first was marked by the 1993 publication of Scott McCloud's *Understanding Comics*,[6] though it was prefigured by Will Eisner's 1985 *Comics and Sequential Art*.[7] Much like Sergei Eisenstein or Dziga Vertov in the history of film theory, McCloud and Eisner represent working artists who sought generalizable insights from their own experiments within the medium. McCloud was trying to distinguish comics as a medium, capable of telling more stories, from its domination by the superhero genre. In doing so, McCloud expanded the historic and cultural context for reading comics, incorporating examples from Asian, European, and American independent and underground traditions, and linking comics to earlier expressive forms, such as Aztec codices and medieval tapestries. McCloud's approach is unabashedly formalist: His key concerns are with the work of the gutter, the construction of time and space, the deployment of expressive lines and color, principles of juxtaposition, and the range between realistic and iconographic modes of representation. McCloud translated his theory back into practice—producing a comic about comics. McCloud's subsequent books[8] expanded his scope to talk more about the technology and economics of comics production. We might see the Center for Cartoon Studies as a logical next development from the model McCloud offered—a place where comics get studied critically in the context of learning to write, draw, and publish new kinds of comics, and where the teachers are veteran comics creators.

During this same period, Art Spiegelman offered a somewhat different picture of what Comics Studies might look like. Spiegelman was busy making the case for why comics deserved artistic and literary respectability, and in the process, often found himself developing an alternative history of the medium, trying to explain the emergence of experimental and independent comics. Spiegelman's *Raw* magazine positioned contemporary comics alongside work by earlier iconoclasts such as Basil Wolverton; he gave lectures and wrote essays on Jack Cole's *Plastic Man*,[9] Tijuana bibles,[10] and the war comics of Harvey Kurtzman.[11] More recently, *In the Shadow of No Towers*,[12] his own graphic meditations on 9/11, also reprinted early twentieth-century comics by artists like Winsor McCay and George Herriman, which inspired him. Spiegelman's Comics Studies is concerned with the project of canon-formation, of making an aesthetic case for the medium through showing how it has been hospitable to a larger tradition of creative experimentation and innovation, how it has been more diverse than previously imagined, and how it has often met the standards imposed on other works accepted into museums or university curriculum. Spiegelman's version is closely linked to the editorial practices of *Comics Journal* and the publication strategies of Fantagraphics or Drawn and Quarterly, including the recent rise of republication of classic comics, such as Spiegelman's own *The Toon Treasury of Classic Children's Comics* (edited with his wife and partner Françoise Mouly).[13] Spiegelman's Comics Studies is one where some comics deserve serious consideration and most do not.

MAPPING A FIELD WHICH DOESN'T YET EXIST

The kinds of Comics Studies modeled in this book build upon (in some cases) but also diverge from these earlier versions of what such a field might have looked like—to no small degree, because the impulses shaping this collection are thoroughly academic—promoting scholarship and supporting teaching—albeit mixed with a healthy degree of fan interest. Most of the writers, after all, were fans first who have sought ways to integrate what they love into their scholarship, though some, we might imagine, are also academics whose other intellectual interests led them to comics research. Television Studies has struggled with these same tensions, and some have complained that the tendency of academics to write about programs of which they are fans have left gaping holes in the field with major programming and programming strategies going unexamined because they are not the kinds of series academics love to watch.[14]

Each of these versions of Comics Studies, then, implicitly or explicitly addresses a series of interrelated questions about the nature of the field. Who participates in the activity of Comics Studies (intellectuals, academics, artists, fans, reformers)? What questions (aesthetic, cultural, ideological, formal, historical) get asked and through what methods do they get answered? What audiences (fans, the general public, would-be artists, students) get addressed and through what channels (popular periodicals, comic books, academic journals, blogs)? We can imagine the McCloud version, say, would raise the question of whether one must create comics in order to critique them, much as Game Studies argues one must play games in order to study them. An academic field modeled on Art History or Film Studies would see such issues as beside the point, since the focus would be on interpretation and evaluation rather than production, on aesthetics rather than poetics.

How might an academic Comics Studies relate to other (sometimes militantly), nonacademic versions? For example, comics fans have constructed their own canon, their own expertise, their own critical vocabulary, their own benchmarks for close reading practices, which have as much to do with preserving continuity as with tracing cultural history or mapping aesthetic norms. Academic conferences on comics can become battlegrounds between different generations of comics scholars with different assumptions about how little or how much respect to pay to the fan tradition. Young Turks spouting credentializing theory stand alongside aging fan-boys mapping the oral culture of the comics industry and collectors speaking with a mix of nostalgia and curatorial sophistication. These very different branches of research need to stop rolling their eyes and snickering behind each other's backs. They need to learn to talk to and with each other and the first step may be teasing out the very different models of Comics Studies which shape their work. We need to proceed carefully since many now feel that academic Film Studies may have gained acceptance within the academy by separating scholars from other groups (artists, cineastes, journalists, archivists) who similarly studied and wrote about their medium.

These competing visions for Comics Studies might be illustrated by two recent collections. Ben Schwartz's *The Best American Comics Criticism*,[15] published by Fantagraphics, brought together the Seldes and Spiegelman clans, collecting writing about comics from journalists (Douglas Wolk), men and women of letters (John Updike, Jonathan Franzen), the fan intelligentsia (Donald Phelps, Jeet Heer, Robert C. Harvey, and Gary Groth) and comics creators (Seth, Chris Ware, Marjane Satrapi), but including no academics. By contrast, Jeet Heer and Kent Worcester's *A Comic Studies Reader*,[16] published by the University Press of Mississippi, includes mostly academic contributors from the United States, Europe, and Latin America. The Schwartz book focused primarily on pieces devoted to specific artists or works; the Heer and Worcester book on larger theoretical issues impacting the general study of comics. Both have titles that are more inclusive than the ground they ultimately cover.

Make no mistake about it, a discipline disciplines. Disciplines define borders and set priorities. Disciplines decide what counts and on what terms. These decisions are, to be sure, made collectively and they evolve over time, but the starting premises for a field matters. Disciplines are defined as much by what they exclude as they are by what they include (and that consists of methods, works, theories, and people). So, the decisions we make right now—as basic as which methods to represent in a book like this one—matter because they represent the road map for a field that is still trying to grab its turf, define its boundaries, and find its way.

A key question is how insular or porous we see the field of Comics Studies becoming. Will Comics Studies be an exclusively academic discipline, a meeting point for all of those intellectually curious about comics, or something in between? We might also ask which comics matter in this new Comics Studies and on what basis they matter. Is Comics Studies to be modeled on Art History or Literature, which have tended to embrace exemplary works, often masterpieces, while excluding much of what is produced? Is Comics Studies to be modeled upon Cultural or Media Studies where there is a desire to be more inclusive, to represent marginalized perspectives but also to reappraise works from the commercial mainstream? The canon of comics represented in McCloud, who sought an inclusive and expansive definition, looks different than the one constructed by Spiegelman, who seeks to define an alternative tradition but has little interest in the commercial mainstream.

The examples chosen to illustrate the methods here are not random or accidental. In theory, each method can speak to a range of comics, but the questions these contributors ask lead them to prioritize the discussion of different kinds of comics. How we justify our objects of study in different disciplines shapes what we can study. The kinds of comics that will be studied in a phase of multidisciplinary research will look different than those which get studied if we somehow coalesce the study of comics into a single, unified discipline.

And so far, I am operating as if we all already agreed upon what comics are—perhaps McCloud's "juxtaposed pictorial and other images in deliberate sequence, intended to convey information and/or to produce an aesthetic response in the viewer."[17] Yet, I remain haunted by those forms of graphic expression McCloud must leave behind—such as single-panel comics like *Family Circus*, to use his example—in order to create this definition. Will whatever definition we embrace be elastic enough to encompass the new forms comics are going to take in the digital era, much as Seldes' focus on the comic strip had to give way to a field now much more preoccupied with the comic book and the graphic novel?

The desire to define a field of research around comics brings with it that whole confounding, frustrating, perplexing history of debates about medium specificity which have charged the early history of research on film, photography, and more recently, computer games. Noel Carroll has offered a series of philosophic challenges to medium-specificity arguments (often really medium-purity arguments) which should be required reading for anyone who wants to promote Comics Studies.[18] Many fields of media studies were stunted by the effort to figure out what their medium did that no other did, to assume that this was what the medium did best, and then to constrain its aesthetics so that what it did uniquely was what it *must* do constantly. These other disciplines are splattered with blood spilled in trying to defend or overturn competing definitions of what constitutes the essence of different media and how we might construct meaningful boundaries between them and other adjacent modes of expression. The emergence of Games Studies was marked by a really nasty debate between the ludologists (who saw games as part of the larger study of play) and the narratologists (who saw games as part of the larger study of storytelling forms).[19] The history of film was shaped by ongoing debates between the formalists and the realists, between montage and mise en scène, between Eisenstein and Bazin.[20]

So, again, I ask, should the reading of comics be disciplined? What is the price we will have to pay in order to become a coherent academic field and are we willing to pay it?

By now, it should be clear that I embrace an approach that is radically undisciplined, taking its tools and vocabulary where it can find them, expansive in its borders to allow the broadest possible range of objects of study, inclusive in who it allows to participate and in the sites where critical conversations occur. Media, I would argue, is best understood through an approach that is broadly comparative, looking across different platforms and modes of representation, rather than seeking exclusivity and specificity. For me, academics have significant roles to play in this process but only if they do not try to monopolize the conversation or try to hold the party captive to their own disciplinary preoccupations; only if they learn to talk in ways that are thoughtful and yet can be understood by a wide array of different publics who share our investments in this truly spectacular mode of expression.

SAMPLE ANALYSIS

Deitch, Kim. *The Search for Smilin' Ed!*. Seattle: Fantagraphics, 2010.

Given this book's focus on testing methods against specific objects of study, I wanted to end this discussion of the field of Comics Studies by focusing on how it might address the conceptual challenges posed by a specific work—Kim Deitch's 2010 graphic novel, *The Search for Smilin' Ed!*[21] To be fair, Deitch's own approach to comics might be described as radically undisciplined. He is highly reflexive about his medium, very interested in exploring and transgressing the boundaries between different kinds of texts, and deeply committed to exploring a broader history of the popular arts. All of this is captured by *Smilin' Ed*'s epigram: "Sifting through the detritus of a lifetime, the search goes on." Not every comic book will raise such a complex set of issues around the borders between media, yet Deitch's work suggests the kind of text which might better be understood through a comparative rather than medium-specific lens, one that rejects cultural hierarchies and embraces intertextuality.

Within his graphic novels, Deitch constructs an image of himself and his wife Pam as consummate collectors who deploy a range of digital technologies and social networks to track down obscure artifacts of America's popular culture heritage, and in the process, often find themselves pulled into strange conspiracies and exotic adventures. Page 17 (Figure I.1) from *Smilin' Ed*, for example, shows Deitch seeking episodes of the actual *Andy's Gang* television series on the collector's market and rummaging through old photographs and microfilms at the Billy Rose Library, searching for clues to the mysteries surrounding the disappearance of a long-forgotten children's television host. Many of Deitch's books lovingly and painstakingly recreate objects from their collection (movie stills, comic book covers, stuffed toys). These are the "stuff dreams are made of," as Deitch titled one of his stories—vehicles of personal obsession and collective memory. Deitch's collector roots link him in instructive ways to other contemporary comics artists, such as Seth,[22] Chris Ware,[23] Harvey Pekar,[24] Bryan Talbot,[25] Ben Katchor,[26] or Dean Motter,[27] each of whom have done stories that speak to their fascination with "detritus" and the residual.[28]

A typical Deitch story, such as *Smilin' Ed*, moves from autobiographical accounts of his own life into fanciful adventures involving time travel and alien visitation, straight from the pages of the grocery store tabloids or, more likely, from the plots of old movie and pulp magazine serials. Across a range of stories, Deitch has created a vast mythology of characters who represent different moments in the history of American popular amusements (from medicine and minstrel shows in the nineteenth century through to contemporary computer games and e-trade sites), embodying the ongoing tension between personal obsession and commercial motives that have shaped each new media form.[29]

Linking the stories together is the figure of Waldo, the big blue anthropomorphic cat who is modeled most clearly after Felix the Cat[30] but standing in for many other cats in the history of animation, not to mention the scatalogical and folkloric associations of cats which the cultural historian Robert Darnton traces in *The Great Cat Massacre*.[31] (Waldo is anatomically correct and often lacks bodily control.) Waldo is often depicted as a mythical, even demonic, figure (the reincarnated spirit of Judas Iscariot inside the body of a blue cartoon cat) who plagues the debauched real-life entertainers whose work he inspired.[32] Page 36 (Figure I.2) from *Smilin' Ed* shows the "real" Waldo responding with pleasure to a variety of "fictional" reconstructions of himself, including a costumed figure who appeared on children's television and advertising in the 1950s. Waldo appears in *Smilin' Ed* alongside a range of other characters from earlier Deitch stories, all of whom take second place to the figures specifically introduced in this book, such as Smilin' Ed, the veteran children's show host and ventriloquist, and his muse/tormentor, Froggy the Gremlin.

Deitch has returned to many of his comic creations again and again, revising them, adding new installments, revising them for different sites of publication, gradually building them up to form the basis of a series of graphic novels, such as *Boulevard of Broken Dreams*,[33] *Shadowland*,[34] *Alias the Cat*,[35] and *The Search for Smilin' Ed!* The first chapter of *Smilin' Ed* was published in Fantagraphic's *Zero Zero* in 1997, before becoming the basis for this graphic novel more than a decade later. If one wanted to trace Deitch's full

Figure I.1 *The Search for Smilin' Ed!* page 17, collected edition Fantagraphics Books, 2010. Copyright 1997–1998 Kim Deitch.

range of writings on collectors culture, one would also have to include a range of prose pieces, including those recently published in *Deitch's Pictorama*,[36] which offers its own unique blend of prose and illustration. *Smilin' Ed*'s focus on early children's television connects it back to the 1989 "Karla in Kommieland,"[37] about what happened when the Army–McCarthy hearings displaced cartoons on afternoon broadcasting, and forward to the 2010 "American Dreamer," a piece on kid-show host Paul Winchell.[38]

Given all of this, it may be impossible to discuss *Smilin' Ed* in any meaningful way within an approach that separates comics off from other media or which adopts too narrow a definition of what constitutes a comic. To understand its publication history, we must examine a range of different sites where comics appear—some self-contained (from underground comics in the 1960s to Fantagraphics today), others part of larger publications (underground and alternative newspapers such as *The LA Reader*, where Deitch published *A Shroud For Waldo*[39] in 1990 and small press magazines such as *McSweeney's*).

Figure I.2 *The Search for Smilin' Ed!* page 36, collected edition Fantagraphics Books, 2010. Copyright 1997–1998 Kim Deitch.

Deitch's biography[40] straddles the histories of American animation (his father, Gene Deitch, was an important cartoonist, best known for his *Tom Terrific* series) and underground comics (Deitch was a regular contributor to the New York-based underground newspaper, *The East Village Other*, starting in 1967). There is a lot we can learn about Deitch by reading his current projects as a continuation of the underground comics (his sexually explicit, politically radical, and off-beat content; his recurring references to drugs, alcohol, and insanity; his tactical deployment of racial stereotypes, and his sometimes intense graphic style all owe something to R. Crumb and his contemporaries). Yet we would also have to acknowledge how deeply he borrows techniques from the 1920s and 1930s cartoons of the Fleischer brothers (including anthropomorphic representations of animals and inanimate objects, a very rubbery anatomy, and "cartoonish" titling and lettering) or how often he builds upon pastiches of earlier styles of drawing, such as the turn-of-the-century comic strip he created for *Alias the Cat.*

Deitch's debts to underground comics and early animation are both visible in the front and back cover art he designed for *Smilin' Ed* (Figures I.3–I.4). Deitch was drawn into comics as a medium through his childhood encounters with the early comic strips of Winsor McCay, though he was also clearly influenced by the dinner-table conversations of his father and his animation studio cronies. And Deitch's work both influenced and was influenced by his romantic involvement with the animator Sally Cruikshank, whose *Quasi at the Quackadero* shows many of the same preoccupations. So, again, minimally, our approach to Deitch would have to address both the medium which influenced his work and the varied corners of media history his work explores.

Deitch is an inheritor of the alternative comics tradition that Spiegelman has been mapping, though he would also have been at home in the "lively arts" tradition that Seldes and his contemporaries constructed. To understand his style, you need to understand experimental comics approaches; to understand his content, you need to be deeply immersed in the history of comics and animation as popular culture. Would our analysis remain a close reading of the graphic novel as a text or would it include oral history with the still-living author and contextual analysis of the industrial factors that shaped his body of work? What would be our goals for this scholarship—to contribute to classroom teaching or to engage in a larger conversation with his fans? And where would we publish it—in an academic journal or in someplace like *Comics Journal* where it would reach many lay readers who might be interested in his work?

A narrowly constituted Comics Studies approach, which studied comics and only comics, would falter at the challenges Deitch poses; his work invites multidisciplinary and transmedia perspectives. If we are going to discipline the reading of comics, I want a discipline diverse and robust enough to be able to do justice to artists like Deitch.

Will we get there? I hope so. Books like this one should help to get the conversation started and everyone reading this book has a potential role to play in determining what kind of field Comics Studies becomes. Let's not repeat the mistakes made by other disciplines studying other pop culture traditions. Let's hold onto what made talking about comics fun in the first place even as we seek admission into the ivy-covered halls. Let's continue to explore the fringes of the medium, including where it starts to get fused into other forms of artistic practice. Let's continue to draw new tools and insights both from related academic fields and from other sectors which share our passion for funny books. And let's get together on Wednesdays when the new comics come into the shops.

Figure I.3 *The Search for Smilin' Ed!* front cover, collected edition Fantagraphics Books, 2010. Copyright 2010 Kim Deitch.

FINALLY COLLECTED IN ONE VOLUME,

Kim Deitch's sprawling whirligig of a yarn "The Search for Smilin'
Ed" chronicles his investigation into the secrets behind the life and
career of a very strange children's show host and his malevolent (in
fact, possibly demonic) sidekick. Aliens turn out to be involved, as
does Abraham Lincoln... and of course Deitch's ever-present protagonist, Waldo the Cat.

The Search for Smilin' Ed also includes a definitive essay on
Deitch's ever-expanding world; a full-color fold-out spotlighting
over 100 denizens of that world; a brand new epilogue, "Consider
the Beaver"; and more. It's the ultimate Deitch-travaganza!

9781606993248   51699

$16.99 USA
FANTAGRAPHICS BOOKS
ISBN: 978-1-60699-324-8

Figure I.4 *The Search for Smilin' Ed!* back cover, collected edition Fantagraphics Books, 2010. Copyright 2010 Kim Deitch.

NOTES

1. Michael G. Kammen, *The Lively Arts: Gilbert Seldes and the Transformation of Cultural Criticism in the United States* (Oxford: Oxford University Press, 1996).
2. Gilbert Seldes, *The Seven Lively Arts* (New York: Sagmore Press, 1957).
3. Bart Beaty, *Frederic Wertham and the Critique of Mass Culture* (Jackson, MS: University Press of Mississippi, 2005).
4. David Hajdu, *The Ten-Cent Plague: The Great Comic-Book Scare and How It Changed America* (New York: Picador, 2009).
5. Jeet Heer and Ken Worcester, eds., *Arguing Comics: Literary Masters on a Popular Medium* (Jackson, MS: University Press of Mississippi, 2004).
6. Scott McCloud, *Understanding Comics: The Invisible Art* (New York: Paradox, 1993).
7. Will Eisner, *Comics and Sequential Art* (Tamarac, FL: Poorhouse Books, 1985).
8. Scott McCloud, *Reinventing Comics: How Imagination and Technology Are Revolutionizing an Art Form* (New York: Harper, 2000).
9. Art Spiegelman, *Jack Cole and Plastic Man: Forms Stretched to Their Limits* (New York: Diane, 2005).
10. Art Spiegelman, "Introductory Essay: Those Dirty Little Comics," in *Tijuana Bibles: Art and Wit in America's Forbidden Funnies, 1930s–1950s,* ed. Bob Adelman (New York: Simon and Schuster, 1997).
11. John Benson, David Kaskov, and Art Spiegelman, "An Examination of 'Master Race,'" in *A Comics Studies Reader,* ed. Jeet Heer and Kent Worcester (Jackson: University Press of Mississippi, 2009).
12. Art Spiegelman, *In the Shadow of the No Towers* (New York: Viking, 2004).
13. Art Spiegelman and Françoise Mouly, *The Toon Treasury of Classic Children's Comics* (New York: Abrams ComicArts, 2009).
14. Henry Jenkins, "Is *Ally McBeal* a Thing of Beauty: An Interview with Greg M. Smith," *Confessions of an Aca-Fan,* February 29, 2008, www.henryjenkins.org/2008/02/an_interview_with_gregory_smit.html.
15. Ben Schwartz, ed., *The Best American Comics Criticism* (Seattle: Fantagraphics, 2010).
16. Jeet Heer and Kent Worcester, ed., *A Comics Studies Reader* (Jackson: University Press of Mississippi, 2009).
17. McCloud, *Understanding Comics,* 20.
18. Noel Carroll, *Theorizing the Moving Image* (Cambridge: University of Cambridge Press, 1996).
19. Noah Wardrip-Fruin and Pat Harrigan, *First Person: New Media as Story, Performance, and Game* (Cambridge, MA: MIT Press, 2006).
20. Peter Lehman, *Defining Cinema* (Piscataway, NJ: Rutgers University Press, 1997).
21. Kim Deitch, *The Search for Smilin' Ed* (Seattle: Fantagraphics, 2010).
22. Seth, *Wimbledon Green: The Greatest Comic Book Collector in the World* (Montreal: Drawn and Quarterly, 2005).
23. Chris Ware, *Jimmy Corrigan: The Smartest Kid on Earth* (New York: Pantheon, 2003).
24. Harvey Pekar, *The Best of American Splendor* (New York: Ballatine, 2005).
25. Brian Talbot, *Grandville* (Milwaukee, OR: Dark Horse, 2009).
26. Ben Katchor, *Cheap Novelties: The Pleasures of Urban Decay* (New York: Penguin, 1991).
27. Dean Motter, *Terminal City* (New York: DC, 1997).
28. Henry Jenkins, "The Tomorrow That Never Was: Retrofuturism in the Comics of Dean Motter," in *Comics and the City: Urban Space in Print, Picture and Sequence,* ed. Jorn Aherns and Arno Meteling (New York: Continuum, 2010).
29. Bill Kartalopoulos, "Auguries of Brilliance: The Kim Deitch Universe," introduction to Kim Deitch, *The Search for Smilin' Ed!* (Seattle: Fantagraphics, 2010).
30. Donald Crafton, *Before Mickey: The Animated Film, 1898–1928* (Chicago: University of Chicago Press, 1983).
31. Robert Darnton, *The Great Cat Massacre and Other Episodes of French Cultural History* (New York: Basic, 1984).
32. Kim Deitch, *A Shroud For Waldo* (Seattle: Fantagraphics, 2002).
33. Kim Deitch, *Boulevard of Broken Dreams* (New York: Pantheon, 2003).
34. Kim Deitch, *Shadowlands* (Seattle: Fantagraphics, 2006).
35. Kim Deitch, *Alias the Cat* (New York: Pantheon, 2007).
36. Kim Deitch, *Deitch's Pictorama* (Seattle: Fantagraphics, 2008).
37. Kim Deitch, "Karla In Kommieland," in *Raw* 2, no. 1, ed. Art Spiegelman and Francoise Mouly (New York: Pantheon, 1990).
38. Kim Deitch, "Mysteries of an American Dreamer," in *San Francisco Panorama,* McSweeney's (2010).
39. Deitch, *A Shroud For Waldo.*
40. Gary Groth, "'It's Gotta Be Real to Me, Somehow': An Interview with Kim Deitch," in *The Best American Comics Criticism,* ed. Ben Schwartz (Seattle: Fantagraphics, 2010).

SELECTED BIBLIOGRAPHY

Beaty, Bart. *Frederic Wertham and the Critique of Mass Culture.* Jackson, MS: University Press of Mississippi, 2005.

Benson, John, David Kaskove, and Art Spiegelman. "An Examination of 'Master Race.'" In *A Comics Studies Reader,* edited by Jeet Heer and Kent Worcester, 288–305. Jackson, MS: University Press of Mississippi, 2009.

Carroll, Noël. *Theorizing the Moving Image.* Cambridge, MA: University of Cambridge Press, 1996.

Crafton, Donald. *Before Mickey: The Animated Film, 1898–1928.* Chicago: University of Chicago Press, 1983.

Darnton, Robert. *The Great Cat Massacre and Other Episodes of French Cultural History.* New York: Basic, 1984.

Deitch, Kim. *Hollywoodland.* Seattle: Fantagraphics, 1988.

Deitch, Kim. *A Shroud For Waldo.* Seattle: Fantagraphics, 2002.

Deitch, Kim. *Boulevard of Broken Dreams.* New York: Pantheon, 2003.

Deitch, Kim. "Karla In Kommieland." In *The Smithsonian Book of Comic-Book Stories: From Crumb to Clowes,* edited by Bob Callahan, 31–39. Washington, DC: Smithsonian Institute, 2004. Originally published in Art Spiegelman and Francoise Mouly, eds. *Raw,* vol. 2, no. 1 (New York, Pantheon, 1990).

Deitch, Kim. *Shadowlands.* Seattle: Fantagraphics, 2006.

Deitch, Kim. *Alias the Cat.* New York: Pantheon, 2007.

Deitch, Kim. *Deitch's Pictorama.* Seattle: Fantagraphics, 2008.

Deitch, Kim. "Mysteries of an American Dreamer." *McSweeney's Issue 33: San Francisco Panorama,* 8. San Francisco: McSweeney's Quarterly Concern, 2009.

Deitch, Kim. *The Search for Smilin' Ed!* Seattle: Fantagraphics, 2010.

Eisner, Will. *Comics and Sequential Art.* Tamarac, FL: Poorhouse Press, 1985.

Groth, Gary. "'It's Gotta Be Real to Me, Somehow': An Interview with Kim Deitch." In *The Best American Comics Criticism,* edited by Ben Schwartz, 320–330. Seattle: Fantagraphics, 2010.

Hajdu, David. *The Ten-Cent Plague: The Great Comic-Book Scare and How It Changed America.* New York: Picador, 2009.

Heer, Jeet and Kent Worcester, eds. *Arguing Comics: Literary Masters on a Popular Medium.* Jackson, MS: University Press of Mississippi, 2004.

Heer, Jeet and Kent Worcester, eds. *A Comics Studies Reader.* Jackson, MS: University Press of Mississippi, 2009.

Jenkins, Henry. "Is *Ally McBeal* a Thing of Beauty? An Interview with Greg M. Smith." *Confessions of an Aca-Fan,* February 29, 2008, www.henryjenkins.org/2008/02/an_interview_with_gregory_smit.html (accessed December 13, 2010).

Jenkins, Henry. "The Tomorrow That Never Was: Retrofuturism in the Comics of Dean Motter." In *Comics and the City: Urban Space in Print, Picture and Sequence,* edited by Jorn Aherns and Arno Meteling, 63–83. New York: Continuum, 2010.

Kammen, Michael G. *The Lively Arts: Gilbert Seldes and the Transformation of Cultural Criticism in the United States.* Oxford: Oxford University Press, 1996.

Kartalopoulos, Bill. "Auguries of Brilliance: The Kim Deitch Universe." In *The Search for Smilin' Ed!,* Kim Deitch, 1–10. Seattle: Fantagraphics, 2010.

Katchor, Ben. *Cheap Novelties: The Pleasures of Urban Decay.* New York: Penguin, 1991.

Lehman, Peter. *Defining Cinema.* Piscataway, NJ: Rutgers University Press, 1997.

McCloud, Scott. *Understanding Comics: The Invisible Art.* Northampton, MA: Kitchen Sink, 1993.

McCloud, Scott. *Reinventing Comics: How Imagination and Technology Are Revolutionizing an Art Form.* New York: Perennial, 2000.

McCloud, Scott. *Making Comics: Storytelling Secrets of Comics, Manga, and Graphic Novels.* New York: HarperPerennial, 2006.

Motter, Dean. *Terminal City.* New York: DC Comics, 1997.

Pekar, Harvey. *The Best of American Splendor.* New York: Ballatine, 2005.

Schwartz, Ben, ed. *The Best American Comics Criticism.* Seattle: Fantagraphics, 2010.

Seldes, Gilbert. *The Seven Lively Arts.* New York: Sagmore Press, 1957.

Seth. *Wimbledon Green: The Greatest Comic Book Collector in the World.* Montreal: Drawn and Quarterly, 2005.

Spiegelman, Art. "Introductory Essay: Those Dirty Little Comics." In *Tijuana Bibles: Art and Wit in America's Forbidden Funnies, 1930s–1950s,* edited by Bob Adelman, 4–10. New York: Simon and Schuster, 1997.

Spiegelman, Art. *In the Shadow of No Towers.* New York: Viking, 2004.

Spiegelman, Art. *Jack Cole and Plastic Man: Forms Stretched to Their Limits.* New York: Diane, 2005.

Spiegelman, Art and François Mouly. *The Toon Treasury of Classic Children's Comics.* New York: Abrams ComicArts, 2009.

Talbot, Brian. *Grandville.* Milwaukee, OR: Dark Horse, 2009.

Wardrip-Fruin, Noah and Pat Harrigan. *First Person: New Media as Story, Performance, and Game.* Cambridge, MA: MIT Press, 2006.

Ware, Chris. *Jimmy Corrigan: The Smartest Kid on Earth.* New York: Pantheon, 2003.

Part I

Form

1

WORDLESS COMICS

The Imaginative Appeal of Peter Kuper's The System

David A. Beronä

In an interview with *Photoplay* magazine in 1927, Mary Pickford, a legendary star of the silent cinema, commented:

> It would have been more logical if silent pictures had grown out of the talkie instead of the other way around. The value of silence in art is its stimulation to the imagination, and the imaginative quality is art's highest appeal.

Technology did not delay the use of text with images in the comic's medium like sound with pictures in the cinema, but the importance of silence in comics and its imaginative appeal can be traced throughout the history of comics. Early examples from the nineteenth century include the silent strips of Adolphe Willette and Theophile-Alexandre Steinlen, where "the lack of words focuses the expressive role of movement which becomes not just farcical, but alternately frenetic and subtly expressive."[1] Early twentieth-century silent strips include the humorous antics of the *Little King* by Otto Soglow and the more sobering strip *Sanmao*, about the squalor of children orphaned following the second Sino-Japanese War, by the Chinese artist Zhang Leping. Graphic novels from this period of time included a distinct form of storytelling evolved from the woodcut, called the "novel in pictures," and later referred to as the woodcut novel, a term used to include the medium of not only woodcuts but wood engravings, linocuts and leadcuts. These wordless books were highly imaginative and realistic stories for adults told in black and white pictures. They were conceived by the Belgian Frans Masereel and the American Lynd Ward and focused largely on social concerns in a growing industrial culture. An example of a contemporary wordless comic with a highly imaginative appeal and similar social themes to the woodcut novel is *The System* (1996), by Peter Kuper.

Up to that time, Kuper's work was published by independent publishers. In addition, Kuper co-founded with Seth Tobocman in 1979 the socially conscious magazine of comics and graphics called *World War 3 Illustrated*, which remains in print today.[2] Lou Stathis, an editor from DC Comics, originally asked Peter Kuper in the mid-1990s to create a work for a new imprint they were launching to reach a mature audience of readers. Kuper had an idea for Stathis that came after a ride on the subway in New York, where Kuper has lived most of his adult life. Seeing all the different people on the subway, he questioned himself about his relationship with these strangers: "Was this trip all we had in common, or might our lives crisscross and later, affect one another in a larger way?"[3] The result was *The System*, originally published by DC Comics under its Vertigo Vérité imprint in a three-issue comic in 1996 and compiled into a graphic novel in 1997.

The setting for this comic was New York, which Kuper has used repeatedly in his work and which he acknowledged as the "muse in my career."[4]

> In a certain way, I didn't have to write to cook up *The System*. Instead, I just took stories I'd read in the newspapers and put them in a pot together. One tablespoon of missing woman, a dash of police corruption, a cup of the bombing of the World Trade Center; all spiced up with some insider trading. Mix in a broth of corporate takeovers and political scandals, then boil together over a high flame for six months with some secret ingredients of my first hand experiences: the woman I saw singing in the subway, the homeless guys I've seen on a daily basis, a crack dealer on my block, and a strip club I once visited.[5]

ARTIFACT SELECTED FOR ANALYSIS

The System is a leading example of the successful flow of action in a lengthy wordless comic and one of the finest examples of overlapping scenes that employs a narrator who is heterodiegetic or "external to the fictional world."[6] This fast-paced comic follows the lives of over 20 people living in New York City over the span of a few months. The characters include three strippers, an interracial couple, a stockbroker, detective, graffiti artist, drug dealer, policeman, homeless old man and his dog, young gay man and his partner, singer in the subway, Indian cab driver, subway operator, terrorist, long-haired skateboarder, evangelist and his son, and a missing woman.

Kuper was clear about his intention with this work: "I decided to tell this tale with no dialogue, and let the images speak for themselves. This eliminated language barriers and forced the reader to interact with the characters and connect the dots."[7] Without dialogue, the images bear a heavier load for the understanding of context and narrative structure. So, how does the reader interact with Kuper's characters in this urban setting? How much of our own social knowledge and stereotypes does Kuper rely on in telling his story? What clues are offered to establish character and narrative?

Many of these diverse characters pass on the streets, sidewalks, bars, subway, hospital, corner newsstand, hotel, and strip club. They are involved in making money, whether legally or illegally, which is displayed in a constant exchange of dollars, whether it is buying a newspaper, sticking a bill in a stripper's g-string, slipping a bill into the hand of a drug dealer or a corrupt policeman, or exchanging virtual currency in an online transaction following insider trading in the stock market. The dollar is one of many visual motifs used in this narrative and is one of the many "dots" that Kuper asks the reader to connect.

While the lives of these characters unfold, two strippers are brutally murdered in the subway. A young African-American male, walking down a sidewalk with his white girlfriend, is killed by a gang of white men. This killing results in a street demonstration that extends to the takeover of a subway car. A drunken subway operator crashes into the stalled car containing the demonstrators, resulting in a catastrophic wreck that kills himself, a stockbroker, and a terrorist. The evangelist's son, who we discover has murdered the strippers, is killed by an Indian cabdriver after being sprayed with mace from another stripper he attempts to kill. The terrorist's radioactive bomb, which was taken from the scene of the subway accident by an old homeless man, is accidentally activated by his dog. This 84-page wordless comic concludes with three disturbing onomatopoeic sounds—"tic tic tic"—displayed in the lower left corner of a solid black page. In the lower right-hand corner of this page is also the words "The End," which has a double meaning. Not only do the words refer to the end of the narrative but, after the bomb detonates, the words suggest the end of many lives.

PROCEDURES

A preliminary reading of this comic provides a simple comprehension of the American economic and cultural system. However, in order to fully assess Kuper's themes, one needs to drill down through this groundwork and draw links to characters and events not only from within the diegesis, but also in the real world. "From the surface or manifestation level of reading, one works through to the deeper narrative level," which Chatman refers to as a process of "reading out."[8]

My reading out of this comic is based on selected critical theories, with special focus on characters and objects, image functions, stereotypes, word images, and line meanings, which are essential elements in any comic, but deserve particular attention in the wordless comic.

UNDERLYING ASSUMPTIONS

Characters and objects, the first of five focused elements in my analysis, play an important role within this diegesis or the "fictional world constructed by the narration."[9] Although this is true in any narrative, without the use of word balloons, other elements are needed to assure the legitimacy of characters and objects. For example, if a suspected killer is easily angered, it is imperative in a textual model like a novel that the writer use adjectives to describe an agitated mood. In comics the text in a word balloon would support the image of the angry killer. In a wordless comic, the use of gestures and facial expressions is an essential mechanism to indicate mood and personal emotions, and so additional importance needs to be placed on body posture and gesture which, Will Eisner observed, in all comics "occupy a position of primacy over text."[10] For example, the corrupt policeman, who is guilty of extortion, uses a hand gesture to imitate the action of a shooting pistol by raising his fist with the index finger and thumb extended. His index finger points at the drug dealer he has just stolen money from and his thumb is then brought down on top of his index finger. This threatening gesture, always performed by the policeman with a smile on his face, suggests the consequences of not "doing business."

The function of images, examined in Duncan and Smith's *The Power of Comics*, is especially important in this narrative. Though sensory diegetic images "which depict the characters, objects, and sensory environment of the world of the story"[11] are predominantly used within the diegesis, like the characters in a subway or a couple in a hospital room, there are within these pages examples of non-sensory diegetic images, which express strong emotion. One example (Figure 1.1) includes a street singer who sings in a subway entrance. The notes of her song are transformed into peaceful birds that glide over a pastoral jungle of flora and fauna. Animals suddenly express alarm when a bulldozer, with a Syco logo, rips open the ground, overturning trees and running over animals. The singer's intense feelings of loss over this environmental disaster function as a non-sensory diegetic image, "which depict specific memories, emotions, or sensations occurring within characters in the world of the story but undetectable by the senses."[12] The singer's emotion is expressed in the transformation of distressed birds back into musical notes and framed inside a jagged image balloon, which extends across the width of the page. The edge of the image balloon, which on closer examination displays burning flames, operates as a hermeneutic image, which is "not part of the world

Figure 1.1 Peter Kuper, *The System*. Copyright 1996 Peter Kuper.

of the story, but instead comment on the story and influence how readers interpret it."[13] This image expresses Kuper's strong personal feelings against deforestation and commercial imperialism.

With the multitude of characters in this comic, Kuper relies on stereotypes to provide a means to anticipate behavior and also challenge these stereotypes. An example of anticipated behavior involves a young man with a red baseball cap who drops coins in the cup of a begging homeless man. The young man, neatly dressed, is next accosted by an evangelist, who points to a red ribbon on the man's coat. The red ribbon is internationally recognized as a symbol of HIV/AIDS activism. The young man buys flowers and visits a man in the hospital. After a tender embrace, we can assume the young man is gay and this man is his partner. Kuper highlights the goodness of this homosexual in a hermeneutic image of the man walking with his bouquet of flowers surrounded in a white circle against a spotted city background.[14] The positive characteristics of sensitivity and neatness are elements of the homosexual stereotype.

Challenging our stereotypes, Kuper presents one of the strippers from the Super Star strip club. She returns home to a loving son after her shift ends, rather than what we might stereotypically infer a stripper does after her shift, like participating in an all-night drug- and alcohol-induced orgy. Kuper portrays heartfelt and tragic events in the lives of his characters to encourage us to question our own prejudices based on a stereotype and take this insight from the pages of his comic into our personal lives. The conclusion supports Kuper's suggestion of looking past the stereotypes to the individual when a dove soars above each good-hearted character like the stripper and her son, the detective, Lil Bro, the long-haired skateboarder, the gay couple, and finally the missing woman.

The next element of analysis is word images, which are a large part of this urban landscape. The device of synecdoche, "using a part of something to represent the whole of the thing,"[15] identifies the city as New York, with recognizable landmarks like Grand Central Station and the Chrysler Building, which in this diegesis is owned by Syco, whose name is also a pun, applicable to the psychopaths and insane behavior associated with this company. New York reflects a cacophony of brand names, advertisements, and news captions. Kuper uses marketing slogans, brand names, graffiti, posters, newspaper headlines, news on television, electronic ticker tapes, and online banking transactions. The use of these word images are essential elements in the plot and provide important clues about characters and events.

One example of word images used in this manner is shown in the legality of products presented at a bodega corner market advertising "Candy" and "Beer," with the implication of childhood dependence on candy and the progression to alcohol. Another example is a poster of a missing woman named Betty Russell, which is an image in the beginning panel and one that surfaces nine times throughout the narrative and is not resolved until the epilogue, which is not conclusive and opens up multiple interpretations.

Finally, an examination of what Scott McCloud calls the "expressive potential"[16] of lines and what Molly Bangs identifies as "emotions and how we see pictures"[17] not only heightens the action but provides additional insight into the characters. Diagonal lines provide a sense of tension in a panel, as with the renegade skateboarder as he races past upset pedestrians on the sidewalk or the eager hands reaching out for a stripper on stage. In another example, the wavy lines in the panels centered on the subway operator indicate his intoxication.

SAMPLE ANALYSIS

Kuper, Peter. *The System.* New York: DC Comics, 1996.

Kuper provides us with an opening panel filled with so many images that are repeated in later pages that it establishes a frame of reference. How important is the opening panel for our understanding of the subtext in this story? From this initial panel, can we assume the amount of attention, whether subtle or blatant, Kuper plans to place on the characters and objects in the remaining panels? How meticulously do we need to read? This analysis will answer these questions by first reading out the opening panel and then identifying details and connections from one scene using my five elements of analysis.

Like a freeze frame in a movie, opening the moment before the cinematic images come to life, Kuper launches the opening panel (Figure 1.2), which contains a blueprint of some important elements for consideration in this diegesis. In the privileged site or "spatial coordinates within the page"[18] a red traffic light in the center of the first panel directs the reader to "stop," and pay special attention to these elements, which contributes to our understanding of the subtext in *The System.*

Reading out this panel we quickly recognize—from the Chrysler Building in the background—a street corner in New York City on a rainy day. Diagonal streaks of rain fall across the panel as puddles rise in the asphalt street. A missing-person poster is hung on a utility pole, showing a picture of a young woman who, upon closer examination, is named Betty Russell. Below this poster is another poster with a blurry face that simply states "Vote." Above, on an electronic marquee, the text "Muir Leads Rex," infers a political election and that Muir and Rex are political rivals. A newsstand occupies a street corner. Directly below the newsstand in the foreground on the opposite corner is a trash

Figure 1.2 Peter Kuper, *The System.* Copyright 1996 Peter Kuper.

can and a fire hydrant placed diagonally between the political poster and marquee. The trash can's visual placement infers that the news is quickly outdated by the time it reaches the newsstand. This observation is in contrast to the news on the marquee, providing an up-to-the-moment delivery of the news. In addition, the trash can, metaphorically, is the place for the loser in the political election and the fire hydrant suggests an upcoming, fiery race.

Walking past the newsstand is a shadowy figure holding an umbrella. On the right-hand side of the panel we can see that corporate logos for Syco and Maxxon—with the "xx" in "Maxxon" linked to Exxon—are identified with specific skyscrapers. Next to these skyscrapers are illuminated signs advertising "girl" and "gir," which provides enough letters to easily decode the word "girls," and the association to a strip club. The close proximity of the corporate buildings and the strip club suggest a male-dominated system of business and pleasure, confirmed later, on the page showing middle-aged businessmen frolicking in the strip club. The emblematic "S," with an association to the bold letter on Superman's suit and the name of the club, Super Star, assumes a certain entitlement for the businessmen to feel like superstars, a term usually attributed to only stars in sports and entertainment. A homeless man and his dog walk directly below these conglomerates and the strip club. The homeless man is hunched over and grasps the front of his coat close to his body to keep himself warm and dry from the falling rain. His slouching figure is in direct contrast to the upright figure at the top of the page, who becomes the leading character in the first series of action that unfolds in the remaining panels on the page. The homeless man is the largest figure in this opening panel, which indicates a character of primary importance. His placement on the lower right edge of the panel indicates the verbal equivalent of living on the edge. Although a manhole and taxi are common objects in New York, their presence in the panel also imbues these objects with importance. From this initial panel, Kuper immediately incites our narrative curiosity with questions. Who is Betty Russell? What importance does this homeless man have in this story? Who is driving the taxi and what is its importance? What role does the political election have in the lives of the characters? As the story unfolds, we discover answers to these questions, and reading out this initial panel provides us with key ingredients for unlocking the numerous characters and events in this comic, which is ultimately "an art of conjunction, of repetition, of linking together."[19]

As the plot unfolds, the importance of these opening objects and characters becomes clear. For example, the newsstand functions not only as a routine activity, like picking up a newspaper, in the characters' lives in this diegesis, but it also serves as an essential source of information for the reader. It provides information on events and outcomes in clearly stated textual terms from newspaper headlines and magazine cover stories displayed on the newsstand shelves. These print headlines provide insight into the political race between the candidates Muir and Rex. As various characters stop and buy a newspaper throughout the story, headlines reveal Muir's sex scandal, his suicide, Rex's landslide win, and questions raised about Muir's suicide and the authenticity of the sex video. Besides this political drama, detailed information is publicized on other events like the subway killings and the merging of Syco and Maxxon into SyMaxx, which is awarded lucrative military contracts by President Rex after he takes office.

Kuper displays the pattern of his comic in the next series of pages, moving from one character to the next, usually in a panel that characters share. Following the opening panel, the stockbroker enters the strip club and in the last panel on the page, he joins other businessmen who are seated around a stripper who has tossed off her top, exposing her breasts to the rowdy crowd. Turning the page, the stripper from the previous panel is now the center of attention and the stockbroker is no longer displayed in the scene. The phallic outstretched arms of the businessmen reach out to the stripper's naked body, with her rump raised high in the air, to take in the bills from businessmen's hands. Her mask promises to keep a fantasy of anonymity alive for the customers. Her wide smile matches the smiles of the businessmen in the audience. In the next panel her expression immediately changes to a tired expression with lowered shoulders; her head in her hands as she steps off stage behind a curtain. We follow this stripper as she leaves the club, picks up a newspaper from the newsstand and walks down to the subway, where she is murdered.

Our need to organize a narrative encourages us to find consistencies. It becomes important to pay particular attention to the panel when overlapping scenes are displayed and we leave one character to follow another. This device not only keeps the visual history of characters alive, but also keeps us intimately connected to the story. When a character resurfaces in the story, we already have information and personal feelings about them from a previous scene. Despite the numerous characters, both primary and secondary, that populate this story, we begin to build knowledge of the characters and events in this unfolding drama, which not only entertains but attests to our innate enjoyment of storytelling.

> Like art, stories can create a place where we can begin to understand or make sense of our world. They circulate beliefs, desires, hopes and dreams and are used to explain ourselves to others and in turn help us understand one another. Stories carry with them the capacity to convey emotions and build community.[20]

One three-page scene that captures all five elements in my analysis—characters and objects, image functions, stereotypes, word images, and line meanings—is a racial murder on Howard Street, which involves an interracial couple being assaulted by a gang of white men.

This scene begins with a personal moment between the graffiti artist and the drug dealer. The artist, Lil Bro, shares his notebook of works with the drug dealer, whose expression of enjoyment suggests a meaningful friendship. The drug dealer looks down at the notebook, and from the notebook we jump to the next panel which is a view of a subway car with graffiti that matches the artwork in Lil Bro's notebook. The words "True Love" are clearly displayed on the outside of the train car under a highlighted window where the interracial couple is seated.

This transition from one set of characters to the next is consistent with Kuper's previous plot transitions. The top panels with Lil Bro and the drug dealer and the bottom panels with the interracial couple display friendship and love through their expressions and the display of the graffiti in the notebook and on the train car. In a three-panel moment-to-moment transition of close-ups, the couple kisses; smile broadly in a gesture of happiness and gaze into each other's eyes; and kiss again, in a convincing expression of "true love." This sequence brings us closer to the couple and we feel part of their intimacy because of the size of the characters within the last panel. The panels are not crowded with other objects or characters. Our focus is solely on the couple.

They step off the train at Howard Street, where another Betty Russell missing-person poster is displayed. The couple walks down the stairs in the train station. A man with a pointed look of disgust gapes at the couple on the stairs. His eyes are sharp with a mouth full of teeth and he appears more animal-like than human in his show of hatred.

The next panel displays the couple walking down the street. The panel gutter cuts the letters of the stores horizontally in half, but the words are easily reconstructed. They pass a liquor store and a store where only the last four letters are partially visible. The letters spell out "ware." This text can be decoded as "Hardware," but could also be interpreted as a warning—"Beware"—anticipating the murderous assault that follows. A group of young white men loiter outside "Tony's Pizza." On a wall next to the pizza shop is a "Reelect Rex" poster and graffiti that spells out the word "BAD," which acts beyond just graffiti and denotes the upcoming assault (a bad event) and infers that the group of white men are evil. The expressions on the white men show anger and revulsion, and in the last panel, the three men walk from the bottom and side gutter into the panel where the couple stand, showing the invasion and entrapment of the couple within the small panel. On the next page, the panels fly off the formal vertical and horizontal placement into diagonal rectangles. A violent struggle ensues in a series of dynamic panels. The black man is punched in the face by a skinhead. He responds by punching his assaulter in the face. The girlfriend is slapped in the face by one of the men. The black man is held by a second man while the skinhead pulls out a knife and cuts his throat. As the black man bleeds profusely on the ground, the three white men race away. The skinhead has a smile of satisfaction on his face as the girlfriend wails and holds her dying boyfriend in her arms. The next panel on the following page shows the stockbroker holding a newspaper called *The Journal*, showing the front-page story, "Racial Murder at Howard Street Sparks Protest."

Use of gestures and facial expressions are readily visible first between Lil Bro and the drug dealer and between the loving interracial couple. Later, there is a marked change in their expressions, during the assault, and in the killer's pointed look of hate after he slashes the black man's throat, and the wide-eyed disbelief of the girlfriend when she realizes her boyfriend has been killed. The sensory diegetic images are familiar to anyone visiting New York, with the subway car and station, the neighborhood liquor store, hardware, and pizza shop. Stereotypes like the interracial couple or the racist gang of white men follow our preconceived ideas, while the tenderness shown by the drug dealer toward Lil Bro is contrary to the generally accepted idea of being unfeeling and ruthless. The use of text in this scene not only identifies places and reads out graffiti and posters, but many words contain hidden meanings that make it possible to project a personal feeling between characters and also to predict events. Line meanings, whether it is the calming horizontal shape of the train with the traveling couple or the tension displayed in the diagonal lines during the assault, visually heighten the mood and drama in the characters and events.

By using these elements of analysis, Kuper's storytelling skills in *The System* can be fully evaluated, especially his remarkable cultural insight. Despite his ominous forecast, Kuper offers us hope in a few characters that live their lives with kindness and compassion or have stepped out of the system and prefer to be "missing," like Betty Russell.

NOTES

1.   David Kunzle, "The Voices of Silence: Willette, Steinlen and the Introduction of the Silent Strip in the Chat Noir, with a German Coda," in *The Language of Comics: Word and Image*, ed. Robin Varnum and Christina T. Gibbons (Jackson, MS: University Press of Mississippi, 2001), 6.

2. An entirely wordless issue of *World War 3 Illustrated* was published in 2009, showing the growing interest in wordless comics by both artists and readers.
3. Peter Kuper, *Speechless* (Marietta, GA: Top Shelf Productions, 2001), 66.
4. Ibid., 24.
5. Ibid., 66.
6. Ann Miller, *Reading BandeDessinée: Critical Approaches to French-language Comic Strip* (Chicago: Intellect Books, 2007), 105.
7. Kuper, *Speechless*, 66.
8. Seymour Chatman, *Story and Discourse: Narrative Structure in Fiction and Film* (Ithaca, NY: Cornell University Press, 1978), 41.
9. Miller, *Reading Bande Dessinée*, 104.
10. Will Eisner, *Comics and Sequential Art* (Tamarac, FL: Poorhouse Press, 1985), 103.
11. Randy Duncan and Matthew J. Smith, *The Power of Comics: History, Form and Culture* (New York: Continuum, 2009), 155.
12. Ibid.
13. Ibid.
14. Kuper's distinct style is vividly demonstrated in *The System*

> My stenciling process is as follows: after I do my pencil drawing on a piece of paper, I photocopy it onto regular photocopy paper, and then I cut the image with an Exacto blade. I then spray the image with regular old spray paint and the paper kind of flutters a little bit. What's produced is a kind of under-spray paint that gives it a little more sort of photographic or slightly realer feel. I then work on that with watercolor and colored pencil and sometimes collage. And maybe it's this process of stenciling that is more "me."
>
> Jarret Lovell, "This Is Not a Comic Book: Jarret Lovell Interviews Graphic Artist Peter Kuper,"
> *Crime Media Culture* 2 (2006): 79.

15. Duncan and Smith, *The Power of Comics*, 158.
16. Scott McCloud, *Understanding Comics: The Invisible Art* (Northampton, MA: Kitchen Sink Press, 1993), 124.
17. Molly Bang, *Picture This: How Pictures Work* (New York: SeaStar Books, 1991), 7.
18. Thierry Gronensteen, *The System of Comics*, trans. Bart Beaty and Nick Nguyen (Jackson, MS: University Press of Mississippi, 2007), 34.
19. Ibid., 22.
20. Andres Peralta, "The Art of Storytelling: The Co-construction of Cultural Knowledge," *Art Education* 63 (2010): 25–30.

SELECTED BIBLIOGRAPHY

Bang, Molly. *Picture This: How Pictures Work*. New York: SeaStar Books, 1991.

Chatman, Seymour. *Story and Discourse: Narrative Structure in Fiction and Film*. Ithaca, NY: Cornell University Press, 1978.

Duncan, Randy and Matthew J. Smith. *The Power of Comics: History, Form and Culture*. New York: Continuum, 2009.

Eisner, Will. *Comics and Sequential Art*. Tamarac, FL: Poorhouse Press, 1985.

Gronensteen, Thierry. *The System of Comics*. Translated by Bart Beaty and Nick Nguyen. Jackson, MS: University Press of Mississippi, 2007.

Kunzle, David. "The Voices of Silence: Willette, Steinlen and the Introduction of the Silent Strip in the Chat Noir, with a German Coda." In *The Language of Comics: Word and Image*, edited by Robin Varnum and Christina T. Gibbons, 3–18. Jackson, MS: University Press of Mississippi, 2001.

Kuper, Peter. *The System*. New York: DC Comics, 1997.

Kuper, Peter. *Speechless*. Marietta, GA: Top Shelf Productions, Inc., 2001.

Lovell, Jarret. "This Is Not a Comic Book: Jarret Lovell Interviews Graphic Artist Peter Kuper," *Crime Media Culture* 2 (2006): 75–83.

McCloud, Scott. *Understanding Comics: The Invisible Art*. Northampton, MA: Kitchen Sink, 1993.

Miller, Ann. *Reading Bande Dessinée: Critical Approaches to French-language Comic Strip*. Chicago: Intellect Books, 2007.

Peralta, Andres. "The Art of Storytelling: The Co-construction of Cultural Knowledge," *Art Education* 63 (2010): 25–30.

2

COMICS MODES

Caricature and Illustration in the Crumb Family's Dirty Laundry

Joseph Witek

Look at the cover of most general-interest books on comics, and you're likely to see a group of famous comic strip and comic book characters looking back at you.[1] These familiar cover designs are a sign of how figures like Superman, Popeye, Snoopy, and Dick Tracy have become deeply embedded into the visual vocabulary of modern culture (Figure 2.1).

But to lump all these fictional beings into a generalized unity called "the comics" makes it easy to forget that those characters are often radically different from one another in the very physical design of their bodies and in the fundamental principles of the created worlds they inhabit. A historical overview or a book summarizing characters and themes

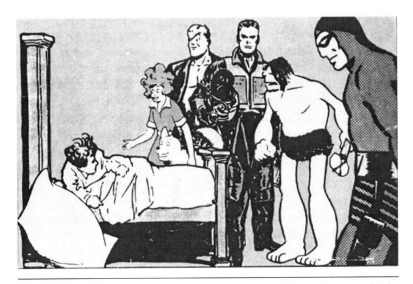

Figure 2.1 Jerry Robinson, The Comics, cover detail. Copyright 1974 The Newspaper Comics Council.

may be able to take "the comics" in general as its field of inquiry, but a close analysis of any individual comic's text requires an awareness of how its specific strategies of visual presentation and storytelling are being deployed. This chapter will discuss how the interaction between different styles of visual rendering and their associated narrative conventions supply comics creators with a series of aesthetic choices, allowing them to adhere to familiar conventions or to modify them in a nearly infinite variety of ways.

UNDERLYING ASSUMPTIONS

Contemporary comics are rooted stylistically in the confluence of two distinct traditions of visual representation. The first grows out of caricature, with its basic principles of simplification and exaggeration, while the other derives from the recreation of physical appearances in realistic illustration.[2] Each of these visual styles also has come to carry with it a characteristic set of narrative tendencies and an orientation toward its themes and subject matter that here will be called its "narrative ethos." Together the visual style and narrative ethos make up what I will call a comic's "mode." Caricature, of course, is most closely associated with verbal humor and slapstick comedy in comic strips and in gag cartoons (what is sometimes called "big-foot cartooning"), while the illustrative style has long been the preferred approach for stories of adventure and domestic romance in comic books and in continuity strips.[3]

To be sure, these categories are by no means mutually exclusive; comics combining elements of both modes are extremely common, including some of the most important achievements in the history of comics. Moreover, many great comics have directly explored the dynamic interactions between the cartoon and the naturalistic modes. For example, Winsor McCay's justly celebrated *Little Nemo in Slumberland* combines McCay's extraordinarily naturalistic draftsmanship and command of visual perspective with the dream logic and associative causation of the cartoon mode; only when Little Nemo awakens in the final panel do the visual style and narrative ethos finally merge. Art Spiegelman's even more celebrated graphic novel, *Maus: A Survivor's Tale*, intertwines the two modes in a complex adaptation of the conventions of anthropomorphic cartooning to a detailed and scrupulously naturalistic account of his parents' experiences in the Holocaust.

Consequently, in the description of the modes below, each categorical statement should be understood to refer to a hypothetical paradigm, to carry with it implied rhetorical qualifiers such as "generally" or "usually," and to acknowledge that many significant exceptions exist. Nevertheless, when taken together, these distinct sets of related visual strategies and narrative conventions constitute different approaches to the artistic problem of telling a story in comic form. As comics scholar Joe Zabel has said,

> [C]ritics are often guilty of taking the values and assumptions that apply to one tradition, and using them to judge work being done in an entirely different tradition. It doesn't make sense to favor one rendering style over another, or one method of using text over another, without regard to the kind of comic you're talking about, and what cartooning tradition it's following.[4]

A basic understanding of the narrative mode in a given comic text, then, constitutes a necessary conceptual underpinning for any kind of reading, whatever its specific critical methodology.

Figure 2.2 Two versions of the comedian Bob Hope. Left, *The Adventures of Bob Hope* no. 109, page 18. Copyright Feb.–March, 1968 National Periodicals Publications; DC Comics. Right, *Real Fact Comics* no. 1, page 7. Copyright March–April, 1946 National Periodicals Publications; DC Comics.

THE CARTOON MODE

The cartoon mode accounts for many of the greatest achievements in the history of comics, from George Herriman's *Krazy Kat* to Walt Kelly's *Pogo*, the Donald Duck and Uncle Scrooge comics of Carl Barks, and John Stanley's *Little Lulu*. Visually, the cartoon mode is marked by simplified and exaggerated characters which are created primarily by line and contour. Panel backgrounds and physical settings are often minimally represented. Little attempt is made to create a sustained illusion of three-dimensional space by such means as shading or the use of linear perspective.

Panel arrangements in the cartoon mode are often based on a regular grid, with few major variations in page layout or panel shapes. The characters tend to be seen as roughly the same size from panel to panel, with their bodies viewed frontally or in three-quarter view and visible at full length (a long shot in cinema terms) or from the waist up (medium shot), with few close-ups, extreme long shots, or abrupt shifts in visual perspective. These compositional strategies lend themselves to plots built on pairs or small groups of characters exchanging dialogue designed to set up a verbal punch line or short passages of physical action. In the cartoon mode, action tends to move from left to right across a single shallow visual plane.

Typical conventions in the cartoon mode include the extensive use of the icons called "emanata," such as the sweat beads, dust clouds, speed lines, and many other symbols that have become closely associated with traditional humor cartooning.[5] The cartoon mode also encompasses conventional gestural tropes such as the "fallout take," where a character reacts to the punch line of a gag by falling backwards out of the panel, leaving only the character's lower legs and feet visible to the reader (Figure 2.3).

Comics in the cartoon mode are so strongly associated with anthropomorphic characters that humorous comics aimed at children have often been labeled "funny animal comics," even when the protagonists are straightforwardly depicted as human beings. Anthropomorphic characters in comics can vary widely in their degree of

Figure 2.3 "Buster Bunny," *Goofy Comics* no. 41. Copyright January 1951 Standard Comics.

animality and in their relation to the human world.[6] Sometimes anthropomorphic characters speak, think, and act exactly like human beings; sometimes they display selective animal characteristics overlaid on primarily human behavior patterns, as in the species-based conflicts between predators like cats and wolves and their mouse or pig prey, all of whom come equipped with the clothes, houses, and other trappings of middle-class domesticity. The ambiguous ontological status of funny-animal characters can be underscored by the presence in the text of "real" animals, as in the famous example of Walt Disney's Goofy, ostensibly a humanoid dog, sharing space in the story world with Pluto, the pet dog of Mickey Mouse. In yet another type of story, the narrative focuses on characters who are capable of speech and rational thought but are otherwise completely animal in form and behavior and who exist in societies parallel to a mostly unseen human world.

In general, stories in the cartoon mode often assume a fundamentally unstable and infinitely mutable physical reality, where characters and even objects can move and be transformed according to an associative or emotive logic rather than the laws of physics. Bodies can change suddenly and temporarily in shape and proportion to depict emotional states or narrative circumstances, as when the body of an outraged character swells to many times its normal size, or appears to levitate several feet off the ground in a cloud of dust. For example, in the opening of the 1953 Donald Duck story "Bee Bumbler," by Carl Barks, Donald first appears to be thrown violently from his chair by a bee sting, then later his face and head elongate and compress in turn to avoid a threatening group of bees. Like the icons of emanata such as Donald's pain stars, sweat beads of anxiety, and the lines tracing the flight of the bees, these transformations of his head exist at a symbolic level, legible to the reader but invisible to characters within the world of the story (Figure 2.4).

Short-form cartoon stories, such as daily comic strips, overwhelmingly are structured to set up and resolve a joke; hence the name "gag strips." In longer form they tend toward episodic narratives which string together an often loosely connected series of gags or physical adventures. In particular, the affinity of the cartoon mode for physical metamorphosis and non-linear logic has made it the most common vehicle for stories set in fantastical landscapes, such as the many direct adaptations of *Alice in Wonderland* and its almost innumerable derivations.

THE NATURALISTIC MODE

In its fully developed form, the naturalistic mode is often called "realism." In this mode, the rendering of figures and objects adheres to (or at least points toward) the artistic conventions for creating the illusion of physical forms existing in three-dimensional space. A significant effort is made to create that plausible physical world using shading, consistent lighting sources, texture, and linear perspective. Backgrounds are rendered in detail, especially in establishing shots, and that background tends to be depicted relatively fully from panel to panel.

Figure 2.4 Carl Barks, *Walt Disney's Comics & Stories* no. 158. Copyright 1953 The Walt Disney Company.

Where the naturalistic visual style derives from the conventions of realism in the visual arts and particularly in photography, its narrative techniques are closely connected to those of cinema. Individual scenes tend to be broken down into more separate panels than in the cartoon mode, and transitions between panels very often correspond to analogous cinematic techniques such as jump-cuts, matching shots, and cross-cuts. The spatial depth created by the use of perspective is available for the movement of characters, who may be seen from a variety of angles and at varying visual distances. Figures likewise remain stable as physical entities, with any changes in shape and size accounted for by the familiar conventions of visual distance and perspective. Though the world depicted within the panels is presumed to be stable, the sizes and shapes of those panels can vary significantly within the story, and page layouts can become fluid and highly complex.

For example, in the page from "The Hanged Man's Revenge," drawn by Howard Larsen (Figure 2.5), the visual perspective ranges from long shots of the running man and the pursuing ape to close-ups of the terrified man's face and the hand ringing the doorbell. Most obviously, parts of the central figure intrude into four separate panels, but he isn't actually grounded in any particular panel at all. Yet despite the unusual organization of the page, each drawing presents itself as a representation of a physical world like our own (Figure 2.5).

Perhaps the most fundamental difference in ethos between the naturalistic mode and the cartoon mode is found in their differing orientations toward causality. Naturalistic comics certainly have depicted extreme physical transformations, fantastical landscapes, and outlandish violations of the known laws of physics. In all these cases, however, the naturalistic narrative accounts for the differences between the fictional world and our own by proffering a technological or supernatural explanation, no matter how notional or scientifically preposterous that explanation may be. On the other hand, the narrative conventions of humor comics derive from the legacy of theatrical and literary comedy, with various elements coming from farce, *commedia dell'arte*, nonsense literature, and vaudeville slapstick. The punch line or pratfall takes precedence over probability, linear plotting, and psychological verisimilitude.

Ultimately, the naturalistic mode makes the implicit claim that its depicted worlds are like our own, or like our own world would be if specific elements, such as magic or superpowers, were to be added or removed. However cursory the attempts to support its truth claim might be, that claim supplies the metaphysical structure underlying the visual and narrative strategies of the naturalistic tradition of comics. The naturalistic narrative ethos presents itself as a developing pattern of represented human behavior, and only when the reader closes the book can the story's ultimate thematic or moral import emerge.

The art form of caricature, on the other hand, specifically disavows any attempt to render the surface appearances of the physical world and makes a very different claim to a very different kind of truth. That is, by stripping away the inessential elements of a human face and exaggerating its defining features, caricature purports to reveal an essential truth about its subject that lies hidden beneath the world of appearances. When structuring caricatures in sequence, the cartoon mode treats the comic's page not only as a loose representation of physical existence, but also as a textual field for the immediate enactment of overtly symbolic meaning. Its images often stand in for concepts rather than for physical bodies, and its narrative strategies are deployed not simply to replicate

Figure 2.5 "The Hanged Man's Revenge," art by Howard Larsen. *Crime Patrol* no. 12. Copyright 1949 EC Comics.

action in space but to embody conceptual relationships. Even though for much of the history of comics the cartoon mode has been associated with juvenile humor and formulaic fantasy, its roots in political satire suggest that the cartoon mode is fundamentally a medium of ideas.

HISTORICAL CONTEXT

For over half a century the cartoon and naturalistic modes were for the most part the unexamined givens of the profession of making comics—a cartoonist simply knew that verbal gags or slapstick humor required the cartoon mode, while genres such as action-adventure, war, and romance used some form of the naturalistic mode.[7] For a variety of technological and commercial reasons, however, by the late 1950s traditional "big-foot" cartooning in comics and theatrical cartoon animation had become almost completely obsolete, associated in U.S. culture with old-fashioned comic strips and juvenile comic book genres. But when a cultural form loses its commercial function, it becomes available for artistic innovation, and in the late 1960s the underground comix movement revitalized the cartoon mode in a cultural salvage operation that Françoise Mouly has characterized as "incorporating the discarded past in the present."[8] As the name "underground" suggests, the intentional violation of societal taboos was central to the ideology of the comix movement, and in the undergrounds the drawing style previously identified with innocuous comics for kids became the preferred mode for the unrestrained depiction of sex, violence, and political rebellion. By exploiting the expressive potential latent in the symbolic nature of the cartoon mode, the underground cartoonists reconnected the style to its roots in social and political satire. In the wake of underground comix, the visual style and narrative tropes and conventions of the cartoon mode have been widely used in alternative and independent comics ranging from Jeff Smith's all-ages humor/adventure series, *Bone*, to Art Spiegelman's celebrated Holocaust graphic novel, *Maus: A Survivor's Tale*.

In contemporary comics, no single figure has done more to exploit the power and flexibility of the cartoon mode than has Robert Crumb, whose trademark amalgamation of the comics and animated cartoons from the 1920s and 1930s became the signature graphic style of the underground comix movement. While Crumb is a highly accomplished draftsman capable of rendering subjects in a variety of styles, the cartoon mode has dominated the vast output of his long career. From his earliest commercial art in the greeting-card industry to the decidedly adult adventures of anthropomorphic cartoon characters such as Fritz the Cat, and of symbolic humanoid avatars such as the Zen guru Mr. Natural and the id-figure Mr. Snoid, Crumb has turned the rounded caricatured figures and absurd metaphysics of the cartoon mode into deeply personal autobiographical stories, abstract experimental pieces, and trenchant social satire.

ARTIFACT SELECTED FOR ANALYSIS

Among the most complex and innovative of Crumb's projects are the *Dirty Laundry* comics, a series of collaborations with his life-partner, cartoonist and comics editor Aline Kominsky-Crumb. Initially conceived as a way to pass the time while Aline Kominsky-Crumb was laid up with a broken foot, the *Dirty Laundry* comics were published from 1974 to 1992 in two comic book issues (1974 and 1977) and in a number of pieces in various newspapers, magazines, and comics anthologies.[9]

Aline Kominsky-Crumb and Robert Crumb were among the earliest and most influential pioneers in developing what has become a vast autobiographical movement in comics and graphic novels, and the *Dirty Laundry* comics are, as the title suggests, autobiographical comics in which the couple candidly depict their personal relationship and domestic life together. But if autobiography is the self writing about the self, the *Dirty Laundry* comics become *selves writing about selves* by deploying a remarkable and highly unusual artistic strategy in which each artist draws the figure representing her or himself; in later years the couple is joined by their daughter, Sophie, who eventually takes over drawing herself.

By depicting the subjective life experiences of more than one person simultaneously, the *Dirty Laundry* project highlights the way that the very notions of *autobiography* and *collaboration* exist in tension with one another. Many autobiographical comics are created by a single artist/writer; in fact, the opportunity for a cartoonist to adopt the auteur ethos of modernist art can be one of the appeals of the autobiographical comics genre. But the disparate drawing styles of Crumb and Kominsky-Crumb refuse to allow the depicted world to resolve into the illusion of a unified whole, and the visual discrepancies within the panels ultimately help to highlight some fundamental aspects of how the cartoon mode works, and to illuminate the reasons why a mode of comics storytelling which is devoted to visual simplification and exaggeration and to an emotive and associative logic has become a preferred vehicle for depicting the truth of everyday human experience.

In the household depicted in *Dirty Laundry*, issues of artistic style, gender equality, interpersonal dynamics, technical drawing skill, individual identity, audience response, professional reputation, and the representation of subjectivity are all bound together in a complex series of interactions that ultimately makes the *Dirty Laundry* comics primarily about the conditions of their own making. A collaborative autobiography created by domestic partners is inherently self-reflexive; when the subject of the comic is their shared experience, the production of that comic becomes a major part of their lives that is finally inseparable from all the others. Both people are cartoonists, but Crumb is by far the more famous (particularly in the early years of the series). His drawing style is instantly recognizable for its distillation of the comics of the past, and he is intensely interested in the craft of drawing and in learning new techniques. Kominsky-Crumb, on the other hand, despite being the only one of the pair who attended art school, draws in a blocky, intuitive style that is, as will be discussed below, almost entirely independent of any fine-art or popular-culture artistic traditions. Crumb has often expressed his admiration for his wife's cartooning but, as she tells us in *Aline & Bob's Dirty Laundry Comics* #2, Crumb's fans criticized her drawings in the first issue so heavily that the second issue ends with her resolution to never draw comics again.[10] On the other hand, the fan letters reproduced in that issue are nearly all positive about Kominsky-Crumb's work, some singling out her style for specific praise.

SAMPLE ANALYSIS

Crumb, Robert and Aline Kominsky-Crumb. *Dirty Laundry Comics* no. 1, Co-op Press, 1974.

This reading of comics from the *Dirty Laundry* series will focus on the ways that Crumb and Kominsky-Crumb transform two aspects of the cartoon mode: the instability of the physical world and the conception of the comic panel as a symbolic field, concentrating on the first comic book issue from 1974. Both artists have complicated relationships to their own and to each other's physical appearance and body structure; they each draw themselves as a number of different personae; and their interactions routinely take the form of physical, often sexualized, roughhousing, making the mutable bodies of the cartoon mode a natural fit for these transient transformations of identity. In the panels, the two artists talk to each other within the story as well as communicate with each other and the audience *about* the story, so the scenes are often laden with identifying labels, comments on the drawings, visual glosses, and commentary about the ongoing development of the narrative. Under these conditions the illusion of represented space in the naturalistic mode would not only be impossible to maintain, the attempt to do so would interfere with the multiple levels of the stories the two artists are telling.

While the characters that initially made Robert Crumb the most famous cartoonist in the underground comix movement were humanoid and anthropomorphic throwbacks to the cartoons of previous decades, he regularly published stories featuring a version of himself as a protagonist. Stories such as "The Adventures of R. Crumb Himself" and "The Confessions of R. Crumb" established what have become the familiar features of the artist: he's thin, stoop-shouldered, wears thick-lensed eyeglasses and old-fashioned suits, with a beak-like nose, unruly cow-licked hair, and a protruding Adam's apple on a long, thin neck (Figure 2.6). His rendering of the Crumb figure can vary even within individual stories to reflect changes in his mood or social role.

Most stories with Crumb as a protagonist set up a baseline depiction of the artist so that the variations from panel to panel appear as temporary embodiments of the character's inner state or his reaction to outside stimuli. Crumb's careful, even obsessive control over his draftsmanship makes it obvious that these variations are intentional effects in the artist's self-presentation.

Figure 2.6 "R. Crumb Presents R. Crumb." Copyright 1973 Robert Crumb.

Aline Kominsky-Crumb's drawings, on the other hand, use an intuitive style that she herself calls "primitive, painful scratching that's not for everybody."[11] Like Crumb's, her drawings are densely wrought and packed with detail, but if the effect of Crumb's notoriously obsessive cross-hatched textures is one of claustrophobic control, Aline's loosely organized and erratic shapes suggest a barely contained chaos (Figure 2.7).

In her early cartoons, particularly the collaborations with Crumb, the figures are often formed by distinct outlines but little interior detail, and in the most significant difference from all previous comics traditions, the figures vary, sometimes radically, in size, shape, and form from one panel to the next.

One of the basic skills of any kind of drawing is the ability to render the appearance of objects consistently, and in comics the expectation is that no matter how stylized or iconic the drawings may be, the figures will look more or less the same throughout the narrative. But here (Figure 2.8) the Aline of panel 1 appears to be a different person than the one in panel 2; the figures in panels 2 and 4 appear to be dressed the same but the slope of the person's forehead in the second panel differs markedly from the one in the panel below it. The figure changes hair color and gains a hat between the first and second panels, but the rounded-top hat in panel 2 becomes more sharply peaked in panel 3 before changing into a flat-topped hat of a significantly different design in panel 4. Her position in the panel relative to Bob remains the same, and her bibbed overalls supply readers with enough cues to determine that it *is* supposed to be the same character, but the rendering of this character's head and face falls well outside the normal range of variation in any kind of professional drawing.

The point is, of course, that the underground comix as well as much cartooning in contemporary comics and graphic novels is *not* professional drawing as it was defined prior to the underground comix, a movement which provided a venue not only for the re-working of obsolescent traditional styles, but opened the way for a wide range of new graphic approaches to enter the visual vocabulary of comics, including those derived from avant-garde art and from psychedelic poster design. In the case of Aline Kominsky-Crumb, her aggressively amateurish art stands at the intersection of two aesthetic

Figure 2.7 "Growing Up As Arnie's Girl," *Weirdo* no. 26. Copyright 1989 Aline Kominsky-Crumb.

movements that specifically bypass the tradition of polished commercial art that Robert Crumb so enthusiastically embraces: primitivism in modernist art and *art brut* (literally "raw art"). In a joint interview, the couple described her art as follows:

> RC: Her comics have no stylistic references to any cartoon tradition, except the most crude stuff you see from the 18th century as drawn by amateur cartoonists. It's just completely her own thing. She went to art school, and it didn't affect her drawing at all, as far as her comics goes. Her whole use of tools and equipment is just completely unprofessional.
> Aline: It's unfiltered artless expression. It's like outsider art.[12]

Many of Robert Crumb's fans, however, seemed to believe that, rather than working in a different aesthetic tradition, Kominsky-Crumb was attempting to draw in a

Figure 2.8 *Dirty Laundry Comics* no. 1. Copyright 1974 Aline Kominsky-Crumb and Robert Crumb.

conventional cartoon style and failing. Their negative responses reinforced her own insecurity about her drawing style, but although her figure drawing became somewhat more regularized as she continued to draw comics, her basic approach never changed: What appears on the page is a function of her psychological state both at the time depicted in the story and at the time the drawing was made, and it is all as unfettered by technical conventions and social inhibitions as possible. The potentially inconstant physical world of the cartoon mode matches the fluctuations of Aline's subjective experience, and the narrative conventions that allow Bob's physical size and facial appearance to alter as he shifts roles from, say, aggrieved homeowner to penitent adulterer can likewise widen to allow Aline to alter her own body image from moment to moment or to change her clothing between panels because Kominsky-Crumb feels like drawing Aline in her newest outfit.

The tension inherent in putting two disparate drawing styles together in a single comic's story-world reflects the conflicts within the bond between these two very different characters. Bob is socially passive but sexually aggressive, alienated from his own slight physique, misanthropic, and fixated on a few long-term concerns like collecting old records. Aline is gregarious, physically active, and robust but attracted to sexual submission, and mercurial in her various interests. Their nonstop verbal exchanges regularly mutate into slapstick physical encounters which are sometimes hostile, sometimes sexual, and sometimes both simultaneously.

The narrative context for one remarkable scene shows why Bob and Aline's relationship requires the absurd logic and indeterminate physics of the cartoon mode. After returning from an alien abduction, the couple sit in front of the fireplace, musing on what to show next in their comic. Stay-at-home Bob uncharacteristically suggests more "swashbuckling adventures," but Aline demurs: "No, I'd rather let the people know our philosophy of life. We hafto share our great insight Robert." She launches into a reverie about a "flash of spiritual ecstasy I had while driving my Honda 90." As she surrenders to her rapture, Bob mounts her for an extended bout of oral sex which ends in a pile of vomit. Rather than objecting, Aline gushes, "Oh Robert you're so sweet. You play with me so good," then requests that Bob hang her from the ceiling in a sexual fetish pose. Bob argues that they should get to work on their farm, but he then reluctantly complies.

In this sequence, Aline takes her revenge after Bob's inadequate handiwork with ropes and pulleys sends her crashing through the floor. In the first panel, Aline's posture is physically impossible, but it sets up her transformation into a pitchfork-armed, double-breasted tank in the next two (Figure 2.9). Fortunately for Bob, the five tines of the pitchfork shrink to four in the third panel, and develop enough width between them to fit around Bob's (admittedly scrawny) neck. The infinitely resilient bodies of the cartoon mode allow the couple's volatile interactions to become visual slapstick; in the naturalistic mode their passions would be simply terrifying.

Such action sequences occur fairly often in the *Dirty Laundry* comics, but far more common are exchanges of dialogue. Even when fantasy sequences in *Dirty Laundry #1* have the characters abducted by aliens and rescued by countercultural guru Timothy Leary, or when an epic flash flood washes their trailer home out from under them, the really important action takes place in their conversation. The two are in fact conducting several conversations simultaneously: the characters speak to one another within the world of the panels; the artists speak to the audience in captions and through identifying

Figure 2.9 *Dirty Laundry Comics* no. 1. Copyright 1974 Aline Kominsky-Crumb and Robert Crumb.

labels written in boxes with arrows pointing to various elements in the panels; and they speak to one another in textual side-notes. Labels in comics panels most famously appear in Chester Gould's classic detective strip, *Dick Tracy*, where from time to time they point toward fictional inventions such as Tracy's trademark "two-way wrist radio." In the *Dirty Laundry* comics such commentary proliferates with abandon, supplying additional detail, artistic second thoughts, and ironic interpretation. In one three-page sequence from the first issue, Aline's body parts are labeled ("hank o' hair" and "crybaby bean body"—the latter being Crumb's term for the particular configuration of his wife's curves); during a sex scene the floating comment "sick relationship" appears; Kominsky-Crumb appends a general footnote lamenting that "Robert doesn't feel like drawing much because the IRS is after him and his ex-wife is hassling him, so I hafto do more stuff than him and its not fair." Aline's clothing ("non-sexist Chinese shoes"), her overall look ("intellectual Bunchimal"), her posture ("irrational pose"), her mood ("indignant," "guilty"), and the strength of her buttocks ("1,000 lbs.") are all labeled; while both artists comment on her drawing (Aline has an "ugly man's face"), Crumb points out a technical error ("shading on wrong side of neck—R.C."). Aline inserts a political challenge to readers that is tied to the local California elections at the time of the drawing ("I'm disgusted… Tom Hayden lost . . Prop. 15 lost… Reagan won… Sheesh! Did you vote? Huh???"). A slumping Bob gets the label "Mr. 4-F," then later turns to the audience and says, rather maniacally, "Hey folks! Aren't we America's most lovable cartoon couple? Hup-Ho!" With the additional effect that the words in their thought balloons are available to the reader and to each other as cartoonists but not as characters within the stories, the result is a multi-voiced, cross-temporal conversation that reverberates in complex patterns throughout the comic and beyond.

As Bob's self-aggrandizing question suggests, readers of these comics are seeing a "cartoon couple" rather than a mimetic representation of a couple of actual cartoonists. Any personal or artistic collaboration is likewise a performance, and the *Dirty Laundry* comics embody the dramaturgy of everyday life as each person adopts one of several different personae or is given others by their partner: Bob's unworked-out body makes him the "Noodle," he's "Mr. 4-F," and a "Superior S.O.B." Aline's identities shift even more restlessly as she's the "Bunch," sometimes the "Bitter Bunch" or "Baldy Bunch"; her name becomes "Arline," and she even transforms into a cigar-smoking man, "Mr. Bunch," who sometimes appears in order to set the couple straight with his cynical and pragmatic advice.

The cartoon mode provides a stage to act out all the multiple roles that people play to each other and to themselves in daily life, and Bob and Aline's shifting visual manifestations are not masks concealing an underlying unified truth but a series of candid but inevitably partial revelations. Aline Kominsky-Crumb told an interviewer: "[O]ur relationship is based on a mutual acceptance of the cosmic absurdity and tragedy of life, and we have no false sentimental illusions that conflict with openly drawing our weirdest thoughts about ourselves and our little lives."[13]

When the absurdity of the traditional cartoon mode was re-worked in the underground comix to encompass the tragedy inherent within the comedy of life, the comics form became a place where caricature, burlesque, and slapstick could become methods to not only depict but to embody the psychic experience of human beings alone and with other people.

NOTES

1. For examples, see Reinhold Reitberger and Wolfgang Fuchs, *Comics: Anatomy of a Mass Medium* (Boston: Little, Brown, 1972); Jerry Robinson, *The Comics: An Illustrated History* (New York: Putnam, 1974); M. Thomas Inge, *Comics and Culture* (Jackson, MS: University Press of Mississippi, 1990); R.C. Harvey, *The Art of the Funnies* (Jackson, MS: University Press of Mississippi, 1994) and R.C. Harvey, *The Art of the Comic Book* (Jackson, MS: University Press of Mississippi, 1996).
2. My discussion of comics modes here is indebted to Joe Zabel's taxonomy of comics styles in "Comics Theory and Comics Traditions." http://amazingmontage.tripod.com/tradition.html. I use the term "naturalistic" instead of Zabel's "cinematic," and I consider his third style, visually spectacular "poster" comics, to be a subset of the naturalistic. Contemporary comics increasingly use at least two additional styles, both derived from modernist art and commercial design, one based on collage and the other on abstraction. For abstract comics, see Andrei Molotiu, *Abstract Comics: The Anthology 1967–2009* (Seattle: Fantagraphics, 2009).
3. The distinction I am making here has been widely discussed in comics criticism using a variety of different concepts and terminology, including "iconic," "minimalist," and "cartoony" for caricature-derived styles, and "realistic," "literal," and "representational" for those derived from illustration.
4. Zabel, "Comics Theory and Comics Traditions."
5. See Mort Walker, *The Lexicon of Comicana* (Port Chester, NY: Museum of Cartoon Art, 2000).
6. In fact, speaking characters are sometimes neither human nor animal, but objects such as trees, stars, and mirrors.
7. The differences between the two modes were satirized in the *Mad* parodies "Mickey Rodent!" *Mad* 19 (January 1955) and "Bringing Back Father!" *Mad* 17 (November 1954).
8. Françoise Mouly, "R. Crumb," in *Masters of American Comics*, ed. John Carlin, Paul Karasik, and Brian Walker (Los Angeles: Hammer Museum, 2005), 282.
9. Collected in Aline Kominsky, R. Crumb, and Sophie Crumb, *The Complete Dirty Laundry Comics* (San Francisco: Last Gasp of San Francisco, 1993).
10. This resolution was short-lived at best; Kominsky-Crumb continues to publish her own comics and to collaborate with her husband.
11. Aline Kominsky-Crumb, interview with Andrea Juno in *Dangerous Drawings* (New York: Juno Books, 1997), 168.
12. Aline Kominsky-Crumb and Robert Crumb, "The Crumbs' Underground Comics," interview with Terry Gross, *Fresh Air*, February 13, 2007.
13. R. Crumb and D.K. Holm, *R. Crumb: Conversations* (Jackson, MS: University Press of Mississippi, 2004), 126.

SELECTED BIBLIOGRAPHY

Crumb, R. and D.K. Holm. *R. Crumb: Conversations.* Jackson, MS: University Press of Mississippi, 2004.
Harvey, R.C. *The Art of the Funnies: An Aesthetic History.* Jackson, MS: University Press of Mississippi, 1994.
Harvey, R.C. *The Art of the Comic Book: An Aesthetic History.* Jackson, MS: University Press of Mississippi, 1996.
Inge, M. Thomas. *Comics as Culture.* Jackson, MS: University Press of Mississippi, 1990.
Juno, Andrea. *Dangerous Drawings: Interviews with Comix & Grafix Artists.* New York: Juno Books, 1997.
Kominsky, Aline, R. Crumb, and Sophie Crumb. *The Complete Dirty Laundry Comics.* San Francisco: Last Gasp of San Francisco, 1993.
Kominsky-Crumb, Aline and Robert Crumb. "The Crumbs' Underground Comics." Interview with Terry Gross. *Fresh Air.* February 13, 2007.
Molotiu, Andrei, ed. *Abstract Comics: The Anthology 1967–2009.* Seattle: Fantagraphics Books, 2009.
Mouly, Françoise. "R. Crumb: It's Only Lines on Paper." In *Masters of American Comics*, edited by John Carlin, Paul Karasik, and Brian Walker, 282–287. Los Angeles: Hammer Museum, 2005.
Reitberger, Reinhold and Wolfgang Fuchs. *Comics: Anatomy of a Mass Medium.* Translated by Nadia Fowler. Boston: Little, Brown, 1972.
Robinson, Jerry. *The Comics: An Illustrated History of Comic Strip Art.* New York: Putnam, 1974.
Walker, Mort. *The Lexicon of Comicana.* Port Chester, NY: Museum of Cartoon Art, 1980.
Zabel, Joe. "Comics Theory and Comics Tradition." *Joe Zabel's Amazing Montage*, http://amazingmontage.tripod.com, accessed December 21, 2010.

3

IMAGE FUNCTIONS

Shape and Color as Hermeneutic Images in Asterios Polyp

Randy Duncan

In 1971, Art Spiegelman was asked to contribute a strip to the underground comic book *Funny Aminals* [sic]. The only editorial guideline was that he had to use anthropomorphic characters. He started working on a horror genre parody about a mouse caught in a mousetrap, but he had no real inspiration or enthusiasm for that idea. After attending a film lecture that pointed out Mickey Mouse's connection to racist minstrel show images, Spiegelman considered doing a strip about race relations in America; perhaps cats lynching mice. He rejected that idea when he realized that "[I] know bupkis about being black in America."[1] However, it led to thinking about the history of oppression in his own Jewish heritage, and particularly his parents' experiences in World War II Germany. He recalled the Nazi propaganda that equated Jews with vermin, and the story was born. Spiegelman's three-page strip for *Funny Aminals* never mentions Germans and Jews, but has cats in uniform rounding up mice and taking them to death camps.

That story was the seed from which the critically acclaimed graphic novel *Maus* grew. In the original three-page story, Spiegelman depicts only mice and cats, but for the graphic novel he adds other animal representations of ethnicity—American dogs, French frogs, Polish pigs, etc. What began as an editorial necessity became consciously applied as a metaphor. Even though once they are a way into the work most readers begin experiencing the characters as human beings and might no longer notice they are drawn as animals, every reader initially encountering *Maus* is confronted with those animal images that are incongruent with the world of the story. When readers realize certain images function not merely as means of showing the story, but also as a commentary on the story, they are forced to consider: Why were these images selected? What are they supposed to mean? Image function analysis, the method employed in this chapter, provides an approach for understanding the various functions of images in a comic book or graphic novel, and examines how those functions can communicate a particular meaning to a reader. In this chapter, image function analysis will be applied to the graphic novel *Asterios Polyp*, by David Mazzucchelli.

Using this unorthodox comic as a focus, this chapter explains how the selection of key images affects meaning. The development and application of image function analysis are based on certain assumptions about the nature of the comic book art form that need to be considered before the method is applied.

UNDERLYING ASSUMPTIONS

The first assumption is that images on the page are a result of author intention. A comic book or graphic novel begins as a blank page or screen. For graphic novels and even for most comic books, it can be assumed that each image is a strategic choice made to communicate a particular idea or effect.

The second assumption is that the meaning you derive from a comic book or graphic novel might not coincide with the meaning the author intended to convey. Whatever the author's intentions and strategic choices, each individual derives a personal understanding of the work as they sift the words and pictures on the page through their own perceptual filter. A perceptual filter consists of beliefs and attitudes that create predispositions and particular knowledge that can contribute to or hinder understanding of the subject matter. For example, in *Asterios Polyp* there is a dream sequence that alludes to the myth of Orpheus' nearly successful attempt to free his dead wife, Eurydice, from the Underworld. Readers unfamiliar with the myth, those who vaguely remember the basic storyline, and those who have studied the symbolism of the myth will each derive very different understandings of the episode. Another important aspect of the perceptual filter is each reader's life experience and how the characters and events of the work relate to that life experience. The main character in *Asterios Polyp* is a 50-year-old college professor. The author of this chapter, being a middle-aged professor, probably experiences greater resonance with the story than would a reader still in high school. The application of image function analysis presented below is an understanding of *Asterios Polyp* as experienced through the perceptual filter of this particular middle-aged professor.

If one wants to consider authorial intent, one can read interviews with the author and learn more about what meaning was intended. Then one can analyze how effectively the author's selection and combination of images communicated his or her intended meaning. However, such interviews are not always available and some authors are reluctant to explain intentions, preferring to let the work speak for itself. *Asterios Polyp* creator, Mazzuccelli believes that "regardless of the ideas you're putting into it, once you make something, it takes on a life of its own" and the artist should not "be following it around explaining what it means."[2] Mazzucchelli acknowledges that "maybe the work is doing something that you don't know it's doing."[3] Even if information on authorial intent is available, you might choose to ignore it and simply do the analysis based on the meaning you derive from applying your own perceptual filter. Either approach, or even a combination of the two, has merit.

The third assumption is that images can function to show the reader the story or tell the reader about the story. In literary theory, the fictional world constructed within a story is called the *diegesis*. The concept of diegesis will be used as the touchstone for identifying three functions of images in a comic book or graphic novel.[4] *Sensory diegetic images* show the physical reality of the world of the story. These are primarily images of what can be seen—characters, structures, objects, etc.—but can include anything, such as sounds and smells, that constitute the sensory environment of the fictional world.

Non-sensory diegetic images show the internal reality of the characters in the story. These images represent thoughts, emotions, and attitudes that are part of the diegesis, but not accessible to the senses. Mazzucchelli seldom uses thought balloons in *Asterios Polyp*, but when a bird flies through the subway tunnel past Asterios, a thought balloon containing a bird and a question mark appears next to his head. Later in the story, little bubbles appear around his head to indicate his state of intoxication. *Hermeneutic images* do not represent either the physical or mental reality of the fictional world; they are not meant to be part of the diegesis. These images are the author's commentary on the story and are often explicit attempts to influence the interpretation of the story. When Asterios sees Hana's studio for the first time and compliments her sculpture, a spotlight shines on Hana in the next panel. There is not literally a spotlight in the studio; it is a way of showing that Hana is basking in the positive attention. Yet, in successive panels, as Asterios pontificates on his interpretation of the themes in her work, the spotlight slowly slides away from Hana and shines on Asterios. The author uses this hermeneutic image to show the reader that Asterios is self-centered, not even aware he is taking the spotlight away from Hana in what should be her moment.

The simple images in the panel reproduced in Figure 3.1 demonstrate all three image functions. The rain and the figure of Asterios are representations of the physical reality of the story that could be seen, touched, and otherwise sensed by other characters in the world of the story. They function as sensory diegetic images. Asterios' thought, "not again," is also part of the diegesis, but because no other character in the world of the story can see, hear, or otherwise sense this thought it is a non-sensory diegetic image. It is a convention of comics that thought balloons are drawn with scalloped borders to differentiate them from the smooth-bordered dialogue balloons, but the shape also evokes the idea of a cloud. Mazzucchelli plays upon that idea by drawing the rain as if it is falling from the thought balloon. However, there are a couple of clues that the balloon–rain

Figure 3.1 The three image functions in a single panel (page 21). *Asterios Polyp* Copyright 2009 David Mazzucchelli.

relationship is not representing a physical aspect of the diegesis, but is operating as a hermeneutic image that nudges the reader to a certain interpretation of the panel. We know from experience that rain clouds are never this close to the ground, and, obviously (as has been shown in previous panels), it is raining all around Asterios, but Mazzucchelli chooses to draw only the rain emanating from the "cloud" and falling on Asterios. This image of a figure with a cloud over his head operates as a visual metaphor used to communicate bad luck, tragedy, or despair. Thus, what this panel contributes to the overall meaning of the story is strongly influenced by how one reads the hermeneutic images.

The fourth assumption is that hermeneutic images are an important agency (or technique) for conveying subtext, the underlying meaning of a story. These images are not just showing the story, but telling the reader something about the story. They are a means for the author to directly address the reader, and they are usually the most purposefully selected images on the page. Therefore, hermeneutic images are often the strongest indicators of the underlying meaning of a story.

APPROPRIATE ARTIFACTS

The author's strategic choices about what to show and how to show it are the creative act, and the resulting comic book or graphic novel is the artifact of that act of creation. The artifact you select for image function analysis should be a complex narrative with a degree of ambiguity. The vast majority of comic books and graphic novels are narratives—that is, they tell a story—but genre adventures intended primarily for entertainment generally have negligible subtext and seldom make significant use of hermeneutic images.

Authors of complex narratives have a seriousness of purpose and communicate their stories with depth and richness. At the surface level there are the events that occur in the narrative, but at the deeper level, or the subtext, there is the consideration of what those actions mean. For example, before fleeing his burning apartment building, Asterios grabs three objects important to him—a lighter that belonged to his father, a unique magnetic watch he bought as a child, and a Swiss Army knife he and Hana found at the beach. Eventually he gives away the lighter and the watch, but he keeps the knife. Those are the surface actions, and one reading of the subtext is that Asterios is severing ties with his previous life and his old values, but he is not ready to relinquish his emotional attachment to Hana.

To come to a full and satisfying understanding of complex, ambiguous narratives, the reader must wrestle with the symbol system used to present the text and the subtext. Analyzing the functions of hermeneutic images can give one a handhold in that wrestling match. The next section lays out a systematic approach for analyzing how hermeneutic images contribute to the layers of meaning in a comic book or graphic novel.

PROCEDURES

The image function analysis method treats a comic book or graphic novel as a rhetorical act by one or more agents. For many graphic novels there is one cartoonist responsible for creating all aspects of the work. Most mainstream comic books are created collaboratively by writers, artists, letterers, etc. In the explanation of the image function analysis method, the term "author" will be used when referring to an unspecified work. For analysis of a particular work you should use the name or names of the cartoonist or writer and artist responsible for choosing the images. To determine the division of responsibilities for a collaboratively created comic you might need to read interviews with the creators or get access to the script from which the artist worked. Some graphic novel and comic book story arcs are reprinted in deluxe editions that include the script. Some writers post their scripts online.

Good critical analysis almost always requires multiple readings of a work. The first reading should be for experiencing the work as a story. You should get immersed in the story, and let yourself be impelled from one action to the next without slowing down to analyze the author's choices. Of course, once you have become an experienced comics critic, you cannot help but notice many of the techniques and decode much of the subtext even in this immersive reading, but as long as this is occurring peripherally it should only increase the pleasure of that initial read.

The next reading should be more deliberate and more analytical. Your first task is to identify the most significant hermeneutic images. Significance is indicated by the frequency of appearance and occurrence at pivotal moments in the narrative. When a particular hermeneutic image—or some slight variation on that image—appears repeatedly, it becomes a visual motif. Such motifs usually have a direct connection to the theme of the narrative. The crucial plot points in a story almost invariably involve a character making choices that lead to changes in the character's circumstances or attitudes. If the author employs hermeneutic images at these pivotal moments, those images usually provide important clues to the meaning the author hopes to convey in the story.

Once you have identified the most significant hermeneutic images, the next step is to determine how they function to contribute to the meaning of the story. Remember, the image is not on the page by accident. Hermeneutic images, in particular, are the result of strategic choices made by the author with the intent to communicate something to the reader. Are repeated hermeneutic images used to communicate something about the personality or morality of one of the characters, or to reinforce a particular theme of the story? For a hermeneutic image used at a pivotal moment in the story, how does the image influence your interpretation of those choices being made by characters?

ARTIFACT SELECTED FOR SAMPLE ANALYSIS

Why choose Mazzucchelli's *Asterios Polyp* as an artifact to analyze? National Public Radio selected *Asterios Polyp* as one of the five best books to share with your friends, referring to it as a "boldly ambitious, boundary-pushing graphic novel [that] synthesizes word and image to craft a new kind of storytelling."[5] According to a review in the *Columbus Dispatch*, "*Asterios Polyp* is a perfect marriage of words and pictures. Every drawing, color choice and panel layout is pregnant with meaning."[6]

SAMPLE ANALYSIS

Mazzucchelli, David. *Asterios Polyp*. New York: Pantheon Books, 2009.

Even on a first reading it is obvious that to understand the subtext of *Asterios Polyp* a reader will have to interpret some of David Mazzucchelli's creative decisions in the use of color and shape. His unconventional and deliberately employed uses of color and shape go beyond merely representing the reality of the world of the story; they function as hermeneutic images through which the author provides a commentary upon the characters and their story. The reader must interpret that commentary to arrive at their own understanding of the subtext of the graphic novel.

Mazzucchelli does not use colors as diegetic images that attempt to realistically represent the colors of people and objects in the world of the story. He uses a limited palette and, for the most part, presents monochromatic characters. Appropriate to a printed medium, he employs the subtractive primaries used by printers: magenta, yellow, and cyan. These colors have essentially the same psychological properties as the three primary colors: red, yellow, and blue. "In the main, the colors of the spectrum are to be associated with two moods, the warm [...] g-ous hues, and the cool, passive, and [...] w is usually a positive color associated [...] he astute reader of the graphic novel [...] th particular characters and time peri[...] sis unfolds we will see that these three [...] es Mazzucchelli uses to communicate t[...]

While less pervasive than color, th[...] t. In most comics the same font and di[...] rs, but in *Asterios Polyp* Mazzucchelli c [...] or each character. Throughout most of [...] s- entational manner, but at a few poi[...] ly different and unrealistic shapes.

Changes in the use of the aforeme[...] al moments in the story, marking the[...] e interpreted to achieve a richly me[...] g application of image function anal[...] ht be conveyed by these hermeneutic images, but focus on the question: How does David Mazzucchelli use shape and color as hermeneutic images to communicate changes in Asterios and Hana's relationship?

Asterios Polyp begins *en medias res.* In the present-time story, Asterios loses everything and begins a new life in a small town named Apogee. His career as a professor and his relationship with Hana are told in ten flashbacks. There is not always a strict chronological order followed within these flashbacks. Some contain multiple vignettes and others contain memory montages or philosophical digressions by the narrator. There are also six dream sequences and a few flashforwards. The complex structure unpacks information in a manner that serves the author's narrative purpose quite well; however, for this analysis the events will be considered in their chronological order rather than the order in which they are presented in the graphic novel.

ASTERIOS AND HANA: COMING TOGETHER, COMING APART

When Asterios and Hana first meet at a faculty party, shape and color are used to accentuate their differences. The precise sans serif font used to depict Asterios' words is enclosed in straight-line dialogue balloons. Hana's font is more cursive in nature and appears in gently curved dialogue balloons. In his chapter on the expressiveness of the line, comics theorist Scott McCloud characterizes such a curved line as "warm and gentle" and the combination of straight lines, such as a rectangle, as "rational and conservative."[8]

These traits are reinforced by the use of color. Asterios is drawn in blue hues. As mentioned earlier, blue is often considered cool and calming. As more flashbacks fill in information about Asterios' career and past relationships, it becomes clear that in his case this coolness manifests itself as intellectual precision, emotional coldness, and detachment.

Hana is rendered in purple, with a hint of magenta in her glass of wine. In the four pages immediately following their meeting, a flashback within the flashback tells the story of Hana's birth and life up to that point. The backgrounds of these four pages are solid magenta, and most of the clothing Hana wears is in shades of magenta or analogous hues. Hana is associated with colors of warmth and emotion. The nonrealistic, and thus hermeneutic, renderings of the characters operate as psychological images that give insight into the personalities and worldviews of the main characters.

In an earlier flashback, the narrator speculates whether "one person's construction of the world [is] an extension of the self" (pages 34, 36). In the mid-twentieth century Kenneth Burke revolutionized rhetorical theory by claiming the motivation for most interpersonal communication is rooted in the desire to overcome the division from other human beings created by each person's unique central nervous system and life experience. Burke believed that much of human behavior was motivated by the need to experience, if only fleetingly, a strong connection with another human being.[9]

When Mazzucchelli re-tells Asterios and Hana's first meeting from Hana's point of view, his bold use of hermeneutic images makes Burke's concepts of division and connection manifest on the page. Hana is a new faculty member who does not know anyone else at the party, and she seems very aware of being different and separate. The form of each party-goer is drawn in a nonrealistic and radically different manner, accentuating the uniqueness that separates all humans. One is composed of wavy lines, another of letters, and another of spirals. Hana's form is outlined by curved, flowing lines, but she and her immediate environment are filled in with the detailed hatching of a sketch style. The hatching is all done in a warm magenta hue. Asterios is diagrammatically drawn in a clear-line style and colored in cool cyan. He is an architectural rendering of a wireframe figure, with arms and fingers composed of cylinders.

As soon as Hana and Asterios begin talking, a few of the magenta lines begin appearing in the rendering of Asterios and his background, and the blue geometric lines begin appearing in Hana's form. By the final panel of the scene, the two rendering styles—sketch and line art—are fully integrated; both figures are composed of cyan wire frames filled in with magenta hatching (Figure 3.2). Hana apparently feels a strong connection with Asterios.

As they begin dating, Hana's outfits become half magenta and half cyan. However, in these early stages of the relationship, there is no hint of warm colors in Asterios' wardrobe or his apartment. When Hana wakes up in Asterios' bed for the first time, there is no trace of magenta; only cyan and purple. She has willingly entered his world. However, when Asterios points out a video camera on the ceiling that has recorded them, her reaction is a magenta exclamation point in a magenta balloon. By the third panel an angry Hana is rendered in the magenta-hued sketch style. Asterios, who has become somewhat defensive, especially after Hana slaps him, is now rendered in the cyan outlined wireframe. Over the next three pages Asterios explains why he has cameras in every room, an

Figure 3.2 Shape and color are used to show emotional connection (page 63). *Asterios Polyp* Copyright 2009 David Mazzucchelli.

explanation Hana finds bizarre but acceptable. As her anger fades, so does the magenta. Mazzucchelli reverts both characters to naturalistic drawing done in a neutral purple (purple, which is used for much of their clothing and environment, is the neutral color for Asterios and Hana because it is a combination of cyan and magenta). The two figures drawn in purple cuddle in a pool of color that is light magenta on her side and light cyan on his, but the colors are so faded they are nearly indistinguishable. They have reconnected.

Mazzucchelli's use of color is a constant marker of the progression of their relationship. The longer they are together, the less often either of them is colored monochromatically. They begin to share the same color palette of purple, cyan, and magenta. The reader learns later that Asterios thought his and Hana's constructions of the world had blended together to create "an edifice of eloquent equilibrium" (page 292). Indeed, just before what seems to be the conflict that ended their relationship, their clothing color schemes show a strong degree of identification and connection with the other. Hana wears no magenta, but has a cyan blouse; Asterios wears no cyan, but has a magenta tie.

Yet, under the stress of conflict, each reverts to the colors and shapes that have been established as representing self. As they return home one evening, Hana is hurt, angry, and uncommunicative. Asterios does not seem to notice, and when he makes a selfish and insensitive remark Hana is shown in a circular panel with a very thick magenta border. As Hana's anger rises, a patch of magenta cross-hatching accents her otherwise naturalistic rendering. As Asterios becomes defensive, part of his naturalistic rendering is outlined by a cyan line. The rendering of Hana transforms into the magenta-hued sketch style as she pours out her feelings. Asterios responds "I don't understand why you're getting so angry," and points out "And by the way, that's a mixed metaphor" (page 227).

The cool cyan, wireframe rendering of Asterios shows he is retreating from the messiness of emotion and turning to the intellectual, geometric precision that structures his architect worldview. Even the background of each character's side of the room is drawn in these styles to emphasize their growing separation (Figure 3.3).

The reader learns about the forming and dissolution of Asterios and Hana's relationship in flashbacks. The present-time story begins after they are divorced and Asterios has "sort of shut down" (page 294). He is unshaven and his usually pristine apartment is in disarray, including empty bottles that seem to indicate he has been drinking. Such is his state when a lightning bolt strikes his apartment building and starts a fire.

ASTERIOS IN APOGEE

Yellow first enters the graphic novel as a fire that destroys Asterios' apartment and, symbolically, his old way of life. Simply walking away from the fire and his past life, Asterios uses most of what little money he has left to buy a bus ticket to a randomly selected small town, Apogee. As he approaches Apogee, yellow increasingly becomes a part of the environment and Asterios is tinged by yellow sunlight coming through the bus window. When Asterios arrives in Apogee, he quickly secures a job as a mechanic at Stiff Major's auto repair shop and rents a room in Stiff's home. As Asterios becomes more immersed in the community, yellow and its analogous hues are used for buildings, clothing, and backgrounds. Even Asterios is occasionally monochromatically rendered in shades of yellow.

Figure 3.3 Shape and color are used to show disparate perspectives (page 226). *Asterios Polyp* Copyright 2009 David Mazzucchelli.

Yellow and golden hues are often used to evoke warm feelings of nostalgia for an idealized vision of rural life in America. The environment seems to have a positive, or at least calming, effect on Asterios. He had been pompous, sarcastic, and attention-seeking in New York, but during his stay in Apogee he becomes increasingly laid-back, polite, and even friendly.

After helping Stiff build a treehouse, a tired, sweaty, but seemingly happy Asterios sits on the front porch looking at his handiwork. Asterios is colored with a richer than usual shade of yellow, indicating perhaps the warmth of the sunshine or his sense of contentment. Throughout the scene there are close-up panels of Asterios eating a piece of fruit. It is beyond the scope of the current analysis, but there are multiple allusions and parallels to *The Odyssey* in the graphic novel—when Odysseus' crew ate the lotus fruit they slipped into a blissful lethargy and forgetfulness. If readers take these panels of Asterios eating fruit to be an intertextual reference to the lotus eaters from *The Odyssey*, it could affect the interpretation of Asterios' entire stay in Apogee.

For a while Asterios does lose himself in a warm haze of sunny days and simple living, with no regrets for his past or concern for his future. Yet, by the time Asterios leaves Apogee, he seems to be better for having been there. From Stiff and his wife, Asterios gets a blend of rustic and new-age wisdom of dubious worth, but more instructive is the example of their loving relationship. Indicating perhaps that it is time for him to think about tomorrow, about the future, Asterios learns the most pointed lesson about relationships from a character named Manana (Spanish for "tomorrow"). Manana leans three coasters against one another while explaining that the coasters represent love, trust, and respect. She lets them go and they stand on their own, but, she cautions, "take any one of those away and the whole thing falls apart" (page 271). This lesson seems to be a true epiphany for Asterios.

Moments later, a drunk smashes a bottle on Asterios' head. Asterios awakes in a hospital bed with a bandage over his left eye. Throughout the graphic novel, duality (thesis/antithesis) has been a structuring principle of Asterios' imagination and worldview. Mazzucchelli uses the presence of a new color to signal that duality has been displaced by synthesis. Green, formed by the combination of the cool cyan of Asterios the architect and the warm yellow of Apogee, appears for the first time in the hospital room. Even though the hospital is in Apogee, there is no yellow in this scene. The scene ends with Asterios announcing "I'm going somewhere" (page 297).

An apogee is the point at which an orbiting object is the farthest away from what it is orbiting. As the name of the town suggests, during his stay in Apogee, Asterios has moved far from the core of who he had been. In the same panel that green appears for the first time, cyan, which had been totally absent from his stay in Apogee, subtly reappears in the form of a blanket on Asterios' hospital bed. Perhaps the cyan signals that Asterios has reached his apogee and is beginning a return to some of what he left behind. However, Asterios is no longer defined by cyan, and the addition of hues of green and tan, along with Asterios' attitude and actions, make it clear he is a different man than the one who left New York. To complete the familiar mythic pattern of journey, transformation, and return, Asterios must go back to his previous life with the boon acquired on his journey. When he is released from the hospital, Asterios drives to Minnesota to see Hana.

RECONNECTING WITH HANA

As he is driving to see Hana, Asterios' solar-powered car stops during a snow storm. In the pages that Asterios walks to Hana's house through a blizzard, cyan is the dominant color. However, once he reaches her home there is a stark contrast to the harsh blue cold. Hana's home is an oasis of comforting colors. Hana is wearing green, the furniture is yellow, purple, or brown, the floor is tan. The previous color palette of their lives is only subtly present. A magenta book lies on an end table. Hana places a cyan blanket over the shivering Asterios, but soon places a tan blanket on top of that, muting the presence of cyan.

The changes in the color scheme seem to indicate a change in the very substance of these two characters. That perception is reinforced by Mazzucchelli's use of shape. The shape of Hana's art has changed. During the time Hana lived with Asterios, her sculptures were shapes abstracted from nature, with the flowing lines of flowers and insects. Now her sculptures are based on the straight-lined Platonic solids, a favorite lecture subject of Asterios and the basis of all his architectural designs.

Mazzucchelli also uses the shapes of the dialogue balloons to show their connection. The borders of the balloons remain as they have been—straight-lined for Asterios and gently curved for Hana—but as they share in recalling a poignant moment during a European trip, the tails of the dialogue balloons become intertwined. On the next page, as they remember an inside joke and speak the same phrase at the same time, the two differently shaped dialogue balloons overlap (Figure 3.4).

This particular application of image function analysis has attempted to answer the question: How does David Mazzucchelli use shape and color as hermeneutic images to communicate changes in Asterios' and Hana's relationship? Mazzucchelli's use of the three printer's primary colors—magenta, yellow, and cyan—individualized dialogue balloon shapes, and sketch and clean-line styles occasionally used to render their forms provide a strong visual representation of the growth, dissolution, and reconnection of Asterios' and Hana's relationship.

When they first meet, the strong primary colors and distinctive shapes used to render the forms of the main characters emphasize their uniqueness and the separation created by that uniqueness. As they grow closer, and particularly as they live together, Asterios and Hana begin to share the cyan and magenta that had defined them, indicating the compromises necessary in a relationship. Yet, in moments of stress, the colors and shapes representing each character's personality and perspective reappear, creating a strong visual division that reflects the emotional divide they are experiencing.

Figure 3.4 Shape is used to convey a moment of connection (page 326). *Asterios Polyp* Copyright 2009 David Mazzucchelli.

Even though they are not able to sustain the relationship, the hermeneutic images used to depict Asterios and Hana toward the end of the graphic novel seem to indicate they have changed for having had the relationship. Early in the graphic novel the narrator suggests that "it's possible for someone to freely alter his own perception of reality in order to overlap with that of another" (page 40). By the time Asterios leaves Apogee, he seems less self-centered and appears to have developed more need and concern for others. The reader has not seen anything of Hana's life after the divorce, but Mazzucchelli uses the shape of her art and the new color scheme of her clothing and environment to indicate that she too has changed. Secondary and tertiary colors, such as green and brown, result from a blending of primary colors. When these new hues are introduced toward the end of the graphic novel, Asterios' and Hana's color palettes are not simply shared, with each wearing the other's color, but truly blended. They have found a common ground that might make reconciliation possible. Near the end of the graphic novel, Asterios and Hana sit quietly side-by-side on the couch, hands almost touching and seemingly at peace with who they have become.

NOTES

1. Art Spiegelman, *Breakdowns* (New York: Pantheon Books, 2008), 13.
2. Brittany Kusa and Jessica Lona, transcription, "David Mazzucchelli and Dash Shaw," *The Comics Journal* 300 (2009): 117.
3. Ibid.
4. Randy Duncan and Matthew J. Smith, *The Power of Comics: History, Form and Culture* (New York: Continuum, 2009), 154–163.
5. Glen Weldon, "The Best Five Books to Share With Your Friends," *NPR*, December 2, 2009. www.npr.org/templates/story/story.php?storyId=120980848.
6. Patrick Kastner, "Tales Delivered in Graphic Terms," *The Columbus Dispatch*, August 23, 2009. www.dispatch.com/live/content/life/stories/2009/08/23/2_GRAPHIC_NOVELS.ART_ART_08-23-09_E3_09EOKSP.html?sid=101.
7. Faber Birren, *Color Psychology and Color Therapy* (New York: University Books, 1961), 141.
8. Scott McCloud, *Understanding Comics: The Invisible Art* (Northampton, MA: Tundra Publishing, 1993), 125.
9. Kenneth Burke, *A Rhetoric of Motives* (Berkeley: University of California Press, 1969), 146.

SELECTED BIBLIOGRAPHY

Birren, Faber. *Color Psychology and Color Therapy.* New York: University Books, 1961.
Burke, Kenneth. *A Rhetoric of Motives.* Berkeley: University of California Press, 1969.
Duncan, Randy and Matthew J. Smith. *The Power of Comics: History, Form and Culture.* New York: Continuum, 2009.
Kastner, Patrick. "Tales Delivered in Graphic Terms." *The Columbus Dispatch*, August 23, 2009, www.dispatch.com/live/content/live/stories/   2009/08/23/2_GRAPHIC_NOVELS.ART_ART_08-23-09_E309EOKSP.html?sid=101, accessed December 12, 2009.
Kusa, Brittany and Jessica Lona. "David Mazzucchelli and Dash Shaw." Transcription. *The Comics Journal* 300 (2009): 88–117.
McCloud, Scott. *Understanding Comics: The Invisible Art.* Northampton, MA: Kitchen Sink, 1993.
Spiegelman, Art. *Breakdowns.* New York: Pantheon Books, 2008.
Weldon, Glen. "The Best Five Books To Share With Your Friends." *NPR*, www.npr.org/templates/story/story.php?storyId=120980848, accessed December 15, 2009.

4

TIME AND NARRATIVE

Unity and Discontinuity in The Invisibles

Marc Singer

A young boy feigns his own death in an imaginary combat with his friends. Then he falls in a real battle as a grown man serving in the British Army. Then he is a child again, lighting fireworks with his father and taking violent abuse from his older brother. Then he is in a hospital, watching his grown brother die. Then he is an infant in a crib, doted on by his mother. Then he is an adult again, attending his mother's funeral. His life continues to cycle between youth, adolescence, and adulthood until the moment of his death, after which he is once again a young boy, dying in an imaginary combat with his friends.

This disordered biography comes from "Best Man Fall," the twelfth issue of Grant Morrison's comic book series *The Invisibles.* The discontinuous scenes and jarring transitions violate our normal understanding of time as a linear and irreversible progression from past to present to future, but they are not at all out of place in the world of narrative, which has the freedom to present time from multiple perspectives and arrange it into a number of possible patterns. *Narrative theory* offers one method for describing and analyzing these manipulations of time and sequence. Also called *narratology*, narrative theory is the study of narratives and the structures that shape them; *narratologists* examine the elements that comprise narratives (the plot, point of view, voice, implied audience, and so forth) with the goal of understanding how meaning develops from and is influenced by these elements. While any narrative in any medium can rearrange its representation of time, comics like *The Invisibles* possess a special potential since their very form presents temporal relationships through spatial and pictorial, as well as sequential, means. Comics have developed their own distinctive techniques for representing the passage of time within single images and between panels, making them ideally suited for experiments with other configurations of time. Although the study of comics requires its own distinct critical tools and terminology, narrative theory has much to offer in exploring the varied operations of time in comics.

UNDERLYING ASSUMPTIONS

Narrative theory generally focuses on the structural elements thought to be common to all stories, although nearly all narratologists will cite specific texts as examples of these general structures. That interest in universal categories is a sign of the field's origins in *structuralism*, a twentieth-century intellectual movement that sought to understand all cultural phenomena, including narratives, as the products of shared systems of rules, relationships, and binary oppositions. As structuralism has lost influence over narrative theory and critical theory more generally, some narratologists have become more interested in exceptional cases, narratives that appear to defy the structures of conventional narratology or suggest those structures are incomplete. Whatever approach it takes, narrative theory offers a precise and expansive vocabulary for discussing the elements that make up narratives, including time, plot, and other *narrative dynamics* that guide the development of a narrative from its beginning to its end.[1]

That vocabulary provides an important set of tools for analyzing departures from linear chronology, which turn out to be surprisingly common. Even the most apparently chronological narratives often depart from strict chronological time. They may begin in the middle of the action, recall earlier events, skip over large periods of time, compress or extend their description of key moments, or present the same incidents multiple times. Many narratologists regard these variations as mere narrative manipulations of events that remain fundamentally chronological: that is, the timeline becomes altered in the telling of the story, not in the story itself. This approach assumes that linear chronology is the only way to represent time and maintain *mimesis,* a realistic imitation of the world. Structuralist narratology supports this approach with its distinction between *story* or *fabula,* the events of a narrative in the (presumably chronological) order in which they happened, and *discourse* or *sjužet,* the manner in which those events are presented to readers. While that distinction has proven invaluable in discussing narrative time, narratology has sometimes privileged the events of the story, which can only be reconstructed from the discourse, as being more "real" than the discourse that creates them. Of course, nonfiction narratives are preceded by a real sequence of events, although Hayden White has argued that even historians plot their works according to narrative conventions, imposing the coherence and structure of fiction upon the raw material of the past.[2] Fictional narratives are less bound to any pre-existing record; they do not even have to obey the laws of time and chronology that appear to govern our lives.

In *Narrative Discourse,* Gérard Genette defines narrative time through three types of relations between story and discourse: the *order* in which events transpire in the story and the order in which they are presented in the discourse; the *duration* of events in the story and the duration of their re-telling in the discourse; and the *frequency* with which these events are repeated in the story as opposed to the frequency of their repetition in the discourse.[3] The discourse can depart from the story in any or all of these areas, leading Genette to regard narrative time as a "quasi-fiction," a "false time standing in for a true time ... a *pseudo-time.*"[4] Privileging the time of the story as the "true time," Genette implies the chronological story is more real and more accurate than the narrative discourse. Because the story can only be assembled from a reading of the discourse, however, its time might just as reasonably be considered a narrative by-product, considerably less real than the discursive time that generates it. Many narratologists now regard story as an ordering scheme constructed through the act of reading the discourse. In *Introduction* to *Poetics*, Tzvetan Todorov dismisses the "representative illusion" that grants mimetic priority to the story: "There is not, *first of all*, a certain reality, *and afterward*, its representation by the text."[5] Todorov observes that readers construct the illusory reality of the story from elements of the narrative discourse, including its presentation of time; Peter Brooks and Jonathan Culler have made similar observations, arguing that the apparent priority of the story is a "mimetic illusion" since the story is a product of the discourse, not its origin.[6]

Recognizing that the story is only a secondary construct and a mimetic illusion, many writers have chosen to exploit narrative's capacity for distorting, rearranging, and otherwise departing from chronology to construct alternative systems of time. Brian Richardson inventories several types of narrative that create nonchronological representations of time, including stories with dual, multiple, conflated, incompatible, or contradictory scales of time and narratives that have no recoverable story at all.[7] Comics writers and artists have also explored alternative temporalities in their own medium. These projects include the circular time of Miguelanxo Prado's *Trazo de Tiza* (*Streak of Chalk*), the backwards time of Alan Moore and Mike White's "The Reversible Man," the differential rates of time's passage that separate the protagonist from his homeland in François Schuiten and Benoît Peeters' *Les Murailles de Samaris* (*The Great Walls of Samaris*), and the eternal present inhabited by Dr. Manhattan in Alan Moore and Dave Gibbons' *Watchmen*. However, even comics that represent worlds of standard linear chronology do so through techniques that confound traditional narratological accounts of time; Genette, for example, speculates that the temporal duality between story and discourse is less relevant to comics than it is to other forms of narrative expression.[8]

Any examination of time in comics must consider the features unique to the form. In *Understanding Comics*, Scott McCloud observes that time in comics is always paradoxical: the images are static, yet they can imply the passage of time within panels through their simulation of sound, action, and motion, and between panels through their establishment of sequence.[9] McCloud concludes that "in the world of comics, time and space are one and the same" since temporal relationships are established through the relationships within and between panels on the space of the page; he also notes that these relationships do not have to follow linear chronology or the standard reading protocols that guide Western readers from left to right and from the top of the page to the bottom.[10] Not only are there other ways of envisioning the passage of time—McCloud represents the circular temporality of the times of day, the phases of the moon, and the stages of birth, growth, and reproduction across the generations (Figure 4.1)—but comics give each moment in the narrative a graphic persistence not found in other, more time-bound media. As McCloud points out, panels are visible on the page before the reader reaches that point in the narrative, and they remain visible after the reader passes them by; gesturing to the panels that surround him, McCloud's cartoon avatar exclaims: "Both past and future are real and visible all around us!"[11]

Time assumes a central role in McCloud's analysis of the narrative dynamics of comics because, like Will Eisner before him, he defines comics as *sequential art*, art composed of sequences of images. By making sequence the constitutive element of comics, McCloud foregrounds the importance of time, especially as it factors into the relationships between images; in his follow-up, *Reinventing Comics*, McCloud simplifies his arguments even further to define comics as a kind of "temporal map" that represents time through spatial arrangements.[12] Other definitions, such as R.C. Harvey's argument that comics are defined by their combination of verbal and visual elements, place less emphasis on time and sequence, although Harvey also acknowledges the role of sequence and panel transitions.[13] Time is an important part of comics under any definition, just as it remains an important part of most approaches to the study of narrative. Any examination of the narrative dynamics of comics should take the form's graphic and spatial representations of time into account.

PROCEDURES

Readers might follow a number of procedures for analyzing narrative time in comics. They could begin by looking at the comic through the lens of structuralist narratology: How does the narrative discourse align with the story? How do the order, duration, or frequency of events change between the story and the discourse? However, many narrative theorists are no longer beholden to these categories, nor do they assume that narrative time is always chronological or that story always takes priority over discourse. Readers could look for other means of presenting time within the world of the story, considering that it may not be strictly chronological, particularly within the fantastic

Figure 4.1 *Understanding Comics* 106 (detail). Copyright 1993 Scott McCloud.

worlds of superheroes, science fiction, and other popular genres. In that case, readers might begin with a different set of questions: How does time operate in this narrative world? What patterns or systems of organization does it follow? How do these systems find expression in the narrative discourse? Which elements of the narrative dynamics reveal the operations of time? How can readers interpret these dynamics to arrive at the narrative's meaning? Finally, a good narratological reading—or any other academic reading—should be able to argue for the significance of its insights.

A narratological reading should also consider how the formal properties of comics shape the medium's representation of time. Readers could examine the graphic techniques that simulate the passage of time within panels, or the spatial and sequential relationships that imply its progression between panels. Those relationships do not always generate a strictly linear progression, however, nor do they occur only between adjacent panels. Comics can also establish connections between discontinuous images and scenes, a nonlinear practice that comics scholar Thierry Groensteen terms *braiding*.[14] Readers may discover temporal relationships that span an entire comic book or graphic novel—or, if the comic has been serialized, those relationships could stretch across weeks, months, or years of publication. The variety of publishing formats affords comics creators many different means of representing time, and furnishes readers with plenty of opportunities for examination.

A narratological reader of comics faces a number of decisions: Do you look for the narrative practices typical of most comics, or the exceptions that break all the rules? Will you survey many different comics, or focus on just one? Will you study a self-contained narrative, or an ongoing serial with multiple installments? Whatever you decide, you can expect to pay close attention to the texts you select. While narratologists also conduct secondary research, surveying what artists and other readers have said about the works they study, putting narrative theory into practice is primarily a matter of conducting an informed, close reading of the text, looking at all the ways the narrative elements contribute to its meaning.

ARTIFACT SELECTED FOR ANALYSIS

The Invisibles is a comic book series written by Grant Morrison, illustrated by numerous artists, and published over three volumes from 1994 to 2000. The series, which chronicles the adventures of a network of anarchists who travel across time and space to battle a sinister conspiracy, presents several challenges to traditional theories of narrative time. *The Invisibles* demonstrates the complex and contradictory operations of time in comics, while it openly violates chronology and asks readers to consider alternative means of perceiving time. Scholars may find it all but impossible to measure the order, duration, and frequency of the narrative discourse against the chronological timeline of the story since the series depicts a world that does not always follow linear chronology. In addition to featuring multiple time travelers and alternate, overlapping universes, *The Invisibles* repeatedly suggests that time does not flow in a simple progression from past to present to future. Several characters are capable of altering their perceptions and viewing their lives from outside the space–time continuum, perceiving time as one *synchronic* unity rather than a *diachronic* succession of moments. In the "Sheman" storyline (volume 1, issues 13–15), an Aztec god tells the shaman Lord Fanny that "All times are the same time" (issue 14, page 1) and that all events happen in an eternal present (issue 15, page 21).

"Sheman" demonstrates this cosmology in its own narrative structure, blurring events from Fanny's magical initiation at age 11 with later ordeals at ages 18 and 23, and shifting the narration between these time periods without regard for chronology. By the end of the story, the 11-year-old Fanny is narrating the 23-year-old's plotline in the past tense, as if it has already happened (issue 15, page 21).

The synchronic time of *The Invisibles* not only abolishes linear chronology, it undermines the distinction between story and discourse. At the culmination of Fanny's initiation, she learns not only to perceive time as a unified whole, but also to alter it:

> And suddenly she is seeing everything all at once—all past, present and future rippling across a trembling hymen. The lightest breath across its surface is sufficient to alter the fragile structure of time and space. And so, against the wishes of the others, she blows gently ... and the membrane shivers.
>
> (Issue 15, pages 16–17)

Blowing on the membrane of time and space, Fanny avoids a grisly fate—the previous issue has shown an omen of her death—and her would-be killer dies in her place. This is only the first of many moments in the series when the characters are able to rewrite their own stories: later instances are even more openly metafictional, suggesting that the entire world of *The Invisibles* is actually a story written by one Invisible, a virtual-reality game developed by another, or even a comic book written by Grant Morrison. When all times are the same time, when characters can change the events of their stories, when the entire universe may be a fiction that can be edited or altered at will, there is no story in the narratological sense—that is, no one chronological sequence of events can be privileged as the correct or true sequence. *The Invisibles* questions the structuralist assumption that all narratives have an underlying chronology that can be recovered from the discourse. Its timeline can be apprehended in any order and characters in one period can affect events in another, the consequences of a synchronic universe.

In the second volume, a scientist named Takashi Satoh attempts to articulate the same ideas in the language of physics rather than mysticism. Like the shamans of "Sheman," he tries to view time from the outside and envisions its unity:

> Think of timespace as a multidimensional self-perfecting system in which everything that has ever, or will ever occur, occurs simultaneously. I believe timespace is a kind of object, a geometrical supersolid. I believe it may even be a type of hologram in which energy and matter themselves are byproducts of the overlapping of two higher systems.
>
> Think of it this way: Where is the past? Where is the future? Undeniably, they exist, but why can't you point to them? The only way to do that is to jump 'up' from the surface of timespace and see all of history and all of our tomorrows as the single object I believe it is.
>
> (Volume 2, issue 5, page 16)

Takashi compares this object to a hologram, a three-dimensional image formed from overlapping light beams (or, in the cosmology of *The Invisibles*, overlapping higher-dimensional universes). Holography encodes the entire image onto each portion of the recording medium, meaning each part contains all the information of the whole. For this reason, holograms often function as metaphors for the structure of *The Invisibles* and other comics by Morrison, in which the part similarly reflects the whole—but Takashi's speech also makes another, more implicit analogy. The extradimensional perspective he describes, in which past, present, and future events are all visible simultaneously, is remarkably similar to the perspective of a reader looking down at the comics page where Takashi delivers this lecture. As McCloud notes, the reader sees events that are narratively located at different points in time (in different panels) yet graphically located in the same continuous space (on the page). In his attempt to visualize time-space, Takashi has unwittingly described the structure of his own comic book and the vantage point of its readers, an analogy that is not lost on his writer. Morrison capitalizes on the distinctive features of time in comics to depict the unconventional time of *The Invisibles*.

SAMPLE ANALYSIS

Morrison, Grant and various artists. *The Invisibles*. 3 volumes. New York: DC Comics, 1994–2000.
Morrison, Grant and Steve Parkhouse. "Best Man Fall." *The Invisibles*, volume 1, issue 12 (1995). Repeated in *The Invisibles*, volume 2: *Apocalipstick*. New York: Vertigo, 2001.

Many of the techniques comics have developed for representing the passage of time, from panel transitions and page layouts to the publication schedule of serialized comic books, are on display in "Best Man Fall," a story published in the twelfth issue of the first volume of *The Invisibles*. Unlike "Sheman" or some of the other, more experimental storylines, "Best Man Fall" appears to present a chronological story (albeit through a nonchronological discourse). Writer Grant Morrison and artist Steve Parkhouse depict the life of Bobby Murray—a security guard and former soldier in the British Army—through a series of discontinuous fragments, and ask readers to assemble them into a coherent biography—a conventional example of how the narrative discourse produces the chronological timeline of the story. This process proves deceptive in "Best Man Fall," however, which manipulates reader expectations through panel and image juxtapositions and the juxtaposition of different installments of the serialized narrative. These juxtapositions produce a sequence of false stories, an accelerating timeline, and ultimately a refusal of linear chronology. The temporal techniques of "Best Man Fall" reflect the concerns of *The Invisibles* as a whole, but they also highlight the complex operations of time in all comics, not just the experimental ones.

In *Understanding Comics*, Scott McCloud speculates that readers are inclined to infer connections between any sequence of adjacent images.[15] "Best Man Fall" absolutely depends on such inferences. Morrison and Parkhouse guide readers through a series of abrupt transitions and disordered vignettes that jump from moment to moment in the life of Bobby Murray, with no regard for chronology. The first page shows Bobby as a young boy playing "best man fall" with his friends—a game in which players take turns simulating their deaths by various imaginary weapons. The second page shows an adult soldier felled by an explosion; later pages will reveal that this is the fully grown Bobby Murray, now in his early twenties and fighting in the Falklands War, but nothing in this scene identifies him. Readers may already suspect the soldier is Bobby, however, since

Figure 4.2 Grant Morrison and Steve Parkhouse, *The Invisibles* volume 1, issue 12, page 3. Copyright 1994 Grant Morrison.

the scene is bracketed on either side by other scenes in which Bobby is the protagonist. These early transitions rely on a form of continuity editing (to borrow a term from film) in which similar images and actions help readers negotiate the shifts between scenes. The pages move from the imaginary combat of "best man fall" to the real battle in the Falklands, then from bursting artillery shells to the exploding fireworks lit by Bobby's father in a scene from his childhood (Figure 4.2). Continuity matching helps readers infer, correctly, that the young boy and the injured soldier are the same person at three different times in his life.

Morrison and Parkhouse do not rely solely on the direct juxtaposition of images to guide readers; they also invite readers to build connections between non-adjacent images and scenes through braiding. Although Groensteen describes braiding as being non-narrative or sub-narrative, "a supplementary relation that is never indispensable to the conduct and intelligibility of the story,"[16] "Best Man Fall" integrates its braided images fully into the narrative and makes their nonlinear connections absolutely essential to the interpretation of the comic. On page 6, for example, Bobby's wife, Audrey, appears with a despondent, beaten expression and a black eye, but the image passes without comment. On page 8, Audrey's oversized sunglasses fail to conceal another large bruise. Her weak excuse, that she fell down the stairs, leaves little doubt as to what she is hiding and suggests an explanation for the earlier injury (even though, chronologically, the scene on page 6 occurs some time after the scene on page 8). Morrison and Parkhouse confirm these implications several pages later when an old army friend asks Bobby how Audrey is doing, and a sudden, silent, single-panel scene transition shows Bobby hitting her (page 15). The braided, disordered chronology often shows effects before revealing their causes, as when a funeral mourner mentions the cancer that killed Bobby's mother (page 8) two pages before Morrison and Parkhouse show her smoking a cigarette in her prime (page 10). The creators count on the reader's memory of earlier scenes to apply the explanations retroactively once they have all the necessary information.

Other connections between panels, pages, and scenes are less explicit, but still provide ample fodder for reader speculation. The obvious similarity between Audrey's features and those of Bobby's mother, for example, goes a long way towards explaining Bobby's initial attraction to his future wife. Some transitions imply judgments or interpretations that elude the characters: Patrick Meaney suggests that an early transition from Bobby's violent bullying at the hands of his brother to Audrey's black eye explains the origins of Bobby's abusive behavior—his brother has instilled "a lifelong association between love and violence."[17] Another sudden transition from Bobby exiting an armed forces recruiting office to lying in the hospital (pages 12–13) encapsulates his military career while highlighting the consequences of Margaret Thatcher's election as prime minister; as Bobby leaves the recruiting office he ignores the newspaper headlines and newsstand conversations that announce Thatcher's victory, yet her enthusiastic pursuit of the war with Argentina will lead to his injuries. In addition to these thematic implications, the issue is filled with so many historical and cultural markers—the moon landing, punk fashions, Thatcher's election, the Falklands, the Live Aid concert—that readers can assemble a chronology of Bobby's life and date it with considerable accuracy.[18]

If the issue were only dedicated to reassembling its fragments into a chronological timeline, then "Best Man Fall" would be a fairly conventional illustration of the differences between story and discourse. In fact, the issue's implied connections are just as likely to mislead readers into inferring false stories. Morrison and Parkhouse play their greatest trick in the opening pages: after Bobby is hit by the explosion in the Falklands, and before the next scene opens on the childhood fireworks, the creators insert a narrow rectangular panel, completely black except for the thought balloon that reads, "I'm dying. Oh fuck, I think I'm" (Figure 4.2). Placed immediately after Bobby's combat injury, the panel invites readers to assume the injury is fatal; they may even assume the entire issue represents Bobby's life flashing before his eyes in the moments before death, providing an in-text explanation for the disordered chronology.

The second assumption proves correct, but not the first. Bobby survives his Falklands injuries, although readers are not given this information until halfway through the issue, in panels that show Bobby being carried off the battlefield on a stretcher (page 14) and recovering in a hospital bed (page 13). (Sharp-eyed readers may have spotted the cane Bobby leans on at his mother's funeral, in the last stages of his recovery.) The black panel after the Falklands scene was a feint, a flashforward to the later moment of Bobby's death; when it reappears at the end of the issue (page 23) it has found its true place in the chronology. Other apparent connections between panels prove equally misleading. Repeated images of a figure digging a grave, introduced during Bobby's mother's funeral and plausibly connected to that event, turn out to be scenes of a teenaged Bobby burying his beloved dog. Whether these misdirections are trivial affairs or literally matters of life and death, they depend on a process of inference and association that, according to McCloud and Groensteen, can happen between any two comics panels. Morrison and Parkhouse exploit this trait of comics, leading readers to combine panels into false narratives and false timelines before disproving and discarding them.

When "Best Man Fall" finally reveals the actual circumstances of Bobby's death, it turns out that readers of The Invisibles have already seen him die once before. Bobby, working as a security guard at a juvenile prison, responds to a break-in and is shot by a mysterious figure in a bizarre mask. This figure is King Mob, one of the protagonists of The Invisibles, and the scene replays his rescue of another hero in the first issue of the series (volume 1, issue 1, pages 34–35). In that issue, the security guards were just so much cannon fodder, unthinking henchmen of the forces of evil and minor obstacles for King Mob to dispatch with righteous violence. After "Best Man Fall" presents that combat from Bobby's point of view and recontextualizes it within the rest of his life story, however, the battle is no longer an entertaining diversion but a tragedy, and King Mob's actions are not heroism, but murder.

By revising an earlier issue, Morrison manipulates another scale of time—the time that passes between issues of a serialized comic book. Not every comic is written and published in serial installments, and Morrison's tactic would read very differently in a self-contained graphic novel, where readers would encounter both renditions of Bobby Murray's death between the same covers. Even the collected editions of The Invisibles allow these scenes to be read within much closer proximity, although they are still separated by two volumes. As originally published, however, the first and twelfth issues of The Invisibles were released one year apart, in July 1994 and July 1995, leaving readers with plenty of time to become invested in the series' initial glamorization of King Mob as a dashing action hero—or to question it. Some of the intervening issues had already begun to raise doubts about the morality of King Mob's actions; in issue 9, for example, he is so efficient and so callous about his murder of a group of enemy soldiers (complete with James Bond-style quips) that even his teammates are disgusted. "Best Man Fall" brings this critique to the foreground and confronts readers with the human cost of King

Mob's cinematic violence; if one of the generic henchmen from the first issue can have such a complex and tragic life, so might any of the soldiers and guards slaughtered by the Invisibles. The temporal manipulations of "Best Man Fall" not only demand that we read the issue retrospectively, they invite us to re-examine the entire series and question King Mob's initial heroic posture.[19]

Just as "Best Man Fall" revises earlier stories, its themes and techniques reverberate into later issues of *The Invisibles*. Early in the second volume, Morrison and new artist Phil Jimenez remind readers that the enemy henchmen are still human beings. As King Mob shoots another luckless soldier, a cascade of panels erupts out of the wound to show a series of fragmented vignettes from the soldier's life (volume 2, issue 3, page 9). The scene repeats "Best Man Fall" both in its disordered chronology—if we read the panels from left to right, we move back in time from the soldier's adulthood through his adolescence, childhood, and infancy, all the way to his conception—and in its reminder that any killing, no matter how much it may be justified by the circumstances or naturalized by the conventions of popular entertainment, still ends somebody's life. However, the storyline is so violent that Morrison must repeat the lesson once more. In the next issue, another soldier mistakes King Mob for a childhood vision of the angel of death (volume 2, issue 4, page 13); the confusion of past and present terrors recalls "Best Man Fall," where Bobby Murray's childhood fear of a bogeyman in a coal cellar—actually just an old gas mask—provides an eerie premonition of his death at the hands of the masked King Mob. The second time around, however, the soldier's humanizing memory is condensed into just a single panel before King Mob executes him.

These successive compressions of the lessons of "Best Man Fall" from an entire issue to a page to a single panel reflect another recurring device in *The Invisibles*—the acceleration of time. Several characters voice their belief that time is moving faster as humanity approaches an impending apocalypse, as seen in this casual conversation from the next issue after "Best Man Fall":

Fanny: Do you feel as though time's speeding up, darling? I mean actually getting faster.
King Mob: Maybe it's like a whirlpool, and the closer we get to the apocalypse or the eschaton or whatever you want to call it, the more things happen in a shorter time.

(Volume 1, issue 13, page 2)

The Invisibles implements this theory in its own structure, gathering speed as the series progresses from the literary and philosophical discussions of the first volume to the action-packed finale of volume three. The final issue compresses events into a rapid-fire montage and replays earlier moments in the series; these quotations include Fanny and King Mob's conversation about accelerating time, a reminder of how long this theme had been building and a theoretical justification for the issue's abrupt and discordant transitions (volume 3, issue 1, page 15). While the final issue recapitulates the series and recalls many of its past highlights, Morrison continues to compress its themes into the final page and then the final sentence. As he told Patrick Neighly and Kereth Cowe-Spigai,

it just keeps condensing. [The final sentence] is the entire series again, but now it's reduced to just words. And then it goes right then in to [the final word], which is the actual word which is telling us what to do. And then it goes right in to the point, which is the universe collapsing completely, and we are liberated by a full stop.[20]

A 59-issue series that has spanned nearly six years is distilled down to its last page, sentence, panel, and period.

"Best Man Fall" is more than just an early stage in this temporal compression; it also reflects the series' accelerating time through its own narrative structure. For the first half of the issue, the vignettes of Bobby Murray's life move at a steady pace, with most scenes lasting around one page. As the issue progresses, the scenes grow shorter. Vignettes collapse to a half-page, a tier of panels, or a single panel, and Morrison and Parkhouse intersperse isolated, silent, mysterious panels (Bobby digging his dog's grave, the door to the coal cellar), whose meanings only become clear later in the issue. The creators begin to nest vignettes inside one another: a scene of Bobby feeding his daughter is interrupted by a flashback to a nurse announcing that she has been born with cerebral palsy, and Bobby's spousal abuse is intercut, with brutal irony, with a panel showing the night he met Audrey. After King Mob shoots Bobby, the pace relaxes into a two-page scene of Bobby proposing to Audrey on an idyllic holiday. But this tranquil scene proves to be a false respite, both in terms of Bobby and Audrey's marriage and the issue's narrative of Bobby's life and death. In both cases, the couple's moment of romantic bliss is overshadowed by the reader's anachronistic knowledge of what will happen next. The marriage will descend into abuse and Bobby, who tells Audrey that he's going to live forever, will grow up to die in the service of a horrible institution. The next panel shows the bullet piercing Bobby's skull.

Following that fatal shot, the pace remains slow as the formal attention shifts to the arrangement of space on the page. As Bobby's life ebbs, the final two pages are increasingly dominated by black panels and white negative spaces (Figures 4.3 and 4.4)—quite a contrast from the full-bleed images of luminous evening skies in his holiday memory. The final page is half-filled by these empty fields, and the final tier of panels is completely filled by them, culminating in a black panel; the expanding black and white areas shrink the amount of space available for representing Bobby's life, a visual and spatial demonstration of his rapidly diminishing time on this earth and the progressively accelerating temporality of *The Invisibles*. The final page also returns to the game of "best man fall" that opened the issue and to the mysterious captions, "It's only a game … Try to remember," that provide its only narration. These repetitions bring the narrative full circle, concluding the issue's temporal shifts and sustaining its challenge to linear models of time and chronology. However, the captions are also variations on another theme that echoes throughout the series as Morrison periodically insinuates that the entire world of *The Invisibles* is just a game, a program, a story, or some other fictional construct—perhaps the virtual-reality game that King Mob develops in the final issue. The individual issue, page, and panel condense the concerns of the entire series, the part reflecting the whole just like the holograms that structure Takashi's understanding of spacetime.

In its form and structure, as well as its cosmology, *The Invisibles* is a comic in which the part always models the whole. "Best Man Fall" exemplifies this design through its creation of circular and nonlinear narratives, its varied and accelerating pacing, its revision of past issues and reappearance in later ones, and its reflections in miniature of the themes that shape the entire series. The issue incorporates these techniques primarily,

Figure 4.3 Grant Morrison and Steve Parkhouse, *The Invisibles* volume 1, issue 12, page 23. Copyright 1994 Grant Morrison.

Figure 4.4 Grant Morrison and Steve Parkhouse, *The Invisibles* volume 1, issue 12, page 24. Copyright 1994 Grant Morrison.

though not exclusively, through its manipulation of time in a manner unique to the medium of comics. While they articulate important arguments about the morality of our actions, the brutality of popular entertainment, and the value of human life, "Best Man Fall" and *The Invisibles* also demonstrate how comic books can creatively represent, rearrange, and exploit time on the level of the panel, the page, the issue, and the series.

NOTES

1. Brian Richardson, ed., *Narrative Dynamics* (Columbus: Ohio State University Press, 2002), 1.
2. Hayden White, "The Historical Text as Literary Artifact," in *Tropics of Discourse* (Baltimore: Johns Hopkins University Press, 1978), 99.
3. Gérard Genette, *Narrative Discourse* (Ithaca, NY: Cornell University Press, 1980), 35.
4. Ibid., 34.
5. Todorov, Tzvetan, *Introduction to Poetics* (Minneapolis: University of Minnesota Press, 1981), 27; his emphasis.
6. Peter Brooks, *Reading for the Plot* (New York: Knopf, 1984), 13; see also Jonathan Culler, "Fabula and Sjuzhet in the Analysis of Narrative: Some American Discussions," *Poetics Today* 1 (3) (1980): 29.
7. Brian Richardson, "Narrative Poetics and Postmodern Transgression: Theorizing the Collapse of Time, Voice, and Frame," *Narrative* 8, (1) (2000): 24–31.
8. Genette, *Narrative Discourse,* 33–34.
9. Scott McCloud, *Understanding Comics* (Northampton, MA: Kitchen Sink, 1993), 95–98. Will Eisner makes a similar observation in *Comics & Sequential Art* (Tamarac, FL: Poorhouse Press, 1990), 28.
10. McCloud, *Understanding Comics,* 100, 105.
11. Ibid., 104.
12. Scott McCloud, *Reinventing Comics* (New York: DC Comics, 2000), 206–207.
13. R.C. Harvey, *The Art of the Comic Book: An Aesthetic History* (Jackson, MS: University Press of Mississippi, 1996), 3–4, 246.
14. Thierry Groensteen, *The System of Comics* (Jackson, MS: University Press of Mississippi, 2007), 146–148.
15. McCloud, *Understanding Comics,* 73.
16. Groensteen, *The System of Comics,* 146–147.
17. Patrick Meaney, *Our Sentence Is Up: Seeing Grant Morrison's* The Invisibles (Edwardsville, IL: Sequart, 2010), 64.
18. A reference to being nine years old during the 1969 moon landing indicates that Bobby was born around 1960, the same year Morrison was. One of the subtle ironies of "Best Man Fall" is that Grant Morrison and Bobby Murray are both born into working-class families in the same year, but Bobby becomes a soldier and a prison guard while Morrison became a countercultural comics writer.
19. King Mob is himself fully invested in that heroic posture. In the issue following "Best Man Fall," he narrates the story of his break-in and rescue to a friend. Artist Jill Thompson draws this re-telling in the style of superhero artist Rob Liefeld, presenting King Mob as a hypermasculine action hero with bulging muscles and big guns (volume 1, issue 13, page 10); the ridiculous presentation suggests that King Mob is exaggerating his story and glamorizing himself. In two of these panels he guns down the security guards—the third rendition of the death of Bobby Murray, a rendition in which King Mob has learned nothing.
20. Patrick Neighly and Kereth Cowe-Spigai, *Anarchy for the Masses: The Disinformation Guide to the Invisibles* (New York: The Disinformation Company, 2003), 214.

SELECTED BIBLIOGRAPHY

Brooks, Peter. *Reading for the Plot: Design and Intention in Narrative.* New York: Knopf, 1984.
Culler, Jonathan. "Fabula and Sjuzhet in the Analysis of Narrative: Some American Discussions." *Poetics Today* 1 (3) (1980): 27–37.
Eisner, Will. *Comics & Sequential Art.* Tamarac, FL: Poorhouse Press, 1990.
Genette, Gérard. *Narrative Discourse.* 1972. Translated by Jane E. Lewin. Ithaca, NY: Cornell University Press, 1980.
Groensteen, Thierry. *The System of Comics.* 1999. Translated by Bart Beaty and Nick Nguyen. Jackson, MS: University Press of Mississippi, 2007.

Harvey, R.C. *The Art of the Comic Book: An Aesthetic History.* Jackson, MS: University Press of Mississippi, 1996.

McCloud, Scott. *Understanding Comics: The Invisible Art.* Northampton, MA: Kitchen Sink, 1993.

McCloud, Scott. *Reinventing Comics: How Imagination and Technology Are Revolutionizing an Art Form.* New York: DC Comics, 2000.

Meaney, Patrick. *Our Sentence Is Up: Seeing Grant Morrison's* The Invisibles. Edwardsville, IL: Sequart, 2010.

Morrison, Grant and Steve Parkhouse. "Best Man Fall." *The Invisibles* 1 (12) (1995). Rpt. in *The Invisibles* 2: *Apocalipstick.* New York: Vertigo, 2001.

Morrison, Grant, and various artists. *The Invisibles.* 3 vols. New York: DC Comics, 1994–2000.

Neighly, Patrick and Kereth Cowe-Spigai. *Anarchy for the Masses: The Disinformation Guide to* The Invisibles. New York: The Disinformation Company, 2003.

Richardson, Brian. "Narrative Poetics and Postmodern Transgression: Theorizing the Collapse of Time, Voice, and Frame." *Narrative* 8 (1) (2000): 23–42.

Richardson, Brian, ed. *Narrative Dynamics: Essays on Time, Plot, Closure, and Frames.* Columbus, OH: Ohio State University Press, 2002.

Todorov, Tzvetan. *Introduction to Poetics.* 1968, 1973. Translated by Richard Howard. Minneapolis: University of Minnesota Press, 1981.

White, Hayden. "The Historical Text as Literary Artifact." *Clio* 3 (3) (1974). Rpt. in *Tropics of Discourse*, 81–100. Baltimore: Johns Hopkins University Press, 1978.

5

MISE EN SCÈNE AND FRAMING

Visual Storytelling in Lone Wolf and Cub

Pascal Lefèvre

To understand the importance of form, you can ask yourself questions such as: What if Hergé had used a photorealistic style instead of his "clear line" style to render the stories of Tintin? What if Chris Ware had used constantly varying baroque perspectives instead of the many slow sequences with a similar framing to show the scenes of *Jimmy Corrigan*? What if Otomo had used cartoony animal characters instead of realistically human characters to tell the science-fiction story *Akira*? Form is anything but a neutral container of content in the comics medium; form shapes content, form suggests interpretations and feelings. Without considering formal aspects (such as graphic style, mise en scène, page layout, plot composition), any discussion of the content or the themes of a work is, in fact, pointless. Paraphrasing film scholar David Bordwell,[1] one could say that the form of a comic consists of materials—subject matter, themes—shaped and transformed by the overall composition (plot structure) and stylistic patterning. The same fabula/story (the chronological sequence of events as they are supposed to have occurred in the time–space universe of the narrative being interpreted) or even the same sjuzet/plot (the actual composition or emplotment of events in the work) can receive a completely different atmosphere and look by a particular use of stylistic elements such as graphic style, mise en scène, and framing. It is via the sjuzet the reader/spectator constructs the fabula or story.[2]

For the purpose of clarity, I will focus my formal analysis of the sample foremost on the relation between mise en scène and framing—but this does not imply that other formal aspects are less relevant. Mise en scène in comics concerns the representation of a scene by a specific organization of its virtual but figurative elements such as décor, props, and characters. Framing in comics refers both to the choice of a perspective on a scene, and to the choice of borders of the image.

To demonstrate that formal analysis can be used for all kinds of comics, a Japanese comic or manga was chosen, namely an episode ("The Assassin's Road") from the long samurai cycle *Kozure Okami* (*Lone Wolf and Cub*) by the scriptwriter Kazuo Koike and artist Goseki Kojima, published in an English translation by Dark Horse Comics in 2000. This episode tells how the protagonist Ogami Itto is stripped of his *kaishakakunin* executioner title by the shogun and is ordered to commit *seppuku,* a kind of ritualistic suicide. The hero, however, chooses to defy the authorities. Then the Yagyu clan challenges him to a duel with Kurato. Though Itto, carrying his toddler son on his back, seems at first in a weak position with the rays of the setting sun in his eyes, he uses it to his advantage by blinding his opponent by means of a mirror attached to the forehead of his child. The most striking aspect of this manga is not the story itself, but the way the Japanese artists tell this story by visual means such as mise en scène, framing, and graphic style.

UNDERLYING ASSUMPTIONS

As aesthetics philosopher David Davies has put it: "In appreciating a work, we must always attend to how an 'artistic statement' has been articulated in a particular artistic medium, and how the articulation exploits the qualities of the vehicle that realizes that artistic medium."[3] It is indeed within the framework of the chosen medium that an artist has to make many choices. In the case of graphic narratives, various constitutive aspects—such as graphic style, mise en scène, the combination of verbal and visual elements, the breakdown (or découpage) of the story in distinct panels, the interaction between panels, page layout, and the plot structure—play a role. The formal options are constrained and constructed by a range of norms originating from formal principles, conventional practices of comics production and consumption, and proximate features of the social context. Moreover, Bordwell[4] explains that through the notion of norms, poetics can be made historical, because in comparison to the prevailing standards, we can better understand the particular workings of a work or a body of works. Since it is not possible to deal with all the stylistic and narrative techniques in this chapter, only graphic style, mise en scène, and framing will be briefly discussed.

First, the particular nature of pictures in a comic needs to be stressed, because in contrast to the photorealistic images of live-action film that deliver a realistic impression, drawings in comics are static and strongly stylized, so the spectator becomes aware of their hand-made quality. Unlike in real life or in photographic images, lines are prominent in drawings. Furthermore, hand-made pictures will leave out unnecessary details and pronounce telling characteristics by means of perceptual factors such as simplicity of shape, orderly grouping, clear overlapping, distinction of figure and ground, and deformation.[5] Stylized images may be less visually analogous to reality, but thousands of years of human art prove that they can very effectively capture the essence of an object or a person. Thanks to their simplified nature, these images are highly communicative, easily and quickly grasped by the viewer. For example, two simple dots can, in a proper context, represent eyes.[6] In contrast to an average photographic image, a drawing is literally and figuratively "signed."[7] An artist does not only depict something, but he expresses at the same time a visual interpretation of the world; every drawing style implies, therefore, a particular visual ontology.[8] The fact that Kojima, in our sample, uses not a cartoony style with lots of deformations (typical exaggerations are big noses, large eyes, or big feet), but a style that respects the real proportions of a human body, gives it a rather realistic look. Nevertheless, lines are still prominent, while in reality people and objects are visible through tonal variations, surface contours, and cast shadows.[9] While the contour lines fixate the main characters and objects quite clearly, Kojima uses, at times, extensively nervous hatching which makes the images vibrate with movement. How and to what extent the reader is influenced by such stylistic variations is difficult to assess,[10] but graphic styles suggest experiences and feelings through their nonverbal qualities.[11]

Mise en scène and framing are also crucial for the reading experience. Though the terms "mise en scène" and "framing" originate from other art forms (such as theater, photography, and cinema), these aspects play an important but somewhat different role in the comics medium. Contrary to mise en scène and framing in film, in comics these aspects are strongly related, because there is in fact no actual scene that a camera registers. In contrast to a photographic image, there are no actors or objects in front of the lens of the camera. A cartoonist suggests only with drawn or painted dots, lines, shapes, and figures in a context. While a camera has no intrinsic problem in registering the same scene in all its details at a rate of 24 frames per second, it can be a very tiresome task for a cartoonist to draw the same scene from the same perspective panel after panel. This is one of the reasons why in comics rather simplified images are quite common and why backgrounds can disappear for several panels.[12] Furthermore, drawing a panel implies realizing at the same time a set up and a choice of frame, but for the sake of a formal analysis one can theoretically differentiate between them.

Mise en scène in comics concerns the representation of a scene by a specific organization of its virtual but figurative elements such as décor, props, and characters. There are millions of ways of showing a scene: The artist has to choose from many options for where and how to position the characters, how to "dress" them, which facial and corporal expressions to use, and which objects and décor to choose.

By framing in comics, we understand two different things: First, the choice of a perspective on a scene, and second the choice of borders of the image. Cinema offers a lot of expressions to define a point of view, such as close-up, long shot, or medium shot. For instance, when the father lets his son choose between the sword and the ball (second panel on page 6, Figure 5.1), the panel shows us this scene from above so the reader has a good overview of the situation: The baby is in front of the father and in the middle between the sword and the ball. The décor is limited to a minimum; even the (supposedly wooden) floor is rendered as one, uniform surface. You can't see any lines indicating the borders of the planks or tatami on the floor because they would needlessly complicate the image. The most essential things (father, baby, ball, sword) must be clearly presented. Though the ball is placed further than the sword from the virtual point of view, the ball is by its volume and its darkness (many hatchings) quite present in the image. Nevertheless, thanks to this particular perspective, the sword is much closer to the father and has more central position in the global panel. That the baby will eventually chose the sword is in some way already suggested by the previous panel; a low angle shows the sword at the left hand, the ball at the right hand and the baby in the center of the panel, but, more importantly, due to the position of the virtual point of view it looks as if the baby is much closer to the sword than the ball, even though, geographically speaking, he is just in the middle between them. So, the mise en scène and the angle can influence strongly how the viewer perceives a scene. The reader does not have another choice than to view the diegetic world in the way the artist has presented it.[13]

Using a formal analysis you cannot only describe the various techniques, but also grasp their role in the visual narration and understand how they try to communicate

Figure 5.1 *Lone Wolf and Cub* page 273 in volume, page 6 of the story, panel 1–3. Copyright 1995, 2000 Kazuo Koike and Gôseki Kojima.

information. The formal variations may be very broad, caused by the creative power of the authors, but also by their context. A comics artist is generally limited by the publication format of his comics,[14] because a publication format poses not only formal and thematic constraints, it implies also a particular cultural space. However, this influence doesn't have to be considered as purely deterministic, because within certain limits enormous variations and creative solutions are still possible.

APPROPRIATE ARTIFACTS

Every comic can be analyzed from a formal perspective: it doesn't matter whether your sample is a recognized masterpiece or a pulp product; it may be a one-shot or it may be a long-running series. Of course, if you are looking for interesting creative devices, not every comic will be equally suitable; some comics artists have created works that from a formal point of view are more challenging or surprising than others. In any case, if you are triggered in one way or another by a comic, this can be an effective motivation to re-read the work and study it in more detail in order to understand more about the basis for your reaction.

PROCEDURES

As with all techniques, practice makes perfect; the more you apply this method, the more results it will deliver. It is of crucial importance to think broadly about the comics medium and put prejudices towards certain genres or traditions aside. Reading good formal analyses[15] can help develop your insight into the workings of the comics medium. It is also advisable to read and analyze quite different comics, because it is only by acknowledging the variations that you will better understand the enormous possibilities of graphic narratives. You have to develop "a good eye" that scrutinizes the panels for interesting aspects or even minor but telling details (as, for instance, the role of the décor in the final duel scene, as demonstrated in the sample analysis below). This visual awareness has to go in tandem with analytical thinking, comparing activities, and formulating and checking hypotheses.

You can apply similar techniques as Bordwell[16] advises for studying film: As you read the comic, write down brief, but accurate, descriptions of various comics techniques that are used. Do not refrain from some quantitative methods such as counting the frequency of some devices, because those data can give a good foundation on which to base a more qualitative analysis. Afterwards, you can identify the most salient techniques, trace patterns of techniques across the whole comic, and propose functions for those techniques. In the end you have to develop some kind of thesis or theory about a particular work, and the empirical data will serve your argumentation. For a particular thesis, you won't need to analyze all the devices, but it is advisable to limit yourself to the outstanding instances of comics technique. For example, how does Chris Ware break down his plot of *Jimmy Corrigan*, or how are the page layouts organized in *Watchmen* or in a *shojo* manga? You can also study the way a device is applied in a group of comics, as I did in my analysis of page layouts of early comics published in Belgium.[17]

ARTIFACT SELECTED FOR SAMPLE ANALYSIS

I have chosen to analyze an episode, "The Assassin's Road" (1970), from the famous samurai cycle *Kozure Okami* (*Lone Wolf and Cub*) by Kazuo Koike and Gôseki Kojima. It was one of the early manga to be published in comic book format in 1986 by First Comics, but the complete translation of the cycle was published in 28 smaller-sized trade paperback volumes by Dark Horse Comics between 2000 and 2002. Originally the series was serialized in Japan between 1970 and 1976 in the *seinen* magazine *Weekly Manga Action*. In Japan, six feature films (starring Tomisaburo Wakayama as Ogami Itto) were released between 1972 and 1974, and two television series were broadcasted (three 26-episode seasons from 1973 to 1976, and another series between 2002 and 2004). The young Frank Miller acknowledged the influence of *Lone Wolf and Cub* on his *Ronin*, and later drew the covers for the first English publication. This all makes *Lone Wolf and Cub* an almost legendary series that has been widely appreciated.[18]

Lone Wolf and Cub was, however, not the first *samourai* manga to be published in Japan. In the 1920s there appeared stories of brave little *samourai* boys, and in the years prior to and during World War II the *samourai* theme fitted well with the reigning militaristic culture. Right after the defeat, militaristic or nationalistic *samourai* stories were forbidden, and till the 1960s *samourai* manga drawn in a cartoony style were targeted at younger audiences.[19] In the 1960s, when publishers started aiming at more mature readers, the *samourai* genre ventured along new roads; in many cases the graphic style became more realistic, the background more historical and the violence more explicit. Sometimes a *samourai* manga became quite political; Sampei Shirato's *Ninja Bugeicho* (1959–1962) stressed class consciousness and reform that appealed to university students and intellectuals in a Japan polarized on issues such as the Japan–US Security Treaty.[20]

Since each publication format contains to a certain degree an aesthetic system with a set of norms that offers a bounded set of alternatives to the individual comics maker,[21] it is important to realize that manga were in the first place destined for the specialized magazines (weekly, bi-monthly or monthly), which were targeted at different ages and genders: *shonen* manga for boys, *shojo* manga for girls, *seinen* for adult men, *yosei* manga for adult women. All these magazines are quite thick and consist of episodes of various continuing series. Unlike the too-few pages in episodes of a European comics journal, episodes in a manga magazine could be 20, 30, 40, or even more than 50 pages. Unlike American and European comics publications of the early 1970s, Japanese publications used full color only in a very limited amount of pages. Most manga were published in black and white or in a monochrome color.

Unfortunately, the Kyoto Manga Museum does not hold the original copy of the *seinen Weekly Manga Action* that published the episode of my sample analysis, but I could consult there another copy from that period (February 4, 1971). This copy of *Weekly Manga Action* consisted of 192 pages in the 18 × 25.5 cm format, which is much larger than the small English edition by Dark Horse (10.5 × 15.2 cm). This is important, because a larger format is much more suited to appreciating the graphic qualities. The copy of *Weekly Manga Action* offered not only four continuity comics, but also various short humor comics. As it was, and still is, the standard practice to print the first pages of an episode in color (while the rest of the episode is monochrome), the first eight pages of the *Kozure Okami* episode were printed with an additional color (red-brown or blue) and the rest of the pages in black-on-white. The other episodes in *Weekly Manga Action* were not all drawn in a style similar to *Kozure Okami*, as most of them used a more deformed and simplified style with less speed lines than Kojima. With explicit violence and some eroticism, this magazine was clearly directed at young men; not only are some nude breasts depicted, but the magazine included two "playmate" fold-outs with half-dressed, blonde Caucasian models. So this is the context wherein the early episodes of *Kozure Okami* were published. As Thompson[22] rightly states, this series is first and foremost a pulp narrative with plenty of sleaze among the death and gore.

For the sake of clarity, the sample analysis limits itself to only one episode, "The Assassin's Road" (published on pages 267–294 of the first volume by Dark Horse), of the more than 8,000 pages of the *Kozure Okami* cycle. Instead of collecting examples from various episodes from various volumes, it is much more efficient to concentrate on only one episode and to go a little more into detail. Moreover, the analysis will focus on the duel scene, because it is a famous scene from the series. Among others, Schodt[23] used an excerpt of this duel scene for an illustration in his first book on manga. I selected this scene because of its creative use of mise en scène.

SAMPLE ANALYSIS

Koike, Kazuo and Gôseki Kojima. "The Assassin's Road." In *Lone Wolf and Cub*, 267–294. Milwaukie: Dark Horse Comics, 2000 (originally published as *Kozure Okami* in 1970 in *Weekly Manga Action*).

The episodes of *Kozure Okami* do not have a fixed length. This episode, "The Assassin's Road," consists of 27 pages (each comprised of 2–7 panels). On average there are 4.8 panels per page, which is relatively few compared to a European comic page and even to that of an American comic page, but quite normal for a Japanese comic of that period.

Like most other story manga, "The Assassin's Road" offers many panels of varying formats and changing perspectives: from close-ups to extreme long shots, with low- and high-angle framing.

As in most comics that opt for a rather visual storytelling method, the choice of the point of view and angle is generally motivated by the necessities of the narration: long shots are used for showing an overview of a situation (as in the already analyzed panel where the baby has to choose between the sword or the ball), close-ups are for important details (as the torn letter or the sign of the shogun).

In a landscape panel (the third panel on page 12, Figure 5.2) Kojima isolates his protagonist somewhat off center, but in a white halo. From the right-and left-hand side of the picture, swords encircle him. The choice of this framing suggests that Itto is alone and there is seemingly little chance to escape from this dangerous position. However, the posture of Itto, with his child under his arm, suggests some kind of meditative calmness, but as we will see in a moment, it is just the stillness before the storm; 13 panels later (first panel on page 15, Figure 5.3), the fight is over—Itto has killed all the guards that tried to attack him. The fight ends with the protagonist in the middle of a landscape panel: while Itto is shown in the foreground in clear light, the background has become darkened by many tiny horizontal lines (that do not respect the outer contour lines of the guards, only those of Itto). At the back, to the left and the right side of Itto, we see two opponents fatally wounded still falling to the ground, as if they are in some kind of slow motion or suspension (their blood is still gushing from their wounds).

A film-like technique of shot/reverse-shot is used at various times to differentiate the hero Itto from his adversaries, who are at various times shown standing next to each other, occupying the complete width of the space of a horizontal panel. One of the panels even runs over the complete spread of two adjacent pages (pages 17–18); in this way the adversaries seem quite imposing and menacing. At least a decade earlier than American or European artists, the Japanese used such complete spreads in their comics. Kojima,

Figure 5.2 *Lone Wolf and Cub* page 279 in volume, page 12 of the story, panel 3. Copyright 1995, 2000 Kazuo Koike and Gôseki Kojima.

Figure 5.3 *Lone Wolf and Cub* page 282 in volume, page 15 of the story, panel 1. Copyright 1995, 2000 Kazuo Koike and Gôseki Kojima.

the artist, uses this broad space of two adjacent pages for other scenes as well, where he opposes two characters: one is placed on the left-hand side of the left page and the other at the right-hand side of the right page (pages 17–18 and 21–22, 23–24). This results in a considerable distance between two figures, a distance that is not only physical or spatial, but also psychological.

Let us now consider in more detail the duel scene between Itto and Kurato (pages 21–26). In the first panel of the scene, the distance between the opponents is partially filled with text (Figure 5.4). Due to the low angle in the next panel, the décor becomes temporally dominant: we see at the foreground the grass being bent by the wind, and in the background a tormented sky with a setting sun. The text suggests to the reader that Itto has chosen a bad position, because the setting sun shines in his eyes. On the other hand, a careful viewer may notice that another nature element (the direction of the heavy wind) is quite in his favor. Though the text does not mention this explicitly, the mise en scène suggests metaphorically that, in contrast to Itto, his adversary has to oppose such a force. On the next page (Figure 5.5) the characters are shown in another long shot; unlike the first time (in the first panel of the scene) this shot is not from eye level but from a high angle; now the characters seem just small figures within a gigantic natural landscape. Moreover, suddenly at the foreground, in the middle of the panel, arise some rocks. These rocks offer not only some depth to the scene, but their vertical, rigid, and motionless forms rhyme with the two characters still fixed at their positions, still without movement. The following panel no longer presents the characters, but instead the rocks in silhouette from a low angle. Moreover, the sky is completely bright and filled with silhouettes of flying birds. The following panels zoom in on the duelists; now they are set against the backdrop of a turbulent sky. These rapid changes of the sky from one panel to another do not seem quite naturalistic, but serve to tell the scene more dramatically. It is precisely the scene of the white sky, seen from a low angle, that introduces the real start of the duel; right after this panel the opponents start to run to each other (movement lines become more visible). Furthermore, the presence of the birds in this pivotal panel

Figure 5.4 *Lone Wolf and Cub* pages 288–289 in volume, spread of two pages 21–22 of the story. Copyright 1995, 2000 Kazuo Koike and Gôseki Kojima.

is quite unexpected, because they were rather absent in the previous panels. These birds appear precisely at the moment the duelists start to move to each other, after a long wait in a static pose. The fact that the rocks and the birds are rendered as silhouettes reinforces their abstract aspect; the representation is not concerned with their individual characteristics, but aspires to deliver a visual shock of these contrasting black and whites shapes and to suggest a sudden burst of energy. It is also remarkable that Kojima no longer uses extreme long shots from the moment the duelists start to run; they are from now on shown in separate panels. And the image becomes even more fragmented by showing only their running feet or the head of Itto. The horizontal movement is stressed by the use of small horizontal frames.

At the moment of the physical confrontation, the reader is placed in the position of the enemy and receives, like him, a blinding light. On the next page (Figure 5.6), a reverse shot shows in close-up the blinking Kurato, immediately followed by a long shot that presents already the end to the confrontation. Though the swords have seemingly finished their job, at this moment the reader cannot be sure about who has won. The image is too vague to form any ideas about the result of the confrontation; the figures are not drawn in clear contour lines, but they seem to be made up of only speed lines. In the following panel the duelists are now shown a little more distant from each other, but explicit cues about the outcome of the fight are still lacking. Only in the very last panel of the page does Kurato fall down. The change of perspective by 180 degrees increases the confusion because the characters seem to have exchanged their position; Itto on the left is now suddenly on the right, and vice versa.

Figure 5.5 *Lone Wolf and Cub* pages 290–291 in volume, spread of two pages 23–24 of the story. Copyright 1995, 2000 Kazuo Koike and Gôseki Kojima.

It is remarkable that for the quite realistic setting and style (the relative proportions are respected, no use of caricatural deformations) that the dimension of the setting sun is strongly exaggerated, especially in the panel where Itto charges into his opponent. The reader no longer sees Kurato; Itto seems to run into a blinding tunnel of sunlight rays. Though Itto seemed from the start to be in an inferior position (the sun shone in his eyes and he had to carry a child on his back), he used all these elements in his favor. By placing a reflecting plate on the forehead of the child, he could surprise and blind his adversary a second before the physical confrontation. When the enemy collapses in the end, the sun is even more brilliant, because it is set against a sky that has suddenly turned gray. As remarked before, these are not realistic atmospheric changes; they are too sudden. Interestingly, the final panel of the sequence offers us again a view of the uni-directional bowed grass, like in a panel before the fight. Nevertheless, two panels before the end of the sequence, the grass momentarily does not bow any longer to the power of the wind, but bend on the left side to the left and on the right side to the right; they rhyme with the movement lines of the duelists. Again, an element of the so-called background is used to dramatize the situation.

Throughout the whole story the circle motif is quite present, from the first till the very last panel, not only in circular objects such as the ball, the blazon, the sun, or the mirror, but also more metaphorically as in the encircling of Itto by swords. Sometimes these round shapes are accentuated by placing them against a flat white or black surface, so they are isolated in the panel. Initially, it is not clear why the opening page shows us two girls playing with a bouncing ball, but it becomes clear in the flashback on the following

Figure 5.6 *Lone Wolf and Cub* pages 292–293 in volume, spread of two pages 25–26 of the story. Copyright 1995, 2000 Kazuo Koike and Gôseki Kojima.

pages where the father places his son in a dilemma; the baby has to choose between the sword or the ball. After hesitating, the toddler creeps to the sword and chooses, naïvely or instinctively, to join the dangerous path of his father, consequently rejecting a more normal childhood. The very last page picks up where we left off at the beginning, the playing girls with the bouncing ball. Since his son has chosen the sword, there is no longer a need for the ball, so we can assume that the father has given the ball to the girls. The story ends where it started, a figuratively round circle.

In conclusion, the same fabula/story or even the same sjuzet/plot could have been visualized by completely different techniques—a different graphic style, mise en scène, framing, page layout, etc.[24] Since the chronological sequence of events as they are supposed to have occurred in the time–space universe of the narrative (being interpreted) is not particularly special, less-inspired comics artists could have realized a quite poor version of it. It is foremost thanks to the clever mise en scène and the framing by Kojima that it looks quite dynamic and interesting. While suggesting a realistic setting, the artist does not hesitate to arrange this so-called realistic environment (unrealistic changes of climate circumstances during the duel, dimensions of the setting sun) to obtain more dramatic effects. The important thing is that the artist uses these formal elements not just for visual effect, but always in relation to the narrative purposes. Even if the reader does not recognize cognitively all these workings, we can assume that he or she is eventually influenced by the stylistic presentation of a story.[25] A thorough formal analysis can make the implicit functions more explicit.

NOTES

1. David Bordwell, *Ozu and the Poetics of Cinema* (London: BFI, 1988), 1.
2. Pascal Lefèvre, "Some Medium-Specific Qualities of Graphic Sequences," *Substance* (forthcoming).
3. David Davies, "Medium in Art," *The Oxford Handbook of Aesthetics*, ed. Jerrold Levinson (Oxford: Oxford University Press, 2005), 190.
4. Bordwell, *Ozu and the Poetics of Cinema*, 1.
5. Rudolf Arnheim, *Art and Visual Perception, a Psychology of the Creative Eye* (Berkeley: University of California Press, 1971), 149.
6. E. Stephen Palmer, *Vision Science: Photons to Phenomenology* (Cambridge, MA: MIT Press, 1999), 428–429.
7. Thierry Groensteen, "Du 7ᵉ au 9ᵉ art: l'inventaire des singularités," *CinémAction HS: Cinéma et Bande Dessinée* (Paris: Corlet–Télérama, 1990), 23.
8. Philip Rawson, *Drawing* (Philadelphia: University of Pennsylvania Press, 1987), 19.
9. John Willats, *Art and Representation: New Principles in the Analysis of Pictures* (Princeton: Princeton University Press, 1997), 128–146.
10. Inez L. Ramsey, "Effect of Art Style on Children's Picture Preferences," *The Journal of Educational Research* 75 (4) (1982): 237–240.
11. Pascal Lefèvre, "Recovering Sensuality in Comics Theory," *International Journal of Comic Art* 1 (1) (1999): 140–149.
12. Lefèvre, "Recovering Sensuality in Comics Theory."
13. Jan-Marie Peters, *Pictorial Signs and the Language of Film* (Amsterdam: Rodopi, 1981), 14.
14. Pascal Lefèvre, "The Importance of Being 'Published': A Comparative Study of Different Comics Formats," *Comics & Culture*, ed. Anne Magnussen and Hans-Christian Christiansen (Copenhagen: Museum Tusculanum at the University of Copenhagen, 2000), 91–105.
15. Among others, David Kunzle, *The History of the Comic Strip: The Nineteenth Century* (Berkeley: University of California Press, 1990); John Benson, David Kasakove, and Art Spiegelman, "An Examination of 'Master Race,'" *A Comics Studies Reader*, ed. Jeet Heer and Kenton Worcester (Jackson, MS: University Press of Mississippi, 2009), 288–305.
16. David Bordwell, *The McGraw-Hill Film Viewer's Guide* (New York: McGraw-Hill, 2001), 20.
17. Pascal Lefèvre, "The Conquest of Space: Evolution of Panel Arrangements and Page Lay Outs in Early Comics," *European Comic Art* 2 (2) (2009): 227–252.
18. Thierry Groensteen, *L'Univers des manga: Une introduction à la BD japonaise* (Tournai: Casterman, 1991), 102–103; Jason Thompson, *Manga: The Complete Guide* (New York: Balantine Books, 2007); Nicolas Finet, "Lone Wolf & Cub," *Dico Manga: Le Dictionnaire Encyclopédique de la Bande Dessinée Japonaise*, ed. Nicolas Finet (Paris: Fleurus, 2008), 313–314.
19. Frederik L. Schodt, *Manga! Manga! The World of Japanese Comics* (Tokyo: Kodansha International, 1986), 68–70.
20. Schodt, *Manga! Manga!*, 71.
21. Lefèvre, "The Importance of Being 'Published.'"
22. Thompson, *Manga*, 192.
23. Schodt, *Manga! Manga!*
24. Lefèvre, "Some Medium-Specific Qualities of Graphic Sequences."
25. Lefèvre, "Recovering Sensuality in Comics Theory" and "Some Medium-Specific Qualities of Graphic Sequences."

SELECTED BIBLIOGRAPHY

Arnheim, Rudolf. *Art and Visual Perception: A Psychology of the Creative Eye*. Berkeley: University of California Press, 1971.

Aumont, Jacques. *L'image*. Paris: Nathan, 1994.

Benson, John, David Kasakove, and Art Spiegelman. "An Examination of 'Master Race.'" In *A Comics Studies Reader*, edited by Jeet Heer and Kenton Worcester, 288–305. Jackson, MS: University Press of Mississippi, 2009.

Bordwell, David. *Ozu and the Poetics of Cinema*. London: BFI, 1988.

Bordwell, David. *The McGraw-Hill Film Viewer's Guide*. New York: McGraw-Hill, 2001.

Carroll, Noël. "Formalism." In *The Routledge Companion to Aesthetics*, edited by Brys Gaut and Dominic McIver Lopes, 87–96. London: Routledge, 2002.

Davies, David. "Medium in Art." In *The Oxford Handbook of Aesthetics*, edited by Jerrold Levinson, 181–191. Oxford: Oxford University Press, 2005.

Finet, Nicolas. "Lone Wolf & Cub." In *Dico Manga. Le dictionnaire encyclopédique de la bande dessinée japonaise*, edited by Nicolas Finet, 313–314. Paris: Fleurus, 2008.

Groensteen, Thierry. "Du 7ᵉ au 9ᵉ art: l'inventaire des singularités." In *CinémAction HS: Cinéma et Bande Dessinée*, 16–28. Paris: Corlet–Télérama, 1990.

Groensteen, Thierry. *L'Univers des Manga. Une Introduction à la BD Japonaise*. Tournai: Casterman, 1991.

Hebert, Xavier and Pascal Lefèvre. "Mise en scene and Framing in Manga: Analysis of the Various Narrative Devices of Hasegawa, Tezuka, Chiba, Kojima, Takahashi and Suenobu." In 『ユリイカ *Yuriika (Eurêka)*, (2008): 234–247.

Jenkins, Henry. "Historical Poetics." In *Approaches to Popular Film*, edited by Joanne Hollows and Mark Jancovich, 99–122. Manchester: Manchester University Press, 1995.

Kunzle, David. *The History of the Comic Strip, the Nineteenth Century*. Berkeley: University of California Press, 1990.

Lefèvre, Pascal. "Recovering Sensuality in Comics Theory." *International Journal of Comic Art* 1 (1) (1999): 140–149.

Lefèvre, Pascal. "The Importance of Being 'Published': A Comparative Study of Different Comics Formats." In *Comics & Culture*, edited by Anne Magnussen and Hans-Christian Christiansen, 91–105. Copenhagen: Museum Tusculanum at the University of Copenhagen, 2000.

Lefèvre, Pascal. "The Conquest of Space: Evolution of Panel Arrangements and Page Layouts in Early Comics." *European Comic Art* 2 (2) (2009): 227–252.

Lefèvre, Pascal. "Some Medium-Specific Qualities of Graphic Sequences." *Substance*, forthcoming.

Palmer, E. Stephen. *Vision Science: Photons to Phenomenology*. Cambridge, MA: MIT Press, 1999.

Peters, Jan-Marie. *Pictorial Signs and the Language of Film*. Amsterdam: Rodopi, 1981.

Ramsey, Inez L. "Effect of Art Style on Children's Picture Preferences." *The Journal of Educational Research* 75 (4) (1982): 237–240.

Rawson, Philip. *Drawing*. Philadelphia: University of Pennsylvania Press, 1987.

Schodt, Frederik L. *Manga! Manga! The World of Japanese Comics*. Tokyo: Kodansha International, 1986.

Thompson, Jason. *Manga, The Complete Guide*. New York: Balantine Books, 2007.

Willats, John. *Art and Representation: New Principles in the Analysis of Pictures*. Princeton: Princeton University Press, 1997.

6

ABSTRACT FORM

Sequential Dynamism and Iconostasis in Abstract Comics and in Steve Ditko's Amazing Spider-Man

Andrei Molotiu

What are abstract comics? In the introduction to *Abstract Comics: The Anthology*, I wrote:

> Of course, abstract comics can be defined as sequential art consisting exclusively of abstract imagery…. But the definition should be expanded somewhat, to include those comics that contain some representational elements, as long as those elements do not cohere into a narrative or even into a unified narrative space.[1]

In the latter sense, abstract comics can be seen to go back at least to R. Crumb's "Abstract Expressionist Ultra Super Modernistic Comics" of 1967 (published in *Zap* no. 1, 1968). Comics featuring nothing but abstract art are more recent, going back to first efforts from the 1980s by artists such as Mark Badger, Benoit Joly, and Patrick McDonnell (though none of them were published at the time, only seeing the light of print in the 2009 anthology). Experiments with abstract art arrayed sequentially can be found earlier outside the realm of comics—for example, in the 1920s work of El Lissitzky and Kurt Kranz; but, while a number of abstract artists (including Jackson Pollock and Willem de Kooning) experimented with sequence in the intervening years, this always remained a very minor aspect of their output, virtually a footnote. As witnessed in *Abstract Comics: The Anthology*, the genre has only taken off in the last decade, turning what was a trickle (or perhaps no more than a dripping faucet), if not into a flood, at least into a medium-sized creek.

Now, being a genre, a kind of artwork, how do abstract comics belong in a book on the methodology of comics scholarship? I don't mean to speak for the editors, who invited my participation in this anthology and suggested the topic, and who thus clearly have their own reasons for including it. As I see it, however, any new evolution in an art form (such as comics) expands the purview, and thereby proposes a new definition of that art form; and any newly expanded definition of an art form implies a new theorization of it. Marcel Duchamp's readymades, for example, shifted the definition of the visual arts from a formal to a conceptual one, and Andy Warhol's later repetition and elaboration of Duchamp's gesture virtually demanded the rise of postmodern art theory to explain it, not to mention Arthur Danto's entire philosophy of art.[2] More to the point, perhaps, modernism in painting from the Impressionists to the rise of abstraction shifted the definition of painting from a representational medium to one primarily concerned with issues of form and composition—as indicated, for example, by painter Maurice Denis' quote: "Remember that a picture before it is a war horse, a naked woman, or some anecdote, is essentially a flat surface covered with colors arranged in a certain order."[3] The advent of modernism, then, already contained *in ovo* the art theories that came to explain it—such as Roger Fry's or Clement Greenberg's (while of course it is also clear that the artistic changes were themselves influenced by earlier theoretical developments, going as far back as Immanuel Kant's aesthetics).[4] Every new artistic development within an art form is, therefore, also a theoretical development in our understanding of that art form, not only demanding new methodologies to understand it, but making those new methodologies available for the reinterpretation of the entire form. For example, to go back to the Maurice Denis quote, by the early twentieth century a painting by Raphael could be interpreted as "essentially a flat surface covered with colors arranged in a certain order," though this view would have been unthinkable to Raphael's contemporaries.

UNDERLYING ASSUMPTIONS

How does the rise of abstract comics, then, change our understanding of the medium of comics? Many definitions of comics see storytelling or the interplay of words and images as *sine qua non* characteristics of the medium. The editors of this collection, for example, proposed in their earlier book, *The Power of Comics*, the following definition of a comic book: "As an art form, a comic book is a volume in which all aspects of the narrative are represented by pictorial and linguistic images encapsulated in a sequence of juxtaposed panels and pages."[5] They went on to define their terms:

> The aspects of the narrative that we are talking about are the people, objects, sounds, sensations and thoughts that play a role in the storytelling. A narrative, of course, is an account of an event or a series of events.

Thus, narrativity (the idea that a comic tells a story) and representationality (the idea that comics necessarily represent elements of the world such as people, things, and events) are unquestioned assumptions of this definition.

Duncan and Smith acknowledge that their definition "functions best in describing typical or pure cases of the art form. There are some cases lying on the boundaries that may vary from the definition but still meet enough of the criteria to be recognized as comic books."[6] But one could question the very notion of "pure cases of the art form," or the rhetorical formation that sees comics that "vary from the definition" as "lying on the boundaries," and therefore marginal. As a matter of fact, in similar developments in other art forms, the previously marginal ended up being exalted as the purest manifestation of that form—as in, for example, abstract painting being seen as "pure painting," instrumental nonprogrammatic music as "pure music," and poetry that focuses mainly on its formal devices as "pure poetry."[7] Even if we don't want to repeat such a modernist gesture, it is worth pointing it out in order to suggest that abstract comics may end up not being such a marginal genre of comics after all.

As to the notion that the interplay of word and images is an essential characteristic of the medium, this has been most forcefully advocated by Robert C. Harvey—for example, in his book *The Art of the Funnies: An Aesthetic History*. In his introduction, Harvey identifies the elements that, according to him, give the comics medium its specificity: "The technical hallmarks of the comic strip are speech balloons and narrative breakdown."[8] Harvey goes on to elaborate on "the nature of the medium":

> Comics are a blend of word and picture—not a simple coupling of the verbal and the visual, but a blend, a true mixture. From the nature of the medium, then, we can draw up one criterion for critical evaluation: in the usual situation, in which both words and pictures are used, a measure of a comic strip's excellence is the extent to which the sense of the words is dependent on the pictures and vice versa ... in the best examples of the art, neither word nor picture makes complete sense without the other.[9]

Thus, while acknowledging that there are comics that do not fit his definition, Harvey too engages in a rhetoric of typicality, seeing examples of the art form that do not fit his definition as substandard (not "the best examples of the art"). Clearly, this poses a problem for abstract comics, which as a rule feature no text at all; and even when letters and words appear, they usually function primarily visually (closer to sound effects), rather than to convey a story or other kinds of verbalizable meanings. Furthermore, when granting that the medium may be larger than this definition, Harvey falls back on the earlier discussed assumption of narrativity as a necessary feature of the medium: "I don't mean to suggest that verbal–visual blending is all there is to the art of comics. Comics do tell stories."[10]

We could go on to discuss other definitions of the medium that are challenged by the rise of abstract comics (such as the one that sees cartooning as an essential feature of comics), but let us look at one that can fully embrace the new genre, though it was proposed before most examples of abstract comics were created. I'm referring to Scott McCloud's definition in *Understanding Comics: The Invisible Art*. Indeed, one can argue that *Understanding Comics* opens up a space for the possibility, and reception, of abstract comics. We can begin with McCloud's definition of comics as "juxtaposed pictorial and other images in deliberate sequence."[11] As opposed to Duncan and Smith's and Harvey's formulations, this one says nothing about narrative, figuration, or words being inherent characteristics of the medium. Later in the book, McCloud also implies the (theoretical, so to speak) possibility of abstract comics. After discussing "iconic abstraction," the simplification inherent in cartooning that may reduce figures to very simple shapes which nevertheless still have meaning, McCloud goes on to address the more traditional sense of "abstraction," which is also the sense it has in the expression "abstract comics":

> Usually, the word "abstraction" refers to the *non-iconic* variety, where no attempt is made to cling to resemblance *or* meaning.... The type of art which often prompts the question: "What does it mean?" ... Earning the reply "It '*means*' what it *is*! In this case ... ink on paper."[12]

To speak of comics as "ink on paper" is to suggest that representation and diegetic space are not necessary for a comic to function.[13] McCloud's insight opens a theoretical realm within which the possibility of abstract comics can be elaborated. Abstract comics are destined to occupy the very top of his triangular schema of "reality, language, and the picture plane." McCloud writes: "This is the realm of the art object, the *picture plane*, where shapes, lines and colors can be *themselves* and not pretend *otherwise*."[14] As can be seen in the large, two-page spread that elaborates this schema, McCloud, at the time of writing *Understanding Comics*, did not have access to any instances that went all the way up to (non-iconic) abstraction. The highest-placed example in his diagram is "Mary Fleener at her most abstract," but that is still fully *iconic* abstraction, thus still "clinging" to meaning and representation. In a way, McCloud works here like a nuclear physicist positing the theoretical possibility of a particle—or, in this case, a genre, a kind of comic—even before having any empirical proof of its existence. (Keep in mind that the few examples of fully abstract comics mentioned earlier that predate the publication of *Understanding Comics*—such as McDonnell's, Badger's, or Joly's—had not been published at the time.)[15]

Despite this fascinating insight, much of the rest of Scott McCloud's theorization of the medium implicitly takes the medium to be a narrative and representational one. This can be seen from the centrality of the notion of the "cartoon" in *Understanding Comics*, as well as from his categorization of panel-to-panel transitions. McCloud's categories imply characters performing actions ("action-to-action") or juxtaposed within a diegetic space ("subject-to-subject"); they imply the possibility of surveying that diegesis ("aspect-to-aspect") or of traveling through it, in either small increments of space and (diegetic) time ("moment-to-moment") or through large spatial or temporal transitions ("scene-to-scene").[16] Every transition that does not refer to a diegesis fostering a narrative and actors is presumably relegated to McCloud's sixth category, "non-sequitur," which is not so much defined positively as negatively ("everything else").[17] Considering abstract comics, then, can help us transform McCloud's categorization—which has become enshrined as a didactic tool in comics classes—by asking how we can study panel-to-panel transitions by looking *beyond* the diegetic and the narrative, and what we can learn of the actual graphic functioning of comics when studying them in that expanded perspective.

From these two questions we can already see how abstract comics can give rise to a new methodology for Comics Studies. To explore this question further, let us look at an important early example of abstract comics—Benoit Joly's "Parcours," from 1987 (Figure 6.1). "Parcours" consists of numerous panels arranged in what we might call three "paragraphs" of three, three, and four tiers, respectively. Inside the panel frames are nothing but brushstrokes, some dots and small circles drawn with a pen, and a few other pen lines. As opposed to other abstract comics, there is absolutely no representational imagery in Joly's. Yet, we clearly still see a sequence, which is secured by the graphic events on the page, by nothing but formal relationships between the panels. So, for example, the first few panels (indented like a paragraph), proceed in a kind of crescendo, from one dot, to a dot and a brushstroke, to a dot and three brushstrokes, and to a more complex grouping of brushstrokes (plus the dot) in panel 4. After this, the reappearance of a panel empty but for that ever-present ink dot signals the end of a phrase, or melody if you will, like an abrupt return to *pianissimo* after a *forte*, from loud to soft (descriptions of abstract comics almost seem to require analytical terms derived from music).

The further periodical recurrence of the single-dot panel, interspersed with panels filled with more brushstroke activity, structures the peculiar rhythm of this first section. The directionality of the brushstrokes also helps: in panels 2–4, and often afterwards, they are angled upward, clearly moving up from left to right, and thus imparting a sense of kinetic energy to the sequence. Sequentiality can also be very clearly seen in the first tier of the third "paragraph," in which a line of horizontal brushworks that starts in panel 1 drifts downward through panels 2 and 3 in a seemingly continuous movement (repeated in panels 5 through 7). Joly's comic seems to be the perfect fulfillment of McCloud's discussion of "the *picture plane*, where shapes, lines and colors can be *themselves* and not pretend *otherwise*." If it chronicles anything, it is nothing but the life of the graphic trace, strewn across the trajectory of reading.

Yet, this life of the graphic trace does not take place in a diegetic space, it is nowhere else but on the paper before us. This being the case, the comic clearly also has no diegetic time, and so we cannot speak of the panel-to-panel transitions as "moment-to-moment" or "action-to-action," and so on. Sequentiality, Joly's comic shows us, is independent of a represented temporality, and the medium of comics can achieve the former without the

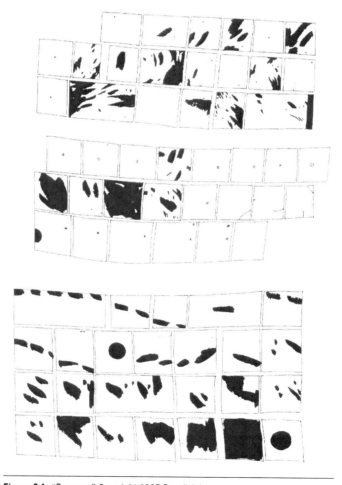

Figure 6.1 "Parcours" Copyright 1987 Benoit Joly.

latter. If that is the case, then, can we still conceive of panels as individual moments in time, arranged along a temporal sequence? Clearly not. Our sense of sequence is derived from the graphic forces on the page, which carry us across the grid of panels; we see a movement, but this movement is only noticeable when we take in, visually, more than one panel at a time.

PROCEDURES AND TERMS FOR ANALYSIS

At this point I would like to introduce a couple of terms that can help us to understand how abstract comics function, and that can also, as I will show, be extended to more traditional representational and narrative comics. The first term is "sequential dynamism." I define this notion as the formal visual energy, created by compositional and other elements internal to each panel and by the layout, that in a comic propels the reader's eye from panel to panel and from page to page, and that imparts a sense of sustained or varied visual rhythms, sometimes along the predetermined left-to-right, top-to-bottom path of reading, other times by creating alternate paths.[18] It is this kind of formal energy that takes us through, and gives a sense of movement to, Joly's page.

Sequential dynamism can clearly be found in narrative comics too, and, interestingly, more often in superhero and other action comics, with their emphasis on movement, on forms hurtling through space, than in alternative comics. Let us look at a page from Steve Ditko and Stan Lee's *Amazing Spider-Man* no. 23, from April 1965 (Figure 6.2). In the first panel, we can see Spider-Man, after a fight with the Green Goblin, falling downward and to the left, from the top-right corner of the panel. In the second panel, his trajectory lines indicate a more complex movement: the down and to the left momentum first continues, then spins around a flagpole, only to then turn up and to the right; in panel 3 it is that up-and-right movement that is continued. Panel 4 reverses the camera angle by 180 degrees, and thus the up-and-to-the-right movement becomes up-and-to-the-left; panel 5 puts a stop to this sequence by showing us Spider-Man's splayed body as he lands, roughly, on top of a water tower.

The Ditko sequence is as melodically arranged as Joly's; and, indeed, one can imagine the page with all representational imagery removed and only the momentum and trajectory motion lines left in, in which case it would very much resemble "Parcours." Joly's, as well as many other abstract comics, can be said to function almost as diagrammatic, formal reductions of the kinds of movements, rhythms, and vectors of force that could be found in earlier, narrative comics. Thus, a kind of sequential dynamism, and therefore a sequential arrangement of abstract forms, already underlay Ditko's comic; therefore, we can see that its sequence did not only depend on a represented temporality. Rather, abstract devices, the arrangement of abstract shapes across the surface of the layout, were used to draw the reader's eye across the page and modulate her reading of the sequence.

To introduce a sense of sequential dynamism into a representational comic is to acknowledge that the medium's purpose is not only narrative and mimetic, basing its sense of sequence on the logic of a represented storyline, and therefore on the progression of diegetic time; rather, it is to understand comics as a means of providing the viewer with a visual aesthetic satisfaction that is not the static satisfaction of traditional painting or drawing, but a specifically sequential pleasure, achieved by putting the eye into motion, and by creating specific graphic paths, speeds of scanning, and graphic rhythms to enliven its aesthetic experience.[19]

Figure 6.2 *Amazing Spider-Man* no. 23, page 18. Copyright April 1965 Marvel Characters, Inc.

The second term I would like to introduce here denotes a quality that has often been noted in comics, yet one for which no single term seems to have been settled upon. Based on the writings and teachings of art historian Werner Hofmann, I will use the term "iconostasis" for the perception of the layout of a comics page as a unified composition; perception which prompts us not so much to scan the comic from panel to panel in the accepted direction of reading, but to take it in at a glance, the way we take in an abstract painting.[20] Hofmann came up with this notion by appropriating the name for the choir screen in Greek-Orthodox churches; etymologically, the terms simply means "image stand," and indeed such choir screens are usually covered in icons, representing various saints and events from the Bible.[21] Arrayed side by side, the icons are arranged in a grid, yet they are not intended to be read sequentially. Hofmann studied such side-by-side arrangements of images from medieval altar pieces and Japanese screens to contemporary art (for example, Andy Warhol's multiple-image portraits), and inquired into the relationship between iconostasis and sequentiality, simply asking: How do we know—how does the art work tell us—when to read a grid of images as sequential, and when to read it as simultaneous? There is no single answer for such a question, of course, but (as Hofmann himself noted on occasion) comics bring a whole new dimension to the inquiry—and this is perhaps even truer of abstract comics.

The iconostatic perception clearly conflicts with a comic's mission to represent a narrative sequentially; if panels are supposed to represent successive moments in, or slices of, time, a simultaneous taking-in of the entire layout defeats that sense of succession. Here, we can note connotative overtones in the term "iconostasis" that go beyond its etymology: specifically the notion—seemingly built into the term—of stasis, of the arrest of movement or time. In some comics the iconostatic effect is barely noticeable: this is true, for instance, of early comic books such as Siegel and Shuster's *Superman*, or of many mainstream European comics such as Hergé's *Tintin* series. In such books, the comic page has no aesthetic unity of its own, but is treated simply as a convenient support for three or four tiers of panels, panels which in other conditions might work just as well arranged in a continuous row (the "strip" of "comic strip," the "bande" of the French term "bande dessinée"). Other artists, from Jack Kirby, especially in his work of the 1960s and later, through Neal Adams, to Chris Ware or Gary Panter, have emphasized the iconostasis by unifying their pages compositionally—for example, through compositional lines that carry from panel to panel, or through balance or symmetry—and even texturally. Since their comics are intended as narrative—and thus, axiomatically, presuppose a temporal succession of panels—what we see in much of this work is a tendency, an impulse toward the iconostasis, yet an impulse which is never fulfilled, or else the narration would stop dead in its tracks. We can refer to this tendency as "iconostatization," the move of a comic toward the stasis of an icon.

Iconostatization, like sequential dynamism, is often at work in Steve Ditko's Spider-Man stories. Simple examples of it are provided by one of Ditko's favorite devices—the repetition of a graphic motif in multiple panels of a page, giving textural homogeneity to the layout. For example, page 18 of issue 22, from March 1965 (Figure 6.3), shows Spider-Man battling a giant serpent. The serpent's coils recur from panel to panel, as does the texture of its body—the scales on its back, the stripes on its ventral region—contrasted with Spider-Man's human form and the web-texture on his costume. The page moves

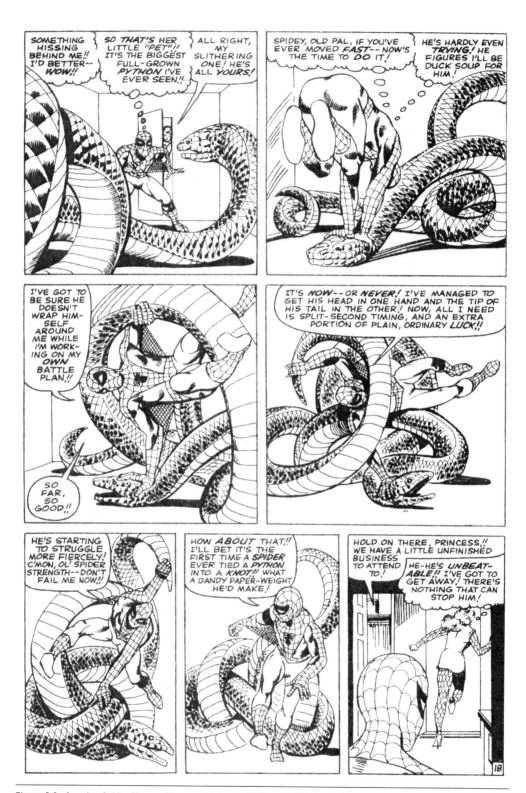

Figure 6.3 *Amazing Spider-Man* no. 22, page 18. Copyright March 1965 Marvel Characters, Inc.

toward a unity of repeated shapes and mark-making that strangely echoes Clement Greenberg's notion of "all-over painting," which the critic identified, for example, in the work of Jackson Pollock. According to him, Pollock's main means of unifying his canvasses was exactly through such repeated textures that covered the entire surface of the work.[22]

And yet, of course, the story can still be read. In this case, visual unity does not impede legibility and sequence. Our attention, when perceiving the comic, is strangely divided: we have one eye, so to speak, on the page's iconostatic effect, and the other on the narrative. This division of attention parallels the division mentioned above between narrative representation and sequential dynamism. Despite the apparent contradiction between dynamism and stasis, they are on similar sides of corresponding dichotomies. How can we reconcile this apparent paradox? Let us look back at our reading of Joly's "Parcours." As I pointed out then,

> our sense of sequence is derived from the graphic forces on the page, which carry us across the grid of panels; we see a movement, but this movement is only noticeable when we take in, visually, more than one panel at a time.

That is to say, iconostatic perception, rather than conflicting with sequential dynamism, is a prerequisite for it; the two go hand in hand.

Indeed, an abstract comic's main aesthetic effect can be seen to reside in this harmonization and reconciliation of iconostasis and sequential dynamism. It subdivides the field of the page into a grid of panels that, through the sequence of compositional vectors, starts moving; or else it offers a sequence of panels that become unified into a greater abstract whole. As we have seen from our *Spider-Man* examples, the same formal structure underlies representational, narrative comics; yet there, the spatial transitions that characterize panel-to-panel movement in abstract comics are overlain with a temporal reading that makes us see (usually) a panel as being later in time than the one that came before it in the spatial sequence; and sequential dynamism is sublated by story and transformed into the arrow of represented time.[23]

ARTIFACT SELECTED FOR SAMPLE ANALYSIS

To study how these elements, in all their complexity, function together in a visually sophisticated narrative comic, let us look at two more pages from Lee and Ditko's *Spider-Man*. Though we have already seen two pages from it, it might be worth at this point saying a few words about the title and its creators. The character of Spider-Man, the superhero alter-ego of meek high-school student Peter Parker, was first introduced in 1962, in the Marvel comic *Amazing Fantasy* no. 15. The following year he received his own title, on which Steve Ditko stayed as artist until issue 38 in 1966. The comic was created following the famed Marvel method: the artist drew the comic based not on a full script, but on a brief plot no longer than a paragraph or two. After the comic was fully penciled, it was sent back to the writer, who "dialogued" it. Thus, some of the most important decisions in the creation of a comic—the breakdown into panels and the layout of each page—were not prescribed to the artist by a pre-existing script, leaving him much more freedom to design the comic visually. While Stan Lee came up with the plots in the beginning, Ditko was credited as plotter beginning with issue 25, and is widely known to have started plotting the comics significantly earlier than that.[24] Therefore, except for the dialogue and caption text, which were added later, Ditko can be seen as the primary creator on the title at the time of the issues we are discussing here. Given free rein script-wise, he used this freedom to explore the visual qualities of the medium—including those we are discussing here, sequential dynamism and iconostasis—to a degree previously unseen within the comics industry.

SAMPLE ANALYSIS

Lee, Stan and Steve Ditko. "The Goblin and the Gangsters!" *Amazing Spider-Man* no. 23. New York: Marvel Comics, 1965.

Our examples come once again from *Amazing Spider-Man* no. 23. Pages 15 (Figure 6.4) and 16 (Figure 6.5) depict a largely aerial fight between Spider-Man and his greatest nemesis, the Green Goblin (for the sake of brevity, we shall refer to the two characters as SM and GG from now on). The two of them crash through a skylight into an impossibly large (for a Manhattan building) room full of ducts and, apparently, heating equipment; there, they whirl around each other and exchange Stan Lee's trademark banter, all while dodging each other's sallies and projectiles, be they pumpkin bombs or webs.

The pages are remarkable for their combination of sequential dynamism and unified compositions, as well as for the complex interweaving they achieve between such formal elements and the story's representational, and even thematic, aspects. Page 15 has three tiers of two, three, and two panels, respectively. The top two and the bottom two panels are of equal size, while the middle tier's narrower three panels are of consistent width. The page is organized as a series of dichotomies and reversals that criss-cross and polarize the surface of the page. If panel 1 shows the two enemies falling from top-left to bottom-right (and slightly forward, toward the reader), with SM atop GG and clearly in control, panel 7, in the opposite corner of the page, shows GG having eluded the hero, who is now falling from top-right to bottom-left (and still toward the viewer), their power relationship momentarily reversed. A similar connection is established between panels 2 and 6, also in opposite corners of the page. In panel 2, SM is shown falling away from GG, from right background to left foreground, along a downward-curving trajectory; while in panel 6 he jumps toward GG, along a similarly downward curve, yet from left foreground to right background. Needless to say, similar symmetries are established between the juxtaposed panels in each tier (1 and 2, 6 and 7). The theme of symmetry is continued in the middle tier, the outer panels of which contain curved motion lines that bracket the tier like parentheses: in panel 3, GG is throwing one of his bombs downward, while, in panel 5, SM is jumping upward. This leaves the middle panel, 4, to function as an almost iconic representation of SM, around which the entirety of the page is organized.

The page is clearly unified visually by this entire network of symmetries; yet because the symmetries in every case involve a reversal, they function dynamically, keeping the compositionally unified layout in constant movement and not allowing it to settle into static form. Of course, the contrasts of direction and movement also refer, symbolically, to the two characters who, as superhero and supervillain, are polar opposites, neatly inscribing the comic's thematic concerns into the very structure of the page.

Figure 6.4 *Amazing Spider-Man* no. 23, page 15. Copyright April 1965 Marvel Characters, Inc.

Figure 6.5 *Amazing Spider-Man* no. 23, page 16. Copyright April 1965 Marvel Characters, Inc.

The dynamic symmetries of page 15 are continued on page 16 and, if anything, rendered even more complex. The page is divided into quarters; the top-left and bottom-right quarters are single panels, while the top-right and bottom-left ones are further divided into two tiers, the top tier of each again subdivided into two equal panels. The criss-crossing structure of the previous page is reinforced here. The two large panels correspond to each other by placing SM in the foreground and GG in the background. In each case, the panel's main compositional lines are curved—SM's motion lines in panel 1, his web (as handled by GG) in panel 8. Yet in panel 1, SM is rising along this curved trajectory, while in panel 8 he is falling against the background of the curled web. The bottom panels in the other two quarters of the page (panels 4 and 7) equally echo each other with curved compositional lines, once again SM's motion lines (as he casts back GG's bomb) paralleling the curve of the web captured by GG. As for the remaining small panels, they make the dynamic symmetries I've discussed clearer than ever. Each pair of panels shows SM and GG, respectively. In panel 2, GG's hand throws his projectile down and to the left (and slightly forward), while in panel 3, this motion is paralleled in the opposite direction by SM's hand and web, which capture the bomb. Similarly, in panel 5, SM casts his web up and to the left, while in panel 6, GG's raised hand grabs the web. In this case, the reversal is not one of direction, but of movement and arrest of movement.

The dynamic symmetries, while drawing attention to the unified layout of the page, do not distract from a sense of sequential dynamism along the predetermined path of reading; rather, that path is inflected with constant motion and energy. Thus, instead of simply proceeding from panel to panel in search of narrative information, our visual attention, on page 15, is pulled down in panel 1, cast back up (despite Spider-Man's downward movement along the same path) in panel 2, given a semi-circular path to follow in panel 3, and so on. Instead of a simple linearity, the visual experience of reading the page resembles more a rollercoaster ride, with a peak, valley, or loop-the-loop in each panel. This sequential experience can be seen mapped out across the page when we take in the layout at a glance, iconostatically. Finally, despite the layouts' formal perfection, the iconostasis is prevented from being arrested into simple *stasis* by the tremendous energy in each panel and by the way such energies find their reflections across the space of the page. As a result, the fight between the superhero and the villain is both highlighted as a formally unified set-piece, and is able to take its place within the longer sequence of the entire story without stopping the narrative dead in its tracks. The attention we bring to these pages is tremendously complex: it is divided bilaterally, between the story on one hand and the formal elements of layout and composition on the other, but also trilaterally, between story, sequential dynamism, and the iconostatic aesthetic unity of the page.

It is in the combination of all these elements that Steve Ditko's artistry in this sequence, and in his work on *Spider-Man* as a whole, consists. Ditko further complicated the relationship between these elements by turning the pages' abstract structure into a virtual metaphor for the conflicting relationship between the two characters. The two pages function almost operatically: abstract form, harmonized into a complex orchestration, not only accompanies but breathes life into the script, the *libretto*. The question remains whether the formal treatment is just subservient to the story or whether—as in much opera—the narrative is primarily an occasion to shape a rhythmically, dynamically, and harmonically complex composition, be that composition visual or musical. It is such questions that a focus on abstract comics, and on the underlying abstract structure of narrative comics, can bring to the fore, helping us to inquire into the very nature of our enjoyment of this formally multifaceted art.

NOTES

1. Andrei Molotiu, ed., *Abstract Comics: The Anthology* (Seattle: Fantagraphics Books, 2009), n.p.
2. Arthur Danto, *The Transfiguration of the Commonplace* (Cambridge, MA: Harvard University Press, 1983); *Andy Warhol* (New Haven, CT: Yale University Press, 2010); and virtually all the books that Danto published between those two volumes.
3. Maurice Denis, "Definition of Neo-Traditionalism" (1890), in Elizabeth Gilmore Holt, *From the Classicists to the Impressionists* (New Haven, CT: Yale University Press, 1966), 509–517, at 509.
4. Roger Fry, *Vision and Design* (1920) and *Transformations* (1926), both of them reprinted many times since; and Clement Greenberg, *Art and Culture: Critical Essays* (Boston: Beacon Press, 1971). Greenberg, especially, often referenced Kant's aesthetics as being the basis of his own formalism. See Immanuel Kant, *Critique of Judgment*, trans. Werner S. Pluhar (Indianapolis: Hackett, 1987; originally published in German 1790).
5. Randy Duncan and Matthew J. Smith, *The Power of Comics: History, Form and Culture* (New York: Continuum, 2009), 5.
6. Ibid.
7. On "pure poetry" and "pure painting," see, for example, Clement Greenberg, *Art and Culture*, 240. The notion of "pure music" goes back to the work of Eduard Hanslick, *On the Musically Beautiful*, trans. Geoffrey Payzant (Indianapolis: Hackett, 1986; first German edition published 1854), where, for example, he sees "all music composed to specified texts as contradictory to the pure concept of music" (83); an equivalent, more widely used term is "absolute music." The notion of "pure poetry" is usually seen to have originated in French Symbolist circles, around the figure of Stéphane Mallarmé; see "Pure Poetry," in *The New Princeton Encyclopedia of Poetry and Poetics* (Princeton: Princeton University Press, 1993), 1007. In English, still with reference to the French Symbolists, it was applied especially to the work of Wallace Stevens. See, for example, Percy Hutchison, "Pure Poetry and Mr. Wallace Stevens" (a review of Stevens' *Harmonium*), *New York Times*, August 9, 1931, available online at www.nytimes.com/books/97/12/21/home/stevens-harmonium.html?_r=1. Hutchison (who seems to disapprove of the idea) defines pure poetry as "a poetry which should depend for its effectiveness on its rhythms and the tonal values of the words employed with as complete a dissociation from ideational content as may be humanly possible." The parallel with abstract comics, and abstract art in general, is clear.
8. Robert C. Harvey, *The Art of the Funnies: An Aesthetic History* (Oxford, MS: University Press of Mississippi, 1994), 8.
9. Ibid, 9.
10. Ibid.
11. Scott McCloud, *Understanding Comics: The Invisible Art* (New York: Harper Perennial, 1993), 9.
12. Ibid., 50. The ellipses indicate breaks from panel to panel.
13. "Diegetic" is the adjectival form of "diegesis." The notion of diegesis, borrowed by Comics Studies from Film Theory, is defined as "In a narrative film [or comic], the world of the film's story. The diegesis includes events that are presumed to have occurred and actions and spaces not shown onscreen." David Bordwell and Kirstin Thompson, *Film Art: An Introduction*, 3rd edn. (New York: McGraw-Hill, 1990), 409. (I am emphasizing the term's origin in Film Theory because it has a different, though related, meaning in classical literary theory going back to Aristotle.) "Diegetic," then, means "belonging to the world of the story."
14. McCloud, *Understanding Comics*, 51.
15. For more on McCloud and abstract comics, see my posts on *Abstract Comics: The Blog*, "Unexpected Precursors, Part I," available online at http://abstractcomics.blogspot.com/2009/10/unexpected-precursors-part-i.html, and "Unexpected Precursors: Scott McCloud, Part II," available online at http://abstractcomics.blogspot.com/2009/10/unexpected-precursors-scott-mccloud.html.
16. For the cartoon, see McCloud, *Understanding Comics*, 29–59; for the types of panel-to-panel transitions, see 60–93.
17. From that point of view, presumably, every panel-to-panel transition in abstract comics would fall under this category. However, once one realizes that McCloud's categories of transitions do not apply universally to all kinds of comics, but only to traditionally narrative ones, the point becomes moot. "Non-sequitur" exists as a category only for narrative comics, describing moments when the storytelling breaks down, when panels do *not* follow *narratively*; therefore it would simply be a categorial confusion to apply the term to the analysis of non-narrative pieces.
18. I first proposed this notion in a paper titled "Sequential Dynamism," that I delivered at the International Comic Arts Forum in 2009. In response to audience comments from Rusty Witek and Charles W. Hatfield, I would like to point out here the difference between the notion I am trying to propose, and the idea of comics leading the reader's eye through the page for purposes of reading comprehension. The two notions can and often do work together but, as I pointed out in my paper as well as in my spoken response, they

don't have to, and their conflict can prove more aesthetically fruitful than their agreement. This could be seen in a 1941 page from Kirby and Simon's *Captain America*, which in my paper I had praised for its usage of sequential dynamism, but which Witek criticized for ending on the left-hand panel of the bottom tier and therefore leaving the reader stranded, as it were, when having to move on to the next page. In my view (which I am probably phrasing much more articulately now than I was able to then), such an apparent problem in no way detracts from the page's aesthetic success; quite the opposite, by problematizing the reading path, it actually opens the reader's eyes to other formal energies hidden on the page.

19. Though I do not have the space to elaborate on this point here, I want to point out that my notion of "sequential dynamism" owes something to Julia Kristeva's idea of the semiotic *chora* (at least in its usage as a term of formal literary analysis), as described in her book, *La Révolution du langage poétique* (Paris: Editions du Seuil, 1974), only partially translated as *Revolution in Poetic Language* (New York: Columbia University Press, 1984). From that point of view, Kristeva's notion of the "semiotic" (not to be confused with the more common usage of the word) corresponds to the formal/abstract dimension of comics that I am trying to outline, while her notion of the "symbolic" is closer to the comics' narrative content.

20. Pierre Fresnault-Deruelle has proposed the term "tabular" for what I call here "iconostatic," opposing it to the "linear" reading of a story. See his article "Du linéaire au tabulaire," *Communications* 24 (1976): 7–23. The two terms seem to derive from the literary theory of the Groupe μ. See their book, *Rhétorique de la poésie: Lecture linéaire, lecture tabulaire* (Paris: PUF, 1977). Of course, the tension between the ("diachronic") linear arrangement of words in a discourse and their ("synchronic") simultaneity on a page had been noticed long before, by literary critics including Gérard Genette, who already in 1970 noted the similarity of this notion to

> how the *roman-photo* or the comic strip function ... which, while making up sequences of images and thus requiring a successive or diachronic reading, also lend themselves to, and even invite, a kind of global and synchronic look—or at least a look whose direction is no longer determined by the sequence of images.

See Genette, *Narrative Discourse: An Essay in Method*, trans. Jane Lewin (Ithaca, NY: Cornell University Press, 1983; originally published in French in 1970 as *Figures III*), 34. Seemingly without knowledge of Hofmann's work, Mark Staff Brandl has proposed the term "iconosequentiality" for the synthesis of the narratively linear and the iconostatic readings; see "Two New Art Terms," posted May 8, 2006, www.sharkforum.org/archives/2006/05/two_new_art_terms_a_new_artist.html. "Synchronic," while important descriptively, is too general for the notion I am trying to outline here, and I would argue that "iconostatic" is preferable to "tabular" both etymologically and from the point of view of the terms' connotations (as argued in my next paragraph).

21. As far as I can tell, Hofmann first introduced the term "iconostasis" (in its French form, "iconostase,") in "Réflexions sur 'l'Iconisation' à propos des *Demoiselles d'Avignon*," *Revue de l'Art* 71 (1986): 33–42. There, in relation to a painting by Adolph Menzel, he refers to narrative (*récit*) transforming into iconostasis, in which "actors and actions form 'fortuitous encounters,' frozen in an enigmatic immobility which is that of the icon." (36). Hofmann greatly expanded upon these notions, especially as applied to "multi-frame" images, in a graduate seminar on narrative art in which I participated, at the Institute of Fine Arts, New York University, in 1991. I base my usage of his term here primarily on his teaching.

22. Greenberg used the term "all-over" repeatedly to describe the work of Pollock and of other New York School artists. See especially his 1955 article, "'American-Type' Painting," reprinted in Clement Greenberg, *The Collected Essays and Criticism*, vol. 3: *Affirmations and Refusals, 1950–1956* (Chicago: University of Chicago Press, 1955): 217–236, and as later revised in *Art and Culture*, 208–229.

23. I use the term "sublated" here in its Hegelian sense, of an entity, quality, or concept being "raised" to another level (usually by synthesis with its opposite), yet at the same time being seemingly negated. Thus, while sequential dynamism is united with the diegetic temporality of the story to create the comic's feeling of sequentiality, it also becomes hidden, less noticeable, in the process.

24. According to Ditko's biographer, Blake Bell, this happened as early as "after about the first ten issues." Blake Bell, *Strange and Stranger: The World of Steve Ditko* (Seattle: Fantagraphics Books, 2008), 65.

SELECTED BIBLIOGRAPHY

Bell, Blake. *Strange and Stranger: The World of Steve Ditko*. Seattle: Fantagraphics Books, 2008.

Brandl, Mark Staff. "Two New Art Terms." *Sharkforum.org*. Posted May 8, 2006, www.sharkforum.org/archives/2006/05/two_new_art_terms_a_new_artist.html.

Duncan, Randy and Matthew J. Smith. *The Power of Comics: History, Form and Culture*. New York: Continuum, 2009.

Fresnault-Deruelle, Pierre. "Du linéaire au tabulaire." *Communications* 24 (1976): 7–23.

Greenberg, Clement. *Art and Culture: Critical Essays*. Boston: Beacon Press, 1971.

Harvey, Robert C. *The Art of the Funnies: An Aesthetic History*. Oxford, MS: University Press of Mississippi, 1994.

Hofmann, Werner. "Réflexions sur 'l'Iconisation' à propos des *Demoiselles d'Avignon*." *Revue de l'Art* 71 (1986): 33–42.

Holt, Elizabeth Gilmore. *From the Classicists to the Impressionists*. New Haven, CT: Yale University Press, 1966.

Hutchison, Percy. "Pure Poetry and Mr. Wallace Stevens." *New York Times*, August 9, 1931, www.nytimes.com/books/97/12/21/home/stevens-harmonium.html?_r=1 (accessed December 20 2010)

Lewin, Jane E. *Narrative Discourse: An Essay in Method*. Translated by Gérard Genette. Ithaca, NY: Cornell University Press, 1983.

McCloud, Scott. *Understanding Comics: The Invisible Art*. New York: HarperPerennial, 1993.

Molotiu, Andrei, ed. *Abstract Comics: The Anthology*. Seattle: Fantagraphics Books, 2009.

Payzant, Geoffrey. *On the Musically Beautiful*. Translated by Eduard Hanslick. Indianapolis: Hackett, 1986.

Part II
Content

7

PHILOSOPHY

"The Triumph of the Human Spirit" in X-Men

Jeff McLaughlin

Philosophy is about wisdom. And wisdom is not usually the first word you think of when you think of mainstream American superhero comic books. Philosophy is also associated with the pursuit of truth and justice, which may sound a bit familiar to fans of Superman. "Truth, justice and the American way" was his calling card; it was his reason for getting up in the morning. While we (i.e., philosophers) might argue strongly about what the social and political connotations of the phrase "the American way" entails, everyone knew what Superman meant by it. At a time when the world was at war, it was a message that gave hope to many and put fear in the hearts of many others. So while philosophers do what they do—search for truth and justice—Superman tried (and presumably continues) to promote these two ideals. It would seem that superheroes and philosophers share some things in common.

Philosophy has many subfields. For example, epistemology is the study of knowledge; in other words: What is truth? Metaphysics asks what the ultimate nature of reality is, while ethics looks at the nature of right and wrong and good and bad behavior. There are also a multitude of "philosophy of" areas: philosophy of science, philosophy of religion, and so forth. The word *philosophy* comes from two Greek words, *philos*, meaning "love," and *sophia*, meaning "wisdom." So philosophy is the love of wisdom. Because of this generality, it is sometimes hard to distinguish philosophy from other intellectual pursuits, but that is because philosophy is at the foundation of all areas of inquiry. When a person gets a doctorate in sociology or economics, she is not granted the title of Doctor of Sociology or Doctor of Economics, but rather a Ph.D. in the relevant area, e.g., one has a "doctor of philosophy in sociology." Philosophy asks questions and seeks wisdom, while these other areas go about trying to find answers.

UNDERLYING ASSUMPTIONS

One of the first philosophical questions we can ask about comic books is: What *is* a comic book? Definitions are an essential part of philosophical analysis. We have to know what something is before we can start discussing it in any proper way. If I said "Beezles are fun," you would not be able to agree or disagree with me until you understood what I meant by the unfamiliar term. Philosophers interested in aesthetics discuss what makes a comic book a comic book and not a novel or a comic strip or even a movie. Can a comic book exist without illustrations? Can it exist if there are no words? How do these two things, that is, illustrations and text, come together to give us a comic book rather than a Sears catalog? What is essential to a comic book such that if it didn't have it, we wouldn't consider it a comic book?

Knowing what a comic book *isn't* is easier to determine than knowing what it *is*. For example, a comic book is not a frozen movie where each panel simply mimics a frame of film. A single page with a 3×3 grid of panels that is typically read from left to right, top to bottom, can have each panel represent something completely different—a different perspective, place, and time. We can have a series of snapshots that gives us not only the outside picture of what is going on, but the inner images, or inner dialogues of the characters. As we move from panel to panel, usually there is a period of time that seems to pass, be it a second or a minute or a millennium. Also, the reader can read the entire comic book as one watches a movie, but then when finished he or she can turn back and re-read a previous page. He or she can also linger over an image or bit of dialogue for as long as he or she wants. Movies might allow this by using the "replay" button on our home theater remote control, but they weren't meant for this degree (or ease) of viewer participation and interactivity.

Since comics tell stories, they have something to say; and because they have something to say, we can discuss them from a variety of perspectives. Of course, some may claim that comic books do not have anything of interest to say to us and so do not deserve our time and energy. Admittedly, this criticism will apply to some, but not all, comic books. Yet one cannot just adopt this position without looking at the question: Do comic books have anything of interest to say? *This question is philosophical in nature.* For example, if they have nothing of interest to say, what does that say about their enduring popularity? If they are mere digressions, is this a bad thing? Is being entertained by tales of heroic deeds, humorous events, love stories, space adventures, and so on unworthy of thoughtful analysis? In other words, rejecting comic books as being philosophically uninteresting requires a philosophically interesting argument! Whatever we think, comic books are finally coming to be recognized for what they are: an art form.

Art can be dangerous—it can challenge the viewer and even the entire culture. It can say things in a way that meticulously and logically constructed arguments cannot. Plato argued that art was useless because you can sit in a chair but not in a painting of one. But, more importantly, he considered art to be dangerous because it was mimicking the real. It could be interpreted by the foolish as being the truth when in fact it was far removed from the truth.[1] Similarly, more than 2000 years later in the 1950s, some people thought comic books were dangerous because they promoted a worldview that was negatively affecting the children who were reading them. Juvenile delinquency, sexual violence, threats to authority, and the promotion of criminal behavior were all perceived to be intentionally drawn on the covers of various comic books.[2] And if the kids were oblivious to these theoretical messages, a lot of their parents were told they were there.

Unless we have certain insights or personal communications with or from the artist, knowing his or her intent will be difficult. Comic book readers have to work at getting more than just entertainment out of comics. One reading will give them the pleasure of the story, a second or third might give them something a bit more. Since the story itself is no longer the focus of attention, the reader can spend more time looking at the book differently.

PROCEDURES

In terms of the philosophical process involved in evaluating and analyzing comic books, one begins with the simple experience of reading the comic book. And after this, a personal reflection: Did you like it? This seems like a pretty basic question, but when you try to answer why, this will be the springboard for your intellectual investigation. Did the story grab your attention? Did you like the artwork? The characters? Be specific. Don't just find examples, find examples and figure out what it is that made you form this opinion. Push yourself a little harder. Perhaps you found it simplistic, or maybe you liked the witty dialogue. Whatever the case, you will have formed a general opinion about the comic book. Now try and articulate the reasons for your opinion.

To support your reasons you should critically read (i.e., carefully and objectively think about) the comic book to look for the supporting evidence. Sometimes it might be possible to find the creators' discussions concerning their work and their intentions (e.g., through outside interviews or commentaries). However, that they express particular views does not mean they are correct regarding whatever meaning they attribute to the comic book. For example, if the comic shows every single woman wearing fishnet stockings or every panel is splattered with illustrated gore, to claim that the comic is about empowering women or is a negative commentary about violence may be disingenuous. These sorts of images (at least at first glance) would not reinforce the position. Yet most of the time you do not have the creators' thoughts, and fortunately most of the time they aren't necessary. Whether you agree or disagree with the comments of the creators, you are actively engaged in a dialogue about their work. Indeed, I will engage in this process in this chapter.

To say there is "meaning" is in one sense to ask if there is a theme in the comic book. That is, can you generalize what it is "about" to someone else? If the comic book or its theme is not really that interesting or does not seem significant, this very determination is actually a useful observation. Let's imagine that you don't think there's anything of merit here and your opinion is that the comic book seems rather dull, yet it is achieving a lot of commercial success. Is there something that you are missing that others are finding? It may seem that the comic book you have chosen to evaluate has failed you, but in fact the reason for its failure in your opinion will open doors to more theoretical issues, such as the nature of subjectivity, the nature of what "success" is, why people enjoy—or hate—comic books, and so forth. It is easy to come up with opinions, but finding good reasons and formulating appropriate questions will direct your philosophical journey. And this journey can take you anywhere.

Although it is probably a safe bet to say that most writers and artists in the comic book industry are not professional philosophers and do not intend their work to be overtly philosophical ("as opposed to being fun," a cynic might say), this does not mean that what they are doing cannot be traced back to some philosophical point of view. Use what is on the pages of a comic book and what you think about what is on those pages to investigate relevant philosophical areas. Yes, the story might be about the possibility of time travel, extra-sensory perception or some superhuman feat, but outlandish concepts and equally outlandish presentations can be grounded in very important ideas—even if the creators aren't aware of this. It is not that difficult to start to think in this sort of way. Why doesn't Superman make better use of his time and just destroy all weapons of mass destruction instead of writing newspaper columns as Clark Kent? Are the technologies created by Tony Stark (Iron Man) good, bad, or ethically neutral? Why does or should Wonder Woman care about what happens in society?

ARTIFACT SELECTED FOR ANALYSIS

There are always examples of ethical issues to be found in most mainstream superhero comics because they involve some sort of conflict between those who wish to harm others and those who try to prevent that harm from happening. More complicated (or perhaps less obvious) are issues such as the nature of reality, which are sometimes directly or indirectly raised. Accordingly, we will examine these two topics within one series.

We will focus our attention on the classic Marvel Comics "Dark Phoenix Saga" that had a main character, Phoenix of the X-Men team, go bad, very bad. Here we have the eternal battle between good and evil, a battle for supremacy between a superhero and a supervillain—all within the same person. In looking at this saga, we will see how comics can be about more than just what is on the page, but it requires the thoughtfulness of both the artist and writer and the reader/viewer to manage this. Comics allow the reader/viewer to be drawn into the action and think about things in a unique way that movies and books cannot. Please note that this observation is a philosophical one. We are comparing different modes of artistic expression and proposing how they are capable of doing (and achieving) different things.

The original *X-Men* comic book was co-created by Stan Lee and Jack Kirby in 1963. In it, a collection of teenagers who possess mutant superpowers are brought under the tutelage of Professor Charles Xavier, who doesn't want them to hide their differences, but to celebrate them and use them to combat various villains. Unfortunately, the series was ahead of its time and didn't have the success of other Marvel titles. After a series of reprints, it ended its run in 1970. It was resurrected in 1974 by Len Wein and Dave Cockrum and has gone on to be a huge hit, with various spin-off titles, movies, animated shows, and more. Many teenage readers saw themselves in these X-Men characters because teenagers often feel awkward and misunderstood (a common feature in Lee's creations). Later on in the series, the depiction of hatred and fear that the general public had for the characters was seen by some readers as an allegory for real inequities in race, gender, and sexual orientation.

One of the characters that continued from the original 1960s run of the series was Jean Grey, originally codenamed Marvel Girl, who possessed the powers of telekinesis and telepathy. She was romantically linked with another original team member, Scott Summers (a.k.a. Cyclops), who suffered the disability of never being able to open his eyes without a powerful energy beam blasting forth.

The Phoenix Saga was a great story to read and remains a classic example of good characters and storytelling. The saga was written by Chris Claremont and penciled and co-plotted by John Byrne. It started with issues 101–108[3] and morphed into the "Dark Phoenix Saga" between issues 129–137.[4] A summary of the saga follows.

Returning from a mission in space, Jean Grey is exposed to the radiation of a solar flare and becomes a being of pure thought. She transforms herself into Phoenix after acquiring god-like abilities, but initially she is able to restrain these powers by creating a series of psychic "circuit breakers." However, after experiencing intense emotions the psychic barriers she has put in place start to give way. Witnessing Cyclops' defeat in battle, her powers finally overwhelm her. Renaming herself Dark Phoenix, she fights her former teammates and transports herself to a distant galaxy. There, she devours the energy of a star, causing it to explode and kill five billion inhabitants on a nearby planet. Members of the Shi'ar alien race now realize that she has the ability to destroy the entire universe and thus is a threat that has to be stopped.

One of her teammates creates a device that will scramble Dark Phoenix's ability to think clearly, thereby weakening her. Professor Xavier is then able to restore the psychic "circuit breakers," thus allowing Jean Grey to regain control. However, because she has killed billions of people, she has been sentenced to death by the Empress of the Shi'ar race. Wanting to defend their now "normalized" teammate from what they see as an unjust punishment of their friend, the X-Men attempt to fight off her would-be executioners, but when all the X-Men fall, Jean Grey's emotions rip through the psychic barriers and release the Dark Phoenix powers once more. Momentarily regaining self-control, Jean Grey ends her own life to save the universe from Phoenix's wrath.

SAMPLE ANALYSIS

Claremont, Chris and John Byrne. *X-Men*, vol 1, issues 101–108; 129–137, Marvel Comics, 1976–1980.

What is the saga's message? Comic book artist and co-plotter John Byrne has stated: "The story was, after all, about the triumph of the human spirit."[5] But is he right? Think about it. You would be hard pressed to think of one story about human beings that *isn't* about the human spirit. But the Dark Phoenix Saga really isn't about the human spirit. At best, it is about the spirit of her friends. Jean Grey is a phoenix, a mythical bird that rises from its own ashes. Ask yourself: Why is she called Phoenix? How does this help me understand her character or our attitudes towards her? Superman is more than a man, he is super—but would he be called "Superman" if he were evil? It doesn't quite have the right ring to it, so perhaps when we think of the word "super" we also have emotional connotations associated with it. And thus we have two more examples of our being philosophical. Do names have any meaning beyond just being an identifier and (as alluded to before) can the person who creates a work of art be wrong about what they think they have created? Does it even matter if the creators are wrong or at least did not intend what we interpret to be true about their efforts? If Byrne and Claremont intended to create a vehicle for philosophical conversation, would it have worked? Probably not. Byrne writes a response to a question on his website:

> But looking back, if I had the power, I would erase the whole thing. Too many people since have, consciously or unconsciously, set the Death of Phoenix as a scale against which to measure their own work. They want to do their own "Death of Phoenix," their own "event," forgetting that what Chris and I did was not *planned* as an event. It just happened.
>
> It has been wisely said that no one ever created a great comic book story by setting out to create a great comic book story. That's a lot of what's wrong with

the industry right now. If you set out to create an "event" (in the sense of something that is truly memorable and not just a sales stunt) you will almost certainly fail.[6]

Likewise, if you start out trying to be philosophical in a medium where the reader isn't expecting you to be overtly intellectual, you will probably fail in terms of constructing an entertaining story, because you are forcing the story into a straightjacket rather than letting it go where it needs to go. If, however, through the natural growth of the characters and the story, philosophical issues arise, then you may achieve greater success. No reader of a superhero comic book wants to have the creative team pushing the action to the sideline so they can hit the reader over the head with their *big message*. The comic has to be driven by the internalities (character, conflict, situation, etc.), and if a reader picks up something else, even something not intended, then that makes the experience all that more enriching. It is this interpretive process that allows us to show how comics can be philosophical. Legendary comic book writer and editor Stan Lee didn't try to be profoundly philosophical when he came up with the "With great power, comes great responsibility" narrative caption in *Amazing Fantasy* no. 15.[7] But it is truly an important statement that not only has external philosophical significance but also captures (in my opinion) what all superhero comic books are really about.

This great responsibility is deeply felt by Jean Grey. Yet, unlike that which her name presupposes, this particular phoenix does not rise from the ashes. She dies. She kills herself after her friends risk their own lives and grapple with their own sense of morality to save her. It is only years later when others take over the writing duties from Chris Claremont that Phoenix actually rises again. When asked by another fan on his website about whether he approves of the 1986 resurrection of the character in *Fantastic Four* no. 286, Byrne posted the following note:

> I actually think the death of Phoenix [not Jean] was made even MORE poignant by the revelation that the thing that killed itself was a doppelganger.... By saying Phoenix was not Jean, we now say the human spirit is so powerful that even a COPY will make the ultimate sacrifice when the circumstance demands.[8]

But what is the ultimate sacrifice that is being referred to? Jean was going to be killed anyway, so she just preempted justice by taking her own life. This doesn't seem very honorable. Moreover, if the circumstance demanded it as Byrne states, how is her compliance in any way ennobling?

In fact, when we learn what the original intent of co-plotters John Byrne and Chris Claremont was, we see that this notion of "the human spirit triumphant" does not fit.[9] The original ending had Jean Grey live:

> Jean [Phoenix was still Jean then, turned evil by Mastermind] flew off into space, had an encounter with a Shi'ar [an alien race] ship, blew it up, and then returned to Earth.... When it came time to draw the key issue, I, as co-plotter, decided Dark Phoenix needed to do something "bigger" than just blow up a Shi'ar ship. Something that would make it absolutely clear that Dark Phoenix was the Meanest Mother in the Valley. So I decided to have her blow up a star, and that that star would have at least one inhabited world in its family of planets.[10]

Co-plotters Byrne and Claremont wanted Jean to survive the ordeal but be lobotomized of her powers and returned to Earth, where her parents would look after her. She would have the mental capacity of a young child, but every once in a while Dark Phoenix would be released and the X-Men would have to do battle with her.[11] Apparently, editor Jim Shooter did not like this idea because she was not being "punished" sufficiently for her crime, so the decision was made to kill her.

Jean's dying, or her being allowed to live—as a child—just doesn't seem to capture a positive sense of the human spirit, nor does having her come back as a recurring villain make it any more heartwarming. So what else can it be about? Or perhaps, more appropriately, what can we learn from this story? Well, if we extrapolate from the specific events to more general concepts, we can see a number of philosophical points. Let's just mention three. First, the saga provides us with an illustration (no pun intended) of the Platonic tripartite nature of the soul. Second, it provides us with a plot point that highlights (and contrasts) two ethical theories. Finally, it gives us a nice example of drawing an important distinction between causal versus moral and legal culpability. These concepts will be explained as we move along.

Plato and Dark Phoenix

Jean's fury is always triggered by harm done to those she cares about—her negative rage actually comes from the positive emotion of love. This power mutates into a potentially destructive force—and the more powerful it is, the less good that comes from it. In other words, the emotional Dark Phoenix is more powerful and thus exerts more negative energy than Phoenix. She does not stop to consider her actions; she does not ponder over the consequences, she merely acts to satisfy her appetites and her passions.

In issue 136, she refers to this:

> Jean: Yes! No! I … hunger, Scott, For a joy, a rapture, beyond all comprehension. That need is a part of me, too. It … consumes me.

And Professor X describes her as having characteristics that require self-control—something that she sorely lacks (Figure 7.1):

> Professor X: Power without restraint—knowledge without wisdom—age without maturity—passion without love.

Yet in times of rationality, Jean attempts to regain this control, which tells us that she knows that although she is a complex person, she knows the proper order of these elements.

> Professor X [to himself]: Would … have lost … but I sensed Jean … fighting her Phoenix-self … helping me …[12]

Plato voiced concern over the proper functioning of the human soul. In *The Republic*, Plato argues that the human soul is made up of three parts: reason, spirit, and appetite.[13] Reason tells us what is good for each part, and for the whole of the soul. So if we thirst, our appetite will push us to drink something and our reason will tell us what we should drink in order to quench it. Think of being lost in the desert and coming across a small oasis. Your appetite will make you want to drink the water, but your reason will tell you to be cautious—perhaps the water is poisonous. Clearly, it is important that your reason be able to win and command your spirit to do its bidding in this situation. Furthermore, the stronger your appetite is, the more difficult it is for reason to rule and the more important it is for reason to rule. If reason is not in control, for example, when we are desperately thirsty, it is harder to say "no" to those things that could harm us. We may desire another beer or cigarette, and if we don't have control over our desires, we will fulfill those desires even if they are not good for us. Reason must rule for our own good.

Figure 7.1 *X-Men* no. 136. Copyright 1980 Marvel Characters, Inc.

When reason is in control, Phoenix is in control. When rage, anger, and other emotions take over, the dark version of Phoenix comes out. For Dark Phoenix, reason does not rule; her spirit and appetite do. And when she seeks to satisfy her own sense of pleasure, she not only destroys worlds, but also destroys her friendships.[14]

In the climatic issue 137, Jean is hit and momentarily brought back to her normal self:

> Jean: Neither [being] can exist without the other. Phoenix provides my life-force while I provide a living focus for its infinite power. So long as I live, the Phoenix will manifest itself through me. And so long as that happens I'll eventually inevitably become Dark Phoenix.... Kill Me!

Cyclops runs after her.

> Cyclops: Jean. Wait! You're not giving us any choice!
> Jean: The choice was never yours to begin with.... Jean to Phoenix to Dark Phoenix a progression as inevitable as death. You of all people should know how I feel.... I'm scared Scott. I'm hanging on by my fingernails. I can feel the Phoenix within me taking over. Part of me ... welcomes it. You want me to fight? I have. I am—with all my strength. But I can't forget that I killed an entire world—five billion people—as casually, as unthinkingly, as you would crumple a piece of paper. I want no more deaths on my conscience. Your way, I'd have to stay completely in control of myself every second of every day for the rest of my immortal life ... if even one more person died at my hands ... it's better this way. Quick. Clean. Final.[15]

The rational Jean sees the difficulty with the Jean who has an unquenchable appetite; she has desires and urges but does not care about their merits. What she wants she takes, regardless of the consequences. This eternal struggle of having wants and desires that we know are not appropriate overrule both reason and right is a drama played out throughout the history of fiction. Dramatic struggles are not just about a battle of "us against them," but also "us against ourselves" (Figure 7.2).

The suggestion has been that the saga has shown how the Platonic argument concerning the different parts of the soul can be dramatized and, even more importantly, *supported*. What if you were one of the X-Men? How would you judge your friend who is struggling in this sort of situation? What if a friend did something wrong—perhaps cheated on an exam or on their boyfriend or girlfriend—and you had the ability to do something about it? Now you are the one who is struggling with a decision that has to be made. Do you say something and to whom? Even if you do not act and do not say anything to anyone, you have chosen to do something: nothing. Dramatic fiction mirrors reality, and comic books often simplify and exaggerate that reality and as such can allow readers to reflect upon the actions and intentions of the characters involved. This sort of question, "What is the right thing to do?" is one that ethicists ask.

Ethics and Dark Phoenix

Utilitarians believe that the ethically right thing to do is to promote the greatest amount of happiness for the greatest number of people.[16] Deontologists believe that the ethically right thing to do is to do one's duty, no matter what.[17] Consider that you promise to go to a movie with your best friend, but then your neighbor invites you over to watch a special one-time-only television event that your best friend doesn't care about, but which you would really like to see.[18] A deontologist would simply state that you have a responsibility to always keep your promises—if you promised you would go to the movie with your friend, then that is what you must do, regardless of how disappointed you might be. Friendship is more than just making yourself happy, and keeping promises requires that you keep your word; otherwise, what point would making a promise be if anyone could break it at any time?

Figure 7.2 *X-Men* no. 137. Copyright 1980 Marvel Characters, Inc.

Utilitarians would only look at the consequences to determine which option would create the greatest amount of happiness for everyone involved. It is not important why you do what you do, so long as more people are happier afterwards than before. If you would be happier by going to your neighbor's house than to the movie and you could schedule the movie night for some other time so your friend wouldn't be too upset, then the utilitarian would say that going to the neighbor's house is the right thing to do. But if your friend would be offended and if you would feel guilty, then the utilitarian would say you should go to the movie: Your friend will be happier and you will be happier (i.e., feeling less guilty).

Consider a more fanciful case. Your house is on fire, as is your neighbor's, and you can only rush in to one home to save its occupants. Your spouse is in your house, but in the neighbor's house there are three brilliant doctors who just discovered the cure for cancer in the basement. The deontologist and utilitarian would disagree on what would be the right thing to do in this situation. On one hand, you have a duty to your spouse; on the other hand, the loss of these doctors would have a severe impact on the welfare of millions. "How many lives would be saved?" the utilitarian would ask. While you would be sad losing your spouse and feel bad for it, you would be indirectly saving the lives of millions. "What's your obligation here?" the deontologist would ask. If you cannot count on your spouse in a time of need, who can you count on? And who knows if the doctors would actually give the drug to the world? Perhaps they would only sell it to a huge pharmaceutical company who would destroy it so they could make billions more by selling their own "cures."

Carry this debate over to the Dark Phoenix Saga. As an X-Man, what would you do? Would you allow your teammate to be killed, or defend her right to live? You might argue that she deserves to be punished for the crime she committed, which would be a deontologist approach. You might further stress that we don't know for certain if she would kill again in the future, but the risk will always be there so there's even more reason to carry out the execution. Since this latter argument is a utilitarian one, we note that both the deontologist and the utilitarian can come to the same conclusion but for very different reasons. Execute Phoenix because she deserves it; execute Phoenix because the risk of not doing so is too great.

The above conclusion is based upon the published ending. If we examine the original ending, the two ethical schools part ways. If Phoenix's powers could be neutralized by having her psychic abilities removed, one presumes that this would be a better thing for her (she's not dead) and for her team (they still have their friend). As this would promote more happiness than her execution, the utilitarian would push for this option if it were available. The deontologist, however, would still demand her execution because she committed the greatest crime of all: murder. The fact that others might be saddened by this is not relevant to the application of justice.

Responsibility and Phoenix and Dark Phoenix

But does Jean Grey deserve to die for what Dark Phoenix did? Surely this question is one that goes well beyond the pages of a comic book when we examine the behaviors of any individual. Moral responsibility and causal responsibility are not equivalent concepts. You don't have to be causally responsible to be held morally accountable for some act. For example, if you tell your child to hit another child, you are to be blamed even though you didn't commit the actual physical act. Yet if the child hits another because they are copying something they saw on television, then the child is causally responsible but not morally responsible. This is because they did the act but were not aware of its ethical significance; they didn't know that it's wrong.

In the legal system a person who commits a crime but is found legally insane is to be viewed like the child who hit without understanding that what they did was wrong. Dark Phoenix is causally responsible for the deaths of billions, but is she morally responsible too? Did Dark Phoenix appreciate the difference between right and wrong? Jean Grey seemed to: She was horrified when told of her crimes and even asked her friends to kill her because of her actions. Perhaps she knew what she was doing was wrong at the time, and Dark Phoenix just didn't care. Perhaps, then, Jean Grey was acting but could not help but do what she did. Did she have an irresistible urge to feed her need? In Platonic terms, did her appetite overrule her reason? Let me offer a possible solution.

When Jean Grey visits her family, we finally witness the intense internal struggle that she is going through to maintain her sanity. This struggle gives us insight into her psyche and allows us to conclude that her will is weak and she is losing the battle against her powerful appetite for pleasure.

> Jean [to herself]: I can't stop reading their minds!
> Jean: I'm fine mom.
> Jean [to herself]: I'm **NOT** fine! Get out of my head! All of you! Get out! **GET OUT!** … Dad's worried about me, but he's as edgy as mom … and Sarah's TERRIFIED … Can't help myself. Don't want to anymore. I'm reacting to their thoughts not their words![19] (emphasis in the original)
> Jean: You fear me. All of you, and with good reasons.… I am what I am. I was your daughter.
> Dad: No. You're not mine. Not any part of me! I deny you. I cast you out!
> Jean [to herself]: Dad, no! Please!
> Jean: Watch your tone with me old man. You dance with death.[20]

Here we have evidence of the "irresistible urge" defense being played out in a comic book storyline and also by the very way that storyline is visually represented on the page!

For the legal court system there would be no good reason for punishing Jean if she is insane—it would be like holding an animal morally accountable for biting you. This does not mean that society cannot protect itself from the future actions of dangerous actors. We could euthanize the animal, not because it deserves to die (which would be a deontological argument), but to prevent it from biting someone else (which is a utilitarian argument).

For Jean Grey, her death may be the only way to ensure that she does not put the universe in further danger. And her death, as opposed to incarceration or being lobotomized, may be warranted since there would always be the risk of great harm if she were ever able to regain her powers and freedom. Thus, the second version of the saga's ending—the one that readers got—is the better one from an ethical perspective. But as we have seen, the best comic book characters always come back to life, sometimes years later. Likewise, good philosophy is eternal, since an old philosophy will always be a new philosophy to someone.[21]

NOTES

1. See Plato, *Republic Book X.*
2. For an excellent discussion of this, see Amy Kiste Nyberg, *Seal of Approval: The History of the Comics Code* (Jackson, MS: University Press of Mississippi, 1998).
3. *Uncanny X-Men* nos. 101–108 (cover dates: August 1976–October 1977).
4. *Uncanny X-Men* nos. 129–138 (cover dates: January 1979– October 1980).
5. John Byrne, www.byrnerobotics.com, posted April 1, 1998.
6. John Byrne, www.byrnerobotics.com/forum/forum_topics.asp?FID=3, posted May 12, 2009.
7. Cover date August 1962.
8. John Byrne, www.byrnerobotics.com/forum/forum_topics.asp?FID=3, posted April 1, 1998.
9. The original ending of the Dark Phoenix Saga was part of a special reprinted version of *Uncanny X-Men* issue no. 137, titled *Phoenix: The Untold Story* no. 1 (1984). It included commentary by those involved with the original story. Byrne summed up his own recent feeling: "I am weary beyond measure of talking about that story! I wish everyone would just forget it! (And you can quote me!)" Personal email communication with the author, April 23, 2010.
10. John Byrne, www.byrnerobotics.com/forum/forum_topics.asp?FID=3, posted May 12, 2009.
11. "The Dark Phoenix Tapes," in *Phoenix: The Untold Story* no. 1 (1984).
12. *Uncanny X-Men* no. 136 (cover date August 1980).
13. Plato, *Republic, Book IV.*
14. This may seem backwards in terms of importance, but turning against one's teammates is a big deal in comic books, since the teams are usually made up of individuals who have common experiences and bonds that go beyond what typical friends share.
15. *Uncanny X-Men* no. 137 (cover date August 1980).
16. John Stuart Mill, *Utilitarianism,* 1861.
17. Immanuel Kant, *The Metaphysical Elements of Justice: Part I of the Metaphysics of Morals,* 1780.
18. Let's assume for the sake of argument that the show will not be repeated and no one is able to record it for later viewing. I throw this scenario in since this could be an option that would make everyone happy.
19. So too is the reader! We are reacting to Jean's thoughts, not her words!
20. *Uncanny X-Men* no. 136 (cover date August 1980).
21. Other long-dead philosophers may have come to conclusions that you will draw for yourself, but the difference now is that *you* are the one thinking them and that is pretty impressive.

SELECTED BIBLIOGRAPHY

Byrne, John. *Byrne Robotics,* www.byrnerobotics.com (accessed on December 21, 2010).

Kant, Immanuel. *The Metaphysical Elements of Justice: Part I of the Metaphysics of Morals.* 1780. Translated with introduction by John Ladd (2nd edn.). Indianapolis: Hackett, 1999.

Mill, John Stuart. *Utilitarianism.* 1861 (2nd edn.). Edited by George Sher. Indianapolis: Hackett, 2002.

Nyberg, Amy Kiste. *Seal of Approval: The History of the Comics Code.* Jackson, MS: University Press of Mississippi, 1998.

Plato. *Republic.* Translated by G.M.A. Grube. Revised by C.D.C. Reeve. Indianapolis: Hackett, 1992.

8

COMICS JOURNALISM

Drawing on Words to Picture the Past in Safe Area Goražde

Amy Kiste Nyberg

Joe Sacco wanted to be a journalist; the tight job market when he graduated from the University of Oregon with a degree in journalism in 1981 thwarted those ambitions. He turned instead to comics, and his early work encompassed satire, biography, autobiography, and travelogue. In the winter of 1991–1992, during a trip to the Middle East, he gathered material for what would become the nine-issue series called *Palestine*, published between 1993 and 1995. Although Sacco had initially intended the comic to be autobiographical, *Palestine* became "something more journalistic."[1]

Sacco is now the best-known of a small group of contemporary comics journalists—creators who employ the comics form for journalistic storytelling. Comics journalism is most closely aligned with the sector of comics publishing referred to as "alternative" comics. The catch-all term describes comics that fall outside of the mainstream superhero comics and manga that remain the dominant market force in comics publishing. Researcher Charles Hatfield notes that alternative comics have their roots in the underground comix movement of the 1960s and 1970s. Changes in comic book distribution and the growth of comics specialty stores gave rise to independent publishers and the development of non-mainstream comics. Today, creators continue to experiment both with "narrative form and thematic content" in a number of genres, most notably autobiography.[2]

UNDERLYING ASSUMPTIONS

As a genre of nonfiction comics, comics journalism combines the form of comics with the conventions of journalism. While separating comics journalism from its other forms (newspaper, magazine, radio, television, online) presents no real difficulties, determining what happens to journalism when it is presented in comics form can provide insight into the creative process that underlies producing journalism in comics form.

GENRE AND FORM

Sacco, and those who followed, faced the challenge of how to negotiate the assumptions and expectations that dictate how journalists go about their work. Journalists adhere to a strict set of rules determined by professional norms, institutional constraints, legal considerations, and audience expectations that are different from those that govern the writing of fiction and most other nonfiction. These rules—the genre conventions of journalism—serve to shape and limit journalistic storytelling.

The application of those rules, both individually and institutionally, go largely unnoticed by the news audience, however. As researcher Richard Campbell notes: "[J]ournalists and their audiences routinely assume that there is little distance between the narrative *product* and the raw experience that the product represents and accept one for the other without questioning the *process* of transformation."[3] This is reinforced by the use of the third-person omniscient voice employed in most journalistic storytelling. Even in television journalism, where reporters appear onscreen, the use of camera distance and the placement of reporters in relation to the action and subject(s) in the story reinforce the detachment of the journalist.[4] Reporters are both authors and narrators, but textual and visual stylistic devices serve to distance journalists from the stories they tell.

What happens, however, when the "product" of journalism—the story—is presented in comics form? As Nick Lacey writes:

> Genre is a concept that appears in many different forms, such as television, literature and film. This makes it a useful concept in the analysis of the media themselves. For instance, if science fiction literature is different from science fiction film, it is likely that the difference is caused by the medium and/or its institutional context. Thus the essential character of a particular medium and its means of production can be isolated by considering differences in the way a genre is articulated.[5]

What separates comics journalism from other forms—the essential character of the comics medium—is the integration of text and image. Comics are written *and* drawn. Other forms of journalism employ text and images as well. However, news audiences generally do not recognize the creativity of language—particularly in journalistic writing—because of its stylistic emphasis on "plain" language. In addition, the dominance of objectivity as the professional norm of the journalistic narrative means the creative process of storytelling is largely hidden by journalistic conventions such as the third-person omniscient narrator.[6] Although language, too, is a creation, we all have some degree of linguistic competency, so we generally do not recognize the creativity of language—particularly in nonfiction writing—in the same way as we do drawing.

Nor do news audiences usually acknowledge the constructed nature of photojournalism, because of its documentary nature and because it is strongly linked to a perceived external reality. John Taylor writes: "[M]ost people privilege natural eyesight over technology. They treat photographs as a time-and-space delayed form of natural eyesight. They never know or conveniently forget that photographs are not equivalent to eyesight but are generated, printed and published."[7]

While comics creators may adopt the plain language of journalism, drawings—however realistic or representational—do not possess the same documentary quality as photographs. They are clearly created by the comics journalist. Thus, what G. Stuart Adam refers to as the "art" of journalism—the creative nature of what journalists do when they transform experience into story—is foregrounded by comics journalism.[8] Reporters who are also artists working in the comics form convey a sense of the constructed nature of news in a way that is unique to the form.

STORYTELLING PROCESS

If we accept the assumption that the form of comics journalism—the integration of drawing and text—reveals the *process* of storytelling in a way that most other forms of journalism do not, we can examine how this is reflected in the way the process of journalism becomes part of the product. In other words, how does the work of the journalist become part of the story itself? Comics journalists are faced with the seeming contradiction between the genre conventions that emphasize the invisibility of the art of journalism and the obviously visible art of comics. How they articulate (or reject) the conventions reveals how they negotiate the tensions between form and genre.

As Rocco Versaci suggests, the work of many comics journalists can be compared to that of the so-called New Journalists, whose work also challenged the genre conventions of mainstream journalism. Their experimentation, beginning in the mid-1960s, with fiction techniques reintroduced a style of narrative journalism that had largely disappeared from American newspapers by World War I.[9] Borrowing a term from John Hellmann, Versaci suggests that comics journalists have embraced the New Journalists' idea of a "shaping consciousness" that acknowledges "the mediation that takes place in any journalistic enterprise" by foregrounding the journalist's role in the story.[10]

One way in which narrative journalism achieves this transparency in the storytelling process is to make the journalist a character in his or her own story. Comics journalists do this both textually and visually, by writing in the first-person and by drawing themselves. What the reader sees is the journalist at work. It is a way of reinforcing the idea that stories have authors—or, as Adam put it, "Journalism is made; it doesn't just happen."[11] In this sense, the character can serve as a stand-in for the reader. Readers are invited to imagine themselves in place of the journalist, to become a part of the "here and now" of the story that is unfolding.

In order to understand what is being represented both visually and textually, we need to know what the "work" of journalism is. Adam provides a useful way to distinguish the work of the journalist from the work of other authors: "[Journalism] is the product of reporting—the gathering and presentation of slices and bits of human experience."[12] He identifies the three primary devices of reporting as: observation, with the journalist as an eyewitness; analysis and summary of documents, particularly public records; and interviewing. Journalists use these materials to construct their stories, and this newsgathering process is at the heart of "doing" journalism.

Journalists distill experience into story. They are not recording or transcribing—they are reporting. It is a selective, creative process guided by journalistic conventions of storytelling, with an emphasis on news values and completeness of information (identified by answering the questions: who, what, when, where, why, and how). Journalists who are eyewitnesses to events often supplement their own accounts with sources who are also eyewitnesses or who are in a position of authority and can provide additional information about the event that journalists judge to be credible and reliable. Likewise, documentary source material can be incorporated into stories—often as an additional form of evidence, as well as for background and context.

But interviewing is at the heart of the practice of journalism. There are two basic types of journalistic interviewing. In the first, journalists select sources that provide information needed to tell the story. Depending on the scope of the story, there may be a single source or multiple sources. The sources are usually identified, and their information is incorporated into the story in the form of direct quotes and paraphrases (known as indirect quotes). In the second type of interviewing, the person being interviewed is the subject of the story. Journalists are either focusing on the experiences of individuals who have their own story to tell, or the interview subjects themselves *are* the story—which is often the case when prominent people are profiled.

PROCEDURES

In this chapter we will examine how comics journalism makes visible the process of storytelling through the use of first-person reporting, focusing on the textual and visual representation (what Versaci calls the "graphic language") of the transformation of experience into story. This will allow us to answer the question: How does comics journalism both articulate and resolve the tension between form and genre?

Any analysis of comics journalism must acknowledge the complex semiotic activity that "reading" comics entails. The text and image are integrated, requiring readers to negotiate both. We speak of reading comics, but that is simply a conventional way of referring to the multifaceted process of generating meaning. One way to approach studying the meaning of a comics text is to employ textual analysis, drawing upon semiotic theory. Semiotics has been defined as "the discipline that studies the nature of any system of meaning."[13] Media scholars have adapted Saussure's concept of the sign, composed of the signifier (material form) and signified (meaning), out of which codes are constructed that can serve both representational and conceptual functions. These codes, or systems of signs, can be as varied as language, the style of drawing, the use or absence of color, the positioning of elements within a panel, and page layout.

Studying any text requires not only the identification and analysis of the various codes or sign systems employed, but also examining the complex ways in which these codes interact to create the meaning of the text. Combining semiotic and genre analysis provides a way to explore the meaning of text and image together within the context of *journalistic* storytelling.

To begin, first-person storytelling goes against the genre convention of journalism's third-person, omniscient voice. While first-person reporting allows comics journalists to present themselves in their work, both visually and textually, it is also important to consider the ways in which comics journalists absent themselves in response to the journalistic norms of objectivity and distance. In addition, to tell stories, comics journalism both adopts *and* adapts the processes of journalism. The devices of journalism as delineated by Adam—eyewitness accounts, documents, and interviewing—are incorporated through words and images. The genre conventions that guide how journalists process information into stories are adopted by the comics journalist—but also adapted to the form of comics.

ARTIFACT SELECTED FOR ANALYSIS

We will look at Sacco's graphic novel, *Safe Area Goražde: The War in Eastern Bosnia 1992–1995*. Sacco made four trips to the Bosnian city of Goražde in late 1995 and early 1996, during the final days of the Balkan war. This largely Muslim enclave was situated in the midst of Bosnian Serb forces and was one of three U.N.-designated "safe areas." During his trips, Sacco went about gathering material for his project the same way as other war correspondents: through personal observation and conducting interviews. He had press credentials that enabled him to travel with U.N. convoys, and he found himself both socializing and competing with his fellow journalists. As he became more familiar with the area, he struck out on his own, with the help of Edin, an engineering student whose studies in Sarajevo had been interrupted by the war. Edin served as Sacco's translator and guide and became his friend.

Although *Palestine* was a ground-breaking work in terms of establishing Sacco as a comics journalist, he was still experimenting with journalistic storytelling. *Safe Area Goražde* reveals a comics journalist who has honed both his own character and his storytelling techniques, which are more consistent throughout the graphic novel than in *Palestine*. The narrative structure of *Safe Area Goražde* is also more complex than that of *Palestine*, probably because it was never intended to be serialized. Sacco's reporting is divided into two kinds of narrative: first, we have Sacco's own observations, told in present tense; second, we have the stories of others, based on Sacco's interviews, that are embedded in Sacco's own narrative.

The analysis of the entire graphic novel is far too ambitious a project for this chapter, so we will focus on just one story from *Safe Area Goražde*, a five-page story titled "15 Minutes." This story incorporates both first-person reporting and interviews, which we have identified as central to the understanding of the journalistic story in comics form, making it an appropriate choice for this analysis.

SAMPLE ANALYSIS

Sacco, Joe. "15 Minutes." *Safe Area Goražde*. Seattle: Fantagraphic Books, 2000.

The story "15 Minutes" employs a common journalistic narrative structure—the introduction of a topic or issue (in this case, the state of education in Goražde) through the use of an anecdote, a transition into information from interviews and documents, and a return at the end to the anecdote that began the story. The focus is on Edin, introduced to readers very early on in the graphic novel (page 8). In the first panel of this story, he is grading papers. As he does so, he comments, "Two out of five. My students are very stupid." In the last panel of the story, readers see Edin in essentially the same position, still grading papers. He reiterates, "Two out of five. Very stupid."

His comment serves to introduce Sacco's larger purpose—to examine the impact of the war on education in Goražde. Edin himself provides one explanation, which Sacco includes as a caption in the lower-right corner of the panel: The students' studies have been interrupted and, as Edin puts it, "Their brains are going soft." This sets up the transition textually, because Sacco goes on to explain how much school the children have missed. The caption also provides a visual transition, because it is positioned to be the last text read in the panel before moving on to the next.

In the final panel, Sacco brings us back to Edin—again both textually and visually. He reestablishes the time and place from the first panel by reproducing Edin's image and words from the first panel. In addition, Sacco provides a transition into this last panel with his first caption, located in the top-left of the final panel—the first thing the readers will see as their eyes move to the last panel. The caption reads: "And Edin?" Here, readers also learn two important pieces of information. First, Edin's education has also been interrupted. He is in much the same position as the students he teaches. Second, Sacco reveals where the title of the story came from in the final caption: "He'd been 15 minutes from his degree for the past three and a half years."

As noted before, this structure is fairly standard in journalism. One introductory reporting textbook labels it the "kabob," complete with an illustration of tomatoes on each end of a skewer (the anecdote), with the meat in the middle.[14] Because the narrative structure of this story is similar to other forms of journalism, our analysis needs to look more closely at other aspects of journalistic storytelling—the use of first-person reporting and the incorporation of interviews.

First-person Storytelling

Like all journalists, Sacco must make a decision about his own role in the story. He can position himself in a number of ways, including as a character in the story, as a stand-in for the reader, as a commentator on the action, or as a neutral observer. His textual voice can indicate he is a participant, can describe for the reader what he sees as an eyewitness, or can employ the third-person omniscient voice commonly used in print journalism. Visually, Sacco can draw himself into the story, or he can create a visual point of view, positioning himself either inside or outside the frame. In comics journalism, the visual and textual voice of the journalist cannot always be neatly separated.

Sacco signals his presence textually in the first panel of the story. The opening caption seems to place him in the room with Edin after he and Sacco have finished "our usual coffee-bar cruising." Edin is speaking, as indicated by the word balloons. Sacco's presence is implied in three ways: First, Sacco suggests that he and Edin have returned together to Edin's house; second, Edin is clearly speaking to someone, and readers might assume he is directing his comments to Sacco; third, journalistic conventions require that in order to report dialogue and quotes, journalists must record what their subjects have said. It is unprofessional—and unethical—for journalists to put words into someone's mouth. However, Sacco stops short of placing himself into the story visually. He neither draws himself into the panel nor answers Edin. Instead, Sacco suggests we are viewing the scene as Sacco himself saw it. He literally becomes the reader's eyes and ears, and readers are invited to watch through his eyes. The artist assumes the same visual position as the camera in broadcast journalism.

This textual presence and visual absence continues throughout the story, with one exception (Figure 8.1). Sacco appears in one panel, where he uses his character to offer a first-person anecdote to illustrate for readers—literally—the difficulties in obtaining school supplies. Young boys follow him, asking, "Pencil?" His only reply is, "Sorry guys." This is a panel without a border, and Sacco is literally shown walking off the page, as if his character is exiting the story. And indeed, readers never see him again in "15 Minutes."

Textually, Sacco uses the first-person to establish he has conducted an interview. Twice, he prefaces a direct or indirect quote with the words "told me." Once is when he quotes a school official who is never visually represented; the second time he uses the phrase is when he is paraphrasing the words of one girl, who also is shown speaking (again, presumably to Sacco himself) in two panels. Visually, Sacco indicates an interview took place by presenting readers with an image of the interview subject speaking—again, much in the same way that broadcast journalists put their subjects on camera but remain out of the frame (or edit themselves out). Sacco even uses the same sort of subject distance as broadcast journalists, drawing his interview subjects in the equivalent of a head-and-shoulders shot in television journalism. The people interviewed either look straight out of the panels as if talking directly to the reader, or they look to the side, speaking to the unseen interviewer outside the panel.

In one instance, Sacco is privy to a discussion involving Edin, an older man, and a boy who is a student in Edin's class. Sacco reports the conversation in a three-panel sequence, using a combination of word balloons (dialogue/direct quotes) and indirect quotes (e.g.,

Figure 8.1 This panel is the only time Sacco appears in the story "15 Minutes" (page 97). *Safe Area Goražde* Copyright 2000 Joe Sacco.

Edin told the boy …), again indicating that he must have been present in order to be able to quote the man and the boy. Edin appears in the first of these panels, but he is given no dialogue. Instead, his remarks are reported as indirect quotes in captions. In the fourth panel, Sacco signals the passage of time with the caption, "After they'd left …," positioned in the upper-right corner of the panel to serve as both a visual and textual transition. Once again, Edin is speaking to an invisible Sacco.

What Sacco accomplishes by limiting his first-person voice and refusing to be a character in the story is to lessen the tension between the form and the genre of comics. As noted in the previous section, comics journalism draws attention to the journalist's role by the nature of the form. Readers are conscious of comics as a creative process, rather than simply a reporting process. The form makes more transparent the creative force behind the story. What Sacco strives for, however, is to mitigate the impact of the comics form by largely deflecting attention away from himself as the journalist, particularly visually. His presence is implied rather than flaunted before readers. In this way, he aligns his work much more with that of mainstream journalism than with the so-called literary or "new" journalists, who called attention to journalism as a creative, subjective process.

Journalistic Process

In addition to his own role in telling the story, Sacco—like most journalists—draws upon reporting devices as the building blocks for creating his narrative. Journalism, as nonfiction writing, incorporates both the observations of journalists and those of their sources. Journalists who are eyewitnesses to events generally provide an account of those events without attribution. When journalists include the observations and opinions of others, those are incorporated into stories as quotations—either direct quotes (verbatim, signaled by the use of quotation marks in print and by the use of the recorded voice in broadcast), or as indirect quotes (paraphrases of the source's words by the journalist). Both direct and indirect quotes are attributed to the source. Broadcast journalists employ audio and visual strategies to accomplish the same thing. When providing eyewitness accounts, broadcast journalists provide narrative over the image (called a "voice-over") or they are on camera. When they wish to provide the direct words of the subjects they interview, they edit visual "clips" of that person into their stories.

The quality of the reporting is judged by journalists' selection of sources to interview. The most common types of sources are individuals who are experts on a topic, those who have been eyewitnesses or participants in a newsworthy event, those whose opinions and observations are sought as representative of "the public," and those acting in an official capacity as a spokesperson. Identification of each source establishes the credibility of the information and opinion being quoted.[15]

Not all information comes from sources interviewed by Sacco. He draws upon the following: (1) dialogue involving Edin, one of his students, and an older man who had befriended the boy; (2) Sacco's personal observation of a bombed-out school building; (3) a personal anecdote where children tail after him begging for pencils; and (4) an illustration of how Edin is coping with textbook shortages. However, Sacco relies heavily on interviewing, incorporating a surprising number of sources into his five-page story: (1) an informal conversation with Edin, which is incorporated into the story; (2) an interview with a student who tells him she didn't attend school for eight months; (3) an interview with the official in charge of sports, education, and culture; (4) an interview with a 17-year-old who no longer attends school; (5) an interview with one girl who talked about attending school only three days a week; (6) an interview with a physical education instructor; (7) an interview with a computer instructor; and (8) an interview with students who had finished secondary school but were unable to attend the university.

These interviews provide both textual and visual material. At least half of the panels he draws are images of his interview subjects, drawn as if they are speaking to an unseen camera and interviewer, typical of the structure of broadcast news (Figure 8.2). He mostly presents his interview subjects tightly framed, with little in the background. This keeps the reader's focus on what is being said. Dialogue and direct quotes are accompanied by little description. This is a convention of mainstream journalism, which eschews the scene-setting techniques employed in literary journalism.

In this way, Sacco adapts the devices of conventional print and broadcast journalism to the form of comics. His own observations are rendered both textually and visually. For example, a drawing of a derelict school building is accompanied by text that anchors the image as a specific secondary school in Goražde. The anecdote about the shortage of school supplies is clearly Sacco's own observation, since he draws himself into the panel. For interviews, Sacco employs quotation marks in captions to signal direct quotations in the same way that print journalists do, as well as using captions to paraphrase information from interviews. Word balloons represent sound in comics, so Sacco substitutes still panels for video clips, with tails of the word balloons clearly indicating who is speaking. However, Sacco also utilizes interview material in a way that is unique to comics journalism—he adds images drawn from the words of his subjects as they describe places and events. Broadcasters can do this by including historical footage, if it exists, but Sacco has no such limitations. He combines his subjects' memories with his own imagination to visualize the past.

Figure 8.2 Sacco frames his interview subjects in the same way a broadcast journalist might (page 98). *Safe Area Goražde* Copyright 2000 Joe Sacco.

The Form of Comics

In the previous section, key questions were posed: What happens when the journalistic story is presented in comics form? How is comics journalism different from other forms of journalism? Sacco adapts the conventions of both print and broadcast journalism in his textual and visual presentation of his story. By refusing to be a character in the story, as well as by incorporating material from interviews in much the same way that print and broadcast journalism do, Sacco distances himself from the "creativity" of the journalistic process foregrounded by the artwork.

In addition, Sacco makes several artistic/stylistic choices in *Safe Area Goražde*, employing other codes that serve to downplay the creative process of journalism. The publication format itself—a graphic novel rather than serialized—marks the comic as a work distinct from mainstream superhero comics. The format connotes a gravitas appropriate to a serious work of journalism nonfiction.

Within the work, four formal sign systems contribute to signifying "15 Minutes" as a work of journalism. First, consider the absence of color. While production and cost factors may dictate whether the artist can use color, it is also a formal choice. Black and white images signify seriousness and have a documentary quality. The drawings become more closely aligned with photojournalism, which is still reproduced primarily in black and white for newspapers, even with advances in color printing. In addition, the lack of color conveys a bleak environment that enhances the representation of a city under siege. And finally, the absence of color makes the image appear as less of an artistic interpretation of the people and places depicted.

A second formal quality that enhances the signification of the graphic novel as journalism is the panel and page layout. Sacco opts for a very traditional panel layout, one that largely reproduces the composition of the print photograph and the broadcast screen. It is very easy to follow the sequence of panels in his page layouts, and he supplements this by providing textual transitions through the use of captions. Unlike many artists working in both mainstream superhero comics and in alternative comics, Sacco eschews visual experimentation that challenges both the reader and the conventions of reading comics, which draws attention to the form as well as the content. Sacco's layout helps to push the form into the background and directs the reader's attention to the content, which is traditionally journalistic.

The drawing style is a third formalistic choice made by the artist. Sacco renders his images relatively realistically—in fact, he has noted that he deliberately modified his artistic style.

> I realized that the drawings had to reflect the weight of the material I was presenting, and slowly but surely I forced more realism out of my pen though I could never shake—nor did I desire to lose—my "cartoony" line.[16]

Finally, the extensive use of captions—similar to the cutline used with photojournalism and to the voice-over in broadcast—serves to explain the image to the reader. Theorist Roland Barthes referred to this process as "anchoring"—closing off some interpretations of the image by anchoring its meaning through employing text. In journalism, images are seldom left to "stand alone"—almost always they are accompanied by text or by the spoken word.[17]

Visualizing the Past

Through these formal choices, Sacco mimics the techniques of print and broadcast journalism. He incorporates the conventions of each of these forms into his story both textually and visually, producing a sort of hybrid of print and broadcast journalism— with one important exception, as noted above. As a comics journalist, Sacco does what other journalists cannot do—visualize the past. The comics form allows him to take the words of his sources and draw the situation or event described.

Sacco does this explicitly in eight stories included in *Safe Area Goražde*. He sets these stories apart visually with black page borders. The artwork adds images to the interview subject's narrative of events. In some cases, narration is presented through the use of captions. Other panels include word balloons, drawing on the subject's memories to create dialogue. The separation of these stories from the others in *Safe Area Goražde* signifies their difference—Sacco is emphasizing the fact that these stories are his representation of the events described by his interview subjects. The first panel of each story introduces the people providing the narrative Sacco draws upon.

However, Sacco also incorporates scenes of the past into "15 Minutes" without explicitly signifying he is doing so in a three-panel sequence narrated by an education official. This information is not set apart by black panel/page borders. The only clues that Sacco has shifted from the present to the past come in the captions, where the official's direct quotes are spoken in the past tense, and in the content of the drawings, which depict scenes Sacco may not or could not have witnessed himself.

The first panel illustrates the quote that reads, in part, "… they would find the empty tables of their friends who were killed or wounded …" Sacco draws students in a classroom, focusing the reader's attention on an empty chair by drawing it prominently in the panel and by leaving that area of the drawing unshaded, as if a spotlight were shining on the empty space. Time is ambiguous in this panel. After interviewing the school official, Sacco could have visited a classroom and observed empty seats, learning that they were once occupied by students who were killed and wounded. More likely, however, is that he depicted the words of his source by populating his imagined classroom with imagined students.

In the second panel, to illustrate "… some of them had to change their living space …" Sacco draws several people carrying suitcases and bundles, walking down a road lined with damaged houses. Unlike the classroom setting, which could be duplicated by an existing space, the exodus of students after an enemy attack is an event that clearly occurs in the past. Sacco could not supplement the source's description with his own observation.

In the final panel, as the official states "… it was very dangerous on the trip from school to home," he depicts the interview subject's information by drawing two boys running (Figure 8.3). Their position in the panel, moving into the panel rather than toward the reader, signifies they are running *away*. One is looking back at the other with a grotesque grimace on his face. The road is marked with shell impacts, and directly in the boys' path is a dead horse. Again, Sacco is not drawing from observation, but creating a time and place populated with characters who stand in for the children the official describes.

Sacco pushes the boundaries of conventional journalism by adapting the journalistic interview to the comics form, as he does with this three-panel sequence in "15 Minutes." While the rest of the story is a hybrid of print and broadcast journalism, the interview

Figure 8.3 Sacco re-creates a scene from the past as children hurry home from school (page 95). *Safe Area Goražde* Copyright 2000 Joe Sacco.

with the school official is uniquely comics journalism. The difference lies in the images. While art and photography are visual sign systems, the work of the photographer and the videographer—particularly the photojournalist—is largely invisible. The images connote reality. The photojournalist presents a window on the world, a faithful *reproduction* of actual people, places, and events. Not so with Sacco's drawings. He is not reproducing what he sees; the words gleaned from interviews are the basis for an *interpretation* of reality, filtered through the creativity of the artist.

The role of the image is the primary source of tension between the form and the genre. Sacco crosses the line between drawing as representation and drawing as interpretation, and by doing so, he calls into question that distinction. In the process, Sacco opens the door for a closer examination of mainstream journalism as well. Comics journalism simply lays bare what mainstream journalism disguises—that journalistic storytelling itself is an interpretive process, no matter what its form.

NOTES

1. Dave Gilson, "Joe Sacco: The Art of War," *Mother Jones*, July/August (2005): 80.
2. Charles Hatfield, *Alternative Comics: An Emerging Literature* (Jackson, MS: University Press of Mississippi, 2005), ix–x.
3. Richard Campbell, "Securing the Middle Ground: Reporter Formulas in *60 Minutes*," *Critical Studies in Mass Communication* 4 (4) (1987): 346.
4. Julia R. Fox and Byungho Park, "The 'I' of Embedded Journalism: An Analysis of CNN Coverage of the 'Shock and Awe' Campaign," *Journal of Broadcasting and Electronic Media* 50 (1) (2006): 48.
5. Nick Lacey, *Narrative and Genre: Key Concepts in Media Studies* (New York: St. Martin's, 2000), 143.
6. Stephen J.A. Ward, *The Invention of Journalism Ethics: The Path to Objectivity and Beyond* (Montreal: McGill-Queen's University Press, 2004), 21.
7. John Taylor, "Iraqi Torture Photographs and Documentary Realism in the Press," *Journalism Studies* 6 (1) (2005): 41–43.
8. G. Stuart Adam, *Notes Toward a Definition of Journalism: Understanding an Old Craft as an Art Form* (St. Petersburg: The Poynter Institute for Media Studies, 1993), 46–48.
9. Rocco Versaci, *This Book Contains Graphic Language: Comics as Literature* (New York: Continuum, 2007), 111; Michael Schudson, *Discovering the News: A Social History of American Newspapers* (New York: Basic Books, 1978), 89–90; Jack Hart, "A Brief History of Narrative in Newspapers," in *Telling True Stories: A Nonfiction Writer's Guide*, ed. Mark Kramer and Wendy Call (New York: Penguin Books, 2007), 232.
10. Versaci, *This Book Contains Graphic Language*, 111.
11. Adam, *Notes Toward a Definition of Journalism*, "Authors Note."
12. Ibid., 12.
13. Lawrence Grossberg, Ellen Wartella and D. Charles Whitney, *MediaMaking: Mass Media in a Popular Culture* (Thousand Oaks, CA: Sage, 1998), 128.
14. Tim Harrower, *Inside Reporting: A Practical Guide to the Craft of Journalism*, 2nd ed. (New York: McGraw-Hill, 2009), 50.
15. Ibid., 71.
16. Joe Sacco, "Reflections," in *Palestine: The Special Edition* (Seattle: Fantagraphics, 2007), ix.
17. Roland Barthes, *Image, Music, Text* (London: Fontana, 1977), 39.

SELECTED BIBLIOGRAPHY

Adam, G. Stuart. *Notes Toward a Definition of Journalism: Understanding an Old Craft as an Art Form.* St. Petersburg: The Poynter Institute for Media Studies, 1993.

Barthes, Roland. *Image, Music, Text.* London: Fontana, 1977.

Campbell, Richard. "Securing the Middle Ground: Reporter Formulas in *60 Minutes*." *Critical Studies in Mass Communication* 4 (4) (1987): 325–351.

Fox, Julia R. and Byungho Park. "The 'I' of Embedded Journalism: An Analysis of CNN Coverage of the 'Shock and Awe' Campaign." *Journal of Broadcasting and Electronic Media* 50 (1) (2006): 36–51.

Gilson, Dave. "Joe Sacco: The Art of War." *Mother Jones*, 2005 (July/August): 80–81.

Grossberg, Lawrence, Ellen Wartella, and D. Charles Whitney. *MediaMaking: Mass Media in a Popular Culture.* Thousand Oaks, CA: Sage, 1998.

Harrower, Tim. *Inside Reporting: A Practical Guide to the Craft of Journalism* (2nd edn.). New York: McGraw-Hill, 2009.

Hart, Jack. "A Brief History of Narrative in Newspapers." In *Telling True Stories: A Nonfiction Writer's Guide*, edited by Mark Kramer and Wendy Call, 230–232. New York: Penguin Books, 2007.

Hatfield, Charles. *Alternative Comics: An Emerging Literature.* Jackson, MS: University Press of Mississippi, 2005.

Lacey, Nick. *Narrative and Genre: Key Concepts in Media Studies.* New York: St. Martin's, 2000.

Sacco, Joe. "Reflections," in *Palestine: The Special Edition.* Seattle: Fantagraphics, 2007.

Sacco, Joe. *Safe Area Goražde.* Seattle: Fantagraphics, 2000.

Schudson, Michael. *Discovering the News: A Social History of American Newspapers.* New York: Basic Books, 1978,

Taylor, John. "Iraqi Torture Photographs and Documentary Realism in the Press." *Journalism Studies* 6 (1) (2005): 39–49.

Versaci, Rocco. *This Book Contains Graphic Language: Comics as Literature.* New York: Continuum, 2007.

Ward, Stephen J.A. *The Invention of Journalism Ethics: The Path to Objectivity and Beyond.* Montreal: McGill-Queen's University Press, 2004.

9

PROPAGANDA

The Pleasures of Persuasion in Captain America

Christopher Murray

In an essay on Charles Dickens, George Orwell, author of *Nineteen Eighty Four* (1949), asserted that "all art is propaganda … on the other hand, not all propaganda is art."[1] In the original context of the quotation, Orwell was considering why Dickens continued to prove popular in the 1930s, noting that his writing was often stifled by his "message." Orwell concludes that the key is the sense of familiarity that readers bring to the stories, the feeling that they are experiencing a fictional world and characters that they are comfortable with. This encourages readers to suspend their judgment, to accept the underlying assumptions of the text, and to allow its message to permeate into their consciousness. To put it another way, "[propaganda's] power lies in its capacity to conceal itself, to appear natural, to coalesce completely and indivisibly with the values and accepted power symbols of a given society."[2] This is the essence of propaganda, which is usually defined as any means by which those in authority control and manipulate the masses.[3]

Any form of representation, whether it be a painting, sculpture, piece of music, poem, play, book, or comic, tells a story of some sort and presents a point of view, and is therefore always political. When Orwell observed that "all art is propaganda," he was warning his readers that all artworks project and legitimize some view of the world, which is partly constructed by the stories we tell about it, about ourselves, and about others. It is therefore extremely important to understand how stories work, what they say, what they omit, and how a story is told, both in terms of structure and style, as in understanding these things a reader can come to a better understanding of the political messages that are being put forward, and the manipulations they attempt to conceal.

While propaganda has been fundamental to most societies in one form or another, it was in the twentieth century, with the spread of mass media, that propagandists came to wield the most power; in the twenty-first century their power may be all the greater. However, while such manipulation is usually practiced by governments in the forms of civic projects, monuments, events, buildings, broadcasting, poster campaigns, and the myriad ways a culture is shaped by official influence and control, including policies and laws, propaganda can also emanate from below, presenting subversive or oppositional messages. By the same token, some of the most striking attempts at persuasion emanating from governments in the last century have actually mimicked popular culture, replicating the form and style of advertising, or using the conventions of genre fiction, and the clichés of pulp magazines, popular cinema, comics, and television, creating a very powerful interplay between entertainment and politics. Regardless of the source or intent, the methodology of propaganda is usually to persuade on an emotional or unconscious level, not an intellectual one, circumventing the reader's or audience's critical faculties by appealing to values and modes of thinking that can be described as "mythic," weaving implicit and seemingly natural values into the story.[4]

Significantly, it was in the context of a rapidly expanding mass culture that Orwell was writing, warning that all forms of representation, including both art and mass culture, carried ideological assumptions and hence were propaganda. As the other half of Orwell's observation ("not all propaganda is art") suggests, the need to be aware of manipulative messages is perhaps all the more urgent in popular texts, which are often presented as "mere" entertainment, but are actually powerful instruments of persuasion. Both forms of propaganda (official and unofficial) encompass, articulate, and even define the seemingly universal values of the culture, forming a metanarrative into which all other narratives can be fitted. Myth, ideology, and propaganda can therefore be seen as almost interchangeable (or at least co-dependent) terms, and in one iteration or another are to be found in all forms of representation. If one were to attempt to draw fine distinctions between them, one could argue that myth defines values over a very long period of time, or at least gives the other two an antique appearance, while ideology is more fluid, representing the ideas that govern an era or specific groups, while propaganda is usually tied to an event, situation, or crisis, such as a war. While obvious and blunt messages reside on the surface of many popular texts, there exists an undercurrent of more complex manipulation, myth-making, and propaganda. This flows between all texts at the level of a shared discourse of signs, icons, symbols, and ideology (culture, in the broadest sense, divorced from contingent ideas of which texts have value, or are deemed artistic, literary, or otherwise). However, when myth, ideology, or propaganda find expression through popular texts, these representations of political discourse become bound up in pleasurable and eager consumption rather than forceful indoctrination, which makes them all the more pernicious.

The fact that mythic/ideological/propagandist messages can be "concealed" in popular texts, where the reader's defense mechanisms and critical faculties may not be primed for them, makes it all the more important that these messages be understood for what they are. This chapter will examine a comic, *Captain America* no. 1 (1941) as an expression of a certain political formulation, which can be interpreted in response to the historical factors that were dominant in the context of its production and reception. This raises issues of power, identity, and interpretation, and how a reader is to determine "meaning" in relation to the original "message." This is content and context analysis as a kind of archaeology, but it does not seek to reproduce the "true" meaning, or to uncover the author or artist's genuine intentions (as these can be partly described and theorized, but never recaptured in their entirety), but rather to locate the text within a larger framework of interrelated texts and discourses.

PROCEDURES

Reading a text in this way situates this kind of approach as Materialist and Marxist, in that the main concern is to reveal the operations of power and political motivations encoded within texts. Of course, form is not divorced from content, and in looking at what comics say, one must also consider how they communicate that message. This requires that any analysis of the "meaning" must begin with a consideration of how the text works as an interplay of different types of "signs," from language use to icons and symbols. In practical terms, this means that when conducting an analysis of a text, a reader should try to find the meanings that exist below the surface through a detailed and careful consideration of the content, which is to say, the methods used to tell the story, including symbolism and iconography, genre, recurring themes, narrative structure, characterization, and so on. From there, a reader/critic forms a view of the surface meaning and implicit or underlying meanings, and situates this in relation to what is known about the political and cultural context of the time, looking for correlations or explanations. From the interrelation of the content and the context the reader should be able to construct a critical appreciation of the text that moves beyond its genre and entertainment value, interrogating the text in terms of its political and cultural significance in order to come to an understanding of how the text can function as propaganda.

UNDERLYING ASSUMPTIONS

One of the assumptions of this type of analysis is that creating a complex understanding of how a text operates, considering what it might have meant in its original context, and the various things it might have signified to different people, while also contemplating the messages that it sends to later readers operating within a different historical framework, is a desirable and effective means by which to combat the processes of simplification and mythologization that propaganda enforces. The text therefore becomes a lens through which to view a political moment, the various formulations of power within it, as well as later historical contexts, and indeed, allows the reader to reflect on the contemporary context they find themselves in. The following examination of *Captain America* no. 1 will serve as an example of how to analyze a text for political meaning in relation to both content and context, describing the narrative and visual strategies employed by the comic (the genre, form, and style), and discussing them in terms of the political message they communicate.

ARTIFACT SELECTED FOR ANALYSIS

In March 1941, Timely Comics (later to become Marvel Comics) published *Captain America* no. 1 by Joe Simon and Jack Kirby. With its bold attacks on the Nazis—and Hitler in particular—*Captain America* was a distillation of all the propaganda messages current at the time. Moreover, the comic was itself a form of propaganda, calling for intervention at a time when America was not yet at war, the first issue appearing several months before the Japanese attack on Pearl Harbor. This first issue was published at a time when superheroes were common, and hundreds were appearing to mimic the success of Superman, who had appeared three years earlier, in 1938. However, while other superheroes had been pitched against war-mongers and fascistic forces implicitly modeled on the Nazis, *Captain America* was explicit about who the enemy were and did not use substitutes for the Nazis and Hitler, as was then common practice in comics. This harder line against the Nazis saw the appearance of "super-patriot" heroes, such as The Shield and Captain America, who were popular icons of patriotic values, re-cast in mythological form for specific ideological purposes.

The Shield provided the model for Captain America, and appeared in January 1940's *Pep Comics* no. 1, published by MLJ, more than a year before Captain America. There were many similarities between them: The Shield was a government agent who wore a costume based on the American flag and reported to J. Edgar Hoover, head of the newly formed F.B.I., and was physically enhanced by a chemical process, as was Captain America. The Shield had a shield motif in his costume and Captain America carried a shield, a symbol that his every attack on the villains was actually a form of defense. The patriotism of the hero was the driving force of these narratives, defending America from enemies who were clearly modeled on fascists and communists (although in these stories it was not clear that there was much difference, as they were all represented as mindless brutes led by blood-thirsty dictators).[5] However, regardless of who came first, when Captain America appeared, he became far more popular than The Shield, emerging as the defining vision of the super-patriot. Perhaps this was because the story and artwork by Joe Simon and Jack Kirby were so striking, or that the timing of Captain America's arrival was perfect, with increasing pressures on Allied and American shipping in the Atlantic in 1941 forcing Americans to consider the wisdom and practicality of their policy of isolationism. Whatever the case, with *Captain America* no. 1, Timely was unambiguously declaring war on the Nazis, and there was clearly an appetite for this kind of story. In fact, *Captain America* quickly became Timely's biggest seller, firmly establishing the careers of its superstar creators, Simon and Kirby.

SAMPLE ANALYSIS

Simon, Joe and Jack Kirby. *Captain America* no. 1. New York: Timely Comics, 1941.

The methods employed in this comic are clearly propagandist, delivering the message that the Nazis were an immediate threat to U.S. interests, and that they were in fact evil, and that it was the moral duty of Americans to combat the threat they represented. This is important, as the comic should be understood as part of a debate that was going on in America at the time. It would be easy to look back from a contemporary perspective and see American involvement in the war as somehow inevitable, and to see this comic as a reflection of universal American hatred toward the Axis powers, but this is simply not the case. At the time of publication, many Americans believed that becoming involved in "the European War," as it was tellingly called, was unwise, fearing a return to the slaughter of World War I. Indeed, America's official policy toward foreign wars was one of isolationism and non-involvement. This was not a view shared by President Franklin Roosevelt, but with an election on the horizon it was difficult for him to argue for intervention.[6] It was also the case that there were Americans, some of them very vocal, who saw the Nazis as a modernizing force, or at least a necessary one given the rise of Communism in Russia. There was also the German–American Bund, as well as anti-Semitic groups, who, for various conflicting reasons, supported the Nazis, or at least wanted to keep America from direct conflict with them.[7] *Captain America* no. 1 is, therefore, not simply a reflection of universal American feeling; it was a contribution to a fierce national debate, and evidence for this is sown throughout the comic, most notably on the cover (Figure 9.1).

The cover of the first issue of *Captain America* shows the hero bursting into a Nazi base and punching Hitler on the jaw (Figure 9.1). Here the reader sees the Nazis surrounded by plans for sabotage of U.S. industry, and, ultimately, invasion. Driving the point home, a caption identifies Captain America as "The Sentinel of our Shores." The message is clear: Americans are in immediate danger and only military intervention can halt the enemy's plans. The image and caption are resolute—becoming involved in the war was a direct response to a clear and present danger to "our shores." This concentration on the U-boats was a means to focus American attention on what was at the time a very real threat. Now the war started to seem less distant, and some argued that the policy of isolationism was becoming untenable, even dangerous. Some superhero comics, like editorial cartoons in newspapers, heightened this sense of looming catastrophe for political effect, picturing invading armies, as well as spies, sympathizers, and saboteurs, all intent on undermining American industry and morale. In other words, the enemy was within as well as beyond American shores, a very specific message that was continued and amplified in the stories contained within the comic.

The first issue of *Captain America* was comprised of four stories, ranging from eight to sixteen pages long, a format that was not uncommon in the 1930s and 1940s. The first story, naturally enough, is the origin story, "Meet Captain America," in which a patriotic young American, Steve Rogers, volunteers for military service. Distraught at being turned down on the grounds that he is medically unfit, Rogers volunteers for an experimental procedure that transforms him into a "super-soldier." During his metamorphosis, a Nazi spy strikes, killing the scientist responsible for the super soldier process. Rogers kills the spy, adopts a costume that recalls the star and stripes, and Captain America is born. On the first page the reader is introduced to the hero, with a full-page image of him waving to the reader, his sidekick behind him, along with the Capitol Building showing the Stars and Stripes flying from a flagpole. The context is immediately established by a banner under the title, announcing that this is "U.S.A. ... 1941." The contemporary setting is further established by narration in the form of captions, which evoke a radio broadcast or newsreel film, communicating the situation in an authoritative tone: "As the ruthless war-mongers of Europe focus their eyes on a peace-loving America ... the youth of our country heed the call to arm for defense."[8]

The conflict is therefore immediately situated in propagandistic terms, with the "peace-loving" Americans and the "war-mongers of Europe." The specific message of the story, that America must be prepared for the coming conflict, is very much to the fore in the first panels, which show a queue of young men at the recruiting station, smiling as they calmly wait their turn to sign up for military service. On one side there is a soldier in uniform, on the other there is a recruiting poster, which is clearly James Montgomery Flagg's instantly recognizable "I want YOU for the U.S. Army" poster.[9] However, the very next panel reveals the extent to which paranoia and fear-mongering will drive this narrative, with two saboteurs in the process of blowing up a U.S. munitions factory while bragging about how easy it was to join the army with forged papers. This is very much an invention of the comic. There was no serious concern that Nazi agents were operating in this manner, and what appears in the comic is a simplistic characterization of the danger posed by the enemy. However, this is also not a naïve view of the war; rather, it

Figure 9.1 Cover of *Captain America* no. 1. Copyright 1941 Timely Comics; Marvel Characters, Inc.

is a deliberate simplification and distortion in order to bring the threat of the war home to the reader, to make it seem less distant, and therefore to justify, at least in narrative terms, the fantasy that is to follow. This message is continued in the first panel on the next page, which takes the imagined threat one step further and is targeted for maximum effect, with the demonic saboteur laughing manically as the munitions factory dramatically explodes in a panel that takes up nearly half the page. This mirrors the image on the cover, of a factory being blown up, and the brutish nature of the enemy is again foregrounded. The next panel shows the reaction of the president (not named, but clearly Roosevelt) to these attacks, and the threat of spies within the army. He ironically suggests that a comic book hero might help save the day, suggesting The Human Torch (a character already being published by Timely, providing advertising for another Timely product), but after laughing this off the president turns to J. Arthur Grover, head of the F.B.I. (and clearly modeled on J. Edgar Hoover), who takes the Army officers to a secret location, a laboratory hidden in an old curio shop guarded by X-13, a beautiful female agent who disguises herself as the shop's aged owner.[10]

It is clear even from the first few pages that several genres are interacting in this story. There are elements of the spy story, as well as crime, horror and science-fiction. Some of the panels even make use of shadows to reveal a touch of film noir and expressionism. This situates the text within a familiar cultural landscape, with an intertextual blend of many genres popular at the time. The added element is the inclusion of overt propaganda, which on the surface has the appearance of being just another generic code among many others; however, it is in some respects the master code which organizes all the others around itself, directing meaning and delivering a clear message. By encircling the propaganda message within familiar and recognizable genres, adding an air of mystery and suspense, and the hint of a romance sub-plot, the ludicrous and childish manipulation becomes accepted on its own terms as it establishes a rationale for the pleasurable fantasy that is to follow. It is doubtful that the manipulation that is occurring was ever designed to make readers believe in the threat in these fantastic terms, but a framework is created in which this narrative at once refers to the real world, wearing the authenticity of its newsreel-style narration and its referencing of well-known posters, while simultaneously exaggerating and parodying these events using caricature and stereotype. The key is that the patriotic sentiments are treated very seriously, so the "message" is delivered, even though the vehicle for its communication is entirely and self-consciously fantastic and unbelievable. Indeed, in the origin story the patriotism of the characters is inextricably bound up in a message about the importance of volunteering and self-sacrifice for one's country, as shown in the most important scene, where Captain America comes into being.

The key point of the narrative comes when a "frail young man" enters and is injected with a "strange seething liquid" (Figure 9.2). He appears dejected and unheroic yet calm as he "allows himself to be injected." This contains several messages. The volunteer is clearly ashamed that he cannot serve his country. He is unable to join the ranks of the fit, smiling men lining up to volunteer in the first page of the story; however, despite his physical limitations, he is patriotic and courageous and finds another way to serve—this time as a volunteer for an experimental process. The panel in which this occurs is singled out as important in three ways: first, due to the fact that it is circular; second, because it is situated between the two other panels in that sequence, overlaid on top of them; and third, due to the caption box in the form of an arrow pointing to it. Quite apart from

Figure 9.2 Detail of page 4 of *Captain America* no. 1. Copyright 1941 Timely Comics; Marvel Characters, Inc.

creating suspense, this panel is sign-posted as important because it shows the volunteer's selfless act of patriotism and his willingness to serve his nation.

The next panel is also extremely important in terms of the "message," as the scientist, Professor Reinstein (clearly modeled on Albert Einstein) gazes out of the panel, while the syringe is directed straight at the reader, who is invited to experience the scene from the volunteer's perspective, and to imagine that it is they who are being injected with the serum. This is crucial in terms of the propagandistic effect of the comic, which is aimed primarily at readers too young to volunteer. The syringe is aimed at them too, suggesting that by reading the comic and being filled with the patriotic message it contains, the reader can be transformed, like Captain America and the nation itself, suddenly prepared for the coming conflict. Here, Simon and Kirby mimic the same form of direct prompt that is achieved by Flagg's "I want YOU for the U.S. Army," with Uncle Sam pointing directly at the viewer. This panel goes a step further, with Reinstein injecting the reader with the means to participate in the defeat of the enemy. It is also significant that Reinstein is modeled on Einstein and is clearly Jewish, as this signifies the importance of the Jewish contribution in the upcoming struggle against fascism, of which this comic is a part (Simon and Kirby are both Jewish).[11] The comic is therefore very much implicated in the Jewish-American response to isolationism. Like many Hollywood films of the time, the comic is aggressive in its anti-Nazi stance, partly because the owners of these companies (the publishers and the Hollywood studio moguls) were Jewish and had a vested interest in promoting this view.

Once the transformation is underway, the panels that show the volunteer picture him surrounded by a strange glow. Significantly, in every panel in which he appears he is seen breaking the frame, as if his growing power cannot be contained.[12] As Reinstein names the volunteer "Captain America" and promises that he is but the first of a new corps of "super-agents," yet another saboteur strikes, killing Reinstein and attacking the officers.

Captain America makes short work of him and in the struggle the villain stumbles into laboratory equipment and is electrocuted. With his mythic origin recounted, the following panels quickly establish Captain America's early exploits against spies and saboteurs through newspaper headlines and a few images of Captain America in action. This is counter-pointed with the introduction of Private Steve Rogers, who the reader will later come to know as an average and often comically inept G.I. who spends much of his time in trouble with his superiors, and a young boy, Bucky Barnes, who serves as the camp mascot at the base where Rogers is stationed. When Bucky walks in on Rogers changing into Captain America, it is "revealed" that Rogers and Captain America are one and the same, but this could hardly be a surprise to the reader as there is no real attempt at mystery. Indeed, the caption "Who is Captain America?" appears in the panel just prior to the introduction of Rogers, which rather gives the "surprise" away. Upon being discovered, the hero is forced to take on Bucky as a sidekick, with the final panel showing them charging into action together.

On the final page of the origin story, the lower half of the page is given over to an advertisement asking readers to join "Captain America's Sentinels of Liberty" for a 10¢ fee, undertaking a signed oath to "uphold the principles of the Sentinels of Liberty" and assist Captain America in his war against spies. As John E. Moser notes, this campaign may have actually prompted many vigilant children to report suspicious activities in their areas to the local police.[13] It is doubtful that any of these activities were actually the work of Nazi spies, put this goes to show just how much the manipulation practiced by these comics influenced readers.

The origin story works as propaganda on a number of levels. It is direct and to the point, clearly identifying the enemy and those who will oppose them: patriotic Americans (which includes the public, the government, the military, the scientific community, and two notable sub-groups, children and Jews). As a broad piece of propaganda, the message is clear—the Nazis are the enemy. But the secondary message is much more targeted at a specific audience: the young reader. Unable to participate directly, young readers are motivated in other ways, and joining the "Sentinels of Liberty" is one way to realize this. Both Captain America and Bucky are wish-fulfillment figures for young readers who, at the time of publication, would be seeing their fathers and older brothers joining the military and might want to feel involved too. This is a shrewd piece of propaganda, as intervention was exactly the difficult political question facing the nation at the time, while a peacetime draft was in the process of recruiting thousands into the military.[14] This points to another reason why the interventionist message was so appealing— not all readers were children, and many of the readers of these patriotic comics were enlisted men.[15] This text pictures intervention as a political and ethical inevitability, and combats the anti-Semitism of some isolationist rhetoric of the time while making clear that the enemy is monstrous and must be destroyed, using gothic imagery appropriated from the horror genre to denote this.[16]

Comics such as *Captain America* were particularly gothic, presenting grotesque visualizations of the war. The second story in the first issue deals with Sando and Omar, a hypnotist and a dwarf who seem able to predict the future, specifically the series of accidents and sabotage that is afflicting U.S. forces. Steve Rogers and Bucky attend the show to gather clues. It quickly transpires that Sando is actually a Gestapo agent, planning the explosions and using the performance to destroy U.S. morale. As a story, this makes no sense whatsoever. It is not explained what role the act has in this plan, other than to attract attention to the saboteurs, which is ridiculous and contrived. With a dressing room full of Gestapo thugs and a ring leader who explains his allegiance quicker than a Bond villain revealing his master plan, the narrative does not work very well as a mystery or as an adventure.[17] The only real purpose of the story is to highlight the fantasy concocted in the narrative that the United States is blighted by brutish saboteurs and spies. As noted, the historical reality is that there was never any serious threat from saboteurs on the U.S. mainland, but if superhero comics like this were to be believed, they posed an enormous threat and lurked around every corner.

The third story continues these themes, increasing the emphasis on gothic horror, opening with the image of a monstrous, clawed and fanged villain named Rathcone playing chess with a skeletal figure, no doubt representing Death. Rathcone has chess pieces for all the major characters, and when one is removed from the board that character is destined to die (the orders are relayed through a radio to "hard-faced foreign agents" who perpetrate the murders). When an admiral is killed prior to a public address, shot through the forehead and propped up on stage, the assembled officers cry for the assassin to be lynched, but Steve Rogers and Bucky do more than talk—they pursue the killer, and upon capturing him, they torture him by strangulation until he agrees to confess. Before useful information can be gained, the killer is shot dead by his own colleagues. Later, another high-ranking officer is murdered, and Rathcone decides that now Captain America and Bucky must die too, but first he wants them brought to him alive. Bucky is lured to the Nazi hideout and captured. In rescuing him, Captain America violently beats the Nazi agents into submission in a fight scene that goes on for several pages. In the aftermath, the heroes find invasion and sabotage plans for both North and South America. This story is more successful than the one that precedes it, as it is longer and gives more time to the key element—the action, which Kirby presents wonderfully. As artist Irv Novick noted, "The fight scenes had impact … when the hero punched the villain [Simon and Kirby] wanted the reader to feel it. They had invented action in comic books."[18]

What links all the stories in this comic is an absurd plot, over-the-top violence, gothic imagery, and blunt patriotic messages mixed with outright scare-mongering. These elements are designed to give the reader pleasure in experiencing an energetic narrative, while demonizing the enemy and presenting patriotism as the ultimate good. These rudiments are very much in evidence in the fourth and final story in the comic, "The Riddle of the Red Skull," which features the first appearance of Captain America's arch nemesis. The story opens with the murder of a U.S. officer, a prominent theme in the last three stories in the comic, this time committed by the mysterious Red Skull, who wears a grotesque red mask shaped like a skull. Clutching his prey, he tells them to "look at death" as they stare into his eyes before mysteriously dying, apparently of no detectable cause. When Captain America goes to investigate, he leaves Bucky behind without any explanation, but once again the sidekick goes looking for the villain on his own and is captured. Another display of violence (which is more visceral than in most comics of the time) again allows Kirby to show-off his skills and sees the Red Skull's thugs captured, though he himself escapes.

The next day Rogers attends a test flight of a new kind of aircraft, presided over by Rogers' superior officer, General Manor, and Maxon, the head of the aircraft corporation that designed the plane. Maxon is portrayed as weak and dithering, a petty and insecure man, which is to say, in the machismo terms of the comic, not a man of action like

Rogers/Captain America. When the aircraft crashes, killing the crew, Maxon bemoans the loss of the plane, but not the men, to Rogers' disgust. Upon expressing this, Rogers is chided for his outburst by his superior. Shortly afterwards, General Manor is killed by the Red Skull. Manor's wife tries to stop the Red Skull but is brushed aside. When Captain America bursts in (rather improbably because he "heard a shot"), the two fight and Captain America is beaten unconscious. Bucky appears and upon Captain America regaining consciousness, the two defeat the Red Skull, only to learn that he is Maxon, the head of the aircraft corporation. They discover that his "death stare" is just murder by poison in a concealed hypodermic needle. In the ensuing scuffle, Maxon rolls over on the needle and is killed, apparently deliberately. When Bucky asks why Captain America did not stop him killing himself he simply answers, "I'm not talking, Bucky," signaling that he wanted Maxon to die, which falls far short of the ideals of the average superhero.

Captain America, then, is not squeamish about death, yet another indication that this is a tougher comic than most others of the time. He is not entirely straight-laced either; he is spirited, emotional, and at times rebellious towards authority, in the true spirit of the traditional all-American hero. This indicates the other cultural mythology driving the comic and the characterization—its celebration of masculinity and patriotism. When the F.B.I. find Maxon's body they also uncover the reason for his terroristic activities, a letter in his pocket from "The Fuehrer" promising him the post of "Minister of All American Industry" once America is "within the fold of the Greater Reich." This time the enemy is not a foreign agent but an American seduced by promises of power from the Nazis. The message here is still that the enemy is within, but now the enemy is also greed, which makes Maxon a powerful and vicious enemy, and the polar opposite of the ideals embodied in Captain America. The Red Skull is also reminiscent of the figure of death seen stalking the battlefields in much propaganda, often as a critique of enemy war-mongering or unscrupulous weapons manufacturers who benefit from war. Despite his death at the end of the story, the Red Skull proved to be a popular villain, and returned again and again to fight Captain America, though this new Red Skull was not Maxon but a Nazi supervillain who is shown inhabiting medieval torture chambers hidden away in basements in New York, just as the same comics would show Hitler and the Nazis in gothic castles, as if drawn straight from a horror film. This is very much the clichéd image of Europe that an American reader is primed to expect by popular culture.

Overall, the first issue of *Captain America* presents two very clear themes: that volunteering is patriotic and empowering and that the enemy is omnipresent, brutish, and horrific. In the face of such an enemy, only their utter defeat will suffice, and Americans must be strong and resilient, even cold-blooded and violent when the situation demands. In this respect, the comic does not simply "reflect" American feeling at this turbulent point in history, but is a contribution to the great debate, and an unequivocal one. As Joe Simon recalled, "the opponents to the war were all quite well-organized. We wanted to have our say too [but there were] threatening letters and hate mail."[19] While later readers would be likely to read the story in the context of their knowledge about America's eventual entry into the war and its outcome, if one wants to consider the propaganda value of the piece, it is important to situate it in its original context, and to consider how all the narrative and formal properties of the text contribute toward the message.

The appropriate stance toward such texts is therefore a healthy skepticism and a critical, questioning manner, sensitive to caricature, exaggeration, satire, or hero worship, the celebration of symbols and icons, and mythologization. Of course, it is impossible to ever be truly outside such manipulation, as there is no privileged position from which to observe it, and all readers are enveloped by culture, language, and history, but it is better to be a willing participant and contributor to such debates than an unaware victim of them. Only by maintaining such a critical stance does any reader have a chance of being a "Sentinel of Liberty," revealing myth-making, manipulation, and ideological espionage when it occurs, and not allowing the pleasure of popular propaganda to obscure its political function.

NOTES

1. George Orwell, "Charles Dickens," 1939, published in *Inside the Whale* (1940), reprinted in *The Collected Essays, Journalism and Letters of George Orwell, Volume 1: An Age Like This, 1920–1940*, ed. Sonia Orwell and Ian Angus (London: Penguin Books, 1978), 492.
2. A. Peter Foulkes, *Literature and Propaganda* (New York: Methuen and Co, 1983), 3.
3. The term "propaganda" derived from the *Congregatio de Propaganda Fide* (Congregation for the Propagation of the Faith), established by Pope Gregory XV in 1622 to counteract the Protestant Reformation. For more on definitions of propaganda, see Jacques Ellul's *Propaganda: The Formation of Men's Attitudes*, translated from the French by Konrad Kellen and Jean Lerner, with an introduction by Konrad Kellen (New York: Vintage Books, 1973).
4. Roland Barthes, *Mythologies*, 1957, translated by Anette Lavers (London: Vintage, 1993), 11.
5. Cord Scott, "Written in Red, White, and Blue: A Comparison of Comic Book Propaganda from World War II and September 11," *Journal of Popular Culture* 40 (2007): 334.
6. David M. Kennedy, *Freedom from Fear* (New York: Oxford University Press, 2001), 454–464.
7. Harold Evans, *The American Century* (London: Pimlico, 1998), 291–294.
8. Joe Simon and Jack Kirby, *Captain America* no. 1, March 1941, reprinted in *Captain America: The Classic Years*, Vol. 1 (New York: Marvel Comics, 1998), 1.
9. This poster was created in 1917 and used for World War I, but due to its popularity it was adapted and re-issued for the World War II.
10. This is an interesting inversion. Whereas other publishers, such as MLJ, named American political figures, Timely did not (although it was obvious who they were). Instead, Timely was clear about attacking the Nazis and Hitler at a time when other publishers substituted imaginary enemies to stand in for the Axis powers.
11. Although Steve Rogers is not signaled as being Jewish—as Danny Fingeroth points out in *Disguised as Clark Kent: Jews, Comics and the Creation of the Superhero* (New York: Continuum, 2007), 58—superheroes of this sort can be viewed as proxy Jews, or at least figures who form a conspicuous response to the anti-Semitic ideology and policies of the Nazis, a democratic Übermensch to counteract the Nazi iconography of Aryan perfection.
12. As Mark Evanier notes in his essay "The Heroes" in *The Best of Simon and Kirby*, ed. Steve Saffel (London: Titan Books, 2009), 12, Simon and Kirby's comics were not the first to realize that "there was no reason to contain [characters] within rigid panel dimensions," but they were the best at executing such effects. He observes that in their comics "activity could spill outside of those panels, projecting beyond the borders and right into the readers' laps."
13. John E. Moser, "Madmen, Morons and Monocles: The Portrayal of the Nazis in Captain America," in *Captain America and the Struggle of the Superhero: Critical Essays*, ed. Robert G. Weiner (Jefferson, NC: McFarland, 2009), 28.
14. Martin Gilbert, *Second World War* (London: Phoenix, 1999), 139.
15. Gerard Jones, *Men of Tomorrow: Geeks, Gangsters and the Birth of the Comic Book* (New York: Basic Books, 2004), 213.
16. Moser, "Madmen, Morons and Monocles," 24–35.
17. Ibid., 28.
18. Irv Novick, quoted in Mark Evanier's "The Heroes," 13.
19. Joe Simon, quoted in Bradford W. Wright, *Comic Book Nation: The Transformation of Youth Culture in America* (Baltimore, MD: Johns Hopkins University Press, 2001), 36.

SELECTED BIBLIOGRAPHY

Barthes, Roland. *Mythologies.* 1957. Translated by Anette Lavers. London: Vintage, 1993.

Blum, John Morton. *V Was for Victory: Politics and American Culture during World War Two.* New York: Harcourt Brace Jonanovich, 1976.

Clark, Toby. *Art and Propaganda.* London: Everyman Art Library, 1997.

Ellul, Jacques. *Propaganda: The Formation of Men's Attitudes.* 1965. Translated by Konrad Kellen and Jean Lerner. New York: Vintage Books, 1973.

Evans, Harold. *The American Century.* London: Pimlico, 1998.

Fingeroth, Danny. *Disguised as Clark Kent: Jews, Comics and the Creation of the Superhero.* New York: Continuum, 2007.

Foulkes, A. Peter. *Literature and Propaganda.* New York: Methuen, 1983.

Gilbert, Martin. *Second World War.* London: Phoenix, 1999.

Jones, Gerard. *Men of Tomorrow: Geeks, Gangsters and the Birth of the Comic Book.* New York: Basic Books, 2004.

Kennedy, David M. *Freedom from Fear: The American People in Depression and War, 1929–1945.* New York: Oxford University Press, 2001.

Orwell, George. *The Collected Essays, Journalism and Letters of George Orwell, Volume 1: An Age Like This, 1920–1940,* edited by Sonia Orwell and Ian Angus. London: Penguin Books, 1978.

Rhodes, Anthony. *Propaganda—The Art of Persuasion: World War Two.* London: Angus and Robertson, 1976.

Saffel, Steve, ed. *The Best of Simon and Kirby.* London: Titan Books, 2009.

Scott, Cord. "Written in Red, White, and Blue: A Comparison of Comic Book Propaganda from World War II and September 11." *Journal of Popular Culture* 40 (2007): 325–343.

Siegel, Jerry and Joe Shuster. *Superman,* no. 10. New York: DC Comics, 1941.

Simon, Joe and Jack Kirby. *Captain America: The Classic Years,* Vol. 1. New York: Marvel Comics, 1998.

Simon, Joe and Jack Kirby. *Captain America: The Classic Years,* Vol. 2. New York: Marvel Comics, 2000.

Weiner, Robert G., ed. *Captain America and the Struggle of the Superhero: Critical Essays.* Jefferson, NC: McFarland, 2009.

Wright, Bradford W. *Comic Book Nation: The Transformation of Youth Culture in America.* Baltimore: Johns Hopkins University Press, 2001.

Part III
Production

10

POLITICAL ECONOMY

Manipulating Demand and "The Death of Superman"

Mark Rogers

In 1971 DC Comics scored quite a coup when Jack Kirby, probably the most well-known comic book artist of the 1960s, left DC's rival, Marvel, to go to DC. Kirby, who had co-created Captain America, The Hulk, The Fantastic Four, and countless other characters, would bring his "Fourth World" concept to DC, introducing Darkseid and the New Gods. The first comic he took over, however, was the moribund *Superman's Pal Jimmy Olsen.* DC heavily promoted Kirby; the cover of his first issue of *Jimmy Olsen* was emblazoned with "Kirby is Here" above the title. Despite this, due to management concerns about how Kirby's distinctive style might impact the value of the Superman license, DC had other artists redraw Superman's head in this issue and throughout Kirby's tenure at DC.[1]

This anecdote is illustrative of two things. First, comics as a medium in the United States have largely been produced within a business environment, where profit is the ultimate goal, and the creation of good comics is a by-product of that goal. This is not to demean the contributions of the thousands of talented creators who have worked and continue to work in the comic book industry, but the second thing illustrated by Kirby's experience at DC is that when business interests conflict with artistic expression, it's usually business interests that win. Looking at how comics are affected by the business and economic environment in which they are produced and consumed is political economy.

In broad terms, political economy studies the relationship between economic systems and social and political structures. The term is often used as a synonym for the discipline of economics. It can imply significantly different things within different fields of study. Political economy has its roots in the development of economics by moral philosophers such as Adam Smith, David Ricardo, and John Stuart Mill, and the subsequent theories of Karl Marx and later Marxist theorists.

Within communication and media studies, political economy has developed from two distinct, though sometimes overlapping, traditions. The first has focused on institutional approaches that examine the development of the media industries and media corporations, while a neo-Marxist strand has tended to view the media and media products as a commodity that is produced and consumed within the larger capitalist system. Neo-Marxist approaches are grounded in a critique of capitalism, and examine how media work to perpetuate a capitalist system. The two approaches are blended in studies of issues like the concentration of ownership within the media industries and cultural imperialism.[2] While neo-Marxist theories are undeniably central to the development of the use of political economy in communication, contemporary use of political economy in studying the media is not necessarily centered on a systemic critique of capitalism.

UNDERLYING ASSUMPTIONS

Two major assumptions underpin the use of political economy in analyzing the mass media. The first is that the media are produced within an economic system. The mass media in the United States are largely financed and created under a free market system and compete for audiences. The overarching goal of media producers in this system is to make a profit, though other factors (ideology, aesthetic goals) may play a role at times. The primary reason for this is that the bulk of American media are produced by large corporations, many of which are publicly held and need to deliver results to stockholders. An additional reason is that, as a general rule, it is ultimately not sustainable to continue creating media products that lose money. In 1991, for example, Fantagraphics, a publisher of "art" comics, added a pornographic line to subsidize its other publications.[3]

The second assumption is that the economic systems in which media are produced impact the media in many ways. Economic factors affect not only which media products get created, but also the content of those products, who is represented in them and how, and which audiences get their interests catered to. In short, television programs, movies, and comic books are all produced and consumed within a material context. Analyzing the impact of that context is political economy.

Though innumerable economic factors have affected the American comic book industry on a micro level, there are three issues that are particularly relevant to political economy and using this approach to study comics. The three key areas of study for political economy in regard to comics are: the practices of licensing and merchandising, through which intellectual property is used to generate additional revenue; the methods of distribution and sales that deliver comic books to consumers; and the systems of production used to create those comic books. The next several sections briefly discuss each of these areas.

LICENSING AND MERCHANDISING

Although licensing and merchandising may seem less relevant to the study of comics than looking at readers or actual comic books, the importance of these practices to the economic structure of the comic book industry cannot be overstated. Licensing involves selling or renting producers the rights to use characters in other media (television, film, advertising); merchandising is the creation and sale of products based on those characters. Licensing and merchandising have played a significant economic role throughout the history of the American comic book industry.

Comic book publishers have licensed their characters to other media products for decades. Superman and Batman, DC's early iconic superheroes, began appearing in film serials in the 1940s, and later in a number of animated and live-action television programs, as well as multiple series of feature films. Media appearances increase both the visibility and the value of Superman and Batman. This allows DC to license the characters' images for a wide range of products and advertising uses. Because comic books, in and of themselves, have a relatively narrow fan base, successful licensing programs are key to generating increased revenue through merchandising.

Three key examples demonstrate the importance of licensing to the comic book industry. The first is the incredible licensing success of the 1989 *Batman* film. The film grossed $405 million worldwide and sold over $1 billion in merchandise. Warner Communications, then DC's parent company, netted at least an estimated $390 million, approximately $90 million more than the gross sales of the entire comic book industry that year.[4] The second significant example is *Teenage Mutant Ninja Turtles*, created by Kevin Eastman and Peter Laird. After making their debut in a small print run, self-published, black and white comic in 1984, Teenage Mutant Ninja Turtles (TMNT) went on to become one of the biggest licensing successes in history. During the late 1980s and early 1990s, more than $2 billion of TMNT merchandise was sold. The last example is the $4 billion acquisition of Marvel by the Disney Corporation in 2009. Robert Iger, Disney's Chief Executive, made clear that Marvel's value was in its character licenses, saying "This treasure trove of over 5,000 characters offers Disney the ability to do what we do best."[5]

These three examples show how comics publishers serve as "license farms" for the larger media industries.[6] Disney's acquisition of Marvel and Time-Warner's continued development of its DC licenses demonstrate the value to the media conglomerates of owning the intellectual property of companies that have essentially been character and concept factories for more than 50 years. The example of TMNT shows that the low barriers to entry in comic book publishing can allow relatively unknown publishers to create marketable characters.

DISTRIBUTION AND SALES

Until the 1970s, comic books (with the exception of underground comix) were largely distributed via newsstand distribution, the same as other general interest magazines. In this system, a publisher sells comic books to a distributor for a relatively high percentage (usually 60–80 percent) of the cover price, on a returnable basis. Because the comics are returnable, and sales to a casual audience are unpredictable, publishers must overprint comics for the newsstand market, usually by a factor of three. Overprinting and newsstand distribution created a high barrier to entry into comic book publishing until the 1980s.

In the early 1970s, newsstand distribution was problematic both for the companies and for the growing comic book fan community. Comics, as a low-cost item, represented a very small profit margin for newsagents, so it was difficult to get space on shelves crowded with higher-priced magazines. What had previously been a major market for comics, Mom and Pop candy stores and corner shops, were disappearing from American cities. Their replacements, supermarkets and other larger stores, often did not carry comics. Furthermore, because comics were returnable, sales were difficult to predict accurately.

This system also did not work well for the growing number of comic book shops that serviced the fan community. Newsstand distributors tended to fill orders with assorted

DC or Marvel comics, rather than allowing stores to specify quantities or titles. It was also very difficult for customers to know when new comics would appear at their local outlet.

A Direct Market system was developed by comics fan and convention organizer Phil Seuling in 1974 to better serve the fan and comics specialty retailer. Seuling went to DC with a proposition to buy comics directly from the company and re-sell them to comic book stores. DC agreed, and Seuling formed Seagate Distributors. Under the conditions of this new deal, Seuling could specify titles and quantities, and received a higher discount than the newsstand distributors, but the comics were non-returnable. This didn't represent a significant problem for the comic book shops; they could now specify the titles their customers wanted and those that didn't sell went into their back-issue stock.

Seagate enjoyed an advantage, being the first in the market and having an exclusive agreement with DC until 1979, but once it lost that agreement, competition in the direct sales distribution market increased considerably. The early and mid-1980s were marked by especially robust competition among distributors. By the early 1990s, two large companies, Diamond and Capital, controlled about 80–85 percent of the market, while a number of smaller companies served the rest. In 1994 Marvel made a disastrous move into distribution by acquiring Heroes World, a regional distributor based in New Jersey, and using it as the exclusive distributor of Marvel comics. This destabilized the industry; by the time Marvel finally folded Heroes World in 1997, Diamond was left with a virtual monopoly on direct sales distribution.

The ruthless competition among distributors in the 1980s improved the efficiency of the comic book industry, allowing publishers to make more money by selling comics to a narrower audience. This audience was willing to pay more for comics, and at times, buy more than one copy of a comic for investment purposes. In addition, competition opened distribution barriers, allowing many smaller publishers to enter the market. Since comics could now be printed after orders for them had come in, and they were not returnable, the profit margin soared.

By the end of the 1980s, direct sales would represent more than 80 percent of all comics sold. Few of the independent companies would ever try newsstand sales, and even fewer would succeed. Only the perpetually struggling children's market (which included Archie, Harvey when it wasn't in bankruptcy, and some licensed comics from DC and Marvel) would derive most of their sales from the newsstands. These changes in the American comic industry during the 1970s and 1980s took place within the context of the overall shift in American economy from Fordism to post-Fordism.

During this period, the comic book industry was gradually transformed from a Fordist mass medium, which sought to sell comics to as large an undifferentiated audience as possible, to a post-Fordist "niche" medium which sought to maximize its profits by efficiently selling to a relatively narrow audience. Fordism, an economic system in which mass production is tied to mass consumption, was the central organizing principle of the American economy from the 1920s through the 1970s. Fordism was based on an economy of scale—the more units produced of a commodity, the lower the cost per unit. To sustain the relationship between mass production and mass consumption, Fordism required stable, cooperative relationships between big business, organized labor, and the state.

The rise of the Direct Market in the late 1970s and early 1980s brought the comics industry a new life. Gross sales would reach new highs in the late 1980s and early 1990s.

Somewhere along the way, however, comic books ceased to be a mass medium. Instead of producing a variety of comics for a variety of people, the industry increasingly produced a single kind of comic for an insular, though devoted, audience.

The American comic book industry's shift from a mass medium to a "niche" medium did not come out of nowhere; the decline of the Fordist economy provided a necessary backdrop for the industry's transformation. In many ways, this transformation reflects larger changes in the nature of mass culture. Many other media, particularly television and the magazine industry, saw considerable fragmentation in their audiences. They then learned to make money by catering to ever-narrower market niches, a process which has continued and accelerated with the introduction of high-capacity digital cable and high-speed internet. Economies of scale have been replaced by structures built on better information and marketing. Comic books, however, deviated from this pattern in that the comic book industry became mostly focused on one niche market, that of reader-collectors, and ended the twentieth century without ever really developing more product lines.

This situation has changed somewhat in the twenty-first century. Driven by the popularity of manga (Japanese comics sold in the United States, mainly as paperback books) and the increasing visibility of graphic novels in American culture, comics publishing has moved strongly into the book distribution market. This exposes comics to a larger, more diverse audience and greater diversity in content has appropriately followed.

PRODUCTION

Focusing on the creation of the content rather than printing, cutting, and binding, etc., comics are made using two distinct methods of production. The industrial process developed in the origins of the industry in the 1930s and continues to be the dominant model for the production of mainstream, color comics. Labor is divided into a number of functions and specialized workers are assigned different tasks. A typical mainstream comic is the creation of a team that includes a writer, penciler, inker, letterer, colorist, and editor. The industrial process originates in the Fordist model of the industry, when characters and titles were more important than creators in selling comics. It functions largely to produce many comics rapidly in order to keep licenses in view, to meet the demands of the fan audience by feeding the Direct Market, and to allow publishers to spread the work of popular writers or artists over several titles.

In the artisan process, which originated mainly in the underground comix movement of the 1960s and 1970s, one person writes and draws primarily black and white comics, designed for the independent comics and bookstore markets. Because the content largely represents the labor of one person, this method almost always takes longer to bring a product to market and is better suited to less-frequently published material, such as limited series, individual graphic novels, and one-shots, rather than the Fordist ideal of regular monthly comics.

There is an enormous amount of variation in both of these processes; they represent more of a continuum than a binary opposition. Nonetheless, they are associated with differing economic models of ownership (work-for-hire vs. creator ownership) and compensation (page rates vs. royalties).[7] The generally higher costs associated with industrial production mean these comics need to sell more copies to break even, which has generally limited the diversity of the industry.

The industrial model survived the comic book industry's transition from a Fordist mass medium to a niche medium largely because it also effectively serves retailers and fans, who became the core audience for comics. The artisan model, with lower costs, has been more idiosyncratic in its content. In many ways, it was the shift from Fordism—which lowered the cost of entry in publishing and better served the comics specialty shop market—which allowed the artisan model to thrive. But because that market was dominated by superheroes and closely allied genres and it was fans of those comics who patronized the stores, the small press, black and white comics created using the artisan method were restricted to an audience of superhero fans who also happened to like other kinds of comics. The growth of the bookstore market has provided a new outlet for graphic novels produced using artisan methods; the audience is interested in a wider variety of content and artisan methods fit within the traditional single-author paradigm common in book publishing.

Licensing and merchandising, sales and distribution, and production are the three most significant economic issues affecting comics and the comic book industry. Other economic and business issues affect the industry as well. Consideration of any economic factors in studying comics is within the scope of political economy as a method.

PROCEDURES

There are three important steps if you want to use political economy in studying comics: establishing an economic context; developing a theory based on evidence; and evaluating the meaning and impact of your theory. You first need to be able to situate the thing you're studying in an economic context by acquiring an overall picture of what the comic book industry looks like. How much you need to understand will vary according to the scale of your project. If you are looking at a specific storyline or issue of a comic, you would want to know something about the publisher's position in the industry at the time. A broader issue, such as the resurgence of the crime genre in the twenty-first century, would need a wider understanding of the history of the industry and the development of the genre and its publishers within that history. Industry websites and fan and trade magazines, such as *Wizard* or Diamond's *Previews* catalog, can help you understand the current structure of the industry, and there are many books and magazines devoted to industry history.

Once you can place your subject within this larger economic context, the second step is to examine evidence and create an argument or theory based on that evidence. Consider how economics may have affected your topic and find out as much economic information specifically related to it as you can. What you are doing here is forming an argument and trying to find information that supports or counters it. The process of doing this will help you modify and sharpen your argument and see if there is evidence to support it. In this sense, a political economist is something of a cross between a historian, who creates a narrative based on evidence, and a scientist, who tests a theory to see if evidence can confirm it.

Sales figures, marketing campaigns, audience demographics, distribution channels, and information about the work experiences and memories of creators and staffers can all contribute to your argument. This type of information can be difficult to find. Using primary sources, such as contemporary newspaper accounts, financial statements, and entertainment trade magazines is key; many of these sources are searchable in large databases. Comics-specific stuff, such as fanzines or older issues of trade magazines, would probably require a visit to a specialized collection, though there is also a substantial amount of material available on the internet at sites such as www.icv2.com and John Jackson Miller's Comics Chronicles (www.comichron.com).

For the third step of evaluation you need to consider the larger implications of your argument. Like the economic context, these will vary according to the scope of your project. You need to ask what your theory means: Does it affect not just your project, but the development of a genre, or a different market, or the comic book industry as whole? By doing the first two steps correctly, you will have created an evidence-based argument regarding the impact of economic factors on your object of study. In this step, you want to answer the "so what?" question—what are the implications of your argument for a larger context of the comic book industry, the mass media industries or even the economy as a whole.

SAMPLE ANALYSIS

Jurgens, Dan. "The Death of Superman, Part 7," *Superman* vol. 2, no. 75. New York: DC Comics, 1993.

In early 2010, a copy of *Detective Comics* no. 27, the first appearance of Batman, sold at auction for $1,075,000, breaking a $1 million record set just three days earlier by a copy of *Action Comics* no. 1.[8] Those amounts of money for ephemeral objects attract attention in the larger media, and several people— knowing that I work on comics—asked me if I had heard about this. Almost invariably, the ensuing conversations would turn to old comics and someone would say that he or she (or their brother or uncle or high-school pal) had a fantastic collection of old comics that got thrown out (almost always) by his mother when they went to college/got drafted/got married and wouldn't it be swell if they still had those since old comics are worth a lot of money.

These people are well intentioned, but are missing two points. First, people grossly overestimate the condition of comics. Much more important, however, is that the reason old comics are valuable is precisely because everyone's (or almost everyone's) mother threw them out. Fundamental economic principles show that value is created by scarcity, an imbalance of supply and demand. There are more collectors who want high-quality copies of *Detective Comics* no. 27 than there are existing high-quality copies. In the early 1990s, the American comic book industry was thriving in general terms. The shift to the Direct Market had created some risks, but the industry was growing due to the expansion in the number of comic book stores. Seeking further growth, publishers and retailers realized that they could manipulate demand. It is in this environment that I want to discuss *Superman* no. 75 and the much-hyped "Death of Superman."

Context

In 1992 the American comic book industry was in a period of fairly rapid growth. Although the 1990–1991 recession in the larger American economy had caused some comic book stores to fold (and taken down early independent publishers Comico and First Comics), the number of retail outlets was growing rapidly. Because of a greater focus on speculation—the practice of purchasing comics to profit by re-selling them when they went up in price—many stores that sold other types of collectibles, like sports memorabilia and trading cards, added comics to their offerings. The situation in the Direct Market was

Figure 10.1 Platinum edition polybag "The Death of Superman, Part 7." *Superman* vol. 2, no. 75, with story and art by Dan Jurgens. Copyright 1993 DC Comics.

relatively stable, with two large national distributors, Diamond and Capital, and several smaller regional distributors. Robust competition between Diamond and Capital created a situation in which credit standards for new and existing retail accounts were relatively lax, contributing to the growth in new comic book stores.

At the beginning of the year, Marvel and DC were by far the largest publishers. The situation was somewhat fluid, as the smaller presses sometimes produced hit comics, but the volume of titles published by the big two kept them in control of 65–80 percent of the total Direct Market. This changed when Image Comics was formed in 1992 by a group of hot artists who were dissatisfied with labor conditions at Marvel. The first comics published under the Image imprint came out in April (Rob Liefeld's *Youngblood*) and May (Todd McFarlane's *Spawn*), and other initial titles by the star artists followed throughout the summer. These first issues and origin stories generated large sales to the collector's market; as a result, Image briefly passed DC as the second-largest publisher. The growth period in the comic book industry continued through 1993, when gross sales reached $900 million, a high-water mark for the industry. There were as many as 10,000 retail outlets at the peak of the market.[9]

Theory

Comic book fans can be divided loosely into three groups: collectors, who value comics primarily as commodity objects; readers, who use comics as a consumable; and reader-savers[10] who both consume and collect comics. Both collectors and reader-savers often fall into one of two overlapping categories: completists and investor/valuationists. Completists seek to own every issue of a title or every comic from a particular creator or publisher. Valuationists are interested in comics primarily because of their perceived value in the marketplace, which is a function of scarcity. These categories are not exclusive and completism often drives scarcity; fans who wish to collect all the comics work of Alex Toth, for example, drive up the price of those comics in the back-issue market.

Prior to the late 1980s, comic book publishing catered mostly to the latter two types of fans; sales of back issues, excepting some re-orders and reprints, did not contribute to publisher revenue. As a result, the publishing industry was mostly focused on the use-value of comics, with a goal of drawing in customers by making comics that appealed to the reading tastes of the audience by featuring popular characters and creators. Comic book stores catered to all three types of fan, carrying back issues (and sometimes rare Golden and Silver Age comics) for the collectors and new and recent comics for the readers and reader-savers.

The growth of the industry in the early 1990s came as publishers and retailers began to focus more on the commodity value of comics, marketing comics as collectibles and an investment. This was not necessarily done at the expense of use-value, focusing on content to attract readers, but as a way to expand the consumption of those readers and to draw in new customers who were more interested in collecting comics than reading them. Many of the collectible stores that had begun to carry comics were especially focused on the commodity-value of new comics. The sports card market, which co-mingled with the comic book industry at a publishing level as well as a retail level, had long focused on collectibility.

Seeking ways to attract new customers and extract greater revenue from existing buyers, publishers began to try to exploit completist and valuational collectors by producing multiple versions of the same comics. The practice of variant covers was successfully used by Marvel in 1991, when the first issue of a new X-Men series came out in five different versions, with four different covers and a collector's edition with a combined version of the other covers. The combined sales were approximately eight million copies, making *X-Men* no. 1 the highest-selling American comic book in history.[11] As a result of the success of *X-Men* no. 1 and *X-Force* (which also debuted that year), Marvel's 1991 publishing revenue was up by $28.2 million, a 40 percent increase over the previous year.[12] Variant covers became common in the industry, along with other practices such as new no. 1 issues, no. 0 issues, and pack-ins such as trading cards or posters.

In keeping with this, *Superman* no. 75 was published in several versions and printings (including a platinum edition retailer premium, a polybagged direct sales edition, a collector's edition that included a commemorative black armband, and newsstand editions that used a different cover). Combined newsstand and direct sales totaled about six million copies.[13] Although it did not end up outselling the 1991 *X-Men* no. 1, the "Death of Superman" is particularly illustrative of the speculation boom. It was both an event comic (like new no. 1 issues), and employed the variant covers and extra collectibles to drive sales. Because of the prominence of Superman in the larger culture, the upcoming death of the character received wide coverage in the media. This brought a large number of naïve consumers; many of whom were sold, both by retailers and by media coverage, a narrative about the historical value of the comic. Customers purchased multiple copies for investment purposes and some retailers held back copies to wait for the price to rise. Resulting high demand created shortages, driving prices up rapidly, especially for the collector's edition.

As noted above, commodity prices rise based on scarcity. During the speculation boom of the early 1990s, comic book publishers and retailers shifted to a focus on commodity-value over use-value. The gimmicks used to create more collectible titles created artificial scarcity that drove rapid, short-term gains in price. Genuine scarcity exists when demand exceeds supply; by marketing the investment value of comics, the price of the commodity lost any rational relationship to real demand. Recent back-issue prices went up because customers were buying them because prices were rising. This circular relationship creates an economic bubble. In 1993–1994, the comics speculation bubble burst.

Evaluation

The collapse of the speculation bubble, coupled with Marvel's catastrophic entry into the distribution business, caused a huge shakeout in the number of retailers as thousands of stores, many of whom had longboxes filled with unopened polybagged copies of *Superman* no. 75, closed their doors. The number of stores dropped to 6,000 by 1995, and was as low as 4,000 in 1996,[14] with sales falling to around $450 million by 1996.[15] Many fans who actually read comics had been alienated during the speculation mania and had given up on comics entirely. Small independent publishers, who had not really profited from the boom, were hurt by the mass closure of comic book stores. Mid-major publishers like Valiant/Acclaim, Topp, and Malibu were damaged by the crash and many ceased publishing by the mid-1990s.

Marvel, the largest publisher of that era, filed for bankruptcy in December 1996. During the 1990s, Marvel had accumulated a tremendous amount of debt by purchasing other companies such as Toybiz, Skybox trading cards, Malibu Comics, and Heroes World Distributors. The debt was leveraged against Marvel's publishing revenue—when that revenue declined, Marvel was unable to service the debt. Though Marvel would emerge from bankruptcy and reclaim its position at the top of the industry, the company was nearly destroyed by the speculation bubble.

Superman no. 75 did not, in and of itself, cause the comic book industry to drastically contract in the mid-1990s. But in many ways, it was the pin that burst the bubble. By bringing in hordes of naïve consumers who believed the get-rich-quick hype surrounding comic book collecting, it exposed what prominent retailer Chuck Rozanki called "the 'Ponzi Scheme' reality of the market for recent back issue comics."[16] Retailers and the public began to realize that the underlying audience for comics just wasn't big enough to maintain demand for an endless stream of collectible new comics.

In conclusion, using political economy to study comics means examining the economic and business factors that shape the comic book industry. Political economy is an appropriate approach to studying many issues in comic books. It can be an end in and of itself, as in Gabilliet's *Of Comics and Men*, but it can also serve as an ancillary method to other approaches. It can provide context to studies of a single comic or story, but it is most often used in studying larger issues such as the evolution of a genre or the development of industry practices. Most analyses of comics that are not strictly formalist, but rather try to place comics into a larger cultural perspective, would benefit from an examination of the economic context of the industry.

NOTES

1. Mark Evanier, "Introduction" in Jack Kirby, *Jimmy Olsen: Adventures by Jack Kirby, Volume 1* (New York: DC Comics, 2003), 3.
2. See, for example, Ben Bagdikian, *The New Media Monopoly* (Boston: Beacon Press, 2004); and Robert McChesney, *Rich Media, Poor Democracy* (New York: New Press, 1999).
3. Richard Seven, "The Misunderstood Art," *The Seattle Times Pacific Northwest Magazine*, March 18, 2001. http://seattletimes.nwsource.com/pacificnw/2001/0318/cover.html.
4. Les Daniels, *DC Comics: Sixty Years of the World's Favorite Comic Book Heroes* (Boston: Bulfinch, 1995), 202; Michael Cieply, "Warner's Wild Card: No Matter How You Count 'Batman's' Payoff is No Joke," *Los Angeles Times*, August 11, 1989, Part 6, 1.
5. David Goldman, "Disney to Buy Marvel for $4 billion: Walt Disney Co. Will Purchase the Comic Book Company behind X-Men and Spider-Man," *CNNMoney.com*. http://money.cnn.com/2009/08/31/news/companies/disney_marvel/index.htm.
6. Mark C. Rogers, "License Farming and the American Comic Book Industry," *International Journal of Comic Art* 1 (2) (1999): 132–142.
7. Mark C. Rogers, "Understanding Production: The Stylistic Impact of Artisan and Industrial Methods," *International Journal of Comic Art* 8 (1) (2006): 509–517.
8. George Gustines, "Batman Beats Superman in the Marketplace," *New York Times*, February 27, 2010, 2.
9. Jan Norman, "Action Guide: The Super Heroes of a Special Genre; Retailing: It's Your Business Takes a Break From Problem Solving to Explore the World of Comic-book Stores," *Orange County Register*, December 16, 1996, D12. See also, Dirk Deppey, "A Comics Journal History of the Direct Market, Part Three," *The Comics Journal*. www.tcj.com/history/a-comics-journal-history-of-the-direct-market-part-three/2.
10. This term comes from Marvel's 1991 form 10-K.
11. John J. Miller, "Comics Sales Records in the Diamond Exclusive Era: High and Low Points in Sales to Comics Shops in North America from 1997–Present," *Comichon*. www.comichron.com/vitalstatistics/diamondrecords.html.
12. Marvel Entertainment Group Inc., Form 10-K, 1991.
13. Daniels, *DC Comics*, 217.
14. Greg Stump, "The State of the Industry 1996," *The Comics Journal* 188 (1996): 31.
15. Norman, "Action Guide," D12.
16. Chuck Rozanski, "Tales From the Database: 'Death of Superman' Promotion of 1992." www.milehighcomics.com/tales/cbg127.html.

SELECTED BIBLIOGRAPHY

Cieply, Michael. "Warner's Wild Card: No Matter How You Count 'Batman's' Payoff Is No Joke." *Los Angeles Times*, August 11, 1989, 6:1.

Daniels, Les. *DC Comics: Sixty Years of the World's Favorite Comic Book Heroes*. Boston: Bulfinch, 1995.

Deppey, Dirk. "A Comics Journal History of the Direct Market, Part Three." *The Comics Journal*, www.tcj.com/history/a-comics-journal-history-of-the-direct-market-part-three/2.

Evanier, Mark. "Introduction" in *Jimmy Olsen: Adventures by Jack Kirby—Volume 1*, by Jack Kirby. New York: DC Comics, 2003.

Gabilliet, Jean Paul. *Of Comics and Men: A Cultural History of American Comic Books*. Translated by Bart Beaty and Nick Nguyen. Jackson, MS: University Press of Mississippi, 2010.

Goldman, David. "Disney to Buy Marvel for $4 Billion: Walt Disney Co. Will Purchase the Comic Book Company behind X-Men and Spider-Man." *CNNMoney.com*, http://money.cnn.com/2009/08/31/news/companies/disney_marvel/index.htm

Gustines, George. "Batman Beats Superman in the Marketplace." *New York Times*, February 27, 2010, 2.

Miller, John J. "Comics Sales Records in the Diamond Exclusive Era High and Low Points in Sales to Comics Shops in North America from 1997–Present." *Comichron*, www.comichron.com/vitalstatistics/diamondrecords.html.

Norman, Jan. "Action Guide: The Super Heroes of a Special Genre – Retailing: It's Your Business Takes a Break From Problem Solving to Explore the World of Comic-book Stores." *Orange County Register*, December 16, 1996, D12.

Rogers, Mark C. "License Farming and the American Comic Book Industry." *International Journal of Comic Art* 1 (2) (1999): 132–142.

Rogers, Mark C. "Understanding Production: The Stylistic Impact of Artisan and Industrial Methods." *International Journal of Comic Art* 8 (1) (2006): 509–517.

Rozanski, Chuck. "Tales from the Database: 'Death of Superman' Promotion of 1992." www.milehighcomics.com/tales/cbg127.html.

Seven, Richard. "The Misunderstood Art." *The Seattle Times Pacific Northwest Magazine*, March 18, 2001.

Stump, Greg. "The State of the Industry 1996." *The Comics Journal* 188 (1996).

11

CULTURE OF CONSUMPTION

Commodification through Superman: Return to Krypton

Ian Gordon

In a 2000 interview, Darren Hayes, the former lead singer of Australian soft rock duo *Savage Garden*, noted that as a young boy he had read American comic books and through that reading began to aspire to things American. Hayes noted in particular the "ads on the back" of comic books and the way this stimulated his imagination about the United States. Hayes' encounter, coming from as far as Australia, may be somewhat different than that of American comic book readers, but it does point to ways we can understand the role of comics and, in particular, comic books in a culture of consumption in which we define ourselves through the sorts of things we buy or want to buy more than through other values.

There are numerous ways comic books can be analyzed. For instance, they are commodities, they of course contain stories, many print fan letters, and they have advertisements. Each of these things can be analyzed separately, but at the same time we need to remember that mostly we experience comic books as a whole. Hayes' experience is a case in point because if the advertisements on the back of the comic books created a desire for goods mostly obtainable only in America, he could at least purchase American comic books and through that satisfy some of his desire. When Hayes read the comic book, he almost certainly would have encountered some of the things that distinguish America from Australia, such as the American idiom and American spellings such as "jail" rather than the Australian usage of the British English "gaol." That later in life he could recall the impact that the ads had on him may well be because they were the most significant marker and/or sound bite he had on hand to explain his fascination with American culture, which he also extended to television and music. For Hayes, comic book ads stood for American culture and he saw that culture as made up of commodities.[1]

UNDERLYING ASSUMPTIONS

Using comic books to understand how American society became a culture of consumption and how that culture operates involves a different set of analytical approaches than, say, looking at the formal properties of a comic, such as how comics work through the use of sequential panels, word balloons, and the like. The focus here is on how comics help us understand change, and indeed the lack of change, over time—the process is essentially historic. Historians are not known for foregrounding their method and theory; rather, they tend to concentrate on offering explanatory narratives. Historians who deal with material culture will have an underlying theory of how such artifacts gain their value and the sorts of functions they perform in society beyond their immediate utility. Likewise, historians who deal with texts will employ some methodology to interpret and interrogate the work. While a political historian will check documentary records against multiple records of a similar event, a cultural historian will contextualize a comic in relation to other comics, related forms such as cartoons and perhaps film and television, which may differ according to era, and will need some understanding of how the storytelling conventions of comics work. For instance, to understand the impact comic books had on Hayes, a historian might examine what he read, the other sorts of American cultural products—like television shows, movies, and music—he experienced and how these fit into the context of an Australian boyhood. Examining a particular comic book can involve a number of approaches, such as a close reading of the narrative, a discussion of the formal properties of comic book storytelling, contextualizing an individual story in a narrative arc, and perhaps putting in the larger framework of open-ended continuity. Similarly, if arguing that comics contain symbolic value for their readers, fans, and collectors, a historian will need some theory about the manner in which that value is inscribed in the comic.

COMIC BOOKS AS COMMODITIES AS CULTURE

The experience of Hayes throws into stark relief the cultural symbolism of certain types of comic books as American, but if they carried that significance for an Australian, it is equally true that they carried a similar significance for Americans. Comic books can be understood, in part, through analysis of their function as a commodity, a good to be bought, sold, and traded. At this abstract level of analysis, a comic book is simply a commodity and the value of it is removed from any immediate link to the story contained therein. The cultural anthropologist Grant McCracken argues that goods, like comic books, help make "culture material." What he means is that we use things to create the values and habits of everyday life that make up our culture. Moreover, goods provide one way of making order within a culture by the sort of processes by which we attach hierarchies of value to them. So, for instance, we may value a diamond more highly than a ruby, or one tennis player more highly than another.[2] This process of making order can be seen in the changes in attitudes to comic books since the 1950s. In those years, the values attributed to comic books has shifted from the moral panic of an anti-comic book campaign led by Fredric Wertham, who linked comic books as a medium to juvenile delinquency and other forms of what he saw as aberrant behavior, to a broad social acceptance as a literary and/or art form, albeit with a requisite name change to "graphic novels."[3]

Mary Douglas and Baron Isherwood noted that the process of naming "and the operations to be performed upon names [is] a means of thinking."[4] In naming the good purchased, then, there is already a shift away from its simple utility as a good and the beginning of meanings embedded by creators and users. The term "comic book" is laden with meaning, as is the term "graphic novel." Numerous articles in newspapers and journals carry on a public discussion about what these terms mean and help reorient the cultural symbolism we attach to the medium of comics. This discussion is not one about lexicographical distinctions, but rather one about basic shifts in the means of thinking. Typically, such articles make an observation along the lines that "comics are not just for kids anymore" and inform readers of the many complex literary works that look and feel like comic books, but are now more appropriately called graphic novels. In these pieces, comic books equal childish simplicity and graphic novels equal adult sophistication and refinement. Consuming comic books as a class of goods, then, carries a different symbolic significance than consuming graphic novels. Indeed, it matters little that 20 years ago these articles sought to establish the non-childish nature of the medium and that now the thrust is to reintroduce the comic art form as something for children as well as adults.[5]

The sort of words used to describe comics are just one part of the way their significance as commodities is shaped. Grant McCracken argues that in addition to embodying the values and meaning people give to their lives, many goods, and our desire for them, serve as a bridge to displaced meaning. By this, he means that when faced with the improbable achievement of some ideal, individuals and societies find ways to displace that ideal to some symbolic representation that operates out of the immediate plane of reality. Thus the meaning at the heart of the ideal is displaced. In consumer societies the never-ending supply of commodities lets individuals displace meaning onto some imagined future purchase or purchases. So long as the means to fully satisfy one's bridges are not immediately present, or it is possible to continually redefine one's bridges, this holds individuals in a state of seeing ideals as achievable. This theory suggests that a person can make up for a disappointment in one's life by working toward a material goal—say, a new car of higher quality—and that it is the process of working toward the goal, rather than attaining it, that provides an ability to live day to day with whatever disappointment one might have experienced. Such a theory explains much about the mechanics of a consumer society in which consumption is a continual process and needs are seemingly never satisfied. Comics, especially those published serially over a number of years, can carry this function as bridges. The materiality of the comic, and the possibility of acquiring a complete run of a series through incremental purchases, can make comics a slow but steady bridge to displaced meanings.[6]

COLLECTORS, FANS, AND READERS

Many commodities are used without giving rise to readily observable groups of people using them, but comics have organized fan groups, professional collectors and sellers, and observable groups of readers. Jean-Paul Gabilliet offers a useful framework for examining different levels of engagement with comics. As he notes, comic book readers may be fans and collectors, but not all readers engage in this level of activity. Likewise, most fans may be collectors, but not all collectors are necessarily fans. And not all fans engage in the same types and array of activities, such as publishing fanzines and attending conventions.[7]

Understanding the complexity of these different relationships with comics is one way to examine the manner in which comics help constitute a culture of consumption. Delineating the distinctions between readers, fans, and collectors is not my purpose here. But these different levels of engagement with comic books point to distinctions about how the comic book as an object is treated by its purchasers. Fans who are collectors may well be using comics as a bridge to some displaced meaning, but collectors who simply collect comics as investments, with little regard for how a particular comic achieved its value, beyond the simple workings of supply and demand, are almost certainly not using comics as a bridge. The point here is that discussing one manner in which comics function as a symbolic commodity that helps constitute a culture of consumption does not exclude other ways of understanding their functions as commodities, nor other ways of understanding why people consume them. For instance, in addition to the symbolic approach, it is possible and useful to examine comic books through their political economy as a commodity (see Chapter 10). Such an approach studies their production and distribution. But at the same time the sort of commodity fetishization of individual issues, say *Action Comics* no. 1, also requires some understanding of how a comic book's story shapes its value as a commodity.

READING THE CULTURE OF A COMIC

There are several possible ways of using comic book stories to analyze their relation to a culture of consumption. Any number of issues of *Richie Rich*, for instance, could be used to demonstrate a variety of points, such as the dangers of conspicuous consumption, the inappropriateness of using things to gain affection, and the duty of *noblesse oblige* that the very wealthy owe the less well off. The comic's subtitle, "The Poor Little Rich Boy," is an obvious tip-off that the comic was a morality tale about the dangers of excessive wealth. On another level, this comic that began in the 1960s and ran, more or less continuously until 1994, offered a notion of limits in an age of mass consumption, in that the solutions to Richie's problems lay not in material wealth, but in other qualities. Alternatively, the comic can be read as affirming that an abundance of material goods does not cripple the soul if one has a moral base and, as such, is a small lesson in American exceptionalism, the concept that only America has the mix of features that makes it a beacon to the rest of the world. But analyzing a comic that is not specifically about wealth and consumption and showing the ways that consumerism is so naturalized in America that it forms the backdrop for a narrative about even the most alien of cultures offers a more complex approach.

ARTIFACT SELECTED FOR ANALYSIS

The *Superman: Return to Krypton* trade paperback collection of related stories was originally published in several Superman titles issued in the magazine format. As the title suggests, Superman returns to his native Krypton, although as it turns out, the return is a dream of sorts designed to kill Superman. This rather simplistic plot device, revealed *deus ex machina*-like in the last episode, is supplemented by the use of multiple layers of Superman's history.

SAMPLE ANALYSIS

Casey, Joe, *et al. Superman: Return to Krypton*. New York: DC Comics, 2004.

There are multiple ways to approach this book. We could ask ourselves what sort of cultural significance there is in magazine-style comic book stories being compiled into a trade paperback. Do comics gain more respectability in the trade paperback form? Is there a greater degree of respectability attached to a book bought from a bookshop rather than a magazine from a newsstand or a comic book from a specialty store? Likewise, questions arise about the economics of production. What sort of business models do comic book companies use these days when such trade paperback compilations are commonplace? And furthermore, how do these volumes figure in the marketing of comics as collectibles? For instance, do fans who collect all published comics of a particular character like Superman feel the need to collect these reprints as well in order to have the satisfaction of a complete collection? And in reading the story we can see the ways in which it assumes and promotes a culture of consumption. From this array of possible ways to approach the comic at hand, I will look at the story and offer two different levels of interpretation: first, looking at the normalization of consumption in the story; and second, looking at the ways in which the story reinforces the symbolic value of Superman and so increases both his status as a commodity and his ability to normalize a culture of consumption.

Seeing Consumption

Superman: Return to Krypton is a vast pastiche of previous Superman stories, comics, and other elements of popular culture. There are easily recognizable elements from Superman comic book stories, the late 1970s and early 1980s Superman movies, *Star Wars*, and even *Mission Impossible 2*. Five writers and eleven artists had a hand in creating the story, which may somewhat explain the abundance of incongruities. For instance, one of the main plot lines is the xenophobic nature of the majority of Kryptonians, and yet in "Atomic Town … the ultimate commerce center on Krypton … free trade and advanced technologies meet in an organic kaleidoscope of cultures." Free trade and xenophobia do not by their nature go hand in hand. Probably such an incongruity occurs because the writers cannot imagine a society without free market consumerism, even as they adopt xenophobia as a plot device. The depiction of Atomic Town comes a page after Lois Lane and Superman visit the "Fire Falls," a "sacred nuptial retreat for Kryptonians," in a scene reminiscent of Lois and Clark's visit to Niagara Falls in the movie *Superman II*. In that movie, Lois and Clark visited to expose a scam of overcharging newly wed couples for their stays at the honeymoon spot, which evoked a mild criticism of an industry that commodified the vows of marriage. In *Superman: Return to Krypton* the notion of taking a honeymoon vacation is raised to a "sacred ritual." Tourism associated with marriage, then, is so natural that a depiction of an alien culture neatly incorporates it and names it as sacred. If we follow Douglas and Isherwood in seeing the naming of practices as important, then in this moment in the comic we see a practice within a culture of consumption lifted from the mere everyday to the sacred. That the practice is a North American one and not, say, the Indian Hindu practice of *Barat Nikasi*, in which a groom leaves for the wedding on a horse or an elephant, is perhaps simply an indication that writers draw on their own cultures for referents, which suggests that Americans find it hard to depict "falls," be it water or fire, without conjuring Niagara Falls and the business of honeymoons. The point here is that such a depiction naturalizes the practices of consumption, which becomes even more obvious on the following page (Figure 11.1) when Lois goes shopping in Atomic Town, a place so rich in its cornucopia of goods that it makes "Metropolis look like … well, Smallville" and tells Superman she will not "max out our credit line."[8]

Figure 11.1 *Adventures of Superman* no. 589, page 11. Story by Joe Casey with pencil art by Duncan Rouleau. Copyright 2001 DC Comics.

Creating and Reinforcing Symbols

Looking for instances such as these in comic books and reading them as naturalizing consumption is easy enough. But consumption also works at another level because Superman himself is a product marketed for over 70 years. Moreover, when the writers of the Superman radio serial had him fight for "truth, justice and the American way" during World War II and DC used him on the cover of comic books to promote war bonds, they named Superman in such a way that he began to acquire a symbolic status as representing American values. The 1950s television series *The Adventures of Superman* further contributed to that naming process by repeating the "truth, justice, and the American way" mantra in the show's opening credits. Part of the symbolism of Superman rests in his longevity, but this has not been acquired simply by hanging around for so long, but by the repetition of key concepts and themes in stories over the years in such a manner that he acquired a mythological dimension.[9] For many years in the 1940s and 1950s nothing ever changed in Superman stories. The Italian academic and novelist Umberto Eco, in an essay on Superman published in the early 1960s, regarded this narrative framework as dream-like.[10] But in the 1960s, with the rise of Marvel Comics, the importance of continuity and a sense of individual stories being part of a greater whole, and the growing importance of fan communities to the health of comic books, this situation began to change. Moreover, a goodly amount of the social change of the 1950s became more and more apparent in the 1960s. For Superman to stand for the American way he had to change as America changed. One way that DC Comics has done this is to reboot the continuity of Superman from time to time to keep the character fresh, but at the same time retain its roots. What this creates is something greater than a simple product—a Superman comic book—but rather a larger cosmology of Superman. Understanding the complexity of any given Superman story, then, can require a wealth of knowledge acquired through an affinity with the character from reading many comic books.

Superman's symbolic status and the density of it is created and reinforced by a culture of consumption in which reading a comic book can transcend a single book and require a whole opus. Indeed, one comic book industry figure, Dallas Middaugh, the head of Random House's Japanese manga division, Del Rey Manga, joked that some comics were "just impossible to read without having a Ph.D. in superhero trivia," which is indicative of the depth of knowledge sometimes required to understand the complex layers in a comic book story.[11] By looking at *Return to Krypton*, we can revisit some of these issues, especially around the different treatments of Superman's father, Jor-El, in these reconfigurations of the Superman story. A double splash page shows Superman meeting Jor-El, who, as the action unfolds, changes from a figure in a green/black/white shapeless oblong shift-with-cowl garment that reveals little muscularity into a muscle-hugging spandex tunic-and-cape suit that displays a physique in keeping with a superhero, or at least the father of one. The transformation is from a mid-1980s version of Jor-El offered by creator John Byrne in the reboot of the character, *Superman: The Man of Steel*, to an updated version of the 1950s depiction of Jor-El.

Trying to balance Superman's Kryptonian heritage with his American life might seem of little matter in the twenty-first century, when diversity is mandated across America, if not always observed in practice. But in the 1950s, Superman did not deviate too far from the accepted social norms of America for several reasons. First, the alien origins of Superman were not particularly prominent in his identity, and for many years simply an explanation for his powers. Second, the anti-comic book campaign instigated by Fredric Wertham in the 1950s and the adoption of a comic code limited the scope for comic book stories. Consequently, writers and artists in the 1950s presented Superman's encounters with his home planet in the most simple-minded fashion, in which Krypton replicated American social norms. In the 1959 story "The Supergirl from Krypton," Kryptonian families bring their children up in what seem to be suburban homes with rooms with curtains and cribs, while in the 1958 story "The Super Duel in Space," Superman meets a scientist who was a "roommate in college" with Jor-El. At one level these representations are risible, but these sort of normative projections of the American Way as a universal way shaped Superman as a symbol of American culture.[12]

Reboots and Maintaining the Symbolism

John Byrne's 1986 reboot of Superman came about as part of 1985's epic continuity fix for DC Comics in which the company tried to simplify the complexity of having different versions of the same characters in a "multiverse" of parallel worlds in a series of comic books later published in the single volume *Crisis on Infinite Earths*. The multiverse and the clean-up of it were attempts to deal with what it meant to have popular symbolic characters with long histories, but who were timeless in appearance. Rebooting the characters from time to time is another solution, as is the sort of self-referential strategy of acknowledging different versions of the character across time. In 1985, DC Comics wished to fix their characters in time and space, but since then they have been happy to see the characters as more free-floating. For a character like Superman, who carries a symbolic reference as representative of the American Way, this might potentially create problems. For DC Comics, who are well aware of the value Superman has to the company in this symbolic guise, the problem is how to keep him a representative figure when the depiction of him has become so varied and diverse.

Superman: Return to Krypton offers a resolution of some of these issues, at least in ways of using different representations of Krypton and Jor-El. Since the story is a dream-like encounter in the Phantom Zone, it can play with the reality of Superman's continuity. The reversion to a 1950s version of Jor-El is internalized in the story as a projection by Jor-El of a warmer historical era in that planet's culture and a period he loved. Such a use of "history" nicely reminds us of our own history, or at least Superman's history, and incidentally projects the 1950s as a warmer, more loving era than 2004. The artifice within the storyline involving both a dream and the Phantom Zone is like the artifice of stories—not quite real, but imagined. This approach harks back to Alan Moore's 1986 work, collected as *Superman: Whatever Happened to the Man of Tomorrow?*, which preceded Byrne's reboot and contained the observation that it was "an imaginary tale ... aren't they all?" Several factors are at work in *Return to Krypton*, including rolling back a little of John Byrne's vision of a cold and chilling, scientifically advanced and very alien Krypton, which built on the depiction in the 1978 Superman film, to a somewhat warmer version. This reversion not only opens the space for this particular story arc to unfold, but helps bring different eras of Superman together through unifying the different representations of Jor-El. And at yet another level, it seems that comic book creators were trying to reintroduce some of the comic—as in funny—elements to Superman comic books, an element that slowly drifted out of the stories during the 1960s. Much of this comes across in the art, with many of the artists employing a more cartoonish style than Byrne's realistic approach.

EXPLAINING THE PROCESS BEHIND THE ANALYSIS

Students reading academic analysis are often puzzled by the array of information academics deploy and the ways in which it is used to make an argument. Such a case is even more likely the less one knows about a particular subject. For instance, a Superman comic book fan reading this piece will probably be aware of most of the different incarnations of Superman I mention and the character's broad history. But they may not accept my analysis and may indeed have counter examples to support another understanding of Superman that is not tied to a culture of consumption. Different analyses may or may not be mutually exclusive.

The two key parts of my analysis, the simple observation of shopping as an act of consumption in *Superman: Return to Krypton,* and the more complex argument about a cultural symbol being both a commodity and a figure that normalizes the values of consumption, are underpinned by an array of academic work that I have not mentioned or explained, but which do shape the way I have approached the subject. For instance, the term "culture of consumption," meaning a society in which the acquisition of material goods is viewed a major defining feature of daily life, is also a theoretical framework for analyzing the impact of such acquisition—and related activities such as advertising—on human social, political, and spiritual life. It is a phrase borrowed from the title of a 1983 book, *The Culture of Consumption,* a collection of essays edited by Richard Wightman Fox and T.J. Jackson Lears. That work analyzed the "commodification" of society—that is, the transformation of virtually everything, from objects to experiences to feelings, into a commodity or brand that can be bought or sold. My approach to the subject of consumption and using comic books to understand it also draws on work by a diverse group of social and political theorists such as Thorstein Veblen (*The Theory of the Leisure Class*), Walter Benjamin ("The Work of Art in the Age of Mechanical Reproduction"), Max Horkheimer and Theodor Adorno ("The Culture Industry: Enlightenment and Mass Deception"), Karl Marx, Herbert Marcuse, Daniel Bell, David Riesman (social theorists), Roland Barthes (French theorist of mythology, structuralism, and semiotics), Clifford Geertz (anthropologist), Guy Debord (French situationist/anarchist), Warren Susman, and Christopher Lasch (American historians). The point here is that shaping an analysis does not rely on one method or one theorist, but on many. For instance, I could have talked about Darren Hayes' encounter with comic books and the advertisements through an analysis that looked at consumption as an ideology along the same lines as Leonard Rifas has done in Chapter 16 of this volume.

My analysis also relies on a familiarity with Superman in all his incarnations. Because many comic book characters, particularly superheroes, appear in ongoing serial narratives that have often run for many years, there are special challenges in trying to look at a single story or story arc and understand all the issues involved. When it comes to Superman, who has appeared in numerous incarnations in movies, television, and radio, as well as comic books and strips, the problem is compounded. My approach here makes a virtue of that problem by looking at Superman's symbolic status. If as a symbol Superman is inconsistent in, say, his ideology, then it may be merely because he is representative of a culture that is not always consistent. Such an approach is not always useful, because you might want to explain why the expression of a particular ideology at a particular time is important and what it reveals about American society. This observation points to some of the limitations of dealing with the long history of a comic book character through an approach that tries to unify every incarnation. There may indeed be good reasons not to do so.

Using the notion of a culture of consumption to analyze comic books is useful in that it can explain some of the ways comics both reflect and help shape American society. Comic books do this through the stories they tell and through being commodities to which people can attribute value. Some comic book characters can transcend the form of comics and become broader cultural symbols, which are useful in helping understand unifying aspects of a culture, or at least the ways in which such characters and the stories about them provide ways of talking about aspects of a culture that seek to unify.

NOTES

1. Katherine Tulich, "Over the Garden Wall," *The Sun-Herald*, March 3, 2002, 10.
2. Grant McCracken, *Culture and Consumption: New Approaches to the Symbolic Character of Consumer Goods and Activities* (Bloomington, IN: Indiana University Press, 1988), 75.
3. See Ian Gordon "Making Comics Respectable: How *Maus* Helped Redefine a Medium," in *The Rise of the American Comics Artist: Creators and Contexts*, ed. Paul Williams and James Lyons (Jackson, MS: University Press of Mississippi, 2010).
4. Mary Douglas and Baron Isherwood, *The World of Goods: Towards an Anthropology of Consumption* (New York: Basic Books, 1979), 51.
5. For examples of these discussions, see Edwin McDowell, "America is Taking Comic Books Seriously," *New York Times*, July 31, 1988, 4:7; Michael Sangiacomo, "Get Your Comics Fill at Columbus Convention," *Cleveland Plain Dealer*, October 3, 2009, E3; Emily Mathieu, "Remember, They're for Kids," *Toronto Star*, May 3, 2008, ID4.
6. McCracken, *Culture and Consumption*, 117.
7. Jean-Paul Gabilliet, *Of Comics and Men: A Cultural History of American Comic Books* (Jackson, MS: University Press of Mississippi, 2010), 256.
8. Casey, Joe, *et al.*, *Superman: Return to Krypton* (New York: DC Comics, 2004), 59–60.
9. Ian Gordon, "Nostalgia, Myth, and Ideology: Visions of Superman at the End of the American Century," in *Comics* and *Ideology*, ed. Matthew McAllister, Edward Sewell, and Ian Gordon (New York: Peter Lang, 2001); Umberto Eco, "The Myth of Superman," *Diacritics* 2 (1972): 14–22.
10. Ibid., 17.
11. Dirk Deppey, "Interview with Dallas Middaugh," *Comics Journal* 277 (2006). http://archives2.tcj.com/index.php?option=com_content&task=view&id=368&Itemid=48 (accessed September 15, 2010).
12. Otto Binder (w), Al Plastino (p, i), "The Supergirl from Krypton," *Action Comics* No. 252 (May 1959); Otto Binder (w), Al Plastino (p, i), "The Super Duel in Space," *Action Comics* No. 242 (July 1958).

SELECTED BIBLIOGRAPHY

Douglas, Mary and Baron Isherwood. *The World of Goods*. New York: Routledge, 1996.
Eco, Umberto. "The Myth of Superman." *Diacritics* 2 (1972): 14–22.
Fox, Richard Wightman and T.J. Jackson Lears, eds. *The Culture of Consumption: Critical Essays in American History, 1880–1980*. New York: Pantheon, 1983.
Gabilliet, Jean Paul. *Of Comics and Men: A Cultural History of American Comic Books*. Jackson, MS: University Press of Mississippi, 2010.
Gordon, Ian, "Nostalgia, Myth, and Ideology: Visions of Superman at the End of the American Century." In *Comics* and *Ideology*, edited by Matthew McAllister, Edward Sewell, and Ian Gordon, 177–194. New York: Peter Lang, 2001.
Gordon, Ian. "Making Comics Respectable: How *Maus* helped Redefine a Medium." In *The Rise of the American Comics Artist Creators and Contexts*, edited by Paul Williams and James Lyons, 179–193. Jackson, MS: University Press of Mississippi, 2010.
McCracken, Grant. *Culture and Consumption: New Approaches to the Symbolic Character of Consumer Goods and Activities*. Bloomington: Indiana University Press, 1988.
McDowell, Edwin. "America is Taking Comic Books Seriously." *New York Times*, July 31, 1988.
Mathieu, Emily. "Remember, They're for Kids." *Toronto Star*, May 3, 2008.
Sangiacomo, Michael. "Get Your Comics Fill at Columbus Convention." *Cleveland Plain Dealer*, October 3, 2009.
Tulich, Katherine. "Over the Garden Wall." *The Sun-Herald*, March 3, 2002, 10.

12

ETHNOGRAPHY OF PRODUCTION

Editor Axel Alonso and the Sale of Ideas

Stanford W. Carpenter

It is August 27, 2003. I am an African-American anthropologist conducting an ethnographic interview of Axel Alonso at a Thai restaurant in mid-town Manhattan. Alonso and I are at this Thai restaurant in mid-town Manhattan because it is around the corner from his office at Marvel Enterprises. He usually eats lunch at his desk. We came here to get away from the ringing of the telephone and the assistants, associates, and production staff that kept wedging their heads through Alonso's office doorway to ask "just one quick question." Alonso is an executive editor at Marvel Comics. As his name implies, he is of mixed Hispanic/German-American heritage. The lunch-hour rush has just ended, the room has emptied, and we are talking about his job.

I describe this tape-recorded encounter as an "ethnographic interview" to reflect the nature of the conversation, my disciplinary training, and my research methods. Ethnographic interviews consist of series of open-ended questions conducted during multiple sittings over extended periods of time.

It has been a while since our last conversation, so it is no surprise when he asks me to describe my thesis. I tell him that I have come to see the comic book creators' jobs in terms of imagining and creating identity; that the creative teams he assembles (and contributes to) start with blank pages, and that in an effort to create a compelling story, they have to create a world that bears enough resemblance to the reader's world that the reader will suspend his or her disbelief. At the core of these imaginary worlds are characters with identities connected to commonly held notions of class, ethnicity, gender, and race. Even the aliens, monsters, and non-human-looking mutants speak and behave in ways that connect them to commonly held notions of class, ethnic, gender, and racial identities. And the same could be said for the imaginary worlds these aliens, monsters, and non-human-looking mutants occupy. I ask Alonso how he feels about being a part of creating these imaginary worlds and, by extension, creating identity.

Looking back at the transcripts of the conversation, it became obvious to me that my phrasing of the question had the potential of eliciting a response from Alonso that could easily be misread. While we had spoken in a variety of private and public venues, this was a taped interview. He knew that he could refuse to answer or have his response removed from the record. The fact that my query came up as I was describing the thesis of my book project, however, must have put additional pressure on him to give me a response I could use.

Alonso has known me since February 1999, when I entered the field. Since our first conversation, my research has evolved from dissertation research to a book project. My experiences in the field have challenged my preconceptions and theoretical frameworks, and altered my theses. Over time, Alonso has observed the changes, given me helpful feedback, and helped me contact comic book creators. Now I am waiting for Alonso's response. How does he feel about being involved in the work of imagining identity in comic books? His words are measured:

> [I'm] not thinking in those terms, what [I'm] thinking about is [that] I want to take care of myself and do some good. I'm not looking to change the world. I'd like to be a decent person and maybe affect the fate of people around me. And maybe those seem to be more realistic goals for me when I'm looking at the medium [in] which I work.

SO WHAT IS THE MATTER AT HAND?

Ethnography (noun) and ethnographic (adjective) research methods were developed by and are closely associated with anthropology. Ethnography is based on prolonged close study of a group of people. While ethnographies contain rich descriptions of group and individual behaviors and interactions, rituals, and social processes, the explicit goal of ethnography is "to understand the culture of a group from within."[1] The main distinctions between ethnographic and other qualitative research methods are that, for the most part, ethnographers conducting fieldwork developed ethnographic methods. Fieldwork is research based on the researcher (ethnographer) becoming embedded for extended periods of time among the people whom they study. Ethnographic research methods can be important tools for a variety of research projects. Still, the use of fieldwork is what distinguishes ethnography from "ethnographic" and/or "qualitative" research projects. This chapter will focus on ethnography as defined by the use of ethnographic research methods in conjunction with fieldwork.

UNDERLYING ASSUMPTIONS AND PROCEDURES

Anthropology, broadly defined as the study of humanity, was originally divided into four fields: archaeology, cultural anthropology, linguistics, and physical anthropology. All four fields have gone through significant expansion and redefinition, and can be divided into many sub-fields. There has been significant cross-fertilization among the four fields and with other scholarly disciplines. Still, each of the four fields is based on some form of fieldwork. Archaeologists and physical anthropologists conduct expeditions that include digging for artifacts. Cultural anthropologists and linguists embed themselves among groups of people, create ethnographies, and have developed concepts and theories that are most applicable to comics scholarship. Cultural anthropologists and linguists have historically borrowed from one another in the development and execution of their research. Archaeology's emphasis on artifacts, especially its use of reverse engineering of the construction of artifacts to understand creative practices and social relations, has implications for the way in which cultural anthropologists address and theorize cultural production.

Historical Considerations

Early ethnographies employed third-person narrative structure. Over time this gave way to instances of second- and first-person narratives. Still, ethnography tended to address the ethnographer as an omniscient narrator. The 1960s and 1970s saw the introduction and recovery of ethnographic accounts and memoirs that emphasized the fieldwork experience.[2] The 1980s saw a series of critiques of ethnography as a mode of inquiry and as a representational form[3] that transformed ethnography. Ethnography began, and continues to experiment with, different media forms with an emphasis on thick description, reflexivity, and multi-sited research imaginaries. Thick description is the use of detailed accounts to show connections between people, places, and things. Reflexivity refers to narrative strategies, usually involving first-person accounts that place the ethnographer in the ethnography to highlight the ethnographer's subject position. A multi-sited research imaginary explores cultural processes and underlying assumptions by "tracing and describing the connections and relationships among sites previously thought incommensurate."[4]

Fieldwork

"Fieldwork is the central activity of anthropology,"[5] "the ritual initiation experience of the discipline,"[6] and the primary context for the development of ethnography. Obtaining a Ph.D. in Cultural Anthropology without conducting a year or more of fieldwork is rare and often frowned upon by anthropologists. The places where fieldwork is conducted are referred to as field sites, the field, or the site. Upon completion of the Ph.D., the cultural anthropologist maintains contact with and/or returns to their field sites throughout their career. A year as a unit of time emerges out of early cultural anthropologists' attempts to see the entire life cycle (holidays, rituals, seasons, etc.) of a culture. Also, it can take months (and sometimes years) to gain the necessary trust of a group of people to have the access required to understand a culture from within. Depending on their research design, cultural anthropologists often live with and/or are assigned positions among the groups they are following.

Entering the Field

Most ethnography begins with the ethnographer's entry into the field. While this conceit gives the ethnography a certain narrative coherence, it obscures the fact that entry into the field is closer to the end than the beginning of an ethnographic project. Before entering the field, the cultural anthropologist is expected to have conducted a thorough literature review of the people they are preparing to study, as well as potentially applicable theories; visit potential field sites; establish relevant networks; and secure living arrangements. This preliminary work is required for most fieldwork grants. These activities, especially in the context of dissertation research, can take years. At the time of entry into the field, a cultural anthropologist should have a thesis, research topics, contacts, and timeline connected to the application of theoretical and methodological approaches. As mentioned in my conversation with Axel Alonso, once in the field, everything is subject to change.

Being in the Field

Ethnographies are methodologically driven. It literally prioritizes relationships with people over relationships to books and, by extension, theory. Fieldwork will challenge theoretical assumptions. Often, the image of an anthropologist doing fieldwork is of someone who is "hanging out." While there is some truth to this, it is primarily due to the inordinate amount of time spent observing and the downtime between activities and interviews. It is nearly impossible to be embedded among a group of people for years and remain a passive observer. The pressure to participate in activities, ceremonies, rituals, etc. increases over time. Rather than addressing this pressure as a negative aspect or conflict of interest, cultural anthropologists take advantage of opportunities to participate to gain insider knowledge of the workings of a culture. This is referred to as *participant observation*. This type of intense engagement is very much part of the reason that doing fieldwork requires one to lean in the direction of cultural relativism. Gaining trust can also involve becoming complicit in the actions of the group one is researching. An example of this is Clifford Geertz getting caught up in a police raid during a cockfight as the seminal event in his gaining the trust of people he was following.[7]

A lot of insights are gleaned from conversation and everyday interaction. Ethnographic interviews tend to consist of open-ended questions and ideally have a conversational feel. For this reason, it is commonplace for an ethnographer to wait until he or she has built a trusting relationship with the interviewee. Also, the presence of recording equipment and note-taking can impact the answers.

When conducting research, I frequently keep a small notebook or note-taking device with me, and I only pull these out when I am alone between conversations and interviews. Most importantly, I establish clear rules of engagement with my interviewees, which are designed to build trust. I give my interviewees opportunities to review transcripts and declare information off the record after it has been gathered. In many instances I send drafts of my publications to people mentioned in the text to get their perspective. There are times when the interviewees disagree with my comments and/or conclusions, but this is a good thing. In fact, negative and positive feedback has advanced my knowledge by forcing me to reassess my conclusions.

Ultimately, the two most important things about doing an ethnographic research project are to have a firm sense of one's own subject position so as not to impose it on others, and to enter under the assumption that your interviewees are the experts, that you are there to learn, and they are there to teach you. This was made clear to me at the beginning of my research, when I had to acknowledge that several of the people I was following were better read than me in some areas of identity politics and cultural production.

Fieldwork Ethics

Cultural anthropologists operate under a series of ethical guidelines that have different applications for different projects. Cultural anthropologists have an obligation to do no harm to the people who grant access, which includes the release of confidential information. This is a key distinction between cultural anthropology and journalism. Cultural anthropologists are beholden to the people they follow. Journalists are beholden to an abstract notion of truth defined by gathering facts. Cultural anthropologists will negotiate 100 percent access to a group in exchange for limits on what they can reveal. This works because, over the course of a year, an incident that could do harm in its revelation will likely re-occur in a manner that can be revealed without doing harm. Also, in some cases, anthropologists will fictionalize, change the names of individuals, and/or attribute the instance in such a way as to protect the identities of people. Cultural anthropologists commonly find themselves in situations where they have information about multiple members of a group that the group members want access to. Ultimately, the ethical dilemmas contribute to the research because they highlight the values of the group that the anthropologist is following.

SAMPLE ANALYSIS

What follows is an abridged account of four days in September—a discrete period of time. Or is it? My ethnographic research involved prolonged engagement with comic book creators. The formal interviews constituted a relatively small part of my research. Much of my time was consumed by conversations, hanging out, observing, trying to get from person to person or place to place, and waiting. I took notes consisting of interview notes, memorable quotes, observations, reflections, and summaries of discussions. Sometimes in the presence of comic book creators, but mostly when I was alone, bored, at the end of the day, or in transit. While this is an abridged account, it embraces elements of thick description and my multi-sited research imaginary.

September 2000. Day 1. New York City. A gray and black skyscraper sits at the corner of 53rd and Broadway. However, the first thing that one notices upon approaching this rather innocuous black and gray building are the lines of people just across the street waiting for tickets under the familiar blue and yellow marquis of the *David Letterman Show.* It is a relatively busy intersection. So busy, in fact, that it is easy to overlook the four-foot tall Superman cardboard cut-out in the sixth floor window of the gray and black building, the only overt indication that this building contains the headquarters of DC Comics.

As African-American assistant editor Harvey Richards and I approach the lobby, we shuffle past the huddled smokers sitting on the concrete steps. We had just finished lunch and I was heading up with him to his office. We were planning on meeting up with two African-American comic book creators, Alex Simmons and Eric Battle, at Jim Hanley's, a popular NYC comic book shop, and we were going to see if either of them had left a message as to when we were to show up. Harvey was still on the fence as to whether he would be able to meet us. He had a 3:00 p.m. editorial meeting.

As we walked toward the elevators, a familiar figure approached. It was Axel Alonso, then an editor at DC's Vertigo Comics line. Walking fast and looking a bit weary, he didn't notice me. I had tried in vain to contact him before I came up to NYC. I was a bit apprehensive as to why I hadn't heard back from him until my earlier lunch conversation with Harvey. Cuban-American artist, Joe Quesada, had recently been made the new editor-in-chief at Marvel Comics. Apparently, Axel had just been promoted in an attempt to dissuade him from jumping ship to Marvel. Axel was a hot commodity, in part for the recent success of *100 Bullets.* I say "in part" because *100 Bullets* is only the most recent successful project developed by Axel for DC's Vertigo Comics line. In *100 Bullets*—just as in *The Unknown Soldier, The Human Target,* and *Congo Bill*—Axel had created a critical and market success using previously unheard-of talent. While Axel is credited for developing new talent and innovative ideas, I would argue that the essential quality of Axel's talents and ideas are rooted in notions of race and identity that are less a part of Axel's personal politics than his personal experiences.

Axel, a Hispanic male in his mid-thirties, with short salt-and-pepper hair and a goatee, grew up in Northern California, where he got his undergraduate degree from UC Santa Cruz. He didn't always want to do comics; in fact, he fell into it shortly after completing his M.A. in Journalism at Columbia University. Still, he wasn't a stranger to comics, citing *Master of Kung Fu, Luke Cage, Iron Fist*, and *Love & Rockets* as titles that left a lasting impression.

When he came to DC's Vertigo line he was put off by the dominance of gothic, horror, and magical themes. "It was the same thing all over ... there is more to life," he recalled. In essence, Vertigo had become a victim of *Sandman's* success. While as editor it is not his role to actually write or draw the books, he describes his role as akin to a Hollywood producer, picking projects and assembling teams. One of his first moves was to do *The Unknown Soldier* mini-series, with the major theme being an exploration of patriotism, for which he tapped Irish writer Garth Ennis. His next project, *The Human Target*, was all about identity crises, in a story in which the protagonists become other people in the literal and racial sense. For this he chose a Croatian artist. Looking through these works while learning about their creative teams led me to the conclusion that identity in comic books is a multicultural construction.

At the same time, Axel was put off by my suggestion that the work was about any kind of overt identity politics. He likens the "political stuff" to high-concept story elements:

> This comics, it's a genre medium ... it can't be about race, [I] can [however] do high concept stuff as long there are enough explosions ... I don't do this to be political ... there has to be a story that people identify with.

In fact, this statement about genre is realized in his descriptions of his projects. For example, he described *Congo Bill* as *Heart of Darkness*[8] meets contemporary African politics. The story emerged out of conversations with Scott Cunningham over beer. According to Axel, "I had been following the news about Mbutu and the Congo." While Axel and Scott had both read *Heart of Darkness*, Scott's take on the whole Congo Bill idea was influenced by his marriage to a primate anthropologist. Ironically, Congo Bill doesn't appear in the mini-series until the last issue. In separate conversations, Axel and Scott both revealed that the heart of the story is not Congo Bill, so much as Congo Bill was the conduit through which to sell the mini-series internally within DC and market it externally to comic fans.

100 Bullets and the upcoming *Codename: Knockout* were and are (respectively) built on the successes of *The Unknown Soldier, The Human Target*, and *Congo Bill*. If not for the fact that Axel had spearheaded three series based on unused, second-tier, already-established DC characters, it would have been difficult to sell either of these concepts internally. Each of these started with two strikes against them. The first being the fact that they would be creator-owned.

But I digress. As Harvey and I got closer to the elevator, Axel motioned to me. Harvey continued on to the elevator, gesturing to me to give him a call. "Hey Stan," said Axel, "Look man, I'm sorry I haven't gotten back to you but things are totally crazy." Axel continued, giving me the details about the bidding war between DC and Marvel. The stress was written all over his face. "It's a good position to be in but it's still a really hard choice,

100 Bullets is finally on its feet...." He told me that he wasn't sure what he was going to do, but that he had a lot to deal with. We exchanged a few pleasantries and I decided not to go up, instead opting to go to my next appointment.

I have done this trip before. Axel at DC, followed by the five-block walk to the top-floor studio on 47th street that Louis Small Jr., at the time, shared with several other African-American cartoonists. The first time, a moment in which I truly realized how small this industry can be, was also one of my first meetings with Axel. I asked for an example of a project in development. "What are some of your main considerations?" I asked.

He told me about this idea that he had for a book that he described alternatively as "a play on the bad girl books, sort of *Thelma & Louise* meets *My Best Friend's Wedding* meets James Bond." Lots of "T & A" but with a gay sidekick whose T & A is also equally present, "Ally McBond." Axel wanted the book to be written by a gay writer. Robert Rodi, the novelist responsible for *What They Did to Princess Paragon* (1994) and *Fag Hag* (1999), was the writer Axel had in mind for the project. Axel was still trying to figure out who the artist would be; he was looking for someone who was good at drawing women, "someone like Louis Small," he said. Ironically, I planned to visit Louis later that same day. Axel asked me to convey his interest to Louis. A moment of complicity. Louis would eventually be offered and accept the job, which was solicited as *Codename: Knockout*. While Axel already had a firm idea of how they wanted the gay male sidekick to be, he pretty much left the female lead as a blank slate. Still, the general assumption was that she would be White.

At the time, Louis was the regular penciler for *Vampirella*—a comic book that blended horror, heroics, and soft porn. Louis is African-American. Vampirella is an Eastern European woman. Louis' primary artistic sources for Vampirella were mostly Asian, Black, Hispanic, and mixed race women who he recruited.

"When I first started I did Frankenstein women," said Louis in reference to the female forms that he composed from various soft-porn magazines. When he started doing Vampirella he decided that he needed to be able to "really draw women." He started by approaching women on the street, in clubs, and Kinko's. In exchange for allowing him to take nude or partially nude photos of them in his studio or on the roof, he offered them an 8½ × 11 drawing, copies of the photos, and the "honor" of appearing as Vampirella. Some women said yes and some referred friends to him. According to Louis, most of these women had never modeled before. Some have become professional models. Some shared the photos with their partners. Louis' use of models was very much a part of his image among cartoonists and his fans, primarily due to the fact that he also paid some of the models to appear with him at conventions and accompany him to other events.

When Louis drew Vampirella, he did a series of thumbnail sketches that he developed into page layouts. Then he had his models pose in a series of positions, many of which corresponded to the page layouts. Later, he used both the photos and sketches to put together the final product. The result was a Vampirella with body types that shift ever so slightly from panel to panel, between that of the broad hips of his Black and Hispanic models to the slighter frames of their Asian counterparts. Still, Vampirella remained perpetually White on the comic book page.

Louis' initial *Codename: Knockout* sketches were based on a mixed race model. For the purposes of the pitch, Louis created several versions of the character, many of which were either White or racially ambiguous. Axel knew Louis was working from a model so he asked Louis to have her sign a DC Comics model release form. I have heard from multiple sources that many heads turned on the day that Louis brought his model in to sign the paperwork. All of this played a major role in the decision to make the lead female character mixed race.

I took the elevator to the fifteenth floor, got off, and walked the flight of stairs to the sixteenth floor of the building that housed Louis' studio. Pictures of naked and scantily clad models are strewn about Louis' desk, alongside corresponding thumbnail and panel sketches. I let myself in through the unlocked door. Louis is on the phone with a potential model. After Louis got off the phone we chatted on the roof. Our conversation is interrupted several times by gestures from the people in the neighboring building. As I looked toward the building across the street, I realized it was the same backdrop as many of Louis' most revealing photos. After a while, I left for my next meeting.

Jim Hanley's Universe sits just across from the Empire State Building. Eric Battle was already there. Eric got started in the business through Milestone comics, but at the time he was most known as the artist for *Aquaman*, a job that few people would instinctively attribute to a dark-skinned, six-foot-tall, African-American male with dreadlocks. But then, even some of the people on *Aquaman*'s creative team didn't realize they were working with an African-American artist (a story for another time). Eric's anonymity is not entirely uncommon. In fact, there are several comic book professionals lurking amid the comic fans and the wannabe cartoonists that frequent this establishment.

Not much time passed before Alex Simmons arrived. Alex is the writer/creator of *Blackjack* and the soon-to-be-released DC mini-series *Orpheus Rising*. As we meet and greet one another, we are interrupted by a regular African-American customer who knows who Alex is and wants Alex to read and critique a story proposal to be submitted to the Batman books. Eric and I drift away, turning our attention to the new comics. I move through the aisles more quickly than Eric, skipping past many of the DC titles I had already seen this morning when I initially stopped by to meet with Harvey.

Alex, Eric, and I make our purchases and head down the street to grab a bite to eat. I missed a cell phone message while I was on the subway. It's Harvey. Axel resigned at the staff meeting. I'm not surprised. Axel's distance begins to make even more sense. Just as in other publishing and entertainment industries, when someone leaves DC for a competitor they are lucky if they are allowed to stay through the rest of the day, let alone two weeks. It's not personal so much as it is a protective measure, especially in the case of someone like Axel, who is being headhunted as much for his Rolodex as his editorial skills. The first priority of DC will be to contact as many people on Axel's Rolodex as possible in order to prevent them from jumping ship. Axel's first priority will be to beat DC to the punch without letting the word get out.

September 2000. Day 2. Just across the Hudson in Hoboken, NJ. I'm staying the night with Eric Battle. We're both tired and ready to collapse when my cell phone rings. It's Brian Azzerello. Axel introduced me to Azzerello at the 1999 San Diego Comic Con. At the time, *100 Bullets* was about to be released. We had since met up at subsequent San Diego and Chicago Comic Cons, but I had not interviewed him. Eventually, we exchanged information and he told me it was okay to give him a call if I was in Chicago and wanted to talk to him. Now *100 Bullets* was a hot property. I was going to be in Chicago in three days and we were arranging an interview.

September 2000. Day 3. I got home to Baltimore. I realized I wasn't remotely prepared. When I made my plans I hoped to see Robert Rodi and Brian Azzerello. I hadn't heard back from Brian until the night before, and while I was prepared to talk about *100 Bullets*, I wasn't prepared at all to address Axel Alonso's move from DC Vertigo to Marvel. But I didn't really have much time. I was only in Baltimore long enough to catch up on some sleep and change bags. I decided it was better to be rested than prepared, especially since I didn't really know Brian or the implications of a high-profile editor leaving a creator-owned book.

September 2000. Day 4. I was in Chicago with Brian Azzerello at a Starbucks just across from Wrigley Field. Brian is concerned. Brian, a White male, grew up in Cleveland. Brian likes working with Axel because he is "attentive" and they are friends. Axel gave Brian his first break. It's a "low-conflict situation," said Brian. Axel spoke to him about it. Brian was open to working with Axel at Marvel. However, DC wanted Brian to sign an exclusive contract to keep him from working for other companies. Brian could write three books a month. He was already doing *Hellblazer* and *100 Bullets*. DC wanted him to write *The Authority*. If he agreed, he might as well sign an exclusive because he would not have time for much else.

Brian spoke with Eduardo Risso, the artist for *100 Bullets*, the night before our conversation. Eduardo lives in Argentina. He speaks very little English and Brian speaks very little Spanish. "It was a lot of Tarzan talk … me Brian … me Eduardo … you good. Axel leaving … bad." Brian sends the edited scripts to Eduardo, who has them translated, produces the images, and sends or faxes them back to the United States. Axel hired Eduardo after seeing some of his published work. Axel and Brian think that Eduardo does some of the best hip-hop imagery in comics. But there was a breaking-in process. The original sketches for the first issue, according to Axel and Brian, looked like something out of a Michael Jackson video. "We saw the original pictures and immediately scrambled to send Eduardo copies of every hip-hop magazine that we could find! Thank god we got them to him in time to fix the first issue." Brian doesn't like working too much from pop culture. Instead, he prefers to go out on the streets and observe. He showed the Dizzy story to some of the kids who inspired the dialogue and "they got into it and gave me some pointers."

All told, it took about two years to develop and publish *100 Bullets*. According to both Axel and Brian, Axel's ability to sell the idea internally at DC was very much a result of the success of previous non-creator-owned concepts. Once they got the go-ahead, they had to get final approval of the first story arc from Karen Berger. They put forth the Dizzy story because it has a female lead, in part to sell it internally to Karen. The fact that this arc featured a woman of color was more coincidence than design.

So where does Brian fit into this? Where do the ideas come from? Why aren't the characters White guys from Cleveland, Baltimore, or Chicago? Brian immediately eschewed any notion of striving for any type of political statement. According to Brian, "the best stories are in the metro section of the newspaper … what would be the fun of writing people like me? I'd go crazy." On the face of it, *100 Bullets* appears to be a lowest common denominator concept. If you had a gun and 100 untraceable bullets, what would you do with it? Yet, Brian has used this concept in order to present stories about a Hispanic woman just released from jail grappling with the death of her child, interracial grifter couples, a White mother struggling with the reality of her absent runaway daughter, and a Black absentee father meeting up with his delinquent son. All of these stories take place against the backdrop of an international conspiracy—as seen through the eyes of the people Brian observes.

Still, *100 Bullets* is very much a group project. Axel described it to me as a reflection of the world—the seedy side, but a reflection nevertheless. The overarching concept of *100 Bullets* insures the requisite level of action expected in the comics, but the book depends on the writing and a diversity of protagonists in order maintain the reader's interest. Axel likens it to the Black, Brown, and White guys that he plays pick-up basketball with—they have different politics, different ways of speaking, and different lives. They aren't all good or all bad. They just are. And they come together to play the game.

WRITING AND DRAWING CONCLUSIONS

Conceptualizing the comic book production inherently lends itself to thick descriptions and a multi-sited research imaginary. I would argue that the value of ethnography in comics scholarship is its ability to look beyond the writing tablet and drawing board and account for the inspirations, experience, and reference used by individuals as well as the negotiations between individuals of similar and divergent visions. The difficulty of such a task, however, is that the compromises born of negotiation create narratives and images that have multiple reads and contain internal contradictions. An Irishman writes about American patriotism, the *Heart of Darkness* meets *Congo Bill*, a White man protects a Black man by becoming Black himself, *Codename: Knockout*, a White man writing about people not like himself getting away with murder. These stories are not the reflection or by-product of political agendas in a programmatic sense. The flashy colors on paper mask the everyday lives and experiences of creative people. *Congo Bill* is every bit as much about world politics, the wrath of nature, colonialism, pulp adventure, identity, and man as beast. *Codename: Knockout* is every bit as much about challenging the gothic horror aesthetic as it is about gay heroes and heterosexual desire. While the printed news tells many extraordinary tales, we often overlook the ordinary, everyday stories of work and play. We forget that identity is the bedrock of our existence precisely because it is at once lived, imagined, negotiated, and constructed.

The story and ethnographic research continue. While the opening description of my interview with Axel Alonso and my subsequent ethnographic account covers one day in August 2003 and four days in September 2000, it is the thick description and multi-sited research imaginary that uses these five days to reference roughly five years of research. Ethnography that is based on long-term engagements with multiple people and field sites has a way of transcending all of the individual methods that are employed. Still, ethnography is methodologically driven. And the methods employed are oriented toward a single goal—understanding a culture from the inside.

NOTES

1. Andrew Edgar and Peter Segwick, eds., *Key Concepts in Cultural Theory* (New York: Routledge, 1999), 133.
2. Antonius C.G.M. Robben and Jeffrey A. Sluka, eds., *Ethnographic Fieldwork: An Anthropological Reader* (Malden: Blackwell Publishing, 2010).
3. James Clifford, *The Predicament of Culture: Twentieth-Century Ethnography, Literature, and Art* (Cambridge, MA: Harvard University Press, 1988); George Marcus and Michael J. Fischer, *Anthropology as Cultural Critique: An Experimental Moment in the Human Sciences* (Chicago: University of Chicago Press, 1986).

4. George Marcus, *Ethnography through Thick and Thin* (Princeton: Princeton University Press, 1998), 14.
5. Nancy Howell, *Surviving Fieldwork: A Report of the Advisory Panel on Health and Safety in Fieldwork* (Washington, DC: American Anthropological Association, 1990), 4; cited in Antonius Robben and Sluka, *Ethnographic Fieldwork*, 1.
6. Roger Berger, "From Text to (Field)work and Back Again: Theorizing a Post(modern) Ethnography," *Anthropology Quartely* 66 (4) (1993): 174; cited in Robben and Sluka, *Ethnographic Fieldwork*, 1.
7. Clifford Geertz, *The Interpretation of Cultures* (New York: Basic Books, 1973); see also Marcus, *Ethnography through Thick and Thin*.
8. Joseph Conrad, *Heart of Darkness* (New York: W.W. Norton & Company, 1988).

SELECTED BIBLIOGRAPHY

Berger, Roger. "From Text to (Field)work and Back Again: Theorizing a Post(modern) Ethnography." *Anthropology Quarterly* 66 (4) (1993): 174–186.
Clifford, James. *The Predicament of Culture: Twentieth-Century Ethnography, Literature, and Art.* Cambridge, MA: Harvard University Press, 1988.
Conrad, Joseph. *Heart of Darkness.* New York: W.W. Norton & Company, 1988.
Edgar, Andrew and Peter Sedgwick, eds. *Key Concepts in Cultural Theory.* New York: Routledge, 1999.
Geertz, Clifford. *The Interpretation of Cultures.* New York: Basic Books, 1973.
Howell, Nancy. *Surviving Fieldwork: A Report of the Advisory Panel on Health and Safety in Fieldwork.* Washington, DC: American Anthropological Association, 1990.
Marcus, George E. *Ethnography through Thick & Thin.* Princeton: Princeton University Press, 1998.
Marcus, George E. and Michael J. Fischer. *Anthropology as Cultural Critique: An Experimental Moment in the Human Sciences.* Chicago: University of Chicago Press, 1986.
Robben, Antonius C.G.M., and Jeffrey A. Sluka, eds. *Ethnographic Fieldwork: An Anthropological Reader.* Malden: Blackwell Publishing, 2010.
Rodi, Robert. *What They Did to Princess Paragon.* New York: Dutton Ginet, 1994.
Rodi, Robert. *Fag Hag.* New York: Plume Book, 1999.

Though their initial goals arn't primarily politically, the political aspect is there still but less direct and also emphasized by the audience

Why do they deny the connection of language to its political aspect?

13

AUTEUR CRITICISM

The Re-Visionary Works of Alan Moore

Matthew J. Smith

There is a fascination with studying not only the cultural artifacts but also the individual artisans who have created them that cuts across the "nine lively arts." Formal study of any of these art forms is likely to focus attention on the genius of the great talents who defined or refined their respective endeavors: Wolfgang Amadeus Mozart in music, Michelangelo Buonarroti in sculpture, Rembrandt van Rijn in painting, William Shakespeare in literature, Frank Lloyd Wright in architecture, Alvin Ailey in dance, Alfred Hitchcock in film, and Norman Lear in television. As for the "ninth art," comics, there has been a steady growth of interest in the creative persons behind graphic narratives. Such attention was initially in short supply since early comic books were typically published either without attribution or under pen names masking the creators' true identities, but the continuing interest of fans and scholars and the increased reputability of the medium have prompted more frequent auteur studies of comics creators.

An *auteur* (French for *author*) is an individual whose considerable talents distinguish that individual's work from others in the field. The approach comes from film studies and was started by French film critic and director François Truffaut in 1954. Writing in the film studies journal *Cahiers du Cinéma*, Truffaut argued that directors could leave their imprint on the films they made. Such a claim would seem to fly in the face of modern film production, most especially the elaborate Hollywood studio system, where hundreds of individual creators from the screenwriter to the film editor exert some influence over the production process. However, Truffaut and a group of critics that followed him pointed to the distinct styles of directors like Hitchcock. In short, there are qualities about Hitchcock films (e.g., *Psycho, The Birds, North by Northwest*) that separate them from all other films directed by all other directors, most especially those who merely translate a story from screenplay to film. Truffaut's approach to film analysis was later picked up by both British and American film critics, notably Andrew Sarris. Sarris advocated for an analysis of the auteur that examined three key elements: the technical competence or ability of the director; that individual's personal style; and interior meaning rising out of the tension between the director's vision and the other competing production forces (from the studio to the actors) at play in the process. In the decades since formal study of the authorial influence on films began, numerous directors, from pioneers like D.W. Griffith to the eclectic Woody Allen, have been the subjects of scholarly inquiry.[1]

The point of such inquiry is to better understand the medium by understanding those who have exerted significant influence on its development. As the value of such an approach has continued and evolved in decades of film studies, it has been embraced by scholars working in other media, but with some consideration for the difference in production methods. For example, television studies has found that the most influence is wielded by executive producers rather than directors, per se.[2] Thus, the critical lens has turned to influential figures such as Norman Lear (*All in the Family, Sanford and Son*, and *The Jefferson*) and Aaron Spelling (*Charlie's Angels, Beverly Hills 90210*, and *Charmed*). In the comics medium, most attention has focused on the contributions of individual artists such as Jack Kirby (*Captain America, Fantastic Four*, and *The New Gods*), though some writers have been the subjects of study as well, most notably Stan Lee (*Amazing Spider-Man, Incredible Hulk*, and *X-Men*) and Alan Moore (*Watchmen, V for Vendetta*, and *From Hell*). In *The Art of the Comic Book*, comics scholar Robert C. Harvey states that attention should be devoted to those who have mastered the creation of both the words and pictures in concert with one another, creators he labels as "cartoonists."[3] Thus, such figures as Will Eisner (*The Spirit, A Contract with God*, and *The Plot*) and Harvey Kurtzman (*MAD, Two-Fisted Tales*, and *Little Annie Fannie*) should receive the most critical attention. There is, as yet, no clear consensus among comics scholars in agreement with Harvey's position, as individual artists and writers continue to be the dominant focuses of auteur studies, with even some editors (e.g., William Gaines of EC fame) and other contributors coming into focus.

Thus, as with film studies, one of the challenges auteur critics working with comics arts studies face is the problem of comics being produced within an industrial system. Most comic book magazines, trade paperbacks, and graphic novels are produced through a division of labor that separates specialized tasks among a number of professionals: a script writer, a pencil artist, an ink artist, a letterer, a colorist, and an editor, among others. Such specialization allows production to move much more quickly: As the penciler is drawing page three, the inker is inking page two, and the letterer is lettering page one. If the penciler sketches, letters, and inks each and every page, the process takes that individual three times longer. Given how many people are contributing to the process, then, it becomes arguable that in such a collaboration, no single effort rises above the rest. For example, Jack Kirby and Stan Lee both appear to be at their best when the two storytellers worked with one another.

As comics scholar Mark C. Rogers[4] notes, in contrast to the industrial system stands the artisan approach to creating comics. Unlike the specialization utilized in the mass market system, artisans tend to take a lot more of the effort to create a single work upon themselves, handling multiple production tasks individually. This usually means investing a lot more time in producing a single work. Although these works can appear online or even in periodical form, many of the best of these efforts have debuted as standalone graphic novels. Alison Bechdel's *Fun Home* and Craig Thompson's *Blankets* are examples of this more independent approach to comics production.

Today's comics publishers are much more savvy about marketing publications by crediting the creators, much as the rest of the publishing industry has done with novels and other mass market publications. For example, in romance novels, the name of bestseller Nora Roberts is emphasized more prominently than the title of any one of her books. Pick up a recent graphic novel and the name of the writer and artist is likely to be a prominent design feature on the front cover, but the dominant marketing strategy for many of the earliest decades of the comics industry was to sell the characters or the titles that featured them. In this tradition, creators were treated as little more than interchangeable cogs in some publishing machine putting out the monthly adventures of Blue Beetle or Archie Andrews. A few creators were savvy enough to contract that their names appear in the strip, such as Batman creator Bob Kane, but most were never fully recognized for their work. While comic strip artists became household names (e.g., *Peanuts'* Charles Shultz), comic book artists largely continued on in anonymity or, at least, obscurity.

It was the interest of the fan community, though, that prompted increasing attention to these unsung creators. According to comics historian Bill Schelly, from the dawn of organized fandom in the early 1960s, comics' most devoted readers were interested in acknowledging—and meeting—the men and women who had brought their favorite characters and stories to print. Early among these efforts was *Who's Who of American Comic Books*, an initiative put forth by fans Jerry Bails and Hames Ware to create a comprehensive bibliography of those who had contributed to the industry. Fan magazines, or fanzines, also took up the cause of identifying and interviewing those creators, including one that Bails founded titled *Alter-Ego*. In time, more elaborate biographies would occasionally appear, such as Frank Jacob's *The Mad World of William M. Gaines* (1972), and more detailed historic research, such as Trina Robbins' *A Century of Women Cartoonists* (1993). By the turn of the twenty-first century, a wave of biographies, art books, booklength interviews, and appreciations were forthcoming from both start-up and major publishers. TwoMorrows Publishing, for instance, has published *The Jack Kirby Collector* as a periodical since 1994, underscoring both Kirby's enduring legacy and the rising interest in material devoted to comics creators.

In all fairness, while much of the material that has been produced in recent years is lovingly assembled, not all of it has risen to the level of scholarly criticism. Many of the efforts have been disappointingly uncritical in the sense that they provide merely a flattering account of the subject's career. Such efforts have value in focusing attention on the creators, but fail to consider the artist's larger historical and cultural context, assessment of technique that accounts for weaknesses as well as strengths, and the deeper possible meanings found in and among the artist's works. More recent efforts such as Denis Kitchen's *The Art of Harvey Kurtzman* (2009) and Annalisa Di Liddo's *Alan Moore: Comics as Performance, Fiction as Scalpel* (2009) address their subjects with more of the sophistication that one would hope to see in an auteur approach to comics criticism, but much more work is waiting to be done in this vein.

UNDERLYING ASSUMPTIONS

One of the fundamental assumptions of auteur criticism is that individual talent and creative innovation can set one's works apart from everyone else in a given medium for expression. The critic adopting this approach works from a position that superior talent, what some might even call genius, can and does break free from the pack of potential practitioners in a given field of endeavor.

A second assumption guiding this method is that close scrutiny can be revelatory. As detailed below, doing auteur criticism involves considering a lot of material and the presumption is that such an in-depth examination will produce insights that are beyond a cursory or superficial reading of the subject's works.

A third assumption is that auteur criticism is not simply a biography but, indeed, a critique. By this I mean that it is characterized by argument and analysis that goes well beyond simplistic appreciation for the creator's output. The critic makes an argument and uses evidence to build a case for the designation of someone as a distinctively talented figure. Using these assumptions as a foundation, the critic is poised to ask questions about the subject's ability and influence.

Most auteur studies begin with a question about what makes a given figure in the comics medium significant, memorable, or enduring. If, indeed, someone has a lasting career in the field, or has a noticeable influence on those who follow, it is entirely appropriate to question what qualities have made such a lasting impression. The critic wants to understand why the auteur stands out from all others in the field.

APPROPRIATE ARTIFACTS

The focus in auteur studies is on the individuals who create comics, so almost any comics form in any genre is appropriate. However, not every creator is necessarily worthy of such an investigation. Those who have a significant body of work and/or who have exerted a particularly noticeable influence are the most likely subjects for such a project. Those who have produced undistinguished work rarely are the subjects of such analysis. However, since a good part of the finished project relies on the critic making an argument, one might be able to advance a lesser-known talent for consideration as an auteur with a well-constructed case.

PROCEDURES

Auteur criticism seeks to understand an artist's works through close reading of published work and typically through consultation with other records of the subject's life and career.

The first step in auteur criticism is to identify the creative individual and that individual's body of work. This is much easier with today's accessibility to data than it once was. Online references like the Grand Comics Database and numerous fan websites can assist in the compilation of a comprehensive bibliography of the subject's published works.

With the bibliography assembled, the critic then begins to locate and read as much of the creator's *oeuvre*—body of work—as possible. Again, this is easier to do today than ever before. Not only are publishers reprinting many early comics in oversized trade paperback editions (e.g., Marvel's Essentials line or DC's Showcase line), but some publishers have made large portions of their catalogs available through online subscription databases. Even if one cannot read everything ever produced by the auteur, reading as many selections from across the body of work as one can is important for establishing context and development of the individual's talent.

The critic attends to the substance of the works, examining for repeated themes that cut across them and the style that the creator demonstrates. These themes might take into account major issues that the creator deals with time and again, character types that are prominent among works, and genres that the artist works within, among other regularly occurring patterns in the body of work. One thematic apparatus that critics might pick up on is a *motif*. A motif is a symbolic element that repeats itself across works. For example, in the works of Jack Kirby, he regularly depicts futuristic "Kirby-tech" used by his characters (e.g., the Mother Box in *The New Gods*). Along with themes, the critic is also attentive for elements of style that emerge in the works. Style refers to the unique character of how the auteur does what the auteur does. For instance, for Kirby, his depiction of anatomy is often distorted, with most characters having noticeably squared fingertips.

In order to place the works in some context, the critic seeks to understand the auteur's career. Certainly, a straightforward literature search can reveal if previous scholars have already done work on this individual in the academic press, but materials from more popular sources, such as interviews given to the comics press, help provide some insight into the creator's background. If the auteur is still alive, contacting that individual to conduct your own interview could be incredibly helpful. Many creators are accessible and eager to talk about their works. If the auteur has died, though, the critic may be limited to previous documentation created about the figure or commentary from collaborators and family. Diving into other documents (such as letters) may provide unexpected insights into the auteur, but it is not absolutely necessary to get a bead on the person.

The final step is to write up the analysis. There are several possible approaches to this task. One could certainly discuss the development of the auteur in chronological fashion; however, the critic wants to be sure to do more than just re-tell the story of the auteur's life. One might also focus on a particular theme (or several interrelated themes) and connect them to the auteur's works, career, and/or other experiences. The key is to go beyond merely documenting the auteur's existence, as if this were a piece of objective journalism introducing the creator to the world. Rather, auteur criticism seeks to identify the sophistication in a body of work and create a deeper appreciation for the talent that created it.

A final caveat, and an important one, is to avoid guessing what the auteur's intent was in any given situation. Critics call such guesswork about motives the "intentionalist fallacy," and it is frowned upon by academics because it presumes knowledge to the auteur's state of mind that one could not necessarily access from the works alone.[5] The only way to avoid committing this fallacy is to confirm any speculated motives with the creator's own words. Otherwise, it is advisable to avoid such speculation altogether.

SUBJECT OF ANALYSIS

The subject of this auteur analysis is Alan Moore, one of the most highly regarded comics writers of his generation. Over the course of three decades, Moore has produced an oeuvre that is both sizeable and complex. It is far beyond the space constraints of this chapter to account for all of Moore's works or all of their intricacies. Instead, what this section will attempt to do is model a few key applications of auteur analysis, beginning with a brief introduction to the auteur himself.

Moore was born in 1953 in Northampton in the United Kingdom, the first son in a blue-collar family. Like many children of his generation, Moore fell in love with comic books and consumed them voraciously. As an adult, he turned from a number of mundane job prospects to the risky proposition of dedicating his life to producing comics professionally. Although he harbored aspirations to be a cartoonist, Moore realized that he couldn't draw fast enough to produce enough material to support himself and his family and so concentrated his career on writing. After a number of other assignments, his work on two features in the United Kingdom's *Warrior* magazine, "Marvelman" and "V for Vendetta," began to draw the attention of American publishers. In 1983, DC Comics recruited Moore to write *Swamp Thing* and the heretofore languishing title became a critical and financial success. Moore and fellow Briton Dave Gibbons would produce *Watchmen* for the publisher in 1986, but differences over creator's rights later led to Moore's estrangement from DC. For a time Moore began to work outside the superhero genre, initiating projects such as "From Hell" with Eddie Campbell and "Lost Girls" with Melinda Gebbie. However, Moore later returned to superheroes with *1963* for Image Comics, *Supreme* for Awesome Comics, and his own line of comics, America's Best Comics, which included *Tom Strong* and *Promethea*. Since then, most of Moore's work in comic book form has appeared in a series of graphic novels in collaboration with artist Kevin O'Neill under the banner of *The League of Extraordinary Gentlemen*.

Moore's work has been recognized with numerous industry awards, including multiple Eisner, Harvey, Kirby, and Eagle awards. In 2005, the editors of *Time Magazine* issued a list of the "All Time 100 Novels" and Moore's *Watchmen* was the only graphic novel considered among "the best English-language novels from 1923 to present." Moore's work has also been adapted into big-budget Hollywood film productions, mostly without Moore's participation or approval. Still, *From Hell* (2001), *The League of Extraordinary Gentlemen* (2003), *V for Vendetta* (2005), and *Watchmen* (2009) have all done respectable business with film-going audiences, introducing Moore's inventiveness, if not his truest gifts for writing comics, to an even wider audience.

SAMPLE ANALYSIS

One of the compelling reasons that Alan Moore is considered an auteur is his ability to make the most of the medium itself, both in terms of its functions and its contents, in telling stories that are pleasing to his audiences. By this, I mean that Moore does more than merely tell stories that happen to be adapted into comics form, but that he intentionally uses the comics medium to tell stories in a way that would not function coherently in other media. When utilized properly, comics exhibit storytelling properties that make them more than just storyboards for films or novels with illustrations. The blending of words and pictures has the potential to make meaning in unique ways, and it is his skill at interweaving these two set of symbols that distinguishes Moore's work from many others. At the same time, Moore is also exceptionally well read in his medium (and beyond) and brings to bear clever references to earlier comics works in terms of his style. While other creators certainly pay homage to their predecessors, Moore's ability to re-envision this material strikes a balance between being reminiscent and yet original in its execution. These are just two of the elements that distinguish Moore's work.

Moore Working in the Comics Medium

Moore, Alan and Rick Veitch. "How Things Work Out." *Tomorrow Stories* no. 2 (pages 1–8). La Jolla: America's Best Comics, 1999.

The complexity of Alan Moore's use of the medium itself is one of the hallmarks of his creative signature. His ability to interweave a tapestry of plots and subplots, to balance the use of words with imagery to tell the story, and to designate intricate fades back and forth in time using layout are all to his credit. One can certainly see all of these elements play out most vividly in his magnus opus, *Watchmen*, but elements of the same creativity can be identified in lesser-known works as well. For this brief analysis, I focus attention on "How Things Work Out," a story in the "Greyshirt" feature appearing in the second issue of Moore's *Tomorrow Stories* anthology. Greyshirt is a tribute to Will Eisner's "The Spirit," and in the hands of Moore and collaborator Rick Veitch, the feature not only seeks to imitate Eisner's violent crime fighter, but also the creative layouts famously introduced by Eisner in his heyday.

The story is about Sonny, a frustrated musician-turned-janitor, who ends up aiding Greyshirt in taking down building owner and mobster "Spats" Katz following decades of mistreatment at his hands. The eight-page story is laid out with four panels per page. On the first and last pages, the year in which each panel takes place is listed: 1999, 1979, 1959, and 1939 in descending order (Figure 13.1). Each panel also takes place on a different floor of the Katz Building. The story progresses along two axes as one proceeds through the pages. Each "floor" panel moves forward chronologically in its own narrative—that is, the story in 1999 is told in the top panel of each page. But the panels on each page relate to one another, too. As one reads down the page, there is a relationship among those panels as well. For instance, all four panels on the seventh page of the story depict something falling out of a window. Indeed, the relationships among the panels in any given page are reinforced by both the visuals and the wording. In one of Moore's signature transitions, the dialogue of one character in one time or place is mimicked or echoed by a character in a different time or place in the subsequent panel. For instance, in the second panel on page 5 of the story, Sonny is lamenting the end of his dream as a musician, saying, in part, "Just let it all go ..." and in the third panel, 20 years earlier, his father is telling him, "Let it go, Sonny." The effect is a story that, with only 32 panels, manages to develop the character of Sonny as a tragic figure, incorporates conflict between father and son, good guy and bad, and creates anticipation for justice to be meted out to the abusive "Spats."

While most comics writers are content to tell one simple narrative in sequence, Moore pushes the boundaries of what one can do with multiple time frames in a single story. Even when constrained by a short page count as in the "Greyshirt" feature, he experiments with using layout to tell an interconnected story developing over four decades. Indeed, Moore's experimentation with the medium is not limited to this one technique. Examples from across his body of work can be cited as clever means to make use of the form; and as noted previously, Moore also makes use of comics content as well.

Moore as Re-Visionary

Moore, Alan, Steve Bissette, and Dave Gibbons. "When Wakes the War-beast!" *1963 Book Two: No One Escapes ... The Fury!* (pages 1–24). Fullerton, CA: Image Comics, 1993.

One of the most recognizable stylistic markers of Moore's work is his frequent homages to previous comics material—as well as other forms of literature. As a life-long reader of comics, both British and American, Moore frequently demonstrates his considerable familiarity with the medium through his works. The breadth of Moore's homages range

Figure 13.1 Alan Moore and Rick Veitch interweave a narrative through time and space in the "Greyshirt" feature for *Tomorrow Stories* no. 2. Copyright 1999 America's Best Comics, LLC.

from the brash to the subtle. For instance, at one extreme is his work on *Supreme* for Image and later Awesome Comics. Cartoonist Rob Liefeld offered Moore the chance to re-work the Superman knock-off in 1996, and Moore re-envisioned the character as a tribute to 1950s Superman stories. Liefeld had developed the character as a violent power fantasy, but Moore took the character and used him to revisit the charm of the Superman comics that featured a family of familiar characters (e.g., instead of a Lois Lane, Supreme romances Diana Dane), all within the context of a commentary Moore seemed to be making about the need for serial characters to be reinterpreted from itera- tion to iteration by different creators and in different eras. A more subtle example of Moore's ability to pull on the wealth of comics lore at his recollection is "The Black Freighter" sequences in *Watchmen*. While the comic within a comic may be read as simply a foreshadowing of events about to play out in the world of the Watchmen, those familiar with the history of comic books recognize the nod to the notorious EC Comics of the 1950s. After public outage forced publishers to restrain their content, EC, who had published some of the most mature and well-produced comics of their day (such as *Tales from the Crypt* and *Weird Science*), attempted to remain in the comics business by experimenting with titles such as *Piracy*. The title lasted only seven issues, but it must have made a lasting impression on Moore.

Indeed, a cross-section of Moore's work shows a familiarity with and ability to incorp- orate references to the medium. Yet while Moore frequently utilizes this technique, he is not its originator.[6] Indeed, the practice has become an integral part of the superhero genre, and a working knowledge of the relationships and intertextual references found in them seems indispensable to, and a source of cultural capital for, comic book readers.[7]

What's remarkable about Moore's work, though, isn't that he does this with any regu- larity, but how well he does it. Almost any comics writer can slap in a guest star, a flash- back, or a thinly veiled character and invoke such intertextual references for the savvy reader's pleasure. Moore exercises far more care than that. As an example of that care, I point to an issue from his *1963* series published by Image Comics in 1993. At that time, comics heroes had taken a particularly dark turn (e.g., Frank Miller's *Batman: The Dark Knight*), with killer anti-heroes dominating the sales charts. Moore, taking partial responsibility for this turn because of his work in *Watchmen*, sought to comment on the loss of innocence and the need for appreciating a less forlorn conception of the genre.[8] In *1963*, Moore revisits a simpler, more hopeful era by recreating the energy and technique of early Marvel comics. Issues in the parody series offer clever imitations of familiar characters such as the Fantastic Four, Captain America, and, of course, Spider-Man. In the *1963* universe, a teenage hero named The Fury fights crime with a combination of athletic skill and a sharp tongue. Beyond the superficial elements like a blue and red full-body costume and a doting maternal figure, though, the pacing, characterization, and structure are all reminiscent of Stan Lee and Steve Ditko's early Spider-Man stories. Moore's *1963* collaborators on The Fury feature, artists Steve Bissette and Dave Gibbons, even frame the panels of the pages in a fashion that original artist Ditko would, and mimic Ditko's distinctive style within each frame (Figure 13.2). Moore emulates all of the familiar elements of Stan Lee's bombastic storytelling approach, from nicknames for each of the contributors to editor's notes from "Amenable Al" himself.

More than just style, though, the *1963* series emulates the format of an early Marvel comic, too. For example, Stan Lee had created a promotional page of text for each Marvel comic, called "Bullpen Bulletins" that featured an editorial column by Lee, "Stan's

Figure 13.2 Alan Moore, Steve Bissette, and Dave Gibbons capture the look and feel of early Marvel comics, including a character who struggles with inner turmoil in "No One Escapes … The Fury" feature in *1963* no. 2. The Fury™ is trademark of and Copyright 1993, 2010 Stephen R. Bissette, by contractual arrangement with the original co-creator.

Soapbox," which here is mimicked in layout and tone as "Al's Amphitheater." The design is complete with era-specific parody ads (e.g., own your own 1,000-foot long nuclear sub) and even full-page "Sizzlin' Sixty-Three Snap-Shots" recalling "Marvel Masterpieces" splash pages of yore. Even contemporary advertisers like Graphitti Designs offer their ads in the house style to make the imitation complete. With the possible exception of having to pay 195 cents instead of 12 cents, the entirety of the 1993 reading experience was a nearly perfect recreation of the 1963 experience.

Moore goes on to do more of this kind of work, a mixture of imitation, parody, and homage in his *League of Extraordinary Gentlemen* series with Kevin O'Neill, incorporating the most minute details from the characters' histories and even period advertisements. The difference, of course, is that *League* pulls on a rich tapestry of late nineteenth-century novels and other popular fiction. Still, it is Moore's attention to detail and commitment to recreating not just any one layer but multiple layers of authenticity that make his works stand out. While other comic storytellers have certainly attempted to create similar homages,[9] their work lacks the attention to detail evidenced in Moore's efforts, distinguishing his body of work over others.

Why there is such a long list of accolades ascribed to Alan Moore is more readily apparent the closer one examines his works. Whether it is in using the medium's conventions or its contents, Moore proves to be a distinguished creator of comics. While there are certainly weaknesses within his body of work (and a fuller critique would explore those in substantive depth), this analysis has attempted to articulate just what some of the possible aspects are that have contributed to his success in the industry. Reflective readers of his works are likely to discover even more to appreciate in his creative output.

NOTES

1. Pam Cook, ed., *The Cinema Book* (3rd ed.) (London: British Film Institute, 2007), 410–411.
2. Leah Vande Berg, Lawrence Wenner, and Bruce Gronbeck, *Critical Approaches to Television* (2nd ed.) (Boston: Houghton Mifflin, 2004), 235.

3.   Robert C. Harvey, *The Art of the comic Book: An Aesthetic History* (Jackson, MS: University Press of Mississippi, 1996), 26.
4.   Mark C. Rogers, "Understanding Production: The Stylistic Impact of Artisan and Industrial Methods," *The International Journal of Comic Art* 8 (1) (2006): 511.
5.   Vande Berg *et al.*, *Critical Approaches to Television*, 237.
6.   Other commercially successful efforts in this tradition include Kurt Busiek's *Astro City* series and Brian Michael Bendis' *Ultimate Spider-Man*.
7.   Matthew J. Pustz, *Comic Book Culture: Fanboys and True Believers* (Jackson, MS: University Press of Mississippi, 1999), 114.
8.   George Khoury, *The Extraordinary Works of Alan Moore: Indispensable Edition* (Raleigh, NC: TwoMorrows Publishing, 2008), 120.
9.   Kurt Busiek's *Untold Tales of Spider-Man* for Marvel and Mark Waid's *The Silver Age* for DC were other projects that attempted to revisit the storytelling of the 1960s, and though they succeeded in some degrees, their total package was not as inventive or distinctive as Moore's at Image.

SELECTED BIBLIOGRAPHY

Cook, Pam, ed. *The Cinema Book* (3rd edn.). London: British Film Institute, 2007.
Di Liddo, Annalisa. *Alan Moore: Comics as Performance, Fiction as Scalpel*. Jackson, MS: University Press of Mississippi, 2009.
Grand Comics Database. www.comics.org.
Harvey, Robert C. *The Art of the Comic Book: An Aesthetic History*. Jackson, MS: University Press of Mississippi, 1996.
Jacob, Frank. *The Mad World of William M. Gaines*. Secaucus, NJ: Stewart, 1972.
Kitchen, Denis. *The Art of Harvey Kurtzman: The Mad Genius of Comics*. New York: Abrams ComicArts, 2009.
Khoury, George. *The Extraordinary Works of Alan Moore: Indispensable Edition*. Raleigh, NC: TwoMorrows Publishing, 2008.
Pustz, Matthew J. *Comic Book Culture: Fanboys and True Believers*. Jackson, MS: University Press of Mississippi, 1999.
Robbins, Trina. *A Century of Women Cartoonists*. Northampton, MA: Kitchen Sink Press, 1993.
Rogers, Mark C. "Understanding Production: The Stylistic Impact of Artisan and Industrial Methods." *International Journal of Comic Art* 8 (1) (2006): 509–517.
Schelly, Bill. *The Golden Age of Comic Fandom*. Seattle: Hamster Press, 1999.
Truffault, François. "Une Certaine Tendance du Cinéma Français." *Cahiers du Cinéma* 31 (1954): 15–28.
Vande Berg, Leah R., Lawrence A. Wenner, and Bruce E. Gronbeck. *Critical Approaches to Television* (2nd edn.). Boston: Houghton Mifflin, 2004.

14

HISTORY

Discovering the Story of Jerry Siegel and Joe Shuster

Brad J. Ricca

In 1970, artist Jim Steranko released the first volume of *The Steranko History of Comics*, an oversized, illustrated, long-form essay about the origins of the comics medium. In the pages devoted to Superman, Steranko makes an interesting new connection between the character and his two teenaged creators, Jerry Siegel (1914–1996) and Joe Shuster (1914–1992). He writes:

> Superman's creators came from similar backgrounds. Siegel's parents ran a men's furnishing store, barely making a living.... The Shusters had it even tougher.... The secret of Superman's existence, of course, lies deep within the psyche of his creators. Described as "two small, shy, nervous, myopic lads," Siegel and Shuster made the Man of Steel everything they weren't: massive, confident, strong, handsome; a being with perfect reflexes and super vision.[1]

Siegel and Shuster had previously been written about in *Time Magazine*, *The Saturday Evening Post*, and other magazines and books, but only in romanticized strokes about their collaborative young genius. Steranko went further: using quotes, anecdotes, drawings, and other relevant biographical and cultural sources, he offered a revelatory new approach to Superman. Steranko's simple "of course" made a lot of sense. *Steranko's History of Comics*, though devoid of footnotes or peer review, opened the door to understanding comics not through its many colorful characters, but through the long, multifaceted history of the medium itself: in publishing, critical reception, the individual lives of its creators, and the study of cultural sources, to name just a few. The practice of studying comics from this perspective is full of variance in terminology, but its goal is uniform: to better understand comics by examining them as products of public and personal *history*.

There are many ways to read comics through the arc of history. One is the approach of putting comics into *historical context*, or understanding them in terms of the socio-cultural circumstances in which they were created. For example, *Captain America Comics* no. 1 (1941), where Captain America is pictured punching Hitler square on the jaw, is not just another isolated narrative of hero versus villain, but a comment on American pre-war jingoism (see Chapter 9). This approach is the most common means of using historical information to read comics in a way that may open them up to more objective understandings beyond isolated reader-response.

Another critical approach is the study of existing accounts of comics history. This method—understanding how history is written and why—is called *historiography*. This approach is of vital importance to comics scholars who must contend with a patchwork historical record of fanzines, rumor, innuendo, and imaginative creator concoctions. These types of histories need to be critically studied not only to confirm their accounts, but also to determine *bias*: do past histories exhibit personal, political, gender, or class leanings that might diminish their objectivity? No history can be truly objective, but the goal of the historiographer is to identify such factors not only to be aware of bias, but to study its effect, intended or otherwise. Historiography is very important to an evolving understanding of comics; as Charles Hatfield argues, its goal is nothing less than to "[clear] away the limiting assumptions of past scholarship."[2]

Overall, the importance of historical approaches to comics lies in their potential for understanding the material within other contexts. Using history to understand comics helps us to understand the often hard-to-measure range of diffusion of comics into culture, the reader's unconscious, and broader social, political, and even religious arenas. More importantly, it brings a level of discipline to Comics Studies that is perhaps not as standoffish and awkward as theory, and thus more approachable to the beginning scholar.

UNDERLYING ASSUMPTIONS

The main assumption of any historical analysis of comics is that comics do not exist in bubbles or vacuums: they are socio-cultural artifacts that must be studied as products—both physical and ideological—within the timelines and cultures they evolve from. As commercial objects designed for certain audiences and economies, comics offer interesting sites for critical interrogation because they often represent multiple creators, different generations of characters, an outer editorial presence, and various other degrees of influence, including (at times) mandated censorship or other cultural pressures based in gender, class, or race. These are all variables that must be examined and understood within historical contexts. Comics may have been imagined as transient pieces of throwaway entertainment, but the ideas and problems of the culture they reflected most certainly are not. Comics may also be understood through theoretical formalism (e.g., Scott McCloud's *Understanding Comics*), but the comics historian is very wary of the ahistorical nature of such apparatus. The underlying assumption here is that everything must have meaning within a historical context, a meaning that may then be subsequently analyzed by the researcher through *evidence*, whether it be through historical artifacts or close readings of the comics themselves.

A second assumption is that primary historical sources should provide a more objective perspective to understanding any specific work or creator. Because of the various ideological bents of theory, grounding readings in history may provide a less subjective means of understanding comics. For example: a contemporary reading of Wonder

Woman as a feminist icon might be called into question after a close historical inquiry into the circumstances of her creation and early appearances as a rope-binding submissive. Both readings provide a history of the character that invites even more analysis: When did she change? Why?

A third assumption, though perhaps a bit bleak, is also opportunistic for the would-be comics scholar: all existing comics histories should be held in question. Part of the reason behind such a somewhat paranoid approach to historiography is the prevalence of non-peer-reviewed material. This is also a given component of any new, evolving history such as that of comics. The field is fairly young, so any history should be treated as evolving rather than authoritative.

TYPES OF QUESTIONS

Though there are many approaches to dealing with different kinds of historical materials, the central questions of historical analysis should, from a methodological standpoint, remain the same no matter what sort of artifact the scholar considers: What is this? What does it mean? Why? These simple critical questions help the scholar understand the meaning of the historical artifact and why it is (or is not) important to the comic(s) at hand.

The central issue behind all of this interrogation is *reliability*. In many enticing ways, the role of the comics historian is essentially that of detective, collecting evidence and carefully determining its factual relevance to the comics being studied. For the historian, determining the reliability of information is of the utmost importance. Every newly uncovered fact or clue should be, as much as possible, *fact-checked* against other sources. This means that if a creator says in an interview that he or she was influenced by the circus, this should be supported by a similar statement from another source: a peer, a witness, or by an objective artifact such as a receipt, newspaper, or (ideally) an artistic swipe from a circus publication.

Another important question centers around chronological focus, or *when*: Where is the work or creator located along any axis of time, culture, or any other factor determined by the scholar? Creating such an axis—either mentally or physically—is very helpful in keeping evidence straight. A common practice is to use an erasable whiteboard to construct a timeline of events if you are trying to, for example, determine the timeline of the creation of a character. Creating visual, parallel timelines of history and culture can help scholars locate artifacts they may want to look for.

The third question is the central directive behind any critical inquiry: *Why?* Historical analysis is a method of constant hermeneutic scrutiny: Even though the researcher is dealing with supposedly objective information in the form of primary materials and histories, it is up to the researcher to uncover these connections and make sure they are reliable ones. Comics, characters, and creators should be approached as if they were short poems to read closely over a period of many hours: every cape, boot, and spit curl is a line to be examined and wondered over.

PROBLEMS

A primary problem of comics history is also related to reliability—and the lack of it when dealing with information produced and perpetuated by fans. Hatfield clarifies that

One of the challenges facing academics who study comics is this very pool of fan literature, which, besides being of variable quality and trustworthiness, is often of uncertain provenance, tough to find, and just as tough to maintain in research collections.[3]

This is the pitfall of historical research on comics: confusing fact with *nostalgia*. This danger cuts to the scholar as well: Most critical readers of comics are also buying fans, and thus perhaps (unconsciously or not) limited by critical views that are tempered and nudged by uncertainty in the form of nostalgia. For example, a scholar who held an *Uncanny X-men* subscription for the entirety of the 1980s may offer a less than objective opinion of his or her favorite characters. There is undeniable treasure in fan-based work, far more than most academic histories, but it needs to be approached with an eye for expansion and corroboration.

The second major problem facing comics scholars is locating artifacts. John Lent notes of early comics historians that "Researchers had difficulties finding resources; scholarly books and articles on comic art were scarce, as were library comics collections, and access to cartoonists was not easy."[4] Though there are now several comics collections across the world and a variety of internet sources (see subsequent sections), these problems still exist today. Oftentimes, comics historians end up having to buy materials from auctions or eBay. To offset this cost, scholars should look into seeing if their academic libraries would be interested in purchasing the material for their use. A general rule in comics history is that the older the timeframe you are trying to research, the more likely the materials being sought will be in the hands of private collectors and not in public hands. Still, this obstacle should not be completely dissuasive: Many collectors are eager to send photographs and scans of their treasures if they are asked nicely.

A touchy subject is the use of *illegal scans*. This is an ethical question for each scholar to consider, but when researching materials that are completely out-of-print, sometimes scans can be the only way to look at such materials.

A related problem is *ownership*. Even if scans of documents or drawings can be coaxed out of the hands of collectors, who owns them? What can be reprinted? Where and when? These questions are surely beyond this chapter, but always consider claiming *fair use* if the material is not in the public domain. However, you should always seek the advice of your editor or publisher first to determine if they are comfortable with a fair-use claim, which empowers writers to use copyrighted images in focused, specific ways for educational, non-commercial use only.[5]

APPROPRIATE ARTIFACTS

The most prized artifact for the comics historian is the *primary source*, which is broadly defined as materials and evidence that are as close (historically, personally, spatially, ideologically) to the source material as possible. These resources may take a variety of forms, including artist materials (sketches, notes), writer materials (original scripts, diaries, personal letters), legal information (court documents, case evidence), historical documents (newspapers, government documents), personal interviews, visual sources (film, photography), and always the comic itself, which may provide historical clues to its own sources through very close reading. *Secondary resources*, in which others offer their own interpretations of the source material, are also important in order to situate one's own thinking in a way that is a part of an ongoing critical conversation.

In many ways, any artifact is "appropriate" if it can provide a new, reliable reading of the material. For example, Joe Shuster was always quoted in interviews as saying he liked bodybuilding. By researching bodybuilding manuals from the early 1930s (mail-order ones, so that he may have seen them), the scholar can look for artistic similarities between the bodybuilding poses and early depictions of Superman. Like much historical research, there is no assurance of success. Because of this uncertainty, the quest for the primary resource can be very frustrating. But there are many places to look and, with patience, connections can be made.

PROCEDURES

The seemingly never-ending practice of the comics historian is *research*. Because of the nature of comics, historians must be able to research in a four-dimensional manner—laterally across the space of a library (across various disciplines) and through time via primary research resources.

The internet provides many gateways to primary resources: Check your academic or local library for access to other networks of materials (WorldCat), newspaper databases (ProQuest), and genealogical resources (Ancestry). Once you locate the center of your research, explore local county and city archives either in-person or with help from someone on-site. As with any kind of research, breadth is helpful: Browse the stacks, make some calls, take a trip. There are also excellent databases of comics-related material online in a variety of formats, such as www.comicsresearch.org, the Comic Scholars Discussion List, and many excellent fan-created websites. There are also several libraries with especially deep comics collections (and helpful people), including Michigan State University, Bowling Green State University, and Ohio State University. Researchers should also acquaint themselves with the people in their field—not only the academics, but the collectors, creators, and webmasters. It is worth noting, however, that though most peers are very helpful, as with any discipline, comics history is very competitive: good peer collaboration is usually a mix of knowing what to give away and what to hold onto.

Once the primary resource(s) has been identified through a combination of good detective work and luck, it must be critically evaluated to see if it is important to the comic in question: Is there direct evidence showing their connection? This is often a fine line in comics criticism that must be navigated with language and deduction. After enough primary evidence has been found, scholars can construct a *narrative* to help explain the importance of the evidence to the comics being studied. The writer here must be careful to connect rather than invent: The scholar at this stage is writing history and should be very sure that there is evidence to corroborate every important detail. Once confident in the reliability of this narrative, the writer can then present it in a public forum such as the Popular Culture Association or a comics arts conference. Or they could move directly to publication. One of the best things about comics history is that it potentially can reach many shores: Consider sharing it in non-traditional ways and mediums such as a poster, a film, an exhibit, or in a magazine or newspaper. Depending on the scope of your research, consider if you have enough for a book, as many academic and trade publishers are interested in books about comics.

SUBJECT OF ANALYSIS

The subject of my analysis is a study of character doubling and how it relates to historical elements in the early comics work of Jerry Siegel and Joe Shuster. Siegel and Shuster, because they co-created Superman, have always been considered the progenitors of the American superhero. Still, the story as to how they came together and started creating comics, much less Superman, is frustratingly sparse. Until Gerard Jones' *Men Of Tomorrow* (2004) began filling in some of these gaps, the accepted story of Superman's creation was that Jerry Siegel simply woke up one night with the idea in his head. But the single-handed nature of the story (where was Shuster?), as well as an ongoing lawsuit with DC Comics, call this instantaneous burst of creativity into question. In fact, a deep and sustained look at Siegel and Shuster may create a more methodological understanding of how these early comics were made, thus providing a deeper understanding of the very beginnings of the Golden Age.

SAMPLE ANALYSIS

The majority of Golden Age comic books, for a variety of reasons, remain both out-of-print and out-of-reach to most scholars. The early comics of Siegel and Shuster—in *New Fun Comics, New Comics, More Fun Comics, New Adventure Comics*, and *Detective Comics*—are no exception. Though these stories are quite obviously designed around the cultural, social, and economic needs of a juvenile male audience—oftentimes by editors themselves—the early comics of Siegel and Shuster also contain a fairly substantial level of historical—even autobiographical—elements to them, which may lead not only to a

Figure 14.1 Jerry Siegel and Joe Shuster, Glenville High School class photo.

better understanding of certain superhero genre imperatives, but perhaps of Superman himself.

The story of Jerry Siegel and Joe Shuster has become so chiseled into the wall of comic book lore that it has become frustratingly immaculate. The facts are that Jerry Siegel, a nerdy kid with dreams of fame, was born in Cleveland during the Great Depression, where he met Joe Shuster, a would-be artist and fitness buff who shared his love of the weird pulp magazines like *Wonder Stories*. Both Siegel and Shuster worked on the *Glenville Torch*, their high school's award-winning newspaper. Frustrated that the *Torch* editors put a rein on their own submissions, Siegel and Shuster launched their own subscription-only stapled magazine called *Science Fiction*. Five issues in, it folded. Filled with ambition, Siegel instead began to write comics illustrated by Shuster. They were finally published in the new comics magazines such as *More Fun*. Cranking out features like "Dr. Occult," "Radio Squad," "Slam Bradley," and "Spy," Siegel and Shuster began work on an adventure hero named Superman, whose 13-page story they eventually sold for $130–$10 per page.[6]

Much of this background information is well-known to general Superman fans and has been reprinted in a wide variety of books and essays. But what frustrated me as I began my own research into Siegel and Shuster was that none of it was very well documented. As a result, the story of Superman's creators was almost never always the same. So I began to track down some of the primary sources mentioned in these accounts. The best source of material proved to be Glenville High School; I found primary sources in the form of yearbooks, photographs, and copies of the newspaper they worked on, which allowed me to corroborate some of the information on their early attempts at publishing. Instead of taking someone else's word for it, I was able to read the actual articles written by Siegel as a student.

But it was their early comics work that proved much harder to pin down. These stories, commissioned (and in many cases co-created) by Major Malcolm Wheeler Nicholson, are a hodgepodge of genres and fantasies. And they have never been wholly reprinted, which led me to hound collectors for photocopies, purchase older reprint editions, and even hunt down pirated scans. Being able to read these early comics first-hand was again a must, because for all of their immaturity, these comics were perched on the edge of the new format of the comic book. These comics could also help answer the Superman question: How did two untrained young men barely out of high school help invent superhero comics?

As I continued to research both these early comics and their lives at school, I began to recognize some direct personal references. For one, Siegel and Shuster populated their early comics with people they knew. Lois Amster, a pretty girl at Glenville High who would later claim to be the inspiration for Lois Lane, appears in an early "Dr. Occult" where she is referred to as "Mrs. Amster" and is put in the role of fainting damsel (in a provocative dress) to be rescued by the main character. She is helpless to act and can only witness the horrific events from a subservient perspective. Amster motivates the narrative, but she is more of an observer as she drifts in and out of consciousness. This role parallels her real-life presence as someone who was admired from afar, though this time she is the victim, not the presumably lovesick Jerry and Joe. I also realized that Siegel and Shuster were setting their comics in real geographical locales rather than amorphous, fictional cities. "Slam Bradley" takes place in Cleveland, not Metropolis. In "Dr. Occult," very specific settings such as Chardon Cemetery represent local landmarks, which I found by cross-checking names on a city map. Similarly, by reading the local Cleveland newspapers on microfilm during the timeline of their early output, I was also able to spot other parallels in their work. Some such references include a knife-wielding maniac who appears in "Dr. Occult" and mirrors the Torso Murderer who was terrorizing Cleveland in the mid-1930s. Other news references include a Goodyear blimp catching fire out of nearby Akron, a tragedy Siegel and Shuster replicate in a one-page splash for "Spy."

If Siegel and Shuster were seeking to recreate some of their real world—through individualized historical elements as opposed to universally shared knowledge (e.g., what a chair looks like)—the question is whether or not there is a more substantial reason behind it. Another common motif in these early Siegel and Shuster comics that may shed light on their use of personal history is their use of doubling, a motif where characters interact with visually similar versions of themselves. Siegel and Shuster characters constantly look at themselves in mirrors, wrestle seemingly identical twins, and frequently present themselves in transformed or disguised forms. This practice can range from the litany of Slam Bradley clones who constantly spar with one another to the hordes of transforming werewolves and vampires in "Dr. Occult." In Siegel and Shuster comics, these pairings are either identical or grossly differentiated. Slam is idealized, while his sidekick, Shorty, looks like a cartoon—there is no middle ground. The greater the differentiation, the more fantastic the other side becomes. Siegel and Shuster themselves even become Legar and Reuths, adopting pseudonyms so they may add variety to the Major's masthead.

The comics themselves are a doubling of the real world; Siegel and Shuster provide an analogous fantasy reality to their own experiences in which everything is directed toward a positive moral outcome. After all, the main narrative imperative of these early comics—besides the fun and girls—is justice. There is always a wrong to be righted, usually through a combination of detective skill and brutal physical violence. This metaworld is linked to the reader's through proper names and places. Siegel and Shuster are anchoring their fiction in personal history.

A good example of how their process might have worked can be seen in a Slam Bradley story from *Detective Comics* no. 5, titled "Undercover in Grade School." In this story, Slam is assigned a job as an undercover teacher at Glen*dale* school to halt a crime spree. The nods to Siegel and Shuster's important but tumultuous years at Glenville High are bludgeoning in their deployment. Even the principal, Miss Davies, is the same in name and likeness. On the first page of the story, Slam is beating up a bully. It is not Slam conducting the mayhem, is it the fantasizing Jerry, who was slight, unathletic, and according to some interviews, the victim of bullies in high school. The same goes for the main narrative itself, as Slam—strong and handsome—is idolized by the same girls who ignored Jerry.

But Jerry is not Slam, so Siegel balances him out with Shorty (Figure 14.2), Slam's diminutive sidekick who is ignored, inept, and can't climb the ropes in gym class. But he is really funny, which Jerry himself was; he wrote many humorous pieces for the *Torch* as well. Joe, too, makes a brief appearance as a patient student trying to learn about physical fitness, which was, according to interviews I conducted with his sister Jean, his absolute favorite subject. The story ends with Slam getting the girl, who is also based on a real teacher who appears in the Glenville yearbook, *The Olympiad* (she is the youngest and prettiest one). In the Slam story, Siegel takes the role of both the idealized fantasy character and the cowardly, nebbish sidekick: He creates the narrative, but is still an observer of it. Siegel and Shuster portray both sides (to be strong, to be laughed it, to get the girl, and

Figure 14.2 Shorty and Slam Bradley from *Detective Comics* no. 1. Copyright 1937 DC Comics.

not get the girl) to create a narrative that serves both reality and the imagination—this is the genesis of the secret identity.

As with "Mrs. Amster," who is the object of affection but removed from play because of her married status (though the fantasy is that after Occult saves her, that status might change), the comic itself provides room for autobiographical hope. The romantic fantasy is out of practical reach, but easily obtainable through fiction. But what did Siegel and Shuster hope to accomplish with all of these local references, since only their Cleveland audience, and those they went to school with, would get them? Autobiographical history, like any act of recording history, is not a genre so much as a process. As Bart Beaty states: "The distinction between autobiographical and fictional work in contemporary European comics production is revealed as more fluid than defenders of the genre might otherwise claim,"[7] which is an observation that may be extended to American works.

The comics themselves are insistent upon the fact that they have secrets to tell. Breaking the fourth wall in comics does not begin with Ambush Bug or Animal Man, but with "Radio Squad." By inviting readers to join their fan clubs (and having Steve Carson look fans right in the eye in the last panel), these early comics wanted their readers to be in on a kind of real-life secret. Siegel takes things even further when, in an episode of "Federal Men" in *Adventure Comics* no. 14, he places himself in the story in the form of a rascally newsboy named (of course) "Jerry." When the square-jawed hero of the story goes down, it is up to Jerry and his pals (all of them Junior Federal Men Club members) to catch the criminal in a sort of Hal Roach escapade in which they stand in for the adult hero and make things right again. Siegel recognizes the merit in allowing his reader to inhabit one of his characters. This is taken to the next logical step a year later in the form of Clark Kent, who is not only Jerry, but every awkward boy who bought *Action Comics* no. 1. Back in "Federal Men," Jerry is later congratulated by his parents, who look eerily like Siegel's real ones. The Jerry character *is* Siegel, but as a youthful iteration who is physically different (age) and morally and fictionally ideal.

Within this context of characters serving double duty between personal history and imaginative fantasy, *Action Comics* no. 1 can be read as a narrative about truth. Because Superman is so strange, Siegel and Shuster understood that if it were not grounded in the truth, it would not work. This reasoning is probably, partially, why the character was rejected so many times; Superman would make sense on Mongo, but not on Earth. Even Superman's strange powers are explained on page 1 in terms of quasi-scientific terms, not magical ones. The truth is important in *Action Comics*. For one, places are not given fake names and addresses—the action takes place in Cleveland and all the crimes are, unfortunately, real ones at real places. In the final act of his first issue, Superman even goes to Washington, D.C. to stop a corrupt lobbyist. There are no Braniacs or Bizarros in sight.

Superman is inextricably a narrative about self: A strong, alien ideal who must hide behind glasses and ineptitude because he is afraid of his powers and success. In Superman, Siegel self-interprets his life of being ignored by girls who don't really *know* him. Just like Clark Kent's famous glasses, I would argue that Siegel and Shuster's early comics are a clumsy disguise that allows for new, quasi-fictional interpretations of the self. The ongoing debate of Superman's so-called "real" identity is not, then, between Clark or Kal-El, but between Siegel and Shuster, nerd and ideal, all hiding behind Legar and Reuths, Shorty and Slam, and smirking all the while. On his first page, Superman says "I" four times, the last one bold and italicized. As Peter Coogan states, "The identity convention most clearly marks the superhero as different from his predecessors"[8] and this "difference" does not change the truth of history (Siegel and Shuster were ostracized in high school), but just hides and disguises it.

For modern graphic artists and writers, the popular domain of choice is, on the whole, nearly always the self: Will Eisner's *The Dreamer*, Harvey Pekar's serialized *American Splendor*, Art Spiegelman's *Maus*, Craig Thompson's *Blankets*—all of these works default, more or less, to the self as their subject matter. Yet this is rarely, if ever, said of superhero comics. Why? Unlike Eisner and Spiegelman, Siegel and Shuster were flying (or jumping) blind: These were funnies, strips, comics they were dealing with, but they alone seem to be the ones who saw that adding elements of personal truth would deepen their story by linking it to the real. So though the standard superhero imperatives of truth, justice, and strength are all present in these early comics, there are also hidden histories of unrequited love and widely differing self-views. All we need do is look past the glasses.

NOTES

1. James Steranko, *The Steranko History of Comics*, Vol. 1 (Reading, PA: Supergraphics, 1970), 39.
2. Charles Hatfield, "Comic Art, Children's Literature, and the New Comics Studies," *The Lion and the Unicorn* 30 (3) (2006): 370.
3. Hatfield, "Comic Art," 366.
4. John A. Lent, "The Winding, Pot-holed Road of Comic Art Scholarship," *Studies in Comics* 1 (1) (2010): 9.
5. The Duke University Center for the Study of the Public Domain has a very helpful, comic-based explanation of fair-use practices. It is online at www.law.duke.edu/cspd/comics.
6. All of the biographical material here about Siegel and Shuster is from my own research as well as from Gerard Jones' *Men of Tomorrow* (New York: Basic Books, 2004). All of the comics material is out-of-print.
7. Bart Beaty, *Unpopular Culture: Transforming the European Comic Book in the 1990s* (Toronto: University of Toronto Press, 2007), 234.
8. Peter Coogan, *Superhero: The Secret Origin of a Genre* (Austin, TX: MonkeyBrain Books, 2006), 78.

SELECTED BIBLIOGRAPHY

Beaty, Bart. *Unpopular Culture: Transforming the European Comic Book in the 1990s.* Toronto: University of Toronto Press, 2007.

Coogan, Peter. *Superhero: The Secret Origin of a Genre.* Austin, TX: MonkeyBrain Books, 2006.

Hatfield, Charles. "Comic Art, Children's Literature, and the New Comics Studies." *The Lion and the Unicorn* 30 (3) (2006): 370.

Jones, Gerard. *Men of Tomorrow.* New York: Basic Books, 2004.

Kemnitz, Thomas Milton. "The Cartoon as a Historical Source." *Journal of Interdisciplinary History* 4 (1) (1973): 81–93.

Lent, John A. "The Winding, Pot-holed Road of Comic Art Scholarship." *Studies in Comics* 1 (1) (2010): 7–34.

Maroney, Kevin J. "Capes, Types, and Prototypes: A Rumination on Genre." *The New York Review of Science Fiction* 215 (2006): 1, 4–7.

Steranko, James. *The Steranko History of Comics: Vol. 1.* Reading, PA: Supergraphics, 1970.

Part IV

Context

15

Genre

Reconstructing the Superhero in All-Star Superman

Peter Coogan

Who created the superhero genre? That's easy, Jerry Siegel in late 1934 was lying in bed when he was hit with a flash of inspiration. He recalled: "I conceived of a character like Samson, Hercules and all the strong men I've ever heard of rolled into one. Only more so."[1] But that's not right. The Superman he envisioned isn't the one we're familiar with—no cape, no tights, no Clark Kent, no Krypton. Maybe the answer is when he shared his idea with his drawing partner, Joe Shuster, who came up with the visuals. But that's not right because it took another four years for anyone to find out what they had come up with. Maybe it was the publication of *Action Comics* no. 1 (cover date June 1938), which established the primary conventions of the superhero genre—the selfless pro-social mission, superpowers, the codename, the costume, the origin, science-fictional science, and the urban setting. All of these answers fit H.L. Mencken's aphorism, "There is always an easy solution to every human problem—neat, plausible, and wrong."[2]

Siegel and Shuster created the superhero, but Vin Sullivan, an editor at Detective Comics, Inc., (later DC Comics) created the superhero genre in early 1939 when he noticed the success of Superman and asked Bob Kane, "Do you think you could come up with another superhero?"[3] Kane enlisted his friend Bill Finger and together they devised Batman. Sullivan created the superhero genre because, instead of asking for another Superman, he recognized that Superman represented a *kind* of hero rather than a singular creation. That recognition, and the imitation and repetition it caused, gave birth to the superhero genre.

"Genre" is French for "kind" or "genus." The superhero genre is a kind of story, one with specific plots, characters, settings, themes, icons, and effects.[4] What Sullivan saw in Superman, and Kane and Finger produced in Batman, was a *kind* of story, one that could be imitated and reproduced over and over again with variation, but which held constant to certain elements. Imitation and repetition are necessary for a genre to come into existence. If Superman were the only hero with superpowers, a codename, and a costume to have been published, there would be no superhero genre. As Richard Slotkin put it,

"The primary audience for any cultural production in modern society consists of those who do the same work, or who participate in its production, reproduction, marketing, or distribution."[5] This primacy is grounded in the fact that only if culture creators see a character, novel, film, or comic book as worth imitating because of potential sales will they create more offerings for consumers to accept or reject.

But imitation and repetition are important for audiences as well. Unlike literature that imitates life, "It is only in the ultimate sense that the type appeals to its audience's sense of reality; more immediately, it appeals to previous experiences of the type itself; it creates its own field of reference."[6] That is, we understand genre stories by comparing them to other stories of the same genre that we have already seen, not by comparing them to our lived experience, which means that understanding a genre is based in repeated consumption of genre stories.

Both the producers and the audience play a role in genre. Genre can be thought of as a kind of conversation between cultural producers and consumers. A genre has a "specific grammar or system of rules of expression and construction," which operate to provide a "range of expression" for its producers and "range of experience" for its consumers.[7] So genre is a dynamic process of creation that involves give and take between cultural producers and consumers.[8]

The purpose of genre theory is to explain how genre plays out in individual stories, in which meaning is constructed by cultural producers and decoded and read by audiences, whose reactions are taken account of by producers in the creation of new stories. Genre, in this view, is a system of interaction between the producers and audiences of a medium embodied in privileged story forms in which basic social conflicts are narratively animated and resolved.

UNDERLYING ASSUMPTIONS

The first assumption of genre theory is that genre is a *relationship*—between the genre and other genres, individual texts and the genre as a whole, creators and audiences, and the reader and texts—both the individual text being read and the corpus of the genre, as well as other genres and other texts. Genre analysis is often a matter of defining and explaining how one or more of these relationships operates in a specific text.

An important consideration in genre study is to situate the individual text within the history of the genre. Genres evolve through an evolutionary cycle, starting with a *pre-genre* stage before the genre formally comes into being, during which certain characters, motifs, icons, and themes come into existence that later play significant roles in the creation of the genre. The genre proper begins with

> an *experimental* stage, during which its conventions are isolated and established, a *classic* stage, in which the conventions reach their "equilibrium" and are mutually understood by artist and audience, [a stage] of *refinement*, during which certain formal and stylistic details embellish the form, and finally a *baroque* (or "mannerist" or "self-reflexive") stage, when the form and its embellishments are accented to the point where they themselves become the "substance" or "content" of the work[9]

and ending with a *reconstructive* stage, during which the conventions of the genre are reestablished in ways that incorporate an understanding of the genre's completed cycle.

These stages map neatly onto what superhero fans have dubbed the "ages" of superhero comics: Antediluvian Age (pre-genre, 1818–1938), Golden Age (experimental, 1938–1956), Silver Age (classic, 1956–1970), Bronze Age (refinement, 1970–1980), Iron Age (baroque, 1980–2000), and Renaissance Age (reconstruction, 1995–present).[10]

Another concept related to the relationship of the individual text and the genre is *intertextuality*. Genre stories, by their nature, are intertextual—that is, they reference other texts. Standalone superhero stories—like *The Incredibles*—or new series that are disconnected from the continuity of Marvel and DC—like *Astro City*—do not directly connect to other superhero comics, but they draw on the superhero genre and its conventions, and they expect readers to have a familiarity with those conventions. *Reader familiarity* emerges from repeated, sometimes almost ritualistic, encounters with the genre through regular consumption. Reader familiarity is often signaled by a reference to some common genre event, as if it is an inside joke, and the superhero comics fan gets a sense of insider knowledge and feels rewarded for it. *All-Star Superman* opens with a four-panel, eight-word version of the character's origin: "Doomed planet. Desperate scientists. Last hope. Kindly couple" (Figure 15.1). This is Superman's origin stripped to its bare essentials. A reader new to Superman should be able to follow this story of the baby's journey to Earth, but a reader familiar with Superman's origin will immediately fill in the details and will appreciate the economy of the origin's re-telling.

Genre conventions operate in two axes: semantic and syntactic.[11] Semantic conventions compose the content of genre stories: character, setting, and icon. Syntactic conventions concern the structure of the story: plot (narrative structure), point of view, theme, and effect. Most generic identification occurs through semantic elements. In superhero comics these include superheroes, supervillains, and the supporting cast (character); the city, the superhero's headquarters, the alter ego's workplace (setting); the costume, advanced scientific devices (icons). Syntactic conventions structure the narrative and provide thematic unity for the stories. A superhero story that does not involve the hero defeating the villain in a physical confrontation does not feel like a superhero story.

The definition of the superhero, and therefore of the superhero genre, includes both semantic and syntactic conventions:

> **Su•per•he•ro** (soo'per hîr'o) *n., pl.* -roes. A heroic character with a selfless, pro-social mission; with superpowers—extraordinary abilities, advanced technology, or highly developed physical, mental, or mystical skills; who has a superhero identity embodied in a codename and iconic costume, which typically express his biography, character, powers, or origin (transformation from ordinary person to superhero); and who is generically distinct, i.e. can be distinguished from characters of related genres (fantasy, science fiction, detective, etc.) by a preponderance of generic conventions. Often superheroes have dual identities, the ordinary one of which is usually a closely guarded secret.—superheroic, *adj.* Also super hero, super-hero.[12]

The second assumption operating in genre criticism is that genre has a purpose. First, genre is a production tool. It acts as a blueprint that precedes, programs, and patterns industrial production, which helps producers to minimize risk and mass produce their products. It also produces a dialectic of standardization and differentiation. In terms of storytelling, this dialectic operates in the convention/invention balance.

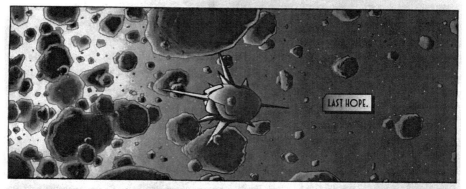

Figure 15.1 Superman's origin. Grant Morrison and Frank Quitely, "Faster," *All-Star Superman* volume 1, chapter 1: 1. Copyright 2008 DC Comics.

This balance connects to two primal human needs—the need for familiarity and the need for novelty.[13] The familiarity need is met through conventional, stereotypical, and even clichéd depictions of plot, character, setting, icon, effect, and theme. Familiar treatments of these conventions help the reader know what they are getting into. Novelty emerges from invention—the depiction of conventions in new and interesting ways. Readers want a certain amount of change and newness in what they read, but not too much. If a story is too conventional, readers will be bored; too inventional and readers will be confused and put off. So the challenge for producers is to balance convention and invention to satisfy both needs.

The social function of genre is a second purpose. There are two basic views of genre among critics and scholars. The first is that genre acts as a system of ideological normalization—as a way of recruiting the mass audience to the goals and ideology of the forces of industrial capitalism that run the culture industries. Usually this is accomplished through stories that depict cultural values as being true and natural. In superhero comics, this is typically done through the villain and his defeat. The second is that genre acts as a form of ritualized collective cultural expression. In this view, genre dramatizes common values and fundamental cultural oppositions that structure a society and narratively animates and ritualistically resolves social problems and inherent cultural tensions.[14] Genre expresses our cultural mythology through narrative, and reconciles binary oppositions that represent irresolvable cultural conflict. Again, in superhero comics the villain represents the method of this dramatization. Villains offer readers a chance to explore and reject tempting but forbidden attitudes and actions, oftentimes culturally positive drives and attitudes that are taken too far.

Genres typically resolve cultural tensions through rites of order and rites of integration. In genre stories, the setting provides an arena for conflict, which is enacted within a community. The characters' identities and narrative roles are determined by their relationship with the community and its value structure. Threats to the social order are represented by physical conflict—whether animated by the antagonist or villain or by the natural forces of the environment—or by a social conflict of attitudes that represent different values. Physical conflict in genre results in the restoration of order, typically through the elimination of the antagonist from the physical setting of the story—in superhero stories this is accomplished by the jailing of the supervillain. Social conflict is resolved through the integration of attitudes within the relationships of the characters— a conflict or argument is resolved.

APPROPRIATE WORKS

Genre criticism is different from other types of analysis because of the view of popular culture studies regarding the inherent literary or artistic qualities of the artifact under study. Genre criticism focuses less on the artistic merit of a single text and more on the relationship between the individual text and the whole body of stories that make up the genre. But the tradition within genre criticism is to examine interesting works that advance the genre by shifting the invention/convention balance more toward the inventional side. Genre scholars often focus on works by auteur creators, who typically have more control over their creations than most of their fellows and are seen by genre critics as artists who can reveal themselves within the confines of industrial cultural production, typically through artistic traits, signature narrative patterns and devices, portrayal of characters and conflict, and other stylistic flourishes that give their body of work a unity lacking in the work of creators with less control.

To produce a valid genre analysis, the reader must have a familiarity with the genre as a whole and the place of the individual text within the genre, as well as some sense of the industrial relations—between creator and publisher, creator and readers, and readers and publisher—that create the context for the production of the individual text. Focusing on the balance of invention and convention can give you a sense of those relationships. The next section lays out a systematic approach for analyzing how convention and invention work within a superhero comic book or graphic novel.

PROCEDURES

Multiple readings are necessary for any critical analysis. The initial reading should just make you familiar with the events and characters of the story. Read it as a reader and just experience the story.

In the second reading you should begin to engage with the text at a deeper level. Note the conventions of the genre—superheroes, supervillains, love interests, the supporting cast, the costumes and superpowers, the settings and equipment, the relationships between hero and villain, dialogue, secret origins, etc.—and see how they are used: Are they treated seriously, humorously, or problematically? Look for structural pairs—events, characters, icons, and settings—that reflect and comment on each other. Identify the ideas about superheroes or society that the conventions seem to point to.

A third reading is often necessary in order to attend to the sequential artistry of the comic book. Too often critics focus on the literary aspects of the storytelling—character portrayals, thematics, point of view—and fail to address the way the sequential artistry—the comics-specific aspects of the storytelling—is used in telling the story and conveying the themes. If you have not read Scott McCloud's *Understanding Comics*, you may want to get a copy, because it is an excellent primer on the grammar and syntax of the comics medium. In the third reading, pay attention to the art style; the panel size, shape, and arrangement of details within the panel; the page layout and panel transitions; the repetition of images; "camera" angles; the on- and off-panel depiction or description of events; the balance of words and pictures; pacing—the number of panels on a page and the relationship of events to the page-turning "reveal"; the presence, location, font, and color of caption boxes, sound effects, and word balloons; the use of color, both the color choices and the choice of the intensity of color; the thickness and thinness of the inking line; and other similar effects produced by the sequential artistry of the artists. All of these effects and techniques affect the way the story is told and experienced, and without paying specific attention to them it is easy to take the sequential artistry of comics for granted and not notice the role it plays in the storytelling. Because most comics critics are not trained in image analysis, it is useful to reserve one reading just to pay attention to the sequential artistry of the comic.

When you have completed these three readings, assemble your notes and try to identify patterns in the story, the use of conventions, and the sequential artistry that lead you to discover the larger thematic concerns of the authors. It can be helpful to situate the book in the genre cycle because of the general tendency of genre works to follow the evolutionary cycle and because it can give you insight into the larger constraints and limitations the authors operated within, as well as the general tendencies of comic books produced at the time the text you are analyzing was published. Next, look for the mediation of structural oppositions—how do the characters represent oppositional attitudes (both semantically and syntactically) and how are these oppositions mediated—through rites of order or rites of integration? Then determine what meaning in the text you are going to examine and how it is constructed—that is, what do you have to say about the story and how does the text support and reveal the points you want to make?

Genre analysis is useful for answering two types of questions. First, what is the comic book saying about society? Is it generally supportive and approving of conventional social mores and values? Or does it critique and question those mores and values? Second, what is it saying about the genre? What attitude does it take toward this history and contemporary presentation of the genre's stories? Does it treat the central concerns of the genre seriously and worthy of consideration? Does it explore the conventions to take them apart or see how they work? The analysis that follows conducts both a social and a genre reading of *All-Star Superman*.

THE ARTIFACT SELECTED FOR ANALYSIS

All-Star Superman is a 12-chapter graphic novel, originally published by DC Comics in installments from 2005 to 2008 as part of the All Star imprint, which was developed to give star creators a chance to experiment with self-contained stories of DC's superheroes outside of continuity.[15] *All-Star Superman* arose from Grant Morrison's take on Superman, as expressed in the "Superman Now" proposal, which was ultimately rejected by DC, but the concepts made their way into other stories, including Morrison's *DC: One Million*, Mark Waid's *Superman: Birthright*, and Mark Millar's *Superman: Red Son*. Morrison has become a leading voice at DC Comics due to his successful revamping of several superheroes and comics series, and he has helmed "event" comics such as *DC: One Million* and *Final Crisis*. As a result of his critical and commercial success, Morrison operates as an auteur, which gives him the freedom to explore and experiment with the genre, resulting in richer, more interesting texts that push the genre envelope and reveal something more about the genre than more formulaic stories.

All-Star Superman covers the final year of the Man of Steel's life. Lex Luthor orchestrates a fatal overdose of solar radiation while Superman is saving Dr. Leo Quintum and his sun-exploration team. Clark Kent interviews Luthor on death row, and Luthor rebuffs Kent's entreaties to change and also introduces him to his pet baboon Leopold, whom he dresses in a Superman suit. With two of his future descendants, Superman visits his own past in disguise to tell Jonathan Kent that his son will grow up to be just fine. Jonathan Kent suffers a fatal heart attack and both the disguised Superman and the young Clark Kent attend the funeral. With his death approaching, Superman completes his to-do list, including relocating Kandor to Mars, cataloging his own DNA, and devising a method of combining human and Kryptonian DNA. Lex Luthor survives his execution with a serum that gives him superpowers for 24 hours; he attacks Metropolis. Superman, who has died, meets his father, Jor-El, in a kind of Kryptonian afterworld, where he is mutating to become solar radio-consciousness. Superman chooses to return to defeat Luthor. Just before his powers expire, Luthor sees the universe as Superman sees it, and Superman knocks him out. With Superman's conversion to pure energy nearly complete, he sets off to save the sun by building a new heart for it. The story closes on Dr. Quintum standing before a door with the Superman chevron with a "2" in place of the "S."

Why choose *All-Star Superman* as an artifact to analyze? Revamping superhero characters has been a mainstay of the genre since the 1980s. *All-Star Superman* sold well—the first two issues ranked number two in sales for their months, with pre-order sales of over 100,000 per issue, and the last issue placed fifteenth for its month, with over 70,000 pre-orders.[16] Critical reception was strong, with both *Time Magazine*[17] and Amazon.com[18] ranking it in the top five for 2007 and 2009, and the series won several industry awards, including the Eisner, the Harvey, and the fan-voted Eagle Award. This combination of commercial, critical, and fan success indicates that the series hit with a wide audience and so reflects their interests in a number of ways. In addition, as a limited series, *All-Star Superman* offers the critic a completed text to examine, which is a useful critical limitation for the purposes of analysis.

SAMPLE ANALYSIS

Genre analysis can be used to look at thematic meaning—the text's message about the human condition—and at its generic meaning—what the text says about the genre. *All-Star Superman*'s theme concerns how we can be better people, and its genre meaning concerns how to make better superhero comics.

The behavioral model of Superman is rooted in Clark Kent, not the bumbling, mild-mannered reporter, but the confident, good-hearted Clark who enacts the philosophy and moral lessons of Jonathan Kent. The first panel of chapter six depicts the sun setting over the Kent farm as Jonathan talks to his son. The sun is the source of Superman's physical power, but his foster father is the source of his moral power; together they combine to make him a superhero. Even his father's death is an important lesson for Clark—he learns he cannot save everyone and that there are limits to his power. Learning that his powers have limits keeps him from overreaching and becoming a tyrant, a lesson Lex Luthor fails to understand. The center of the superhero genre is the dialectic of power and responsibility, encapsulated in Stan Lee's dictum from the origin of Spider-Man: "With great power there must also come great responsibility."[19] At the funeral, Clark sums up the lessons he learned from his father:

> Jonathan Kent taught me that the strong have to stand up for the weak and that bullies don't like being bullied back. He taught me that a good heart was worth more than all the money in the bank. He taught me about life and death. He taught me that the measure of a man lies not in what he says but in what he does. And he showed me by example how to be tough and how to be kind and how to dream of a better world.[20]

Superman puts this philosophy into action through his career as a superhero. He acts specifically as a role model when he saves a teenager from suicide, telling her "You're much stronger than you think you are."[21] Morrison believes that human beings, as opposed to animals, are particularly adaptive, that we have a particular instinct for and ability to imitate what we experience, and that this talent thrusts upon us a responsibility to live up to our ideals.

> Instead of indulging the most brutish, vicious, greedy and ignorant aspects of the human experience, we can, with a little applied effort, elevate the better part of our

natures and work to express those elements through our behavior. To do so would probably make us all feel a whole lot better too. Doing good deeds and making other people happy makes you feel totally brilliant.[22]

Since we "live in our stories," *All-Star Superman* is a way to present a role model for readers to follow to elevate the better part of their selves, to show that we are stronger than we think and can be better than we think.[23]

Structural Oppositions

Lex Luthor and Superman act as a structural pair; each man's behavior comments on the other's, and through contrast convey the theme of becoming better people. Where Superman is the model of responsible use of power, Lex Luthor is the power fantasy gone wrong. Luthor is selfish where Superman is selfless; like all supervillains, he is egotistical and solipsistic. The opposition between the two is set up visually in the first chapter, while Superman is rescuing Leo Quintum's solar expedition (Figure 15.2). Superman is depicted looking in through the round hatch in a blue-inflected background, whereas Luthor is depicted underneath Superman in a rectangular panel with a red tint.[24] Round vs. rectangular, blue vs. red, top vs. bottom—the juxtaposition of these images, which is the heart of sequential art, establishes the oppositional stances of Luthor and Superman.

The hero's journey concerns the transformation of the selfish child into the responsible adult. Superman has completed this journey, which is why his upbringing in Smallville is so central to his superhero career—we see how he was raised and how he enacts his father's values, but we also see him move from his boyhood agrarian home to the larger adult field of Metropolis, with its greater opportunities for meaningful action.

The transformation from selfish, powerless child to responsible adult has to be accompanied by an understanding of how power must be used. In his final empowered moments, Luthor comes to enlightenment, "It's so obvious. I can actually see and hear and feel and taste it and … the fundamental forces are yoked by a single thought." The consequence of this realization is: "It's all just us, in here together. And we're all we've got."[25] But Luthor's realization of the unity of creation does not lead to the transformation of his character. That comes after Superman has departed in order to save the sun. Following the memorial service for Superman, Luthor is described as faded and small now that he has gotten his wish for a world without Superman. Superman's departure does not result from Luthor's victory over him, so Luthor is lost and purposeless. Quintum defines the absence of Superman as "a challenge to human ingenuity," and Quintum himself is the result of Luthor accepting that challenge.[26]

The central figure embodying the theme of *All-Star Superman* is not Superman, but Lex Luthor/Leo Quintum. There are many clues that support the theory that Luthor, in the future of the story, traveled back to the past and created the identity of Leo Quintum in order to atone for his sins. Mythology performs the cultural work of mediating or reconciling cultural tensions, which in genre stories are represented in binary oppositions of convention—character, setting, icon, etc. Mediation is accomplished through rites of order or rites of integration. *All-Star Superman* ends with Luthor in prison—order is restored. But Luthor's transformation into Quintum posits a rite of integration—the supervillain is integrated into the community as a productive scientist.

Figure 15.2 Superman and Lex Luthor. Grant Morrison and Frank Quitely, "Faster," *All-Star Superman* volume 1, chapter 1: 10. Copyright 2008 DC Comics.

Luthor and Quintum are positioned as opposites—Luthor represents the "bad" scientific spirit, using scientific knowledge and advancement for selfish purposes. Quintum represents the "good" scientific spirit—"the rational, enlightened, progressive, utopian" use of knowledge.[27] The connections between the two are subtle, but omnipresent throughout the novel.[28] Luthor and Quintum wear similar coats and clasp their hands behind their back as they walk. Quintum's coat is suggestive of his role as a mediator—Superman's costume is red, yellow, and blue (primary colors), whereas Luthor's supervillain costume is purple and green, and his prison uniform is orange (secondary colors). Quintum's rainbow coat therefore is a clue to his past—secondary colors, as well as an assertion of his present—primary colors. Quintum wears glasses and has hair; Lex is the opposite, but hair and glasses are two primary ways Superman distinguishes himself from Clark Kent. Quintum's name includes clues as well. "Quint" derives from the Latin for the number five. Chapter five of the series focuses on Luthor, whose prison jumpsuit number is 221 ($2 + 2 + 1 = 5$), and which starts with the judge in Luthor's trial reading a list of five of history's greatest villains, with Luthor as the fifth: Attila the Hun, Genghis Khan, Al Capone, Adolf Hitler, and Lex Luthor.[29] Finally—though there are many other clues for the attentive reader—Quintum's name is Leo, a tic-tac-toe inversion of Lex (o is the opposite of x). In his cell, Luthor introduces Clark to his pet baboon Leopold, who is dressed in a Superman costume. If Quintum is Luthor, taking a monkey's name demonstrates that he has humbled himself and reformed. If Quintum is the reformed Luthor then he has also completed the hero's journey and embodies the book's thematic message.

The generic message—that *All-Star Superman* is a model for how to make superhero comics work—locates the book firmly in the reconstructive stage of the genre, the Renaissance Age, the thrust of which has been rebuilding the superhero genre following the darkness of the Iron Age. The cover of the first issue and of the collected trade paperback signals this intent, as do the covers of chapters six and ten. The first cover shows Superman sitting on a cloud above Metropolis (Figure 15.3).

This cover signals to the reader that the book is a kind of idyll for thinking about the meaning of Superman. It differs from most comic book covers, which feature scenes of action drawn from the book. Bright and sunny, the cover promises a positive view of Superman and of the genre as a whole. Superman is shown to be above the fray and on his own—Superman as a special superhero who is not caught up in ordinary concerns. The covers to chapters six and ten (Figures 15.4–15.5) are similar.

Covers are conventions of effect—they are intended to produce an emotional effect upon the reader and to shape the tone or feel of the story. Chapter six's cover shows Superman contemplating his foster father's grave. He is halfway through his hero's journey in the metaphorical land of the dead, so his contemplation of death at night is appropriate. Chapter ten's cover places Superman in a divine role—he has the whole world in his hands. This cover links him and the *All-Star* story with the divine realm of myth. These three covers elevate the series from the action orientation of the rest of the chapter covers and from the genre as a whole to signal that *All-Star Superman* is an extended think piece on the meaning of Superman and the superhero genre.

Morrison and Quitely put down several markers to instruct readers, including other comics creators—remember that genre functions as conversation among creators and between producers and consumers. The first marker is that the whole of the superhero's past should be taken as valid and be made to work. The *Daily Planet* staff portrayed

Figure 15.3 Superman above Metropolis. Grant Morrison and Frank Quitely, *All-Star Superman* volume 1, cover. Copyright 2008 DC Comics.

Figure 15.4 Superman at Jonathan Kent's grave. Grant Morrison and Frank Quitely. "Funeral in Smallville," *All-Star Superman* volume 1, chapter 6: cover. Copyright 2008 DC Comics.

Figure 15.5 Superman holds the world in his hands. Grant Morrison and Frank Quitely. "Neverending," *All-Star Superman* volume 2, chapter 10: Cover. Copyright 2009 DC Comics.

in the story runs the gamut of Superman's history and media. Lois is present from the beginning. Perry White and Jimmy Olsen both come in from the radio program in 1940. The characterization of Jimmy as a young adult who takes on daring assignments touches on his "Action Man" portrayal from the 1970s. The first page of Olsen's focus issue covers his career from the 1940s through the 1960s, showing him as Superman's pal, as an escape artist, in a turtle costume, as the Kandorian superhero Flamebird, closing with him in drag, which references several transvestism stories from this period. Jimmy's transformation into Doomsday connects with many superpowered transformations. Sports reporter Steve Lombard first appeared in the 1970s when Clark Kent transferred to television; gossip columnist Cat Grant debuted in 1987 and appeared as a character on *Lois and Clark: The New Adventures of Superman*; and reporter Ron Troupe, who seems to be the only black man in Metropolis, debuted in 1991. Even a minor character like Luthor's niece Nasthalthia ("Nasty"), who was a minor Supergirl villain in the early 1970s, is a way of referencing the whole of the past and showing that everything in the history of the character can be included.

The second marker is the referencing of specific stories and resonant images. The specific stories that are referenced are two Imaginary Stories written by Jerry Siegel that explored the meaning of Superman.[30] In "The Death of Superman," Luthor successfully poisons Superman with green kryptonite and is tried and sentenced to eternal imprisonment in the Phantom Zone.[31] In "The Amazing Story of Superman-Red and Superman-Blue!" Superman decides to cross several items off his to-do list and so creates a machine that expands his intelligence and splits him into two versions of himself, one with a red costume and the other with a blue one.[32] He enlarges the Bottle City of Kandor and creates and anti-evil ray that rehabilitates Lex Luthor. With the world's problems solved, the Supermen reveal their secret identities to Lois Lane and Lana Lang, marry them, and start families. *All-Star Superman* mirrors the Imaginary Story relation to continuity, and several of the events in *All-Star* imitate or touch on plot points in these two stories.

All these echoes and references to past stories, including many of the sillier aspects of the Superman mythos, point to an all-encompassing attitude toward the character's past and future. No specific bit of lore is off limits, and anything can be rehabilitated and reconstructed to work in a new story. The final panel conveys the generic message directly (Figure 15.6).

Quintum's assistant Agatha asks him what they will do if Superman never returns from his mission to fix the sun. Quintum tells her not to worry, "Now that we know how it's done, I'm sure we'll think of something."[33] Diagetically, Quintum is referring to possessing Superman's DNA and the understanding of how to clone Superman and combine Kryptonian and human DNA to initiate the Superman Dynasty, as demonstrated in various descendants of Superman who have appeared in the story. But metaphorically, Quintum's pronouncement is aimed at other Superman creators. Here he conveys Morrison's message that through *All-Star Superman* he has instructed them how to revamp Superman—Quintum and Morrison have both figured out the formula for Superman and others can follow in their wake.

Figure 15.6 Superman 2. Grant Morrison and Frank Quitely. "Superman in Excelsis,"
All-Star Superman volume 2, chapter 12: 22. Copyright 2009 DC Comics.

NOTES

1. Quoted in Ron Goulart, *Over 50 Years of American Comic Books* (Lincolnwood, IL: Publications International, 1991), 174.
2. Henry Louis Mencken, *Prejudices: Second Series* (New York: Alfred A. Knopf, 1920), 158.
3. Quoted in Will Murray, "Epitaph for Robert Kahn," interview with Bob Kane, *Comic Book Marketplace*, December 1998, 30.
4. In genre theory, an icon is an object with meaning that is specific to a particular genre. In the superhero genre, the most obvious icon is the superhero costume, which signifies the wearer's status as a superhero and announces their identity. A more familiar icon is the use of white hats and black hats in Westerns to

indicate moral standing, i.e. whether the character is a hero or a villain. Effects are the techniques specific to a medium. In comics, effects include drawing and inking styles, covers, coloring, page layout, panel transitions, word balloon font and design, and other aspects of sequential artistry.

5.   Richard Slotkin, *The Fatal Environment: The Myth of the Frontier in the Age of Industrialization, 1800–1890* (Middletown, CT: Wesleyan University Press, 1985), 30–31.

6.   Robert Warshow, *The Immediate Experience* (Garden City, NY: Anchor, 1964), 85.

7.   Thomas Schatz, *Hollywood Genres: Formulas, Filmmaking, and the Studio System* (New York: McGraw-Hill, 1981), 19–21.

8.   Raphaëlle Moine, *Cinema Genre*, trans. Alistair Fox and Hilary Radner (Malden, MA: Blackwell Publishing, 2008), 128; Schatz, *Hollywood Genres*, 38.

9.   Schatz, *Hollywood Genres*, 37–38.

10.   Peter Coogan, *Superhero: The Secret Origin of a Genre* (Austin, TX: MonkeyBrain Books, 2006), 193–194. The Iron and Renaissance Ages overlap because the Iron Age had ended at DC Comics by 1995, but it hung on at Marvel until 2000.

11.   Moine, *Cinema Genre*, 55–59.

12.   Coogan, *Superhero*, 30.

13.   John Cawelti, *Adventure, Mystery, and Romance: Formula Stories as Art and Popular Culture* (Chicago: University of Chicago Press, 1976), 16.

14.   Schatz, *Hollywood Genres*, 29–31.

15.   Continuity is a primary concept of mainstream superhero comics published by Marvel and DC. The basic idea behind continuity is that since all the stories published each month by the comic book companies occur in the same universe, there should be consistency across the company's line regarding the events that occur in it. Since the 1960s, continuity has become a very important element of superhero genre comics.

16.   Figures from monthly sales reports on www.icv2.com.

17.   Lev Grossman, "Top Ten Graphic Novels," *Time Magazine*, December 9, 2007, www.time.com/time/specials/2007/article/0,28804,1686204_1686244_1692109,00.html.

18.   "Best Graphic Novels of 2009," ICv2, December 15, 2009, www.icv2.com/articles/news/16491.html.

19.   Stan Lee and Jack Kirby. "Spider-Man!" *Origins of Marvel Comics* (New York: Simon and Schuster, 1974), 150.

20.   Grant Morrison and Frank Quitely, "Funeral in Smallville," *All-Star Superman*, volume 1 (New York: DC Comics, 2008), chapter 6, 18–19.

21.   Grant Morrison and Frank Quitely, "Neverending," *All-Star Superman*, volume 2 (New York: DC Comics, 2010), chapter 10, 13.

22.   Quoted in Zack Smith, "All Star Memories: Grant Morrison on *All Star Superman*, 6," *Newsarama*, October 28, 2008, www.newsarama.com/comics/100828-Morrison-Superman6.html.

23.   Quoted in Zack Smith, "All Star Memories."

24.   Grant Morrison and Frank Quitely, "Faster," *All-Star Superman*, volume 1 (New York: DC Comics, 2008), chapter 1, 10.

25.   Grant Morrison and Frank Quitely, "Superman in Excelsis," *All-Star Superman*, volume 2 (New York: DC Comics, 2010), chapter 12, 15.

26.   Grant Morrison and Frank Quitely, "Superman in Excelsis," chapter 12, 21.

27.   Grant Morrison, quoted in Zack Smith, "All Star Memories: Grant Morrison on *All Star Superman*, 3," *Newsarama*, October 23 2008, www.newsarama.com/comics/100823-Morrison-Superman3.html.

28.   I am deeply indebted to Neil Shyminsky's blog post "Leo Quintum is Lex Luthor" for the pieces of evidence connecting Luthor and Quintum. Neil Shyminsky, "Leo Quintum is Lex Luthor," *Guilty Displeasures*, September 26, 2008, http://neilshyminsky.blogspot.com/2008/09/leo-quintum-is-lex-luthor.html.

29.   This list is a direct reference to a famous "Imaginary Story" by Jerry Siegel, "The Death of Superman" (Superman no. 149, November 1961). Luthor's "Hall of Heroes" consists of statues of Attila the Hun, Genghis Khan, Captain Kidd, and Al Capone. In this story, Luthor successfully kills Superman with green kryptonite and becomes king of the world, only to be stopped by Supergirl.

30.   Imaginary Stories tell stories that for various reasons could not be depicted within the regular Superman continuity.

31.   Jerry Siegel and Curt Swan, "The Death of Superman," *Superman* no. 149, October 1961.

32.   Jerry Siegel and Kurt Schaffenberger, "The Amazing Story of Superman-Red and Superman-Blue!" *Superman* no. 162, July 1963.

33.   Grant Morrison and Frank Quitely, "Superman in Excelsis," chapter 12, 21–22.

SELECTED BIBLIOGRAPHY

"Best Graphic Novels of 2009." *ICv2*. December 15 2009, www.icv2.com/articles/news/16491.html.

Cawelti, John. *Adventure, Mystery, and Romance: Formula Stories as Art and Popular Culture*. Chicago: University of Chicago Press, 1976.

Coogan, Peter. *Superhero: The Secret Origin of a Genre*. Austin, TX: MonkeyBrain Books, 2006.

Goulart, Ron. *Over 50 Years of American Comic Books*. Lincolnwood, IL: Publications International, 1991.

Grossman, Lev. "Top Ten Graphic Novels." *Time Magazine*. December 9, 2007, www.time.com/time/specials/2007/article/0,28804,1686204_1686244_1692109,00.html.

Lee, Stan and Jack Kirby. "Spider-Man!" *Origins of Marvel Comics*. New York: Simon and Schuster, 1974.

Mencken, Henry Louis. *Prejudices: Second Series*. New York: Alfred A. Knopf, 1920.

Moine, Raphaëlle. *Cinema Genre*. Translated by Alistair Fox and Hilary Radner. Malden, MA: Blackwell Publishing, 2008.

Morrison, Grant and Frank Quitely. *All-Star Superman*, Vol. 1. New York: DC Comics, 2008.

Morrison, Grant and Frank Quitely. *All-Star Superman*, Vol. 2. New York: DC Comics, 2010.

Murray, Will. "Epitaph for Robert Kahn." Interview with Bob Kane. *Comic Book Marketplace*, December (1998): 29–30.

Schatz, Thomas. *Hollywood Genres: Formulas, Filmmaking, and the Studio System*. New York: McGraw-Hill, 1981.

Shyminsky, Neil. "Leo Quintum is Lex Luthor." *Guilty Displeasures*, September 26, 2008, http://neilshyminsky.blogspot.com/2008/09/leo-quintum-is-lex-luthor.html.

Siegel, Jerry and Curt Swan. "The Death of Superman." *Superman* 149, October (1961).

Siegel, Jerry and Kurt Schaffenberger. "The Amazing Story of Superman-Red and Superman-Blue!" *Superman* 162, July (1963).

Slotkin, Richard. *The Fatal Environment: The Myth of the Frontier in the Age of Industrialization, 1800–1890*. Middletown, CT: Wesleyan University Press, 1985.

Smith, Zack. "All Star Memories: Grant Morrison on *All Star Superman*." *Newsarama*. Ten parts. October 21–November 3, 2008, www.newsarama.com/comics/100821-All-Star-Morrison-01.html.

Warshow, Robert. *The Immediate Experience*. Garden City, NY: Anchor, 1964.

16

IDEOLOGY

The Construction of Race and History in Tintin in the Congo

Leonard Rifas

A seemingly ordinary panel in *Marvel Two-in-One* no. 88, from a story featuring The Thing and Savage She-Hulk, has stuck in my memory since I first read it in 1982. A neatly groomed, red-headed, mustachioed man in a disproportionately large gray suit is pushing open the door to his uncluttered private office. While doing so, he gives an order to his secretary, a woman in a magenta turtleneck sweater (and, as seen in the previous panel, matching pants) who is wearing make-up and hoop earrings. She must see to it that he will not be disturbed. The sign on his office door, drawn in unconvincing perspective, identifies their group as "People To Protect Our Environment" (Figure 16.1).

This fictional, Los Angeles-based anti-nuclear group leads the opposition to the "Diablo Reactor" that "Pacific Energy and Utility Corporation" is getting ready to bring online. At the time of its original publication, the topical reference seemed unmistakable. The previous year 1,900 protesters had been arrested at a protest against Pacific Gas and Electric's (PG&E) nuclear power plant, which was nearing completion at Diablo Canyon on the California coast. My response to this superhero comic book was shaped by having participated since 1976 in the movement against PG&E's Diablo Canyon reactors. I was amazed to see that outsiders could misrepresent the anti-nuclear movement in so many ways in a single comic book panel.

The real anti-nuclear movement proposed not only a new energy policy, but also a new way to work for change. Portraying this largely countercultural, eco-feminist, consensus-based, non-violent, volunteer movement as just another organization in which men in suits give orders to women in make-up seems part of a larger pattern of erasing from mainstream entertainment any sympathetic, ready-to-try visions of how society could be organized differently.

Re-reading that comic book story in 2010, I rediscovered the context for the one panel I had remembered. The leader of the anti-nuclear group wanted privacy for a telephone conversation with a supervillain he had been secretly giving the group's money to. "The Negator" had been poisoned by radiation when working as a uranium miner and now, as a

Figure 16.1 Activism represented as though a mainstream business in *Marvel Two-in-One* no. 88, story by David Anthony Kraft and pencil art by Alan Kupperberg. Copyright 1974 Marvel Comics.

supervillain dying of radiation poisoning inside his rocket-powered metal suit, he seeks his revenge by murdering electric utility officials and planning to cause a nuclear power plant disaster which would destroy millions of lives and stop the whole nuclear power industry.

The idea of turning a victim of radiation pollution into a dangerous villain, a criminal madman who must be violently opposed, reminded me of something *Howard the Duck* had done in 1980 with the humorous supervillain "Greedy Killerwatt." I had invented the Greedy Killerwatt character for my own comic book, *All-Atomic Comics*, in 1976 to represent the nuclear power industry. (His name was inspired by the electric utilities' talking-lightbulb cartoon mascot "Reddy Kilowatt.") The writer of *Howard the Duck* borrowed Greedy with my permission and then (to my dismay) created a new origin story for him.

In the *Howard the Duck* version, Greedy Killerwatt began as a man who had been poisoned by radiation while working at the Three Mile Island nuclear power plant and had then mutated into a powerful, living light bulb. The worker renamed himself Greedy Killerwatt, and he planned to cause a meltdown disaster at the North Pole's nuclear power plant and thereby destroy the whole world to gain revenge against those who had mocked his freakish appearance.

Comic books, even fantasy stories, frequently comment on struggles in the real world. How do we recognize and interpret this commentary? How might such stories influence their readers? What forces help to determine which side of a struggle a comic will condemn and which side it will support? *Ideological analysis* interprets comic book stories in terms of where they fit into the larger battles that go on within and between societies.

This chapter will illustrate how an ideological analysis works by using as its main example what seems to have become the most controversial comics-format book ever published, Hergé's *Tintin in the Congo*. An international uproar over this book began in

Figure 16.2 Hergé, *Tintin in the Congo*, translated by Leslie Lonsdale-Cooper and Michael Turner. Copyright 1946, 2006 Casterman, Paris and Tournal.

July 2007, north of London, when human-rights lawyer David Enright, shopping with his young mixed-race children, found a copy of a new edition of this old book on sale in the children's section of a chain bookstore. He reported feeling "aghast to see page after page of representations of black African people as baboons or monkeys, bowing before a white teenager and speaking like retarded children."[1] In response to his complaint, the bookstore moved *Tintin in the Congo* to the graphic novels section. The taxpayer-supported Commission for Racial Equality released a short statement that repeated Enright's concerns. The issue was kept alive when a Swede of Congolese descent, Jean-Dadou Monya and (with greater persistence) a Congolese man in Belgium, Bienvenu Mbutu Mondondo, sued its publishers for violating laws against racist publications. The issue was revived once more when the Brooklyn Public Library responded to a complaint that this Tintin book includes racially offensive images of Africans drawn to look like monkeys by moving the book to their special collections section. Web-posted comments greeted the news that some people had complained about alleged racism in Tintin with a howl of anger against those who had complained.

A bit of background on Tintin helps explain the intensity of the response. Hergé's Tintin stories about a world-traveling boy reporter have been Europe's most influential and widely read comics series, with over 200 million books sold worldwide in more than 50 languages. Two months earlier, Steven Spielberg and Peter Jackson had announced their plans to film three Tintin movies. *Tintin in the Congo*, the second Tintin adventure, was originally serialized in a conservative, Belgian Catholic publication from 1930 to 1931. Hergé's editor had asked him to send Tintin to the Congo to promote Belgium's role in their colony to young readers.[2] Hergé re-wrote and re-drew the story in 1946, and it was the re-publication of this revised edition which David Enright had seen. Hergé (the pen name of cartoonist Georges Remi) was a master of the art of comics, which makes his work especially interesting to read and to study as an ideological statement.

The web-posted comments that defended *Tintin in the Congo* quickly fell into a familiar pattern. Rather than standing up in favor of "racism," people leapt to the defense of "freedom of expression." People argued passionately that if a comic offends you, the simple solution is for you to not look at it. If you complain about an offensive comic, then there's probably something wrong with you personally, rather than with the comic itself. If you persist in trying to *do something* about an offensive comic, then you are guilty of trying to interfere with an artist's right to free expression. In these ways, arguments supposedly raised in favor of complete "freedom of speech" functioned, quite ironically and quite deliberately, as a way to inhibit further discussion about it.

IDEOLOGICAL ANALYSIS

In the popular understanding of the word, *ideology* roughly means "the enemy's false ideas." Anyone who looks for evidence of an "ideology" in the comics that we enjoy as *our own* entertainment, then, becomes instantly guilty of a hostile act. Teun A. van Dijk has devised a different and more rigorous theory of ideology. He sees "ideologies" as composed of three interrelated elements, which he calls "Cognition" (involving some of the systems of ideas that individuals share with other members of their groups), "Society" (referring to the way that these systems of ideas promote a group's interests, for example, in their competitive struggles over scarce resources), and "Discourse" (the words through which these ideas are expressed, shared and taught, and to which we can add images and other nonverbal carriers of meaning).[3]

Stuart Hall has suggested that ideology works by linking ideas together in certain ways and denying or ignoring other kinds of links that might be made. Ideologies, then, like living bodies, are constantly breaking down, being renewed and being repaired.[4] "Ideological struggle" over how to picture the world can be observed in conversations, writings, comic book stories, and in the arguments I make in this chapter.

In the case of *Tintin in the Congo*, first impressions divided sharply between those who thought its racism was obvious and those who thought the idea of calling it racist was absurd. An ideological analysis does not work like a legal case to prove who is right, but brings a clearer understanding of how this comic participates in larger social conflicts. I will argue that the concepts that dominated the first years of the controversies over this book—censorship, effects, and racism—have not provided the most useful tools for understanding this story.

UNDERLYING ASSUMPTIONS

When I describe ideological analysis in this chapter, I am presenting my own, informal version of it. Studies of the ideological content of texts, and especially of comic books, lack a standard, step-by-step methodology.

The most basic assumption of ideological analysis of comics may simply be that the characters, places, and events in fictional comic book stories can *represent* actual people, places, and events. In this way, stories can and often do take sides in actual cases of conflict, with a freedom to twist things around so they conclude in satisfying ways.

Sometimes the comics make such real-world connections directly, using real place names, as when the Belgian character Tintin travels to the Congo. Sometimes the names are slightly disguised, as when the Diablo Canyon Nuclear Power Plant becomes, in a superhero story, the "Diablo Reactor." Even comic book characters that cannot be linked to identifiable, real-world individuals can provide material for examining how comics generally picture the relations between different *categories* of people, such as men and women, whites and blacks, old and young, rich and poor, rulers and ruled, and so forth.

Defenders of *Tintin in the Congo* who deny this first assumption argue (or perhaps merely exclaim) that "it's only a comic book!" and that critics need to back off and respect comics as simply a realm of fun and fantasy. The idea that comics exist in their own off-limits universes from which all analysis, but especially ideological analysis, should be banned fails to recognize that play remains entangled with the real world.

A second assumption holds that comic books and other mass media do not present a simple, consistent "ideological position," but rather an arena in which heroes, villains, and other characters continuously work through issues and conflicts in the form of stories. Some ideas usually come out on top, winning *hegemony*, the status of being accepted without much argument and repeated (or, better yet, assumed) enough times to appear as common sense; "Perpetual war is necessary to defend world peace" would be a contemporary example.

Although defenders of *Tintin in the Congo* raised a strong alarm against "censorship," this idea of hegemony better explains how a bookstore re-shelving a comic from its children's section to its graphic novels section could spark such a sharp international outcry. That act did not make *Tintin in the Congo* less available. That move *did*, however, signal that a book designed to support white power over black Africans would no longer be accepted as ordinary, non-controversial, suitable-for-children entertainment. This sent tremors through the body of common sense assumptions that holds our social arrangements in place.

The idea of hegemony also explains how an even more racially offensive *Tintin in the Congo*, based on the 1931 edition instead of the 1946 edition, could have been republished without incident by Last Gasp just a few years earlier. Because Last Gasp specializes in material for freethinkers and does not sell its comics as children's books, its edition was simply accepted as an early work by a master cartoonist published for a subculture of adult comics fans.

A third assumption states that both children and adults *interpret* stories, instead of passively absorbing their "effects." Ideologies rarely appear in comics as explicitly stated principles, but rather in words and pictures from which readers, consciously and unconsciously, pick up hints for building mental models of how the world works. These models often last a lifetime. Comics can provide some of the most clear, enjoyable, and memorable materials from which we assemble our own personal versions of that body of ideas which we share.

Those who spoke out against *Tintin in the Congo* opposed letting the old idea that Africans resemble apes slip back *into* the status of socially acceptable opinion. Defenders of the comic looked in the opposite direction, by asking whether this book would turn a child into someone whose words and actions would slip *out of* socially acceptable limits. Examples of racist actions that go beyond socially permissible boundaries might include contributing to the rising level of violence against African immigrants in Europe, though I don't recall anyone explicitly making this connection.

A fourth assumption emphasizes that ideology can support domination of one group over another. The ideology of "racism" in the nineteenth century made the domination of white Europeans over the world's non-white peoples appear to reflect a biological hierarchy established by nature, in which blacks held a position between whites and apes. Memories of the horrors which this theory supported make any visual suggestion that blacks resemble apes, baboons, or monkeys scandalous. This kind of biological racism once existed at the height of academic respectability, but survives now only as the most despised of fringe beliefs.

Tintin in the Congo includes many drawings of apes and many of strange-looking Africans. Someone unfamiliar with the history of visual racism might not think to connect them, but these were the kinds of cartoon images of blacks that were popular during the heyday of "scientific racism." Although the complaints have focused on this book as a carrier of this out-of-fashion version of racism, the story works even more effectively as a promoter of a more modern and still "normal" kind of racism.

Modern racism leaves behind biological rationalizations for human inequality, but holds on to the idea of white cultural superiority. This comic supports the idea of white superiority by showing white civilization as superior to Congolese culture in every way.

A fifth assumption, which might seem much too obvious to mention, holds that fictional comic book stories are not documentary accounts of what has actually happened, but artistic creations. One cannot analyze the ideological content of a comic book simply by staring hard at it, but only by seeking out evidence found in history books and other sources to see how the story relates to its larger context. In a surprising number of cases, though, arguments defending the free circulation of *Tintin in the Congo* against censors who would try to eliminate "politically incorrect" material have slipped unconsciously from arguments against destroying historical evidence into arguments which referred to the book *Tintin in the Congo* itself as though it provides reliable information about the history of the Congo.

King Leopold of Belgium's rule over the Congo (which he held as his own personal possession from 1885 to 1908) became such a notorious horror-show that he was forced to surrender control of it. When he turned the colony over to Belgium, he burned the archives of his ironically named "Congo Free State" to destroy the evidence of his crimes.[5] Those who become agitated over the possible loss to "history" of "censoring" this comic fail to recognize that the *actual* documentary history of that place vanished as completely as though it had been sucked down a memory hole in George Orwell's *1984*.

Some claim that comic book content passively reflects the society in which it was made, and so an artist has no personal responsibility for including in stories the dominant assumptions of the period in which the works were created. The irritating foreword in the English-language re-publication, for example, explains that

> In his portrayal of the Belgian Congo, the young Hergé reflects the colonial attitudes of the time. He himself admitted that he depicted African people according to the bourgeois, paternalistic stereotypes of the period—an interpretation that *some* of today's readers *may* find offensive. The same could be said of his treatment of big-game hunting (emphasis added).[6]

Others regard the content of a comic as entirely the consciously intended personal statement of an artist. Both interpret criticism of *Tintin in the Congo* as an unjustified personal attack on Hergé. In the case of *Tintin in the Congo*, Hergé actually did not volunteer to create this book, but was told to do so by his editor, for the propagandistic purpose of providing Belgian children with a story that would make them proud of Belgium's constructive role in the Congo.

Stories include both social assumptions and creators' inventions. Just as we use shared words to speak original sentences, cartoonists use shared ideas to create original stories.

APPROPRIATE WORKS

A work becomes appropriate for an ideological analysis if it can be interpreted as dramatizing a conflict that is going on in the society, such as the recently revived fight between anti-nuclear activists and electric utility executives. Any story that shows relations between characters who represent groups that are tied by unequal power relations in real life can be studied for evidence of whose side the story sympathizes with, even if that story does not portray a conflict between those characters.

A work created under one set of social assumptions, such as Hergé's *Tintin in the Congo*, may find itself closely re-examined decades later in a world in which some assumptions have changed. Defending the comic on the grounds that it was created in a different time misses the point when we are discussing what place that comic will have in our own time.

When analyzing the ideological content of a comic book story, either a major commercial success expressing mainstream ideas or a small-circulation 'zine challenging those ideas can be chosen, as long as we remember to consider how that story fits into its larger context. The social status of the ideas in a story cannot be assumed just because they have appeared in a comic, but must be evaluated by independent evidence. Did the portrayal of a corrupted anti-nuclear group in *Marvel Two-In-One* express the mainstream opinions of its day? The answer requires research. In some periods of their history, Marvel comics have had mass circulation, and in others they have shrunken to a specialty literature read primarily by fans.

PROCEDURES

I recommend as a first step to ideological analysis that you remain (or become) active in some campaign to make the world a bit more fair. That provides a basis of experience for looking at how your particular issues are dramatized, a clearly felt reason to care about these portrayals, an immediate community that may find your analysis useful for your shared work, and something to do while waiting for a new ideologically interesting comic to appear. In addition, you might even win some larger successes. In other words, do not begin with a comic to be analyzed, but with a look at your own position.

This step can be broken into smaller components. As a classroom assignment or on your own, you could begin by writing answers to these difficult questions:

1 What struggles going on in the world seem most important to you? What decisions being made now do you think will have the most consequences 100 or more years in the future?

   Do not limit yourself to choosing between conflicts that have gained attention from the mass media. For example, you might feel that the issue of who owns and controls the industry that produces our news and entertainment (including comic books) has vital consequences for the discourse that appears in them, our cognition (what we know, think, believe, and feel), and on what we can accomplish as a society. This may be the case even if the mass media has never alerted you to the ongoing struggle over how the media will be organized or shown you any attractive possible alternatives to the current system.

2 Do you feel a personal stake in any of the struggles that you listed? The side you support results from your individual choice, and not from whatever social categories (ethnicity, gender, nationality, religion, class, and so forth) have been assigned to you. (People who defended *Tintin in the Congo* sometimes pointed to the popularity of this book in the Congo itself, and some who posted comments defending Tintin identified themselves as black.)

3 Do you believe that participating in a struggle has any possibility of success? Can you name any examples of people winning an important fight to reduce unfairness or promote their common interests?[7] Any recent examples?

   Some people believe they have a chance, however small, of making a positive difference in the world by working together. They try to defend what they would like to preserve and to promote the changes they would like to see. Part of that shared work includes looking critically at how media represent those efforts.

SAMPLE ANALYSIS

Hergé. *Tintin in the Congo*. Translated by Leslie Lonsdale-Cooper and Michael Turner. 1946. London: Egmont, 2006.

When reading a comic as an ideological statement, anything in it that can be interpreted can be used as evidence. To show how this works, I will interpret three incidents from the re-published 1946 edition of *Tintin in the Congo.*

Example One, Pages 19–20

Tintin drives a Model T Ford, with his dog, Snowy, and his Congolese servant-boy, Coco, as his passengers. Coco (and all the other Africans pictured in the story) has clownishly thick lips which extend to the bottom of his face, examples of the caricature tradition associated with blackface minstrel shows. They accidentally become stuck on a railroad track. Before Tintin can get the car unstuck, a train comes down the track and crashes into the car. Comically, the car remains unscratched, but the train is derailed (Figure 16.3).

Photographs confirm that Hergé's pictures were closely based on the actual train that was built to carry the natural wealth of the Congo from the interior plateau to the port, where it could be exported. This railway greatly increased the economic value of Congo's natural resources by making them cheaper to get to market. Rather than bringing prosperity to the Congo, this railroad intensified the scramble for Congo's resources and took the tremendously destructive forced labor system there to peak levels.

The train in the story had been carrying Africans. They are dressed in cast-off European clothing, which they wear in ridiculous ways (for example, a collar, necktie and shirt cuffs but no shirt).

Tintin apologizes to the passengers: "I'm so very sorry!" A Congolese man scolds Tintin as a "Wicked white man" for the damage he has caused, and an angry Congolese woman says, "See what you do to poor, little black boy," pointing to the bump on the boy's head. Throughout this story, characters address and refer to each other in racial terms, as "black" and "white." This bump on the boy's head is the only harm to an African that Tintin or any other white character causes in this story. The trivial nature of this injury is emphasized, considering that in Tintin books characters are hit on the head all the time, and usually lose consciousness. This boy is still on his feet. Thus, the only time this story blames a "white" for harming a "black," we see both that the harm is insignificant and that the blame seems somewhat unfair (because Tintin had already apologized for failing in his attempts to prevent the accident).

The Congolese passengers are too tired, lazy, and afraid of getting dirty to help get the train back onto the tracks. Tintin takes command and shames them into doing the work.

Figure 16.3 The hero is accused of harming a native boy in the Congo. Hergé, *Tintin in the Congo*, translated by Leslie Lonsdale-Cooper and Michael Turner. Copyright 1946, 2006 Casterman, Paris and Tournal.

The stereotype of the lazy black African, like the visual stereotype of the ape-like African, has a special meaning. Historically, the supposed laziness of the natives provided the public rationalization for the forced labor system that enslaved the people of the Congo, and this stereotype justified the atrocities committed against the natives when they failed to produce as much rubber as was demanded of them.

Example Two, Pages 24–27

Because even a simple comic can offer such a dense array of material to be interpreted, a person might easily become lost in contradictory details and lose sight of the larger story. A quick way to gain an overall sense of the political meaning of a story comes by figuring out who the heroes and villains are, and what they represent.

In *Tintin in the Congo*, the enemies of the hero (Tintin), are not the Congolese people in general. Unlike what we would expect from an old-fashioned "racist" story, the natives as a group do not attack Tintin with spears or put him in a cannibal's pot. Instead, they greet him warmly as a celebrity on his arrival, praise him and thank him, and two groups choose him as their leader. The characters who scheme against Tintin are a black witch doctor and white Americans working for Chicago gangster Al Capone.

We know that Muganga, the witch doctor, is the enemy because we overhear him thinking about Tintin: "Little white man getting too big! Soon black people not listen to me, their witch-doctor. I must put finish to little white man." This makes him the story's clearest representative of the principle of African self-determination. We know a white American is a villain because he says "The little white man is my enemy, too. If you want, we'll get rid of him together" (Figure 16.4). The American crooks stand as the clearest representative in the story of other developed countries that might compete with Belgium for the resources of the Congo.

Figure 16.4 The two villains challenge Belgian control over power and resources in the Congo. Hergé, *Tintin in the Congo*, translated by Leslie Lonsdale-Cooper and Michael Turner. Copyright 1946, 2006 Casterman, Paris and Tournal.

The two main villains frame Tintin on the charge of stealing and profaning the village's idol, and the witch doctor condemns Tintin to death. Coco rescues him. Using a phonograph to secretly record their voices and a camera to secretly film their images, Tintin reveals to the villagers that their witch doctor has plotted to keep the people "ignorant and stupid" to hold them in his power, and that the American gangster has defiled their idol. The natives throw their spears at the projected movie images of these villains, and their spears go through the bed sheet hanging on the wall, through the straw wall of that hut, and hit the actual witch doctor and gangster in their butts. As a fun bit of cartooning it works tremendously well, and the lesson that bad rulers' power relies on the ignorance and the superstitions of the people seems valuable, as does the suggestion that people can be harmed by attacking their media images. The story does not suggest, though, that being enlightened in this way puts the natives any closer to self-government.

The gangster and witch doctor flee. The villagers bow down to Tintin and invite him to be their new chief. He accepts.

Example Three, Page 36

On page 36, the missionary who had rescued Tintin from the crocodiles introduces him to their mission: "That's the hospital … And there, the farm school … This is the schoolroom … And there in the middle is our chapel … When we arrived here a year ago this was all bush…" Tintin's dog Snowy responds "Missionaries are the tops!" The missionary looks saintly in a clean ankle-length white robe, and white pith helmet, with a fluffy white beard and a crucifix (Figure 16.5).

This scene, seemingly copied from missionaries' promotional material, provides the heart of the book's argument about why Belgian children should feel proud of their African empire: The whites brought to the Congo health care, education, and the true religion (plus the economic development represented by the railroad and a justice system

Figure 16.5 "Missionaries are the tops!" Hergé, *Tintin in the Congo*, translated by Leslie Lonsdale-Cooper and Michael Turner. Copyright 1946, 2006 Casterman, Paris and Tournal.

and security system, as suggested on other pages). This version leaves out a lot. Rather than improving the people's health, when King Leopold established his rule over the Congo the population fell to half, by eight million or more lives. As for education, when the Congo achieved independence in 1960, it became clear that the Belgians had provided the natives with neither advanced educations nor the practical experience they would need for running a self-governing nation-state.

The Way Things Are

You might, by this point, want to ask of critics of the ideological content of comics, "Well, what did you expect?" Yes, this comic prettifies the history of the Congo, but how could a cartoonist possibly expose horrific conditions in another country and still create a popular, successful, children's comic? Actually, though, Hergé himself, in his first Tintin book, the one immediately before *Tintin in the Congo*, had sent the boy reporter to the recently established Soviet Union, and he showed himself able to expose horrible conditions in a long adventure story that even a child could understand and enjoy. The right-wing paper Hergé drew for opposed the Soviet Union, which made this possible.

Still, you might remain skeptical that a children's comic book story would be able to explain as children's entertainment something as difficult as the relation of racism to socio-economic exploitation. Actually, though, Hergé himself, in his third Tintin book, the one immediately after *Tintin in the Congo*, included a brilliant scene in which Tintin, in America, discovers a huge oil well. The American businessmen swarm around, bidding furiously for the rights to the oil, but when Tintin explains that the oil belongs to the Native Americans whose land it is, the oil men offer the Indians a ridiculously low price and then quickly drive them off their land at bayonet-point.

Even if you concede that in the hands of a great cartoonist, comics could be much better than they are, you might still believe that it does no good to complain. Once again, Hergé's career provides the best counter-example. Tintin book *The Blue Lotus*, his first recognized classic, came about after a fan who had heard that Tintin was planning to go to China wrote a letter encouraging Hergé to avoid the kind of racial stereotyping he had been using, and arranged for him to meet a young Chinese artist as an advisor, a man who would become one of the most important friends of Hergé's life.[8]

For an American, to write critically about an anti-American comic like *Tintin in the Congo* and the evils of King Leopold of Belgium should be only a first step. This nation's own crimes against the Congo deserve closer investigation. For example, the United States generally supported the spectacularly corrupt anti-communist Mobutu Sese Seko's ruinous rule of the Congo from 1965 to 1997. Misery in the Congo continues. America's own "jungle comics" remain largely unexamined.

At the time the uproar over *Tintin in the Congo* started in 2007, the recent Second Congo War had just killed five million people. Those who feared that re-shelving *Tintin in the Congo* or requiring a warning label on it would lead to totalitarian control over information seemed happily unaware of how much news of the world we are already missing.

CONCLUSION

An ideological analysis of a comic provides an interpretation. It does not uncover that comic's one "correct meaning." The historical contexts for understanding the ideological content of a comic cannot be reduced to one true story either. The history books we rely on have their own biases, omissions, and distortions to consider. As a further complication, we most readily accept statements that confirm our preconceptions. Because ideological analysis takes a special interest in critically examining our shared preconceptions, the results of this kind of work can easily remain unconvincing, even when they provide the most coherent account of the evidence. This uncertainty and incompleteness and resistance to revising our beliefs do not make ideological analysis a hopeless project.

People usually study how stories are connected with larger struggles because of a commitment to those larger struggles. Without that larger commitment, such analysis becomes tedious *busywork*. If done simply to support a favored side, however, the result becomes *propaganda*. If done simply to repeat the claims of different sides, the result becomes *stenographic journalism*, a mere record of existing positions with no higher ambitions than to quote accurately, spell names correctly, and to provide a balance between different views. By contrast, an ideological interpretation intended as a work of serious *research* aspires to weaken the grip of harmful illusions wherever they might be found and open a view to greater possibilities.

When an ideology sustains a society that behaves in ways the Earth cannot much longer sustain, we must ask with a personal sense of urgency how ideologies adapt. If we love comics, we can also ask what roles the discourse in and about comics could play in helping us to change our thinking and our society.

NOTES

1. Jack Malvern, "Tintin Book is Crude, Racist and Must Be Banned, Says Watchdog," *The Times*, July 12, 2007, http://entertainment.timesonline.co.uk/tol/arts_and_entertainment/books/children/article2062157.ece.

2. Pierre Assouline, *Hergé: The Man Who Created Tintin* (New York: Oxford University Press, 1996, 2009), 26.

3. Teun A. van Dijk, *Ideology: A Multidisciplinary Approach* (New York: Sage, 1998), 5.

4. The statement from Stuart Hall that I am interpreting here holds that:

   Ideologies do not consist of isolated and separate concepts, but in the articulation of different elements into a distinctive chain of meanings.... One of the ways in which ideological struggle takes place and ideologies are transformed is by articulating the elements differently, thereby producing a different meaning.
   Stuart Hall, "The Whites of Their Eyes: Racist Ideologies and the Media," in *The Media Reader*, ed. Manuel Alvarado and John O. Thompson (London: British Film Institute, 1990), 7–8.

5. Adam Hochschild, King Leopold's Ghost: A Story of Greed, Terror and Heroism in Colonial Africa (New York: Houghton Mifflin, 1998), 290.

6. Leslie Lonsdale-Cooper and Michael Turner, "Foreword," Hergé, *Tintin in the Congo* (London: Egmont, 1946, 2006).

7. The Congo Reform Association, founded in 1904 to publicize terrible conditions in King Leopold's Congo, was formerly credited with having successfully improved conditions for people in the Congo. According to Hochschild, *King Leopold's Ghost*, 277–278, the full story weakens this reputation.

8. Alan Riding, "Chang Chong-Jen, 93, Model for Character in Tintin Comic," *New York Times*, October 10, 1998, www.iht.com/articles/ap/2007/07/12/arts/EU-A-E-BKS-Britain-Tintin.php.

SELECTED BIBLIOGRAPHY

Assouline, Pierre. *Hergé: The Man Who Created Tintin.* New York: Oxford University Press, Inc., 2009.

Duncan, Randy and Matthew J. Smith. *The Power of Comics: History, Form and Culture.* New York: Continuum, 2009.

Hall, Stuart. "The Whites of their Eyes: Racist Ideologies and the Media." In *The Media Reader,* edited by Manuel Alvarado and John O. Thompson, 7–23. London: British Film Institute, 1990.

Hergé. *Tintin in the Congo.* Translated by Leslie Lonsdale Cooper and Michael Turner. 1946. London: Egmont, 2006.

Hochschild, Adam. *King Leopold's Ghost: A Story of Greed, Terror and Heroism in Colonial Africa.* New York: Houghton Mifflin, 1998.

Kraft, David Anthony, Alan Edward Kupperberg, and Charles Eber Stone. *Marvel Two-In-One* no. 88. New York: Marvel Comics Group, 1982.

Mantlo, Bill and Gene Colan. *Howard the Duck II* no. 3. New York: Marvel Comics, 1980.

van Dijk, Teun A. *Ideology: A Multidisciplinary Approach.* New York: Sage, 1998.

17

FEMINISM

Second-wave Feminism in the Pages of Lois Lane

Jennifer K. Stuller

In 1966, the same year that the National Organization for Women (NOW) was founded, DC Comics' *Brave and the Bold* title printed a story called "Revolt of the Super-Chicks" (Figure 17.1), in which Supergirl and Wonder Woman shirk their responsibilities as crime-fighters and run off to Paris to model high-fashion and make out with French men.[1] Even though the "chicks" do return to crime-fighting, the not-so-subtle message is that women are really more interested in romance, shopping and other more tradition-ally gendered pursuits than in heroics.

The feminist movement known as the "second wave of feminism"—a 1960s–1970s women's political movement that addressed real-life women's social issues such as legal and workplace inequalities, sexuality, and reproductive rights—had been in the popular consciousness for several years already, what with the landmark publications of Helen Gurley Brown's *Sex and the Single Girl* (1962), Betty Friedan's *The Feminine Mystique* (1963), and Gloria Steinem's expose on working conditions in Playboy Clubs.[2] Yet while stirrings of feminism had already manifested in popular culture by way of television, a feminist consciousness had yet to reach mainstream comics.[3]

DC's best known female character, other than Wonder Woman or Supergirl, was Lois Lane—a character that predated even Wonder Woman. She received her own comic book title in 1958, and it ran for 137 issues before ending in 1974. *Superman's Girl Friend Lois Lane* was part adventure, part romance, and of course, was written from a man's idea of a woman's perspective. While the series generally detailed Lois' schemes to either convince or trick Superman into marrying her, by the late 1960s the concerns of the women's movement couldn't help but find their way into her comic for better or worse. This was most pronounced in issues 121 and 122 of *Superman's Girl Friend Lois Lane*. These will be analyzed in the second half of this chapter.

Figure 17.1 "Revolt of the Super Chicks," *Brave and the Bold* no. 63, story by Bob Haney, art by John Rosenberger. Copyright 1965 DC Comics.

UNDERLYING ASSUMPTIONS

Feminist analysis can be rooted in a specific school of thought or critical approach. Examples include: Marxist Feminism, Jungian Feminism, Black Feminism or Womanism, Radical Feminism, Transnational Feminism, Ecofeminism, Chicana Feminism, Post-Colonial Feminism, and Postmodern Feminism. These approaches can be further complicated by the application of various lenses such as Queer or Disability studies, theory, or activism.

A more general, yet equally important, method for critiquing the representation of women in popular culture—and for the purposes of this exercise, in comics—involves considering the following in our investigation: How do we look at women? Do we see them as fractured body parts (e.g., breasts, buttocks, legs) or as whole figures? Do we see them as sexual objects for the pleasure of others, or as individuals with agency? How are women represented in popular culture, and what might that say, if anything, about a culture's ideas about gender, femininity, and sex roles at a given point in time? Further, can we determine how our own personal and cultural ideas about gender and sex roles inform our readings?

To make this determination we must consider a number of questions. How are women dressed and how are their bodies positioned? Consider the *male gaze*—a term popularized by Laura Mulvey in her work "Visual Pleasure and Narrative Cinema." The idea of the male gaze is that women are portrayed from a man's point of view, placing the viewer in the position of the male subject, with the female as object—regardless of said viewer's sex. As Andi Zeisler points out, "seeing the visual cues of the male gaze, in turn, affects how women understand images of other women on screen."[4]

Learning how to recognize, understand, and critique these visual cues is essential to our analysis. The bodies of women in mainstream comics tend to be fetishized, receive more focus than their narrative, are shown as parts rather than an active whole (i.e., panels focus on cleavage or derrière rather than a whole body), and are typically drawn in physically impossible positions that manage to display both their breasts and their rear ends. Their bodies are twisted, distorted, and exaggerated. Even a cursory survey of contemporary comic book covers reveals women's faces drawn facing away from the camera, suggesting their passivity in relation to the male protagonist—whose gaze strongly faces the reader.

In recognizing and paying attention to the differences in representations of male and female bodies, we can conclude that the focus on male bodies in comics emphasizes the power of their physique, whereas the focus on female bodies in comics is meant to titillate the presumed male reader, as well as privilege his interests as consumer and audience.

Additionally, make note of the differences in how male and female characters are depicted in action sequences. You will likely find that women are more often drawn in ways that emphasize their bodies as sexual objects—or that the violence itself is of a sexual nature. In fact, depictions of violence enacted against female characters in mainstream comics—rape, torture, kidnapping, disempowerment—is so prolific the trope has a name: Women in Refrigerators (WiR) syndrome. Coined by comic book writer Gail Simone, the term refers to a story in which the Green Lantern's girlfriend, Alexandra DeWitt, was strangled and stuffed in a refrigerator by his nemesis, Major Force.[5] This example reinforces the idea that female characters merely serve as motivation for the hero's journey, rather than as characters of substance in and of themselves.[6] So it's important to ask in our inquiry: In the narrative, is a woman the protagonist, if not, how is she positioned in relation to the main character? Are the women included in the story the nemesis or temptation, the love interest or the damsel, the daughter or mother, the sidekick or spin-off—as in the Supergirl to the Superman? These are more often than not the roles filled by women in comics. They are peripheral to the (presumably heterosexual) male hero and only relevant to the story through their relationship with him. Even when a woman character is intended to be the protagonist of the story—or perhaps, at the very least, on a semi-equal level to the protagonist— WiR syndrome still rears its head, often in extremes. The brutal, highly fetishized depiction of the sexual assault and torture of Batman character Stephanie Brown—a one-time protégée of Batman known as the Spoiler and briefly as Robin—was a particularly gruesome example that inspired an activist campaign from female fans and their male allies.[7]

Another way to assess representations of female characters is to look at how relationships between women are presented. The "Bechdel Test," which originated in Alison Bechdel's comic *Dykes to Watch Out For*, has become a commonly referred to litmus test for the representation of women in movies and television, and it also applies to comic books. Like WiR, the Bechdel Test is a more colloquial than academic term, yet one which proves useful in a critical context. The test requires that the story has:

- two or more women;
- that these women talk to each other; and
- that they talk to each other about something other than men.[8]

This is useful because most stories featuring one or more male characters will have a token female who serves a traditionally feminine, and often less important, role: love interest, damsel in distress, caretaker, family member, or femme fatale.[9]

Also necessary in our feminist analysis is to incorporate elements of *media literacy*, which allows us to analyze and evaluate messages. We must ask: Who is creating and/or producing the text? Can we find, or initiate, interviews with the creative team regarding their intentions?[10] How have the people these texts claimed to represent responded to them? For example, the Diana Prince era of the *Wonder Woman* series (1968–1972, with the creative team of Denny O'Neil, Mike Sekowsky, and Dick Giordano) was meant to reflect the modern woman and the values of the women's liberation movement. And yet notable feminists of the period, including Gloria Steinem and other editors at *Ms.* magazine, felt the character had been de-powered.

We must ask: Who is the intended audience? And we can speculate an answer to this question by researching the advertisements included in a comic book. Is the marketing clearly gender-based? Are the ads directed at boys, girls, women, men? What age range? Do the advertisements within the issue reflect or contradict proclaimed creator intention?

How have audiences' themselves reacted to the artifact? Impressions can be sourced from letter columns in individual issues, as well as from the internet in blogs, articles, and discussion boards.[11] Be sure to also note the writers and audience of each source—a feminist webzine will likely have a different reaction than, say, a male-dominated discussion board. We can take this particular investigation further still by finding out the age range and the location of the respondents. Do 15-year-old males react differently to the presentation of women in comics than a 30-year-old man? What about the response of gay men, many of whom have a fondness for superheroines? What about the differences between female readers in Japan and the United States of America? Remember, there is no single all-encompassing feminism—and therefore no single proper feminist analysis. To reiterate, the ultimate goal is to determine from our artifact how women are represented in popular culture, and what that might say, if anything, about a culture's ideas about gender, femininity, and sex roles at a given point in time. Additionally, we can investigate whether or not the artifact is representative of entertainment media of its day, or if perhaps it has elements that somehow make it progressive, subversive, or even more conservative than its contemporaries.

Since so much of our entertainment, media, and popular culture is produced by men (and also, arguably, film, comics, and video games are in particular marketed with an eye to perceived heterosexual male tastes), it is important to look at how women influence production and reception of culture. Consider the gender of the creator of the artifact. Men and women may write and draw female characters differently. Does this affect how female characters are represented physically or narratively? What about in the character's dialogue and interactions?

Finally, make use of secondary sources. As already noted, an interview with any or all of the creative team on an artifact will provide insight into intent and context for its production.[12] Magazines, articles, blogs, and books of the era will help situate your artifact in the social and political climate in which it was produced. It is not enough in your analysis to say, for example, that Stan Lee and Jack Kirby created superhero teams during the changing political climate of the 1960s, or that the *Wonder Woman* comic underwent a radical transformation that reflected the feminist movement, and expect your audience to know exactly what you mean. You must also provide context by explaining the political climate of the 1960s, the key players, how the comic was influenced by the Cold War, etc., and what the women's liberation movement was, as well as how this change with Wonder Woman both reflected and conflicted with feminist politics.

APPROPRIATE WORKS

Appropriate works for analysis can be anything that proclaims to explicitly attempt to address femininity, feminist politics, female representation, or behavior, as well as those that don't. You'll want to address anything that has a woman character (or women characters), or that talks about women. The objective is to use a feminist consciousness—i.e., an understanding and a critique of the ways that gender (and media representations of gender) construct women's lives, combined with elements of media literacy, in order to evaluate women's representation in comics. The analysis can be of a single issue, a story arc, individual panels, comic strips, or graphic novels. Comparisons and contrasts can be made between different eras, or different authors or illustrators tackling the same property.

PROCEDURES

A summary of possible steps for our approach is as follows. Note that not every step will necessarily be applicable, appropriate or achievable.

- Once you've chosen your artifact, be sure to read it through several times.
- While mainstream comics have rarely been in and of themselves feminist texts, comics are influenced by the culture and politics in which they are produced. Therefore, it may be helpful to consult material of the era in which your artifact was produced, e.g., newspapers, blog posts, magazines, etc., which can provide insight into cultural context. This is especially important if you are evaluating an artifact from a different culture.
- Possibly compare the artifact to others of the era, or of other eras, as part of your evaluation. For example, one could examine William Moulton Marston's original *Wonder Woman* of the 1940s to the more recent *Wonder Woman* written by Gail Simone, or perhaps how DC Comics addressed race in the 1970s as compared to Marvel Comics of the same era.
- Attempt to discern both creative intention and narrative result. For example, how well does a story that attempts to address issues of gender or ethnicity actually reflect the complexity of the issues it confronts. Does it rely on stereotypes?
- Ask questions about how women are presented in the story in relation to male characters. What roles do women play? Are they peripheral characters? Are they used to further the hero's story?
- Make note of how women's bodies are visually represented. What are they wearing? How are they depicted in action sequences—especially in relation to how male bodies are depicted in similar scenes?
- How do women interact with each other? Do they have relationships with other women independently of men?
- Who produced the artifact? How was it marketed? What was the audience response?

Many of these questions can, and should, also be asked about representations of race, class, sexuality, ethnicity, and disability in addition to gender—further complicating a feminist approach.

THE ARTIFACTS SELECTED FOR ANALYSIS

J.P. Williams notes that "analysis of the significance of popular culture in contemporary society requires an understanding of the importance of fictional characters as embodiments of cultural values and concerns."[13] Lois Lane, a character that has been a staple of the Superman mythos since its inception in comics in 1938, has reflected societal attitudes toward women—particularly career women—for over 70 years. This makes her a unique marker of changing American ideas about gender, perhaps even more so than her contemporary, Wonder Woman.[14]

Though the story inside isn't particularly empowering, the cover of *Superman's Girl Friend Lois Lane* no. 80, from January 1968, shows Lois ripping the words "Girl Friend" from her title, suggesting that DC had come to terms with the fact that Lois was indeed something more than that.[15] But it wasn't until 1972 that DC Comics and Lois Lane really embraced the feminist movement in issue 121, which will be analyzed, along with issue 122, below.

Issue 121 begins with a recap of the death of Lois' younger sister, Lucy Lane, from the previous issue. We learn that since then, Lois has been missing for several weeks, and though it appears she has been walking the streets of Metropolis in a daze, no one, not even Superman, seems able to locate her.

When an African-American woman named Julie saves Lois from a mugging attempt, the altruistic act jolts her back to reality. Further, when Lois discovers that Julie's parents have fallen prey to a retirement scheme that has left them missing, she has a rare moment of self-awareness thinking:

> I'm so ashamed of myself! For weeks, I've been carrying on like I'm the only one in this world who suffered a terrible loss! Julie's sick with worry! But she still had time to help me out.... It's time I started taking a good look at this muddled world around me and tried to help people in trouble. Like Julie!

Lois decides she needs to help her new friend, and additionally, it seems the opportunity to use her skills as a reporter once again gives her a sense of purpose. But Lois, in coming out of her grief, has decided to approach her career differently.

Wanting to do more with her life than take assignments dictated to her by editor-in-chief Perry White, she decides to use her career to help others, and perhaps make a difference in honor of her sister. She quits the *Daily Planet* to become a freelance journalist and thus determine what she writes about on her own terms—both a declaration of her independence and a commitment to devoting herself to social justice issues.

Leaving behind a full-time steady paycheck, Lois gives up her luxury apartment and moves into an apartment building for singles with three other women. Julie, an overweight woman named Marsha Mallow, and a woman named Kristin who claims she is easy to live with and keeps to herself. In the meantime, she also quasi-breaks up with Superman, telling him that though she loves him, she doesn't want to live in his shadow and that she needs to live her own life. (He, of course, continues to rescue Lois from her trademark habit of getting in over her head.)

Lois infiltrates a retirement scheme by posing as an elderly woman interested in teaming up with the villainous man who runs the racket. He recognizes her as Lois Lane, "that snoopy reporter," and tries to kill her. Superman arrives just in time, saves Lois, as well as the elderly that were taken advantage of. Lois reports on the scam for the *Daily Planet*, and Perry White believes that working freelance will make Lois a better reporter.

In issue 122, Lois investigates the workings of the mob-like organization called "The 100" with the help of The Thorn (a.k.a. Rose Forrest of *Rose and the Thorn*, a feature that occasionally appeared in the back of *Superman's Girl Friend Lois Lane*; letter columns were also addressed to Lois and Rose). Lois masterminds a plan to expose The 100 and is aided by Superman and her roommate, Julie.

SAMPLE ANALYSIS

Bates, Cary, Werner Roth and Vince Colletta, *Superman's Girl Friend Lois Lane* no. 121 (April 1972), New York: DC Comics.

Cameron, Don, John Rosenberger and Vince Colletta, *Superman's Girl Friend Lois Lane* no. 122 (May 1972), New York: DC Comics.

Considering the objective of our analysis, what can these particular issues of *Superman's Girl Friend Lois Lane* tell us, if anything, about how women are represented in popular culture, and what they might say, if anything, about American culture's ideas concerning gender, femininity, and sex roles at this given point in time? We will apply as many of our bullet-pointed steps from above as we can to our investigation.

Social Issues of the Era Reflected in Comics

The 1960s and 1970s were a time of social change. Political movements including civil rights, the youth movement, the feminist (or women's liberation) movement, and the gay rights movement influenced the changing cultural landscape and were thus necessarily reflected in American entertainment media.[16]

Prior to Lois' feminist consciousness-raising, DC Comics had attempted to integrate feminist values into the *Wonder Woman* comic. During what is now referred to as the Diana Prince era (1968–1972), Wonder Woman gave up her Amazonian powers, changed her style, became the owner of a mod clothing boutique, and practiced martial arts. DC felt this "new" Diana captured the tone of the women's movement, but this new Diana Prince contradicted the values of the original Wonder Woman. She had no qualms about killing, was fashion-obsessed, a little boy-crazy, and wasn't sure she enjoyed the company of women. She was no longer a superhero, and there were so few women superheroes to begin with.[17] This drastic change of character alarmed the editors of the then fledging *Ms.* magazine, who saw what had happened to one of their spiritual sisters and feminist inspirations as a travesty. They championed, successfully, for her return to iconic form.[18]

DC's main competitor, Marvel Comics, also made efforts to address women's changing roles and struggle for equal rights. As comic book writer and legend Stan Lee wrote in *The Superhero Women*, "for too many years the females have been relegated to mere supporting roles [and w]e think it's time to change all that."[19] Yet, characters such as Sue Storm of *The Fantastic Four* still cried, fainted, and exhibited powers that were lesser than her male counterparts. The uneasy relationship to feminist ideas is even more pronounced in the December 1970 story, "Come on in, the Revolution's Fine!" from Marvel's *The Avengers* no. 83, written by Roy Thomas. It's a cautionary tale filled with stereotyped feminist catchphrases such as the unfortunate, "Up against the wall male chauvinist pigs!" and in which the alleged feminist heroine turns out to be a villainess. The dissatisfaction with the status quo that women express in the story is referred to as "women's lib bull."[20]

How is Lois Depicted?

Lois Lane has always been a feisty and tenacious reporter. She began her career as a "sob sister"—handling the romance column for the *Daily Star* (later the *Daily Planet*). Her desire for the opportunity to tackle more serious journalism has repeatedly led her to get in over her head and necessitated her rescue by the Man of Steel. In fact, it is almost as if her ambitions reflected real women's ambitions for respectable careers, while simultaneously trouncing such notions by illustrating that such work is too much to handle and better left to men—like Clark Kent. When Lois quits her job in issue 121, she tells her editor, "From now on, I work freelance! No one tells ME what to write about—I pick MY OWN stories," adding "I'm a journalist. Everything I write reaches millions of people! I have a responsibility to those people! There's far too much injustice all around us to be ignored any longer!"[21]

Here, Lois has asserted herself as an independent journalist, and woman, rather than just a dedicated, if marginalized, career girl and girlfriend. She is no longer dictated to by Perry White, and in fact, he praises her work and notes that he has "a hunch working freelance will make Lois a better reporter than ever."[22] (One has to wonder if Perry has the self-awareness to recognize that perhaps Lois had the skills all along, and that he, as editor, never bothered to utilize them, preferring instead to support Clark's career.) And while it seems as though Lois is no longer burdened by her ties to Superman, her tenacity leads her to trouble and she must be saved by her hero. As she says after a rescue, "I owe you my life again, as usual! Oh, Superman! I just can't seem to live without you!"[23]

How are Other Women Depicted?

Lois' career change means she can no longer afford her apartment and so she moves into a singles residence with three other women. One is Julie, the woman who saved her life. Julie spouts a combination of clichéd blaxploitation and woman power dialogue like: "I dig that chick!" and "Freedom Day sisters!" While Julie debuted just prior to the short blaxploitation heyday, she is still a stereotype that exceeds even the most clichéd characterizations of black America in the 1970s.

The other roommates include a blonde named Kristin, and a slightly heavy woman named Marsha Mallow—as in "marshmallow." As if her name being symbolic of her physique wasn't enough to reinforce the fact that she is overweight, and that this is meant to be funny, Marsha herself lets us know she eats too many calories, has no will power, and is on a new diet every week.[24] Julie calls her a "butterball" and attempts to enforce an immediate diet (Figure 17.2). The girls continue to take food away from poor Marsha.

Figure 17.2 *Superman's Girl Friend Lois Lane* no. 121, page 24, story by Cary Bates, pencil art by Werner Roth. Copyright April 1972 DC Comics.

The reference to her weight through her name may be intended as a playful nod to "Etta Candy"—the charming, and pudgy, ally of Wonder Woman, first introduced in the William Moulton Marston era of *Wonder Woman*. Regardless, it reinforces the idea that any woman who doesn't conform to a cultural ideal should be shamed.

How is Lois Presented in Relation to Superman and Clark Kent?

Lois Lane, Superman, and Clark Kent have had an occasionally loving, occasionally tumultuous 70-plus years together. Comics historian Les Daniels writes in *Superman: The Complete History* that Superman creator Jerry Siegel viewed Superman's disguise as Clark Kent as a joke on Lois Lane.[25] While Lois had perhaps traditionally been the butt of a joke, there have in recent years been moments of true tenderness and affection. Regardless, in the 1960s, Superman still took glee from watching Lois fail, especially when it involved a beatdown from Wonder Woman, as in *Superman's Girl Friend Lois Lane* no. 93. Even though it's not really Wonder Woman, but an imposter, the pleasure he derives from the catfight, and the fact that he makes no attempt to stop it, is disturbing. That he leaves with Diana further demonstrates his capacity for cruelty.[26]

In issue 121 we see a temporarily more sensitive Superman—one who has been desperately searching for his lover all over Metropolis. When Lois returns to the *Daily Planet* to make her grand exit, his thought bubble reads: "I won't waste time greeting her as Clark—when I can do the welcome bit as Superman!"[27] Who knows if it's insecurity or ego; nevertheless, "a heartbeat later, not a word is spoken as anxious eyes meet for the first time in weeks."[28] Lois breaks up with Superman anyway, telling him that they each have to make a difference in the world and that, "I can't live in your shadow—I've got things to do."[29]

In the next issue, Superman displays his typically patriarchal temperament. He orders Lois to stay clear of trouble, specifically The 100, and that tending to such matters is "a MAN'S job!" (He says this even though Lois has already pointed out that The Thorn has captured 23 members of the organization, while he hasn't caught one.) Superman's sexism allows Lois to respond with her new liberated consciousness and say things like:

> What would you like me to do, Superman? Spend my life cooking in the kitchen? Living only for my Master ... Man? ... I love you Superman. But I want to be treated like a woman—not like a toy doll! I have a brain. A heart. A soul! ... Goodbye Superman! And take your super-male ego with you![30]

She's asserting her independence, but her dialogue leaves her coming off like a temperamental adolescent. (At least Superman's is just as bad, and gives the same impression.)

How is Lois' Body Presented?

In the first image of Lois in her new attire she wears red thigh-high boots with matching red hotpants. In the next panel (Figure 17.3), we see the reactions of Jimmy Olsen ("Wow! Lois—you're a knockout! You never looked like *this*!") and editor-in-chief Perry White ("There's a desk-load of assignments waiting for you!").[31] Lois is depicted facing them, while her derriere, hugged by hotpants, faces the reader and viewer. When Jimmy exclaims that Lois never looked like *this*—he is almost echoing the sentiments of Wonder Woman when she adopts a new fashion style ("Wow! I'm gorgeous! I should have done this ages ago!").[32]

Figure 17.3 *Superman's Girl Friend Lois Lane* no. 121, page 12, story by Cary Bates, pencil art by Werner Roth. Copyright April 1972 DC Comics.

Lois' style had changed in 1968—at roughly the same time as Wonder Woman—to reflect more contemporary fashions. Gone were her pill-box hats, page-boys, gloves, and Jackie Kennedy suits. In were mini-dresses, a new hair-style, hotpants, wide ties, and thigh-high boots. As Jacque Nodell observes, youth in America during this time forged their identities through fashion, "which became an increasingly important factor in youth culture." She adds that, "Romance comics of the period kept pace, as did Lois, Linda, and Diana. Together, the romance comics and hybrid titles *Wonder Woman, Superman's Girlfriend Lois Lane* [sic] and *Adventure Comics* reflected the styles of the day."[33] But clearly, there is a tension between pleasing the alleged female audience of the romance comics with fashion, while attracting a male audience by focusing on Lois' sex appeal. (Though one wonders whether this is intentional, or the simple fact that in this era most of the art was drawn by men, for a male audience, and thus the idea of the male gaze is intact.)

How Do Women Interact with Each Other (If at All)?

There appears to be a refreshing (if perhaps stereotyped) spirit of sisterhood. For example, Lois, Julie, Marsha, and Kristin toast their new living arrangement and friendship with "Here we are. All for one and one for all!"[34] Later, when Lois fears her escapades will endanger the women, she volunteers to move out (Figure 17.4). They respond by

Figure 17.4 *Superman's Girl Friend Lois Lane* no. 121, page 14, story by Cary Bates, pencil art by Werner Roth. Copyright April 1972 DC Comics.

insisting she can't leave them, "What's woman power for?" asks Julie. Kristin adds, "We chicks have to stick together!" Lois, is glad to be reminded of their motto "One for all and all for one!"[35]

In her past, Lois' relationships with women have tended to involve rivalry for the affections of Superman (Lana Lang, Wonder Woman, she's even gotten into it with Catwoman). Here, her friendships with women help solidify her identity as something other than someone's girlfriend. These two issues also pass the Bechdel Test. While the women do talk about Superman, they also talk about their families, their eating habits, and Lois' career and volunteer work (such as leading "blind kids" on a tour of the zoo—"a big job," says Kristin, "Looking after blind kids"[36]).

Who Produced the Artifact and Can We Determine Audience Response?

DC Comics produced the artifact, and we know that in the comics industry of the time, the majority of writers, artists, and editors were men, leading us to question just how capable, or at the very least, interested, male staff were of addressing true female sensibilities. Additionally, comics were marketed to a male audience, including, it seems, even those in the romance genre (a genre that would typically have a female audience). In *Superman's Girl Friend Lois Lane*, this is evidenced not only by so many advertisements for army men and body-building kits, but a particularly telling ad for a pillow printed with the image of sex symbol Raquel Welch ("What man wouldn't enjoy spending a night with Raquel Welch? Well, we can't deliver her, but we can deliver that next best thing....")

The letter columns printed in this era of *Superman's Girl Friend Lois Lane*, and specifically for our analysis those in issues 124, 125, and 126 that are printed in response to issues 121 and 122, suggest that the publication did, in fact, have both male and female readers. More importantly, they provide insight into conflicting attitudes toward the women's liberation movement. One reader appreciates the "Diana Prince-ish" direction that Lois adopted, referring to the pseudo-liberated *Wonder Woman* storyline of the late 1960s and early 1970s, adding that Lois' character "needed it" and that "very seldom have

Figure 17.5 Advertisement for inflatable Raquel Welch pillow that ran in issues of *Superman's Girl Friend Lois Lane.*

any of her positive qualities been accented."[37] In issue 125, Gerard Triano—who appears to be a frequent letter writer—says:

> About the subject of Women's Lib, Lois is carrying it too far and Superman not far enough. He must realize that "woman power" means more than fisticuffs and inane clichés, and that being loved and needed doesn't mean being enslaved. Her actions in the last two issues show that she must believe this. Her crack about "cooking in the kitchen" is the reason that some of the women I know hate the movement. It makes the woman who wants to fulfill herself "just" as a wife and mother feel worthless. What Women's Lib should boil down to is the right of every woman to be able to choose the life she wants for herself and be able to live it. I hope Lois and Supie both wake up.[38]

While Triano's observation is that women's liberation is a movement intended to secure the right for every woman to choose the life she wants for herself, it misses the social, cultural, political, and financial complexities that serve as obstacles to this achievement. Regardless, his letter also reveals that some readers were disturbed by the clichéd dialogue and stereotyped depictions of sex and gender in the comics.

Oddly, Triano's letter was not printed in the regular feature "Letters to Lois and Rose," but in a new "Mystery Columnist" segment allegedly meant to address the tremendous reader response to the "new" Lois Lane.[39] The columnist, known only as "Alexander the Great," responds to Triano with over-the-top misogyny: "What's the matter, kid, have you fallen for Lois or something? There is only *one way* to do things, and that's the *man's* way!"[40] It's difficult to tell if this attitude actually reflects the feelings of the columnist, is meant to reinforce the validity of the women's movement (and thus its inclusion in the storyline), or is simply meant to be sarcastic.

Regardless, "Alexander's" response to a woman that praises Lois and Superman for finally catching up with the times is equally hostile (as well as off-topic): "You must be going bananas! Superman is *exactly* that—Super-*man*. If we start to change the power structure, you females will be the losers. Lois is getting out of hand and it's time Superman did something about it!"[41] Alexander then announces that he is "forced to give some [column] space to a mere woman"—the woman being DC Comics editor, Dorothy Woolfolk, who playfully asks a letter writer to call her "Ms." not "Miss," further confusing the intentions of this particular letter page. This one page alone illustrates the tensions, confusion, hope, and anger surrounding the women's liberation movement, and one has to wonder if DC Comics really intended to reflect the spirit of change, or if the politics of the era were something they didn't take seriously. Alexander writes that he'd "get together with Superman and form Men's Liberation to free us from those nutty Women's Libbers," refers to Lois as "a dummy," "nuts," and "stupid," and suggests in response to a request for a *Lana Lang* title that "one girl-adventure reporter mag is *enough*."[42]

While Alexander suggests that "women should know their place"[43] he also jokes that the storyline is a mess because "it was edited by a woman! (BLEECH!)"—the woman being his editor.[44] When one reader questions how can a medium that sports men in underwear doing impossible feats hope to deal seriously with something so real as women's liberation, Alexander responds with "Who knows what evil lurks in the heart of Editor Woolfolk? Women's freedom is one of them, of course, and crusader that Ms. W. is she'll use any medium to fight for her sense of justice. So fellow (male)-leaders … duck!"[45]

Is Alexander's tone meant to suggest that men are unenlightened Neanderthals who need a healthy dose of consciousness-raising? Is it meant to make the politics (however sloppily handled they may be) less threatening to a male audience? Is it all tongue-in-cheek, and if so, is the audience sophisticated enough to pick up on this? It's hard to tell, but we do know that the majority of the letters printed in the "Mystery Columnist" and "Letters to Lois and Rose" in issues 124–126 are from men—most of whom complain about the women's liberation storyline.[46] A representative comment from no. 126 suggests that:

> *Lois* has become much too oriented toward "social causes," "minority groups" and so on. A comic book must primarily be a source of entertainment if it is to sell and it is easy to jeopardize its success in this respect by over emphasizing moral messages. This applies to *Lois'* Women's Lib convictions also. She should be confident and ambitious—and a bit of uninhibited cockiness makes her all the cuter as a character, but I'm sure the great majority of both men and women readers would not like her as a militant Women's Lib Extremist.[47]

This letter is particularly interesting because comics have always addressed social causes (just look at any American superhero comic from the World War II era) and because the author takes specific issue with social causes that involve minorities (i.e., people of color and women). Additionally, the assertion that Lois should be cocky enough to be cute, but not independent or empowered enough to be threatening to the status quo reeks of sexism, privilege, and the assumption that comics are for a specific audience—one which we can deduce from the letter is specifically male, white, and quite likely, heterosexual.

Summary of Analysis

Our goal here is not necessarily to label these issues as feminist or not-feminist. Rather, we are using the above findings from our analysis to comment on women's representation, as well as the handling of real-world politics of the women's liberation movement, in *Superman's Girl Friend Lois Lane* during the second wave of feminism. Though the dialogue is contrived and stereotyped, with talk about "woman power" and "chicks sticking together" and clichés that trivialize feminist politics, these particular issues of *Superman's Girl Friend Lois Lane* do pass the Bechdel Test. Additionally, none of the women are victims of WiR syndrome.[48] Rather than focus on the affections of Superman, Lois is focused on her career and her friends—making her much more independent, and suggests the dynamic character she's capable of being. Additionally, Lois is the subject of the publication, and while Superman rescues her, her tenacity fuels *her* adventures, not necessarily his.

On the other hand, Lois is referred to in the narrative as a "female reporter" rather than a reporter, suggesting that while attempting to make the title relevant to a changing cultural consciousness, the creative powers at DC weren't quite clear on some of the complexities of the concepts.[49] This is also evident in reader responses, such as the one that suggests that in the storyline we've analyzed Lois might be interpreted as a "militant Women's Lib extremist." While Lois is certainly temperamental, and has always dabbled in extremes (both trademarks of her personality), these issues certainly do not portray her as anything close to radical in her politics or position.

In following the steps outlined in the first section of this chapter, we have gained insight into how gender and feminist politics were reflected in DC Comics' *Superman's Girl Friend Lois Lane* in the early 1970s. The storylines in the publication, as well as the artwork and the conflicting responses from readers, suggest what we could only suspect—that reflecting real-world politics and a changing culture will be both embraced and resisted. But it is only in analysis that we have a language and a method to determine some of the reasons why.

NOTES

1. Bob Haney and John Rosenberger, "The Brave and the Bold presents Supergirl and Wonder Woman: Revolt of the Super-Chicks," *The Brave and the Bold* no. 63, New York: DC Comics, December 1965–January 1966.
2. Suffrage is usually considered the first wave of feminism.
3. Anne Francis played the title character of *Honey West* (1965–1966)—and was one of the first female action heroes on American television. The stateside premiere of the British spy-fi series *The Avengers* in 1966 featured the extraordinary Mrs. Emma Peel (Diana Rigg).
4. Andi Zeisler, *Feminism and Pop Culture* (Berkeley, CA: Seal Press, 2008).
5. One of the main rebuttals to the WiR argument is that men in comics suffer just as much violence as

women do, and that it's the nature of the superhero genre—fighting crime is inherently violent. But the difference lies in the way in which violence is depicted according to gender. Women tend to encounter a graphic, sexualized form of violence that men aren't subjected to. Batman had his back broken, but has since healed, whereas Barbara Gordon (a.k.a. Batgirl) was shot in the spine, crippled, and sexually assaulted without a miraculous comeback.

6. This has also been referred to by some feminist comics readers as the "you-touched-my-stuff" syndrome, meaning that the male hero is motivated by an act of violence against his family or girlfriend, suggesting that women and children act as the property of the hero and that violation of this property sets him on a path of vengeance (e.g., The Punisher, the Spider-Man story, "The Night Gwen Stacey Died," the murder of Elektra in *Daredevil*, and so on).

7. See http://girl-wonder.org and Jennifer K. Stuller, *Ink-Stained Amazons and Cinematic Warriors: Superwomen in Modern Mythology* (London and New York: I.B. Tauris, 2010) for more.

8. It's also useful to note whether or not the women have names.

9. For example, in the 2010 film *The A-Team*, Jessica Biel's character is a love interest and antagonist who doesn't speak to any other women throughout the movie. Even in the recent Spider-Man films, when love interest Mary Jane and caretaker Aunt May converse, it's about the male lead, Peter Parker.

10. In your choice of artifact for analysis, it's essential to take into account that women in underground comics—such as those of the Wimmen's Comix Collective (1972–1992), as well as writers of autobiographical or indie press comics, such as those by Marjanne Satrapi, Diane DiMassa, Ellen Forney, or Julie Doucet, are going to have different production restraints, intended audience, and themes than a mainstream superhero comic published by DC or Marvel. The latter are more likely to be produced by men, who therefore have little or no insight into female experiences or identities.

11. For example, in response to *Beware! The Claws of The Cat*—Marvel Comics' attempt at a feminist superhero in the early 1970s—one reader sent in a missive, printed in issue 3 (April 1973) expressing praise for their having created a "smartypants, wise-cracking, strong, brave-courageous-and-bold, bouncebackable WOMAN" that was the hero and not the love interest. Another, printed in issue 4 (June 1973, and the last issue to see print) called the publishers "radicals" and "Communists" for embracing Women's Lib—a movement they claimed was a plot to overthrow the country by destroying family values. The point is, do not underestimate the contextual value of letter columns. They contain great insight.

12. Take, for example, "The Dark Phoenix Tapes"—a roundtable conversation between the creative team on the now-classic, and still influential, *X-Men* story "The Dark Phoenix Saga." The conversation, printed in April 1984, provides an insightful, if startlingly sexist—even misogynistic—look into the creation of the story and feelings on the character.

13. J.P. Williams, "All's Fair in Love and Journalism: Female Rivalry in *Superman*," *Journal of Popular Culture* 24 (2) (1990): 103.

14. Stuller, *Ink-Stained*, 23.

15. Alternatively, and more likely, it suggests that within the issue Lois would have yet another fit of temper and hysteria. And, in fact, there is a scene within the issue where Lois goes quite mad.

16. Civil rights was addressed in *Superman's Girl Friend Lois Lane*, no. 106 (November 1970), titled, "I Am Curious (Black)!," and written by Robert Kanigher. The story involved Lois' attempts to report on the "nitty-gritty" of Metropolis' predominately black neighborhood, "Little Africa." No one will speak to her, as they are mistrustful of "Whitey"—as she is referred to by an activist. At her behest, Superman uses his "Plastimold" machine to transform her into a black woman for 24 hours so she can complete her investigation and story (which Lois is sure will win her a Pulitzer Prize). Lois learns many, many "lessons" about racial prejudice and ends up befriending the very activist who misjudged her for *her* color. When he is wounded protecting her, Lois discovers they are the same blood-type and saves his life by donating her blood. When he discovers Lois is actually white they seal their friendship with a handshake and the issue ends with a panel depicting a well-intentioned, yet very contrived, white hand shaking a black hand. There is also a scene in which Lois asks Superman if he'd marry her if she were black. He doesn't answer.

17. Jennifer K. Stuller, "Emmapeelers, Disco Divas, and The Feministas of Justice: A Look at Superwomen in the American 1970s," presented at WonderCon, 2009.

18. Stuller, *Ink-Stained*, 37–39.

19. Stan Lee, *The Superhero Women* (New York: Simon and Schuster, 1977): preface.

20. Stuller, "Emmapeelers."

21. Cary Bates, Vince Colletta, and Werner Roth, "Everything You Wanted to Know about Lois Lane (*But Were Afraid to Ask!)" and "Lois Lane Free-lancer," *Superman's Girl Friend Lois Lane* no. 121 (New York: DC Comics, April 1972) 12.

22. Ibid., 23.

23. Ibid., 21.
24. Ibid., 24.
25. Les Daniels, *Superman: The Complete History* (San Francisco: Chronicle Books, 1998), 20.
26. Robert Kanigher, *Superman's Girl Friend Lois Lane* no. 93 (New York: DC Comics, July 1969), 11–12.
27. Bates, "Everything You Wanted to Know about Lois Lane," 13.
28. Ibid., 13.
29. Ibid., 15.
30. Vince Colletta and John Rosenberger, "77 Coffins," *Superman's Girl Friend Lois Lane* no. 122 (New York: DC Comics, May 1972), 6.
31. Bates, "Everything You Wanted to Know about Lois Lane," 12.
32. Dennis O'Neil and Mike Sekowsky, *Wonder Woman* no. 178 (New York: DC Comics, September–October 1968), 10.
33. Jacque Nodell, "Sequential Crush Presents 'The Look of Love': The Romantic Era of DC's Lois Lane, Supergirl, and Wonder Woman," 10, http://sequentialcrush.blogspot.com/2010/04/look-of-love.html.
34. Bates, "Everything You Wanted to Know about Lois Lane," 24.
35. Coletta, "77 Coffins," 14.
36. Ibid.
37. Lon Wolfe, "Letters to Lois and Rose," *Superman's Girl Friend* no. 125 (New York: DC Comics, August 1972).
38. Robert Kanigher, Vinnie Colletta, and John Rosenberger, "Death Rides the Wheels!" *Superman's Girl Friend Lois Lane* no. 125 (New York: DC Comics, August 1972).
39. Cary Bates, Vince Colletta, and John Rosenberger, "The 100 Strikes Again!" *Superman's Girl Friend Lois Lane* no. 124 (New York: DC Comics, July 1972), 17.
40. Kanigher, "Death Rides the Wheels."
41. Ibid.
42. Cary Bates, Vince Colletta, and John Rosenberger, "The Brain Busters," *Superman's Girl Friend Lois Lane* no. 126 (New York: DC Comics, September 1972).
43. Bates, "The 100 Strikes Again."
44. Bates, "The Brain Busters."
45. Ibid.
46. At least two men wrote in to praise Lois' "groovy threads" and great hair.
47. Bates, "The Brain Busters." The editors note that they voted this letter "Best Fan Letter of 1972 … so far!"
48. With the arguable exception of Rose Forrest's alter ego, The Thorn, an identity forged out of her vengeful unconscious.
49. Bates, *Superman's Girl Friend Lois Lane* no. 121, 24.

SELECTED BIBLIOGRAPHY

Daniels, Les. *Superman: The Complete History.* San Francisco: Chronicle Books, 1998.
Lee, Stan. *The Superhero Women.* New York: Simon and Schuster, 1977.
Mulvey, Laura. "Visual Pleasure and Narrative Cinema." *Screen* 16 (3) (1975): 6–18.
Nodell, Jacque. "Sequential Crush Presents 'The Look of Love': The Romantic Era of DC's Lois Lane, Supergirl, and Wonder Woman," http://sequentialcrush.blogspot.com/2010/04/look-of-love.html (accessed July 13, 2010).
Stuller, Jennifer K. *Ink-Stained Amazons and Cinematic Warriors: Superwomen in Modern Mythology.* London and New York: I.B. Tauris, 2010.
Williams, J.P. "All's Fair in Love and Journalism: Female Rivalry in *Superman.*" *Journal of Popular Culture* 24 (2) (1990): 103–112.
Zeisler, Andi. *Feminism and Pop Culture.* Berkeley: Seal Press, 2008.

18

INTERTEXTUALITY

Superrealist Intertextualities in Max's Bardín

Ana Merino, translated by Elizabeth Polli

What is the secret to understanding a complex comic book? Can we find certain ways to analyze a sophisticated work with cryptic allusions? This chapter travels through the artistic mind of Spanish artist Max and his character Bardín in an effort to show a way to perceive and connect cultural influences in a comic. Sometimes, reading a comic we discover allusions to other pieces of art or literature. I remember the 1985 story by Gilbert Hernández, entitled "Love Bites," in which his character Heraclio, the teacher of Palomar, is trying to explain to his wife Carmen the importance of books. She is very jealous about him reading books all the time and not paying attention to her. She tries to throw one of the books Heraclio is reading into the sea. Heraclio stops her, begging for her understanding. Carmen asks him why this book, *One Hundred Years of Solitude* by Gabriel Garcia Marquez, is so great. Heraclio explains to her that the book is in some ways about them (Figure 18.1). For many scholars, the works of Gilbert Hernández are linked with the Magic Realism literary tradition, especially the works of Gabriel García Márquez. In "Love Bites," Gilbert Hernández uses intertextuality to develop a personal homage to Marquez's work.

There is an interesting element behind this allusion. Years ago, I asked Gilbert why he did this intertextual reference to Gabriel García Márquez. He told me that in the early 1980s, when he started publishing the stories of Palomar in *Love and Rockets*, many people commented about the similarities the stories of the village of Palomar had with Macondo, the village in Marquez's *One Hundred Years of Solitude*. Gilbert found this interesting because he had not read *One Hundred Years of Solitude*. Curious, Gilbert read the book in 1985. He realized his work and the work of Marquez are connected by a common understanding of their cultural heritage and the tradition of storytelling. The direct reference to and even visual representation of the book by Marquez in "Love Bites" is Gilbert Hernández's personal homage to this connection.

Figure 18.1 An intertextual homage in "Love Bites," *Love and Rockets* no. 16, Fantagraphics Books. Copyright 1986 Gilbert Hernandez.

UNDERLYING ASSUMPTIONS

A critical analysis of the cultural connections and intertextualities in a comic is based on certain assumptions. First, no text is created in isolation. Creators are influenced by the literary, artistic, political, religious, and philosophical traditions to which they have been exposed in their culture, education, and life experience. Second, no text exists in isolation. Each reader brings his or her own experience with literary, artistic, political, religious, and philosophical traditions to the reading of a comic. As Andrew Edgar explains:

> A text (such as a novel, poem or historical document) is not a self-contained or autonomous entity, but is produced from other texts. The interpretation that a particular reader generates from a text will then depend on the recognition of the relationship of the given text to other texts.[1]

"Text" can be anything that conveys information, from another comic book, to an opera, to a well-known event. Third, the critic must have some understanding of the influences and traditions exhibited in the work. Developing and applying that understanding constitutes the procedures of this methodology.

PROCEDURES

To be able to do a productive reading of a comic containing many intertextual references, you first need to understand a little of the personal background that defines the artist and his production in his country of origin. Researching this background will entail reading biographies of and interviews with the creator(s) of the comic being analyzed. Because most comics professionals are both accessible and generous to their fans, you might be able to conduct a personal interview with the creator(s).

Second, you need to contextualize the piece of work that you will analyze, developing an understanding of the tenants and techniques of the various literary, artistic, political, religious, and philosophical influences that the work exhibits. Depending on your background, some of these influences might be obvious to you, but you will probably have to rely on creator biographies and interviews to point you to the movements you need to research.

Third, you should connect these influences and traditions with the specific elements of art, literature, cinema, philosophy, or even religion that are referenced in the comic. After doing an initial reading of the comic to simply experience and enjoy the story, read the work again and make notes about intertextual references. Some of these references will be obvious to you, but you should also make a list of statements, images, or incidents that need to be researched because you suspect they refer to concepts from other texts.

Finally, your ultimate goal should be to explain how the meanings borrowed from these other texts enrich the meaning of the comic. In the application that follows, I will show you how to navigate through the influences of the European Surreal Art Movement of the early twentieth century and demonstrate the way that Max, in the early twenty-first century, appropriates these elements to create comics stories that explore the consciousness, or phenomenology, of his main character, Bardín, and, by extension, of human existence.

SAMPLE ANALYSIS

Max. *Bardín the Superrealist.* Seattle: Fantagraphics Books, 2006.

Max (Francesc Capdevila Gisbert) is one of the most intense and versatile creators of comics in the European panorama. His artistic sensitivity and creative intuition transcend the vignette and have turned him into one of the great narrators of sequential art of our times. Max is an artist who delves into all the possibilities that comics have to offer without limiting his universe to one single character. Max was born in Barcelona in 1956, and as a young child he lived and breathed the world of comics of the Bruguera School, Walt Disney movies, and television cartoons produced by Warner Brothers and Hanna Barbera. During his adolescence he was nurtured by the adventures of Tintin and Asterix, and by the pop scenes of the Beatles' "Yellow Submarine." At 17 he discovered the underground comix of the United States, and when he began to study at the Faculty of Fine Arts in Barcelona, he encountered a significant group of people involved in the world of comics. Max began to adopt the language of comics quite naturally as part of his own expressive vocabulary, as he recognized in the medium a multifaceted communicative dimension that unleashes his storytelling prowess. Even though he thought of himself as a pictorial artist as a child, Max discovered that it was within sequential art that his illustrative talent could express the stories he invented.

Max's production has been cutting edge, risky, and innovative over the span of his career. In his early period, the characters Gustavo and Peter Pank stand out. These two marked the coming of age of comic book readers during the Spanish transition after the Franco dictatorship. Gustavo is the aesthetic son of Robert Crumb's *Mr. Natural,* as well as the Franco-Belgian clear-line drawing tradition. The wild plots of these stories were the fruit of the impulsive, bright ideas of a Max who experimented with the spontaneous alienation of the underground. At the same time, however, the artist committed himself to the social problems of the transition in a Spain immersed in budding ecological debates and the reinstitution of labor unions.

In *Peter Pank*, Max introduced parody directly aimed at messing around with Walt Disney. The parody is affectionate in that it blends Max's passion for the aesthetic value of the Disney movies with a criticism of the ideological content intrinsic to the plots of those movies. The story vignettes of the anti-hero Peter Pank define the traits characteristic to the urban tribes that flourished in Spanish society during the 1980s. The punks, hippies, rockers, mods, *siniestros*, and preppies represent the parody of lost childhood, and express within the vignettes Max's aesthetics and his life philosophy.

Fortunately, Max didn't simply resign himself to the success of *Peter Pank* and the counterculture universe he had created. He toyed with other plots and literary possibilities within the genre of comics, and was one of the pioneers in the development of the graphic novel. Fascinated by the intensity of the graphic testimonial novel and influenced by the narrative model initiated by Art Spiegelman in *Maus*, Max created *The Extended Dream of Mr. D* in the late 1990s. This magnificent work of graphic fiction signals a before and after in the history of the genre within the Spanish context. It is a story of great breadth, in black and white, that breaks with the general humoristic style of comics in order to delve into a realist plot. In this work, the characters live inside a dark and reflexive scenario from the point of view of the artistic execution, but in a very intuitive and melancholy one in its narrative development. The graphic fiction is marked by psychoanalysis, the world of dreams and the subconscious. Max once again redefined the genre and challenged his readers by introducing philosophical and literary elements that demanded a refined and cultured sensibility. The work took the prize for best script at the Barcelona Comics Salon and won an Ignatz Award for the English translation.

In 2007 Max won the National Comics Award with a stunning recompilation of the adventures of his character, Bardín the Superrealist. In the same year this collection also received the prizes for Best Work, Best Script, and Best Drawing at the Barcelona International Comics Salon. Once again, Max appeals to an educated, refined reading public, but he also puts pressure on his readers by reclaiming a type of comic illustration that evokes the Bruguera School.[2] Bardín lives very naturally in every plane of reality while he humorously navigates through the metaphysics of the trials and tribulations of daily existence. His character is full of expressive dimensions that combine different traditions but that take risks and bring forth the originality of the vanguard.

It becomes clear at this point that Max is one of the most revolutionary and well-rounded artists in the European scene, not only because of the high quality and variety found in his oeuvre—or body of work—but also because he has contributed as an editor to the creation and maturity of the genre. He founded and co-directed the magazine *Nosotros Somos los Muertos* (*We Are the Dead*), offering his support to young authors and promoting the exchange of ideas and styles from both an aesthetic and an ideological perspective. In addition, he also dedicated his time to creating illustrative works of extremely high quality for children, such as the album, entitled *La Biblioteca de Turpín* (*Turpín's Library*), which reflects very clearly his literary vocation and his preoccupation with educating new, young readers. In 1997 Max won the National Award for Child and Adolescent Illustration (*Premio Nacional de Ilustración Infantil y Juvenil*) for his work illustrating the story of the series *Popof y Kocatasca*, by writer Teresa Durán.

Max's trajectory is diverse and coherent at the same time, and it is full of literary intensity that shows signs of the universe of myths and legends. Max rediscovers mythology and constructs dreams that evoke things that no longer exist. Because of this, his work should occupy a privileged location on the bookshelves of the true lovers of comics, art, and literature.

Bardín and the Intertextual Phenomenology

In May 2006, Fantagraphics Books published a hardcover compilation of the adventures of Bardín for the English-speaking market. With a tip of the hat to the literary genre of the picaresque, *Bardín the Superrealist* carries in its subtitle an allusion to the existential framework of his everyday life: "His deeds, his utterances, his exploits and his perambulations." The image on the front cover and the large, introductory vignette hold many similarities, presenting a Bardín who is walking through a type of marine-like desert with a face in his arms that is looking at him, while at his side there is something of an anthropomorphic, fully dressed dog carrying a fish in its mouth. This first vignette is loaded with intertextual graphic references that show Max's ability to connect with different graphic traditions and elements invented by other authors. Max has already warned us about the iconographic significance of this page,[3] explaining in a caption at the top of the page that he is presenting herein the "official guide to the phenomenology of BARDÍN," alluding to many elements that will appear throughout the book. This phenomenology links the basic human experience with Bardín and "attempts to describe how the world must appear to the naïve observer, stripped of all presuppositions and culturally imposed expectations."[4]

The reader must approach *Bardín* with an innocent eye, trying to make sense of the images and elements on the page. At the same time, Max's character, Bardín, will discover his own pure essence in a new dimension. Max then offers us the essence of Bardín, playing with the subjective conscience of his personality that combines imagination, sensation, and memory. Through his intuition, Bardín is capable of going deeper into himself to discover particular feelings, desires, and sensations that define him. The reader must approach this comic and the character of Bardín aware of the multiplicity of images that are defining him. The panels by Max combine artistic, literary, or philosophical elements that create a complex landscape where the reader needs to investigate the different levels of meaning within each panel.

In the preface of his book, *Discerning the Subject*, Paul Smith reminds us that "subjectivity is caught up in the set of philosophical terms and problems which are familiar from Descartes, Locke, Hume, Hegel, Heidegger, and many others."[5] Smith explains how "the 'subject' is generally construed epistemologically as the counterpart to the phenomenal object and is commonly described as the sum of sensations, or the 'consciousness' by which and against which the external world can be posited."[6] Max links his character Bardín to a phenomenology replete with intertextual elements in which the reader recognizes numerous traditions. There is a mixture of elements where the reader can create a rich interpretation that combines multiple influences and traditions. Bardín's vignettes, seen from the suggestive perspective of Julia Kristeva who understood that each text acquired its form through a mosaic of references that were the result of the absorption and transformation of other texts—would be a mosaic of graphic references where each new image alludes to other images. Andrew Edgar explains Kristeva's perspective in a succinct fashion by affirming that:

Figure 18.2 Max, *Bardín the Superrealist* (page 7), Fantagraphics Books. Copyright 2006 Max.

A text (such as a novel, poem or historical document) is not a self-contained or auto-nomous entity, but is produced from other texts. The interpretation that a particular reader generates from a text will then depend on the recognition of the relationship of the given text to other texts.[7]

The comics of Bardín must be read as a graphic text that associates different elements connected with multicultural aspects of society. Because of Max's strong artistic and literary background, the reader will find a wide range of themes, from philosophy to religion, circulating in the imaginary space of Bardín's character.

The Surreal Dimension in Bardín

Max's comics function as sophisticated graphic texts that combine words and images, which allude to, pay homage to, and are heirs to different aesthetic, ideological, and literary traditions. Bardín is a stubborn man who reminds us of some of the characters of the Bruguera School, of the tradition of children's comics in Spain during the 1950s; he also reminds us of Chris Ware's Jimmy Corrigan or Charles Schultz's Charlie Brown. In his arms he carries a snail with an eye inside that is looking at him. A caption with an arrow pointing to the snail reads: "Ceci est une pipe" (This is a pipe). In this case, he is alluding to the Belgian surrealist painter René Magritte and one of his pieces, "Ceci n'est pas une pipe" (*This is Not a Pipe*), in which a phrase accompanying the painted image of a pipe appears. This ordinary object, a pipe, changes meaning when accompanied by the sentence that negates its existence. Max inverts this intertextual allusion, transforming the snail with an eye into a pipe since the sentence indicates "Ceci est une pipe." The phenomenology of Bardín is intimately linked to surrealism; this trait has already been presented in the subtitle that accompanies the character, defining him as "the Super-realist." The word *superrealism* in this case is equivalent to *surrealism*. Max is reclaiming a term that was frequently used during the 1930s to define a creative movement that became part and parcel of Western cultural imagery with the publication in 1924 of André Breton's *First Surrealist Manifesto* (*Le Manifest du Surréalisme*). Breton played at constructing a definition of a word which had previously appeared in a 1917 work by Apollinaire, but it is Breton who first tries to conceptually articulate its meaning by establishing its characteristics:

SURREALISM, noun, masc., Pure psychic automatism by which it is intended to express, either verbally or in writing, the true function of thought. Thought dictated in the absence of all control exerted by reason, and outside all aesthetic or moral preoccupations.

ENCYCL. Philos. Surrealism is based on the belief in the superior reality of certain forms of association heretofore neglected, in the omnipotence of the dream, and in the disinterested play of thought. It leads to the permanent destruction of all other psychic mechanisms and to its substitution for them in the solution of the principal problems of life.[8]

Clearly associated with literature in the quote, the movement also found an expressive space in the plastic arts. In Spain its influence was felt on painters such as Joan Miró and Salvador Dalí, as well as on the film director Luis Buñuel, and Max is very conscious of this fact. In his guide to phenomenology, presented in the introductory vignette, we find at the bottom-right, below the horizon, a half-sunken boat, which according to the caption indicates that it was called the Salvador Dalí, and it's been there since 1929: "The 'Salvador Dalí' ran aground in 1929" (page 7).

From the Surreal Gaze to the Interior Struggle

Another clear reference to the surrealist movement would be the caption, which indicates that the lighthouse with the eye is "Max Ernst," the German artist and pioneer in both the Dadaist and surrealist movements. Ernst's artistic as well as written works help to give meaning to this creative movement that permeates and inspires the vignettes of Bardín:

> Departing from a childhood memory in the course of which a false mahogany panel facing my bed played the role of optical *provocateur* in a vision of near-sleep ... I was struck by the obsession exerted upon my excited gaze by the floor—its grain accented by a thousand scrubbings. I then decided to explore the symbolism of this obsession and, to assist my contemplative and hallucinatory faculties, I took a series of drawings from the floorboards by covering them at random with sheets of paper which I rubbed with a soft pencil. When gazing attentively at these drawings, I was surprised at the sudden intensification of my visionary faculties and at the hallucinatory succession of contradictory images being superimposed on each other with the persistence and rapidity of amorous memories.[9]

Ernst's reflections seem to speak to this obsessive vision of the symbolic gaze that appears in the vignettes of Bardín. Many of Bardín's stories develop through the absorbed gaze of this character who imagines and who has a visionary ability to merge images in a hallucinating game of curious contradictions. For example, in the self-contained, one-page story entitled "Bardín imagines," Max informs us how, when Bardín feels extremely lonely, "irredeemably alone" he visits the Prado Museum "and lingers in front of 'The Triumph of Death' by Brueghel the Elder" (page 13). This exercise of intense staring at the painting by this Dutch master from the sixteenth century provokes him to empathize, to feel differently, and at that moment "He imagines himself to be one with the figures in the painting" (page 13). We are presented with a fragment of the painting as a vignette, while Max explains that Bardín can spend hours at this exercise of empathetic gaze. Then the readers will see how, in one of the fragments of Breughel's painting, Bardín's face appears among the terrified bodies of the individuals in the painting. The caption that accompanies this vignette, in which Bardín sees himself in the painting, indicates that this type of hallucinating vision comforts him: "Bardín feels less alone" (page 13). After this curious and obsessive experience with the painting at the Prado Museum, Bardín goes out into the streets and feels much better: "And then, as he takes a stroll downtown, Bardín feels less unfortunate" (page 13). He now breathes, relieved, and walks along the streets without realizing, it seems, that he has found comfort in the symbolic space of death. This story offers a disquieting contradiction because the loneliness that makes Bardín feel so ill-fated finds refuge in a collective death. Of all the paintings in the museum, Bardín contemplates and empathizes with the one that depicts the tragic scene that a bloodcurdling battle leaves on a region. It is a surprising canvas bursting with scenes of crimes and corpses. To the right, death is laying siege to a group of terrified people. Here, death appears represented by hordes of skeletons with knives cruelly throwing themselves at this group of people, whose faces reflect their horror and whose open mouths scream out their fear. Bardín's terrified face also appears, yet he finds comfort in the possibility of imagining a death en masse, surrounded by the panic of other human beings.

The Andalusian Dog as a Tribute to Surrealist Cinematography

As is clearly indicated in the caption, the dog that accompanies Bardín in the first vignette of the book, dedicated to the phenomenology of this character, is the Andalusian dog. The animal is dressed in a plaid jacket, a white shirt, and bow tie, he is wearing a red hat and has human facial traits, and as mentioned earlier, he is carrying a fish in his mouth. The fascinating complexity of this canine character is clearly exposed in the first story of the book, whose title is simply "BARDÍN the Superrealist." It is here that the surreal dynamic strongly crystallizes through this dog character capable of discussing the artistic terms of surrealism with Bardín.

Bardín is strolling along the street in the first vignette, only to find himself in another dimension in the second and third vignettes. His head has been placed in a sort of marine-like desert, with an endless beach with no sea, full of snails with eyes and other shells. The same dog with the jacket, white shirt, bow tie, and hat from the previous large vignette, which introduced the phenomenology of Bardín, is there, waiting for him. The dog has been waiting for some time, and he reprimands Bardín for arriving late and explains emphatically who he is: "I am the **ANDALUSIAN DOG**" (page 7). Much to the dog's surprise, Bardín doesn't recognize the place at all and thus it is the dog who has to explain to Bardín that he is in the superreal world, which means "That it exists on a plane **above** the real World, i.e., that it's even **more** real, see?" (page 8). The dog explains the planes of reality, emphasizing that the world above the real world is even more real. Bardín, however, is not able to understand the metaphysical implications of this reality and tries to give meaning to what he perceives visually: "How come there's no water on this beach?" he says, alluding to the surrounding marine-like desert scenery and snails (page 8). The Andalusian dog begins to lose patience with Bardín: "Where'd you get the notion this is a beach?!! There's no water here, there wasn't ever any water here, and there never will be!" (page 8). This absurd dialogue between the two characters needs an intellectualized explanation in order to contextualize the symbol. The dog begins to define himself, highlighting his intertextual plane: "**I am the Andalusian dog**, the **universal** inheritor of and custodian of **superrealist powers** since the year 1929, when ..." (page 9). The dog is referring to the film *Un Chien Andalou* (*An Andalusian Dog*), made jointly by the painter Dalí and the film director Buñuel. The movie is 17 minutes long and was filmed in one week in March 1929:

> The opening sequence, which is notorious, shows a man [Buñuel himself] sharpening a razor next to a window. As he observes a wisp of cloud passing across the moon, he slices open the eye of a woman sitting passively next to him [an ox's eye in actual fact].[10]

This charismatic surrealist scene becomes, in *Bardín*, an intertextual, graphic homage presented by Max to Luis Buñuel. A two-page, wordless, autonomous, self-contained story appears in gray tones, evoking the black and white texture of the 1929 film. In it we see Bardín walking through the desert of the surreal world, surrounded by the scenery of the lighthouse, which refers back to Max Ernst, and the boat that represents Dalí, half-sunken in the sand and shells. The character's peacefulness is disturbed when disquieting eyes floating through the sky and posing here and there on different elements in the vignette begin to appear. Bardín cannot avoid feeling the sadistic desire to yank an eye from one of the snails and cut it in half through the center with a straight-edge razor. This homage reproduces in an expanded form the same frames of the film. Nevertheless, on pages 16–17, the eye that is being cut turns into the moon with a cloud passing over it. The dream-like intensity of the film, interpreted here through code in a sequential vignette, develops a disturbing continuity through panels that capture the reader's attention. The reader of *Bardín* cannot escape the surreal world and the entire story of the "homage to Luis Buñuel" remains on this superreal plane.

The Articulation of Imaginary of Powers

Returning to the encounter between Bardín and the Andalusian dog, the plot thickens when the dog details his complex relationship with surrealist/superrealist Spanish artists Buñuel and Dalí. The dog has already indicated to Bardín that he is the heir to and custodian of the "superrealist powers," although he admits in a low voice that he had robbed such powers from Buñuel and Dalí after a fight. The disagreement also cost the dog: He was expelled from the film set, from the film he considers his own and which Buñuel and Dalí named after him to annoy him: "They kicked me off the set of my own movie … then adding insult to injury, just to be dicks, they stuck my name on it as the title!!" (page 9). Nevertheless, the Andalusian dog explains how he took vengeance by snatching their powers from them. Even though he couldn't steal all of Buñuel's powers from him, he was able to seize all of Dalí's: "But Dalí, haw! Dalí got himself **reamed**! Haw haw! I left the ol' paranoid-critic **scraping the barrel**! Melting watches, mountains of cheese! Haw haw haw haw!!" (page 9). In this case, the dog's perspective clearly sides with Buñuel, who was able to develop a long and varied career as a film director, while at the same time it criticizes Dalí, considering that he went down somewhat of a laughable path by converting his surrealist perspective into an aesthetic of the "bland."

Buñuel and Dalí were very close friends during their youth, sharing their passion for surrealism, but the Spanish Civil War (1936–1939) and the different ideological positions prevalent during this period separated them radically. Buñuel exiled himself to New York, where he worked at the Museum of Modern Art, but Dalí wasn't satisfied with this American exile of his former friend, and thus denounced him as a communist. Consequently, Buñuel had to abandon New York for Mexico. The surrealism of melting objects and Dalí's great commercial possibilities will mark the aesthetics of this successful artist who settles comfortably into the directives of the Franco regime. The Andalusian dog's laugh when referring to Dalí and his melting clocks and mountains of cheese seems to relate indirectly to this aesthetic conformity marked by a virtuosity which easily adjusted to success and fame. But what worries the Andalusian dog right now is making Bardín understand that he, Bardín, has been chosen to take charge of the superpowers of surrealism. And even though Bardín is not interested in these powers, the dog indicates that it is already too late to categorically deny them because they have been transferred: "The transfer's already been set in motion…!" (page 10). Initially, Bardín doesn't feel anything, but when the Andalusian dog tells him to use his in-sight, everything changes and a giant eye grows inside Bardín's head. This eye discovers with horror that Bardín has three tumors, and thus he falls to the ground reeling from the overwhelming sensation of a giant lobster on top of him. Then, that lighthouse with an eye, which was labeled as Max Ernst in his phenomenology advises him not to panic because "You've been granted some extraordinary powers. Use your imagination: Examine your problem dis-pas-sion-ate-ly!" (page 10). And so, Bardín calms down and observes in an objective and impartial fashion the health problems that his in-sight has detected. Indeed, he has three tumors, which are growing curiously slowly. His prostate cancer is in stage one, his lung cancer is in remission, and his brain tumor is in a state of fossilization. Bardín's fear turns to relief, and the serenity he feels provokes him to remember. Now his power, as the snail with the eye indicates (the snail, which in his phenomenology was indicated by a pipe), is memory: "You have the power to remember **all** that you've **forgotten**!" (page 11). Max ends the story with a final vignette in the super-realist world where Bardín is astonished by his new and incredible capability to remember and see things from new perspectives. The spirit of the gaze was clearly expressed in Max Ernst's essay "Beyond Painting." The construction of extremely intense images was the fruit of this new surrealist stimulus, revolving around the gaze:

> I saw myself with the head of a kite bird, knife in hand, in the pose of Rodin's *Thinker*, so I thought, but it was actually the liberated pose of Rimbaud's *Seer*.
> I saw with my own eyes *the nymph Echo*.
> I saw with my own eyes the appearances of things retreating, and I experienced a calm and ferocious joy. Within the bounds of my activity (passivity) I have contributed to that general overthrow of the most firmly established and secured values which is taking place in our time.[11]

Ernst explained this visionary ability as a new and powerful instrument capable of questioning established values and putting forth new existential forms. Bardín transcends this dialect through a gaze, which gathers together the time of memories and establishes new forms of understanding reality.

Concluding the World of Bardín as an "Exquisite Corpse"

There is a caption in the phenomenology of Bardín, which states "Exquisite Corpse," indicating a car sunk in the sand, with a gigantic eye sticking out of the open trunk. This refers to a creative game of the surrealist universe defined by André Breton:

> Exquisite Corpse: Game of folded paper placed by several people, who compose a sentence or drawing without anyone seeing the preceding collaboration or collaborations. The now classic example, which gave the game its name, was drawn from the first sentence obtained this way: The-exquisite-corpse-will-drink-new-wine.[12]

Max's depiction of Bardín's world combines dreams, literary, pictorial, and philosophical homages, in addition to profound existential and ideological reflections with religious undertones. Toward the middle part of the volume we find two pages in which eight long vignettes point out poetic scenery of the superreal world, presented as "Bardín's description of the superreal world" (pages 48–49). Here Max's little game combines suggestive images with the surreal or superreal dialectic. The sentences, which accompany the vignettes, denote a poetic rhythm to the reading, demarcating its characteristics:

The superreal world is all horizon and nothing but.
There are lighthouses sporting eyes that never stop turning.
There are eyes hidden in the sand or within the snails.
Eyes and more eyes.... Not a lot of privacy in the superreal world.
There are many grounded vessels, smokestacks still smoking.
At midday the battling titans wrestle in the sand.
And what is there to say about the spectacle of the fingerprint-fish schools at dusk?
In the superreal world the endings and the beginnings are the same.

(Pages 48–49)

The permanent gaze, the interior struggle, the sum of multiple identities, and circular time are some of the images evoked through these beautiful yet worrying vignettes. Max is a creator who digs deep into expressive chasms of the imagination and does not settle for linear narrative constructions. He wants to stimulate an educated reader so s/he can transcend the dimensions of comics and navigate along all the possible scenarios of thought as a metaphor for human existence. The superreal or surreal world is an excuse to poeticize his angst and define his own existence. Bardín is not only the result of a transcendent voyage through a parallel surreal world where the reader delights in this framework of metaphors and dreams. It is in addition a graphic dialectic effort that proves that when a comic artist longs to transcend his discursive essence, he is capable of generating a new aesthetic philosophy, which merges with the legacy of the great traditions.

NOTES

1. Andrew Edgar, "Intertextuality," in *Key Concepts in Cultural Theory*, ed. Andrew Edgar and Peter Sedgwick (New York: Routledge, 1999), 197.
2. The Bruguera School is a group of comic artists that worked for the Spanish publisher Bruguera during the 1940s, 1950s, and 1960s. Some of the most notorious authors were Escobar, Peñarroya, Cifré, Vázquez, and Ibáñez. They invented numerous characters that reflected with sharp and sometimes irrational humor on the hardships of the Spanish society under Franco dictatorship. Created with a childhood audience in mind, the Bruguera comics were also enjoyed by adults of different ages.
3. Max, *Bardín the Superrealist* (Seattle: Fantagraphics Books, 2006), 7.
4. Andrew Edgar, "Phenomenology," in *Key Concepts in Cultural Theory*, ed. Andrew Edgar and Peter Sedgwick (New York: Routledge, 1999), 271.
5. Paul Smith, *Discerning the Subject* (Minneapolis: University of Minnesota Press, 1988), xxvii.
6. Smith, *Discerning the Subject*, xxvii.
7. Edgar, "Intertextuality," 197.
8. André Bretón, "First Surrealist Manifesto," in *Surrealism*, ed. Patrick Waldberg (New York: Thames and Hudson, 1997), 72.
9. Max Ernst, "Beyond Painting" in *Surrealism*, ed. Patrick Waldberg (New York: Thames and Hudson, 1997), 97.
10. David Hopkins, *Dada and Surrealism* (Oxford: Oxford University Press, 2004), 93.
11. Ernst, "Beyond Painting," 100.
12. André Bretón, "The Exquisite Corpse," in *Surrealism*, ed. Patrick Waldberg (New York: Thames and Hudson, 1997), 94.

SELECTED BIBLIOGRAPHY

Bretón, André. "First Surrealist Manifesto." In *Surrealism*, edited by Patrick Waldberg, 66–75. New York: Thames and Hudson, 1997.

Breton, André. "The Exquisite Corpse." In *Surrealism*, edited by Patrick Waldberg, 93–95. New York: Thames and Hudson, 1997.

Edgar, Andrew and Peter Sedgwick, eds. *Key Concepts in Cultural Theory*. Routledge: New York, 1999.

Ernst, Max. "Beyond Painting." In *Surrealism*, edited by Patrick Waldberg, 96–100. New York: Thames and Hudson, 1997.

Hernandez, Gilbert. *Palomar: The Heartbreak Soup Stories*. Seattle: Fantagraphics Books, 2003.

Hopkins, David. *Dada and Surrealism*. Oxford: Oxford University Press, 2004.

Max. *The Extended Dream of Mr. D*. Montreal: Drawn and Quarterly, 2000.

Max. *Bardín the Superrealist*. Seattle: Fantagraphics Books, 2006.

Smith, Paul. *Discerning the Subject*. Minneapolis: University of Minnesota Press, 1988.

Part V

Reception

19

CULTURAL STUDIES

British Girls' Comics, Readers and Memories

Mel Gibson

My interest in researching audiences and comics was initiated by three key incidents that made me want to explore how the reading of comics is, and was, understood within British culture. Two of them stem from my experiences as a school-girl reading super-hero comics. The third, in contrast, comes from my work as a literacy professional. All three are, in turn, linked to broader national debates about the medium.

I am beginning with these incidents, as they offer illustrations of how questions you might want to research can emerge from personal or professional experience. My first critical incident took place when I was five years old and my class was asked to take our favorite reading material into school. I took a *Batman* comic, only to be told to go home and return with what my teacher described as proper, appropriate reading material. This made me keen to read more comics, as a rebellion against being told that I should not. It also led to my fascination with why comics were considered improper and inappropriate. One initial question that might lead into research could be, quite simply, why was that teacher so upset by comics?

To frame that more formally, a project starting from this incident would involve exploring professionals' views of the medium through interviewing them about comics and analyzing what those interviews revealed. The background to the research which would help one make sense of the interviews would be that, in Britain, comics have his-torically been tied to a perception of popular culture as insignificant in comparison to high art, such as painting, opera, and the like. The views the teacher expressed could be linked, potentially, with a number of issues. These might include censorship, class, fears about comics weakening literacy skills, fears for (and of) children and youth, and what can be described as moral panics.

The next critical incident also concerns superhero comics. In my early teens, I enjoyed reading about female characters, especially as part of teams. I was particularly attracted to titles that featured women who were more than just romantic interest, victims, or in peril. I was, simultaneously, involved in a number of feminist activist groups, including several focused on media. An argument with a member of one of those groups made me realize that people can see texts in very different ways. When I said I liked comics, she said they should be banned because they were sexist, that male readers would simply see women as objects as a consequence of reading them, and that I should not buy or read them. I attempted to fight back, explaining that while some superheroines were traditionally feminine and vulnerable (some periods of *Supergirl*, perhaps, being an example), others, like Storm of the *X-Men* were much more assertive. She countered that it was how they looked, with tight costumes and buxom figures, which was important. I was offended by her stereotyping, for, as a reader, I was aware of a diverse range of characters who behaved in very different ways. I left the group, but remained insistent that I was a feminist (although at that time I didn't realize how diverse and complex feminism(s) actually was/were). I also continued to believe that women and girls could enjoy reading comics. This incident flags up a number of issues, among them that there is a huge contrast between understandings of a text that emerge from stereotypes and those that come from close textual analysis. Another major issue is the way that ideology has an impact upon perspectives on texts. The clash of ideologies over a particular element in a comic might well make a good focus for your research. If a character is seen as controversial, for instance, he or she could be the focus of interviews exploring both how and why.

In addition, the view of the person I was arguing with was about media influence, another powerful theme in research. She felt there was a direct link between what someone read and how they acted. This insistence that texts do things to people is what can be described as a media effects viewpoint. In contrast, my 13-year-old self was arguing against media effects by saying that comics couldn't be straightforwardly creating male sexism, because I was both a girl and a feminist, yet still found much to enjoy. This childhood assertion, while simplistic, is an embryonic version of what audience research is about, in the sense that it is concerned with what people do with texts.

My final critical incident is tied to my professional practice supporting the development of graphic novel, comic, and manga collections in UK schools, libraries, and elsewhere. As a children's librarian in the early 1990s, a female-dominated profession in Britain, I noted that the majority of my peers had a huge lack of confidence around comics and graphic novels. I was also intrigued by assertions that these were problematic, or even dangerous, texts whose sole value was to increase the literacy skills of young, male non-readers, or that they were not actually books at all. As an adult female graphic novel reader and a student of Cultural Studies, the medium's classification as non-book (with collections sometimes found in music and film sections) and the continuing concerns about both the medium and supposed audience seemed a good area for research. What you observe in work settings, then, can generate research questions.

This led to my becoming part of a small working group, part of the Youth Libraries Group in Britain, which produced a book edited by Keith Barker, focusing on graphic novel collection development and working as a trainer in the field.[1] Barker's book was a response to previous writing by teachers and librarians in Britain, which was often generated by moral panics and media effects theory, such as George H. Pumphrey's work in the 1950s and 1960s.[2] Professional writing about comics, then, could be a starting point for your research. You might have located articles in teaching magazines about reading and manga, for instance, and then decided to interview teachers about how they feel about what those articles contain.

Another thing that intrigued me about the fear and hostility expressed toward comics by some of these female professionals was that they appeared to have forgotten or, to use a term which emerged later in interviews, "buried," their own positive experiences of reading comics as children. They were likely to have read girls' comics, which were the dominant popular reading material in Britain for girls between 1950 and the mid-1980s. There were over 50 weekly publications for girls, partly or wholly consisting of comic strips, of which the most popular circulated between 800,000 and one million per week.

A question that led into research here was about exploring why they had forgotten memories of their own engagement with the comic book. In interviewing people about comic reading, I found I was awakening memories of those texts and of childhood. At the same time, in my training work, I discovered that concerns about the medium could be addressed through working with memories of comics. Connecting the personal and the professional, especially when combined with sessions where the staff could read some of the new titles they had previously felt concerned about, proved very powerful. A wider knowledge, plus remembering that they knew how comics worked, often combined to give them more positive perspectives on the medium. Your work with audiences, then, may develop from specific questions about attitudes and assumptions, but may also seek to have an impact upon an audience, making what you do an approach that can be described as "action research."

In my own research, I attempted to address this lost female history in terms of the texts and production, along with the perceptions, attitudes, assumptions, and memories that women had regarding their childhood reading and the wider cultural perception that these were texts for male readers. This necessitated having a good grasp of the history of the texts that interviewees were likely to mention. Similarly, if your focus is a superhero, read around the production history of that genre. This knowledge will help you analyze your interviews, which are the primary texts of your research. This is especially significant if you are working with people who are likely to mention texts you do not know. In my case, I had to research the British girls' comic as well as interview people about their memories of them, simply to make sense of what people, particularly those considerably older than I was, were talking about.

To conclude, ideas for research about audiences can emerge from personal or professional experience, national debates, or even media accounts. For example, if you see a newspaper article about a parent complaining that they found material unsuitable for children in a comic and demanding it be banned, that complaint reveals a perspective on what comics are and who they are for. If you wanted to explore this view of comics, you might interview parents or children, especially if you have a particular comic in mind (always taking care to follow ethical guidelines, of course), or talk to professional, fan, or other groups about their views of either the critical article or the original comic. Alternatively, if an article suggests that comics are growing up (such language has appeared in articles introducing graphic novels to a wider audience), that reveals a mistaken view of the comic as originally being only for children. That, too, might make a good topic for research.

It is a matter of choosing a focus. Audience work, finally, can be developed with any audience for any type of comic. This is a huge field. The first step is deciding what your focus is, so stay aware of debates around the comics medium and audiences, and if something really grabs your attention, think of it as a possible research subject and read more about it.

UNDERLYING ASSUMPTIONS

In engaging with notions of gender and audience, as well as text, my work can be seen as having, in Britain, a disciplinary and theoretical location within Cultural Studies. However, like many working within Cultural Studies, I take an interdisciplinary approach because my interests mean I need to draw upon a wide range of theoretical writing. The writers who have had an impact on my work are, themselves, from a number of disciplines and occupy a range of theoretical spaces, including Cultural and Media Studies, Communications, Education, Women's Studies, Sociology, Literature, History, and Childhood Studies. Some are interested in analyzing girls' and young women's experience, others popular culture (in the sense of a set of practices, activities, or texts) and yet others the British girls' comic. The latter is the focus for the remainder of this chapter because of my interest in researching girlhood, women professionals, and comics. Depending on your research focus, you will probably find yourself drawing upon a different group of writers.

Of the many researchers in this wider area, one of the most significant for me became Angela McRobbie, whose earlier work, from the late 1970s and onwards, was largely created at the Centre for Contemporary Cultural Studies (CCCS) at the University of Birmingham.[3] This work engaged with three key themes: lived experience, subcultures, and popular culture. McRobbie's work differed from previous work in that she did not research boys, but instead looked at how girls "interpreted some of the structural determinations of age, class and gender in the context of their own lived experience."[4] McRobbie also engaged with popular culture, typically that perceived as working-class. Like her work on subcultures, the emphasis was on girls' engagement with popular culture, femininity, and youth culture.

As part of this work on girls' culture, McRobbie[5] analyzed the very popular title for teenage girls, *Jackie*.[6] This textual analysis did not include interviews, while her work on both lived experience and other popular culture generally did. The semiological analysis of *Jackie* seemed to conclude that these were problematic texts; just like the conclusions about superhero comics I had been offered as a teenager by the feminist media group member. McRobbie saw *Jackie* as offering a problematic ideological message, described as "doubly pernicious" for working-class readers because it "bound them to a future which revolved round finding, as soon as possible, and holding onto, 'a fella,' since life without such a person was synonymous with failure."[7] What seemed to be underlying this analysis was a view of media as directly influencing girls. However, in another piece of research, McRobbie did make reference to how readers of *Jackie* use the title.[8] This contrasts dramatically, for, as Barker points out, in that work *Jackie* is used as a resource for resistance to authority figures and even boys, acting as an element in girls' friendships.[9]

Of the other work on girls' comics in Britain, Valerie Walkerdine is also significant.[10] Her research was textually based too, employing a post-structuralist approach. Walkerdine, in thinking through how comics might speak to girls' desires and internal conflicts looked at titles for slightly younger readers than those of *Jackie*. Walkerdine focused upon the titles *Bunty*[11] and *Tracy*,[12] suggesting that girls' comics direct them, albeit with a battle, into passivity, victimhood, self-sacrifice, and waiting for masculine rescue. Here, again, despite struggle, the girl is depicted as susceptible to the messages offered in the comics, which are seen as negative and sexist.

While British girls' comics were analyzed and the impact upon the reader speculated about, this rarely involved interviews with actual readers. As McRobbie's work hints, interviews often reveal very different views of texts like *Jackie* and their place in people's lives. One of the few exceptions is the work of Elizabeth Frazer, which attempted to respond to notions of ideology and influence through analyzing discussions between readers.[13] Her approach drew on the idea of discourse registers from sociolinguistics, analyzing ways of talking about topics.

McRobbie's, Frazer's, and Walkerdine's work, among that of others, was explored by Martin Barker, who "reconsider[ed] claims about media-effects, by looking closely at the theories advanced by others, and their methods of investigation and analysis,"[14] adding that he

> wanted to review all the main kinds of claims about media-effects, but in a way that would enable me to look back at the original materials about which the claims were being made. And comics, it turned out, almost uniquely gave me that opportunity.[15]

Barker's exploration of the limits and possibilities of theoretical approaches to comics, for instance, led to his rejecting McRobbie's view of *Jackie* as "a 'unified' text."[16] Instead, he emphasizes the way that *Jackie* changes over time. In his close textual analysis of samples taken from various eras, he discovered a complex and shifting picture. He argued that in getting to grips with comics, "we need two interlocking approaches. The first must explore the nature of a 'contract' between readers and the magazine; the second has to consider the production history which enables that contract to be met—or may fail."[17]

Barker's notion of the contract is, he argues, similar to that of the implied reader—so working with textual devices—but is extended beyond the text to "the implied social relation to readers," being "part of a conversation with some aspect of the readers' lives."[18] He summarizes his overall hypothesis as

> (1) that the media are only capable of exerting power over audiences to the extent that there is a "contract" between texts and audience, which relates to some specifiable aspect(s) of the audience's social lives; and (2) the breadth and direction of the influence is a function of those socially constituted features of the audience's lives, and comes out of the fulfilment of the contract; (3) the power of "ideology" therefore is not of some single kind, but varies entirely—from rational to emotional, from private to public, from "harmless" to "harmful"—according to the nature of the contract.[19]

All of the approaches outlined above offer ways of looking at comics, but rarely at audiences for comics. In Barker's case, however, he offers ways of analyzing the relationship between reader and text which you can employ, as we shall see.

CULTURAL STUDIES AND USES AND GRATIFICATIONS

I must emphasize that, despite the diversity within Cultural Studies work in this area, it generally differs from that of uses and gratifications research.[20] The two do have some cross-over, for as Shaun Moores states, "uses and gratifications … reversed the question posed by effects studies—asking 'what people do with the media' instead of 'what the media do to people," adding that both "reject any view of audiences as passive and highlight what they see as the productivity of consumption."[21] Uses and gratifications moved toward the idea of an active reader (particularly regarding television) because it claimed that audiences used mass media to meet individual needs, which, as Denis McQuail outlines, were initially seen as "learning and information, self-insight and personal identity, social contact, escape, diversion, entertainment and time-filling."[22]

However, Moores, among others, insists that "the differences between them outweigh this apparent similarity,"[23] defining uses and gratifications as mainstream communications research and as "outside of the critical paradigm."[24] Barker flags these tensions through looking at one of the few pieces of comic research located in this tradition; that by Katherine M. Wolfe and Marjorie Fiske.[25] He argued that their research contained a number of problematic elements: "timeless needs, which 'explain' why people use the media; unargued distinctions between 'reality' and 'fantasy'; and naïve classifications of media-content."[26]

To depict uses and gratifications research in this way is to argue that it, as Moores says, "is a psychological conception of human personality which focuses narrowly on the media's functions for the individual."[27] Nor, as Barker suggests, does it take the specifics of era or place into account. Ien Ang adds that it "generally operate(s) within a liberal pluralist conception of society where individuals are seen as ideally free, that is, unhindered by external powers."[28] So, in uses and gratifications research, media consumers may be seen as free or powerful. In contrast, Cultural Studies tends to see media consumption as central to everyday life and as a site of ongoing cultural struggle over meaning and pleasure. The two can lead, then, to very different kinds of results.

The Cultural Studies "critical paradigm" is described by Moores as a social theory of subjectivity, power, and meaning construction, a sociologically grounded semiotics of the text–reader dialogue.[29] Also, as Ang argues, "in cultural studies, following Marxist/(post)structuralist assumptions, people are conceived as always-already implicated in, and necessarily constrained by, the web of relationships and structures which constitute them as social subjects."[30] Both approaches, then, are engaged with notions of exploring maps or webs. Uses and gratifications research can be said to create generalized formal "maps" of all the possible dimensions of audience activity. Such a map could be quite static. In contrast, Cultural Studies can be seen as about processes and notions of social power. This means it looks at ongoing and changing cultural practices and relationships, so the Cultural Studies map moves all the time.

Thus, despite some points of connection (and in response to attempts to draw the two approaches together), Cultural Studies in the mid-1980s and onwards continued to develop different definitions and perceptions of work with audiences.[31] It is this Cultural Studies approach that I started to work in during the 1990s. Like me, what you want to find out about in terms of how texts fit into people's lives will determine which is the most suitable approach for you to use.

PROCEDURES

Researching both audiences and texts offered me a challenge and opened up spaces that chimed with both my personal experiences as a comic reader and my professional experiences of comics. The idea that growing older or becoming a professional might change how one interacted with the contract that Barker proposed seemed a way of exploring what I had observed and experienced. The following offers a brief summary of some aspects of the research, although it cannot encompass the full range of responses and understandings the interviews revealed.

I needed, as you will to use this approach effectively, to work with both texts and readers. My understanding of British cultural views of the comic in general and of the girls' comic in particular had to broaden to get a picture of changes in the titles and the genre, as well as possible changes in the contracts offered to readers. Once you have chosen your focus, you will do the equivalent for your chosen area, partly through looking at production history. I chose a ridiculously big area and would advise you to think on a smaller scale, which is why I suggested earlier focusing on people's responses to a character in a particular era and place, or on a specific title. This is much more manageable given the length of the typical dissertation. You also have to have a grasp of the general historical and cultural context. This may not make it into your final written work, but is a necessity, as mentioned, to make sense of what people say in interviews.

Further, as Barker had done in analyzing *Jackie*, I read samples of as many titles as possible over as wide a period as possible to get a sense of the evolution of each title, thus avoiding over-generalizing. Another key issue regarding work with audiences, then, is to have a good understanding of the specific comics you wish to explore perspectives on, as well as the general and production history surrounding them.

So, having got informed about your particular focus, where do you start with actual readers? The first element is finding willing participants. In my case these came from several sources, including some generated by my involvement with a number of newspaper articles, radio shows, and television programs. There are many other options, again depending on the nature of the project. You may, for instance, find yourself talking to other students, or contacting Facebook groups that center on a particular comic. My media involvement came in three forms. First, sometimes I was used as a commentator on a minor moral panic over literacy and comics or a specific comic or genre. Second was what could be described as "feel-good" stories about British girls' comics. My role could vary from being questioned rigorously to explaining nostalgia for a specific title or character. The third could be summarized as a "they let them study that at university!?" story, where I would be asked to defend researching comics. All three types of story led to contacts with individuals who were prepared to be interviewed, including some male readers of girls' comics. Other contacts came from the many professional and parent-led groups I worked with across Britain. This included, among others, teachers, librarians, art and literacy workers, authors, and artists. In all, I interviewed over 200 people in some depth and received letters and emails from many more.

It is important to remember that the interviews you gather are texts for analysis, just like comics. I found that there were many differences between what was remembered and what was actually in the texts when it came to analyzing interviews. This revealed a lot about how texts are re-written and relocated in autobiography. I took a qualitative research approach, using open-ended interviews with individuals, although you might choose to work with small groups and record their conversations. I created an interview schedule that incorporated a range of follow-up questions, but which allowed flexibility. I recorded and transcribed the interviews, color-coding particular themes when they appeared. There is now software available that will help with this kind of analysis.

I chose to use actual comics toward the end of interviews (although even a mention of a title could elicit a whole series of narratives). I made notes about how the use of artifacts initiated other narratives and sometimes resulted in the modification of previous ones. The tactile nature of responses to texts, to the artifact, as well as what was contained within it, was reflected in the way the feel of the paper of a specific title, or the smell of the ink, were often mentioned in the interview before an actual comic book was introduced. You may find, as I did, that physical aspects of the text are as important as content.

Nearly every British girls' comic was mentioned at some point during interviews, along with many from beyond that genre. The most commonly mentioned titles were *School Friend*,[32] *Girl's Crystal*,[33] *Girl*,[34] *Jackie*, *Bunty*, and *Twinkle*.[35] This made having a wider understanding of the genre and the medium very important. How far you allow the interviewee to talk about material that may seem beyond the research is up to you. In my case, allowing people to talk about their wider experience of comics proved important in countering the dominant discourse that girls only read comics for girls.

The majority of interviewees cited narratives focused on adventure, investigation, or education, or about girls' participation in sport and dance, particularly ballet.[36] Others cited narratives that could be located as science fiction and horror. Romance was more dominant in titles for older readers. Typically, interviewees mentioned characters by name, the titles of comics or specific narratives, not artists or writers. This is partly because British titles for girls were anthology comics containing a number of narratives in single-story arcs that each ran for around 14 weeks, along with a small number of gag strips. It is also because of the publishing practice of not giving the names of the artists and writers involved. This applied to the majority of the British girls' titles. Had I not known something of the production history of these texts, these omissions in interviews would have puzzled me.

SAMPLE ANALYSIS

It is often said that if you get the results you expect when researching audiences, then something has gone wrong. It is also true that you may well find yourself dealing with a very wide range of views and attitudes. There is unlikely to be a common response or simple map. You may, all the same, find some broad themes emerge, as I illustrate below.

Theme 1: Personal versus Professional Experience

Analysis of the interviews, in my case, revealed a range of responses regarding the theme of personal versus professional experience. In some, there were explicit tensions between the remembered girlhood experience of readers and professional and academic responses. Professional views here were often tied to wider perceptions of the medium regarding, in particular, gender and literacy. Here, female professional identity meant entering into a different kind of contract with the medium, intertwining identity and text in different ways. Negative discourses from earlier life (often from teachers) were remembered as things to kick against, but later formed the basis for concerns about the medium.

In other cases, forgetting—or burying—childhood memories of these texts was tied in with broader cultural discourses about leaving childhood behind, a different kind of shift in the text–reader contract in that it was imposed from without. Some reported being told that they were "too old" for such texts, which were then destroyed, typically by parents. Loss of a collection was frequently depicted as a culturally enforced form of growing-up.

These were not the only way of thinking about the texts, however. Other interviewees held two views of the texts simultaneously, using notions of current texts as more "dangerous" as a way of separating and isolating the two experiences of reading. This construction of current texts as all one kind and all historical texts as another could be said to reveal the action of nostalgia (although the comics of the past may have been seen as problematic in their time).

Others recalled having been forbidden from reading British girls' comics (or any at all) and either tended to assume that the medium was in some way dangerous and avoided it, or had become passionate readers in secret, rebelling against authority-imposed limitations.

Still other readers had retained memories of how important their comics had been to them and focused on their significance rather than notions of loss. This tended to make the interviewee more likely to be positive about contemporary comics and their readers. This experience was, interestingly, more commonly reported by those who had chosen to read comics that were not primarily associated with girls; typically humor comics or superhero titles. Their oppositional reading position regarding British girls' titles was often expressed by characterizing the girls' titles as "soppy." These readers were the group most likely to have gone on to become adult readers in the medium. As a consequence, they added another identity, that of comic reader or fan, to their professional and childhood selves. They also tended to have a working knowledge of the medium that informed, for instance, collection development in libraries.

Theme 2: Class and Social Relationships

The role these texts played in wider social relationships was frequently mentioned. Some interviewees suggested that these titles were used to establish or cement relationships within peer groups, but others said they were used to exclude (leading, in some cases, to negative memories of specific titles or genres). For instance, one interviewee recalled having characterized readers of *Girl* as "snobs" in comparison to those who read the same title as herself, namely the girls' comic *Bunty*. This interviewee's perception of class was articulated through her choice of both personal and oppositional text. *Girl* was quite expensive, produced on higher quality paper, contained more work in color, and was in a broadsheet format. While generating snobbery was not the intention of the publisher, it is true to say that *Girl* was often bought for, rather than by, girls; that the cost made it more likely to be, or be seen as, addressing a middle-class readership; and that the emphasis on career narratives could also be seen as aspirational.

Bunty, in contrast, was printed on very inexpensive paper, with limited use of color, had a tabloid format, and was cheaper. The softer paper of *Bunty* was described as "friendly" in some interviews, which also reflects a link between artifact, the tactile, and ideology. While this reader did not know anyone who read *Girl*, she made judgments on the basis of production issues and cost, thus articulating effectively who she felt the implied reader was for her comic and for one which she saw as Other. Such an analysis would only have been relevant during the brief period of production which both texts shared, a period covering 1958–1964, when this interviewee was one of the readers of *Bunty* and was around ten years old.

Here, then, the contract offered by *Bunty* was one that this reader had been prepared to enter and possible contracts elsewhere were rejected, in part informed by conclusions drawn from a physical analysis of the text, rather than content. This explicitly related the personal to the social, via class cross-cutting girlhood, and to production.

Theme 3: Cultural Practice

Reading together, swapping and handing on titles to younger siblings, friends, or other relatives were all themes in interviews.[37] One reader, for instance, said: "For me the very best of *Bunty* was the cut out doll and clothes on the back page, but I could not get it until all members of the household had had their read." Handing on comics, or moving on to different ones, sometimes reflected the way the contract of a specific title was no longer relevant due to age or changes in friendships. For example, one woman, speaking of her daughter's reading, said: "My youngest loved *Twinkle* when she was little. From 13–14 years of age she progressed to *Jackie* for teen girls—[it] explained girls' problems, also how to kiss a boy."

Such practices were also ways of establishing a contract with a title that would not be bought for an individual, as, for example, when parental purchases were dependent upon assumptions about gender.[38] For instance, as one woman stated, possessively, about one of her favorite titles, "My brother read the *Eagle*. He got it every week. He's younger than me … well, he didn't *read* the *Eagle* … he couldn't read it. So it was mine really."[39] *Eagle* was aimed at boys, a partner to the title *Girl*. While not bought for her, her contract is made through a claim of seniority and reading skill, both used to counterbalance her reading of a gender-inappropriate text.

Retaining and reading titles seen as for younger readers was also quite common, for a variety of reasons. Sometimes this was characterized as "comfort reading," but in several cases it was an initial recognition of sexual orientation. In these cases the intense friendships between girls in some of the narratives in titles for younger readers were important. These comics were preferred to those which focused on heterosexual romance.

Theme 4: Family Reading

The way in which the comic was positioned within the family was another major theme in interviews. As shown, there was frequently an opposition to the medium and some interviewees stated that their parents had seen the entire medium through the lens of class, seeing all comics as "lower-class" and, therefore, to be dismissed and avoided. Notions of contamination from reading them, of becoming "vulgar" irrespective of the actual content of the titles, were also common. However, some reported sharing titles across generations and gender, often in households where the comic was seen hugely positively. This could sometimes be positioned as a narrative of family, where freedom within the home was contrasted with opposition and criticism experienced outside.

Theme 5: Aspiration and Inspiration

That many of the women I interviewed self-identified as having been working-class, yet had often ended up both with qualifications and professional identities was also at odds with dominant cultural and academic discourses about girls' titles limiting aspirations. Again, a very complex picture emerged from analysis of the interviews. When someone engaged with a specific title—as titles changed over time—and what a specific individual read were both relevant. Even titles seen as non-aspirational by some were inspirational to others. This depended on what cultural capital the individual brought to his or her reading. In many cases the comics were cited as suggesting possible future directions, partly because many of the earlier titles included narratives about working lives and partly through less explicit means. The cut-out dolls that were printed on the back of *Bunty*, for instance, were stated to have influenced three interviewees who later had careers in fashion.

To conclude, this summary of methodology, theoretical and disciplinary location as applied to British girls' comics can only offer a thumbnail sketch of the approach taken. Work on audiences needs to be quite tightly defined, as I've shown here by working with a specific country, gender, and age group.

In my research, I established that British girls' comics can be seen as very much part of a girl's culture, frequently contributing to a sense of belonging, but one that might be cross-cut by age and class, and shift according to period and location. They could be part of a family culture or be used as an oppositional statement to authority in households and professional settings where the medium was disapproved of. These titles could also be seen as aspirational or as entrapping, depending on both childhood and adulthood contracts with the medium. Adults had produced these texts for children, but how they were consumed and understood by children revealed a role, for some, in rejecting adult values. How memory, professional practice, and wider cultural assumptions about the medium relate to the content of actual titles varies and often takes contradictory forms. Looking at cultural practices and locating the titles as part of a comic-reading autobiography involved exploring processes and notions of social power and relationships which were constantly changing over the period of the existence of the genre.

You should expect to find diverse voices and perspectives when working with audiences. There is not a single homogenous audience for any comic. For instance, the girl readers of superhero comics that I worked with had perspectives on their chosen texts which undermined many assumptions about gender and comics that are common in relation to that genre, something my own experience suggested.

The picture formed as a consequence of this approach to audience is usually very complex in that it focuses on the interplay of a range of discourses about identity and power across generations, as well as across both public/private and adult/child divides. The discourses concerning the medium in general, and British girls' comics in particular, that emerged in interviews emphasize some potential roles of comics in relation to subjectivity, power, and meaning construction.

NOTES

1. Keith Barker, ed., *Graphic Account* (London: Youth Libraries Group, 1993).
2. George H. Pumphrey, *Comics and Your Children* (London: Comics Campaign Council, 1954); George H. Pumphrey, *Children's Comics: A Guide for Parents and Teachers* (London: The Epworth Press, 1955); and George H. Pumphrey, *What Children Think of Their Comics* (London: Epworth Press, 1964).
3. Angela McRobbie, *Feminism and Youth Culture: From Jackie to Just Seventeen* (London: Macmillan, 1991).
4. Angela McRobbie, "Introduction," in *Feminism and Youth Culture: From Jackie to Just Seventeen* (London: Macmillan, 1991), x.
5. McRobbie, *Feminism and Youth Culture*.
6. *Jackie*. Dundee: DC Thomson, 1964–1993.
7. McRobbie, Introduction, xiv.
8. Angela McRobbie, "Working Class Girls and the Culture of Femininity," in *Women Take Issue: Aspects of Women's Subordination* ed. Women's Studies Group, CCCS (London: Hutchinson, 1978), 96–108.

9. Martin Barker, *Comics: Ideology, Power and the Critics* (Manchester: Manchester University Press, 1989), 248.
10. Valerie Walkerdine, "Some Day My Prince Will Come: Young Girls and the Preparation for Adolescent Sexuality," in *Gender and Generation,* ed. Angela McRobbie and Mica Nava (London: MacMillan, 1984), 162–184.
11. *Bunty.* Dundee: DC Thomson, 1958–2001.
12. *Tracy.* Dundee: DC Thomson, 1979–1985.
13. Elizabeth Frazer, "Teenage Girls Reading Jackie," *Media, Culture and Society* 9 (1987): 407–425.
14. Martin Barker, "Introduction" in *Comics: Ideology, Power and the Critics* (Manchester: Manchester University Press, 1989), ix.
15. Ibid., ix.
16. Ibid., 159.
17. Ibid., 195.
18. Ibid., 258.
19. Ibid., 261.
20. As exemplified by Jay Blumler and Elihu Katz, eds., *The Uses of Mass Communications: Current Perspectives on Gratifications Research* (Beverly Hills, CA: Sage, 1974) and later by Karl Erik Rosengren, Lawrence A. Wenner, and Philip Palmgreen Rosengren, eds., *Media Gratifications Research* (Beverly Hills, CA: Sage, 1985).
21. Shaun Moores, *Interpreting Audiences: The Ethnography of Media Consumption* (London: Sage, 1993), 7.
22. Denis McQuail, *Mass Communication Theory: An Introduction* (London: Sage, 1994), 319.
23. Moores, *Interpreting Audiences*, 7.
24. Ibid., 6.
25. Katherine M. Wolfe and Marjorie Fiske, "The Children Talk about the Comics," *Communication Research 1948–1949*, ed. Paul F. Lazaerfeld and Frank N. Stanton (New York: Harper & Bros, 1949), 3–50.
26. Barker, *Comics*, 246.
27. Moores, *Interpreting Audiences*, 7.
28. Ien Ang, *Living Room Wars: Rethinking Media Audiences for a Postmodern* World (London: Routledge, 1996), 41.
29. Moores, *Interpreting Audiences*.
30. Ang, *Living Room Wars*, 41.
31. Jay Blumler, Michael Gurevitch, and Elihu Katz, "Reaching Out: A Future for Gratifications Research," in *Media Gratifications Research: Current Perspectives*, ed. Karl Erik Rosengren, Lawrence A. Wenner, and Philip Palmgreen (Beverly Hills, CA: Sage, 1985), 255–273.
32. *School Friend.* London: AP, ran 1919–1929 as a story paper and 1950–1965 as a comic.
33. *Girls' Crystal.* London: AP, 1935–1963. Ran 1935–1953 as a story paper and then as a comic from number 909 in 1953–1963.
34. *Girl.* London: Hulton Press, 1951–1964.
35. *Twinkle.* Dundee: DC Thomson, 1968–1999.
36. Mel Gibson, "'What Became of *Bunty*?' The Emergence, Evolution and Disappearance of the Girls' Comic in Post-war Britain," in *Art, Narrative & Childhood*, ed. Eve Bearne and Morag Styles (Stoke on Trent: Trentham Books, 2003), 87–100; and Mel Gibson, "On British Comics for Girls and Their Readers," in *Consuming for Pleasure*, ed. Nickianne Moody (Liverpool: University of Liverpool John Moores Press, 2000), 210–227.
37. Mel Gibson, "What You Read and Where You Read It, How You Get It, How You Keep It: Children, Comics and Historical Cultural Practice," *Popular Narrative Media* 1 (2) (2008): 151–167.
38. Mel Gibson, "'You Can't Read Them, They're for Boys!' British Girls, American Superhero Comics and Identity," *International Journal of Comic Art* 5 (1) (2003): 305–324.
39. *Eagle.* London: Hulton Press, 1950–1969. A later version was produced by IPC/Fleetway, 1982–1994.

SELECTED BIBLIOGRAPHY

Ang, Ien. *Desperately Seeking the Audience.* London: Routledge, 1991.
Ang, Ien. *Living Room Wars: Rethinking Media Audiences for a Postmodern* World. London: Routledge, 1996.
Barker, Keith, ed. *Graphic Account.* London: Youth Libraries Group, 1993.
Barker, Martin. *Comics: Ideology, Power and the Critics.* Manchester: Manchester University Press, 1989.
Blumler, Jay and Elihu Katz, eds. *The Uses of Mass Communications: Current Perspectives on Gratifications Research.* Beverly Hills: Sage, 1974.

Blumler, Jay, Michael Gurevitch, and Elihu Katz. "Reaching Out: A Future for Gratifications Research." In *Media Gratifications Research: Current Perspectives*, edited by Karl Erik Rosengren, Lawrence A. Wenner, and Philip Palmgreen, 255–273. Beverly Hills: Sage, 1985.

Frazer, Elizabeth. "Teenage Girls Reading *Jackie*." *Media, Culture and Society* 9 (1987): 407–425.

Gibson, Mel. "On British Comics for Girls and their Readers." In *Consuming for Pleasure*, edited by Nickianne Moody, 210–227. Liverpool: University of Liverpool John Moores Press, 2000.

Gibson, Mel. "'What Became of *Bunty*?' The Emergence, Evolution and Disappearance of the Girls' Comic in Post-war Britain." In *Art, Narrative & Childhood*, edited by Eve Bearne and Morag Styles, 87–100. Stoke on Trent: Trentham Books, 2003.

Gibson, Mel "'You Can't Read Them, They're for Boys!' British Girls, American Superhero Comics and Identity." *International Journal of Comic Art* 5 (1) (2003): 305–324.

Gibson, Mel. "What You Read and Where You Read It, How You Get It, How You Keep It: Children, Comics and Historical Cultural Practice." *Popular Narrative Media* 1 (2) (2008): 151–167.

McQuail, Denis. *Mass Communication Theory: An Introduction* (3rd edn.). London: Sage, 1994.

McRobbie, Angela. "Working Class Girls and the Culture of Femininity." In *Women Take Issue: Aspects of Women's Subordination*, edited by Women's Studies Group, CCCS, 96–108. London: Hutchinson, 1978.

McRobbie, Angela. *Feminism and Youth Culture: From Jackie to Just Seventeen*. London: Macmillan, 1991.

Moores, Shaun. *Interpreting Audiences: The Ethnography of Media Consumption*. London: Sage, 1993.

Pumphrey, George. H. *Comics and Your Children*. London: Comics Campaign Council, 1954.

Pumphrey, George. H. *Children's Comics: A Guide for Parents and Teachers*. London: Epworth Press, 1955.

Pumphrey, George. H. *What Children Think of their Comics*. London: Epworth Press, 1964.

Rosengren, Karl Erik, Lawrence A. Wenner, and Philip Palmgreen Rosengren, eds. *Media Gratifications Research*. Beverly Hills: Sage, 1985.

Walkerdine, Valerie. "Some Day My Prince Will Come: Young Girls and the Preparation for Adolescent Sexuality." In *Gender and Generation*, edited by Angela McRobbie and Mica Nava, 162–184. London: MacMillan, 1984.

Wolfe, Katherine M. and Marjorie Fiske "The Children Talk about the Comics." In *Communication Research 1948–1949*, edited by Paul F. Lazaerfeld and Frank N. Stanton, 3–50. New York: Harper, 1949.

20

ETHNOGRAPHY

Wearing One's Fandom

Jeffrey A. Brown

I recently taught a senior seminar entitled "Comics and the Superhero Genre" which had an interesting mix of students. Approximately half of the class were die-hard comic book readers, and the rest were divided evenly between casual comic book fans and those who had never read a comic and only knew of superheroes through recent Hollywood films. It was easy to spot the life-long fans because almost every one of them wore a different superhero T-shirt to class all term. For every student with "American Eagle," "Abercrombie and Fitch," or our university logo written across their chest, there was one with a picture of Batman, Spider-Man, or Iron Man on their shirt. Occasionally the students who were new to comics would joke about not feeling like part of the club since they did not wear the unofficial class uniform. When four students brought in pictures of themselves costumed as their favorite superheroes for Halloween, half of the class were impressed, the other half were baffled. None of our discussion about the genre's historical development, structural elements, gender depictions, or readings about ethnicity, sexuality, hegemony, or patriotism helped the comic book novices understand their colleagues' devotion to wearing superhero clothing.

What the novice students were learning was that, perhaps more than any other genre, comic book superheroes are not restricted to a single medium. The genre is also fundamentally intertwined with a subculture of devoted consumers to such an extent that consideration of the fans is an essential element for understanding the cultural significance of the genre. Analytical methods applied to superhero stories can reveal a lot about how the medium expresses various cultural beliefs, but textual analysis alone cannot account for the various ways that dedicated fans use superheroes to establish a sense of community, express ideological identification with characters, or how they use the genre to project a sense of their core personal identity. In order to understand the importance of comics for a large portion of their readership we have to move beyond textual analysis and into the realm of "ethnography." Ethnography is a qualitative methodology that involves a researcher interviewing subjects, participating in events, and sometimes even living within a given community in order to explore how real people embody and express cultural ideals. We have to consider the fans themselves and how they relate to the comics and to each other. It is only by focusing on the subcultural practice of comic fandom that we can begin to understand why wearing superhero-adorned clothing and specific Halloween costumes allows individuals to express communal affiliation and present an idealized version of their own personalities.

UNDERLYING ASSUMPTIONS

Ethnography is the dominant methodology used in cultural anthropology in order to gather empirical data and first-hand (indigenous) insights into a social group or community. As a methodological approach, ethnography came to dominance in anthropology in the 1920s. In its most conventional sense, ethnographic fieldwork consists of a researcher living among a clearly defined community (both culturally and geographically), often a village or tribe, in order to gain an accurate and humanistic interpretation of the group and their cultural principles. Central to the ethnographic method is the use of participant-observation, formal and casual interviews, and questionnaires. The resulting study, or ethnographic monograph, was usually written up as an interpretive text heavily dependent on detailed observations about the lives of the subjects and with an emphasis on what Clifford Geertz famously referred to as "thick description,"[1] which is providing detailed examples of behavior in a context that helps explain the complex cultural meanings they enact. The emphasis on description is an effort to present cultural analysis which does not efface the humanity or the complexity of the subjects, and which is all the more authentic for its relatively unmediated presentation of facts. The objective of ethnography is to understand a culture from the native's point of view. Debates about the authenticity of ethnographic practices, and questions about the ability of foreign anthropologists to truly speak for the natives, have circulated since the 1980s.[2] Contemporary ethnographers are increasingly cognizant of the need to recognize their own ideological positions and how they may affect the interpretation of their subjects' culture.

Ethnography was eventually adopted by scholars working in the areas of media and cultural studies because the methodology facilitates a better understanding of how and why people from specific cultural groups see the world. A group such as American comic book fans may seem worlds away from Trobriand Islanders, but as a methodology, ethnography is an equally effective tool for understanding how both groups of people make sense of their world. The impetus for incorporating ethnographic techniques into the study of subcultures in Western societies is generally credited to the group of scholars associated with the Centre for Contemporary Culture Studies (CCCS) at Birmingham in the 1960s and 1970s.[3] Most of the CCCS scholars and their contemporaries shared an interest in subjects like youth subcultures, media consumption, and everyday uses of popular culture. In an era obsessed with moral panics about radical youth styles such as rockers, teddies, mods, and punks, these scholars turned to ethnography in order to come to grips with what these new youth subcultures revealed about styles, material consumption, and predominantly working-class, post-war beliefs. Likewise, the group was interested in discovering how real people consumed and interpreted media texts in a myriad of ways that ran counter to the dominant, Frankfurt School-inspired assumption that the media indoctrinated the masses into adopting specific ideological and hegemonic beliefs.[4] It was these twin interests in subcultures and the use of media texts that resulted in ethnographic techniques being used to consider what real people do with popular culture. And by interviewing, participating in communal events, observing their daily behaviors and activities, and sometimes even living with their subjects, these cultural studies scholars refuted the assumptions that youth was becoming increasingly corrupt for no good reason and that media consumers were automatically incorporated into dominant worldviews. Instead, they discovered that people from all walks of life use and interpret mediated messages and the materials of popular culture in myriad ways that reveal individuality, creativity, and ideological resistance.

Building on the question of "What do real people do with media texts?" ethnographic approaches to fandom became the next logical step. Landmark studies have considered a wide range of fan groups as diverse as Harlequin romance readers,[5] Trekkers,[6] and *Cagney & Lacey* viewers.[7] In recent years there has been a great deal of ethnographic work done on fandoms devoted to such cult favorites as *Dr. Who, The X-Files, Buffy the Vampire Slayer*, and *Xena: Warrior Princess*, as well as fans of specific musical groups like The Grateful Dead, The Dave Mathews Band, or Phish, and book series including *Harry Potter* and *Twilight*.[8] Subcultures of fans are an ideal subject for ethnographic considerations of media use for a variety of reasons. First, fans are passionate about their consumption of popular culture and are especially active in their use of the texts (for example, making Halloween costumes based on favorite characters). Second, serious fans are easier to identify than more casual consumers because they often share similar styles (such as superhero T-shirts). And third, they are usually easier to locate in that they often gather at events/locations such as concerts, conventions, or specialty stores. Fans are an extreme example of how people consume and interpret popular texts such as comic books. By using an ethnographic approach we can begin to understand what the texts actually mean for the reader rather than just theorizing possible meanings assumed to be inherent in the text and only accessible by critics using learned analytical methods such as Marxism, semiotics, or psychoanalysis.

OBJECT OF STUDY

This chapter is not concerned with the content of any actual comic books. It is concerned with a larger understanding of how comic book superheroes function for fans as a crystallization of ideals and beliefs, and how these concepts are expressed through subcultural fashions. This research was inspired by the students who were baffled by their classmates' consistent superhero T-shirts and elaborate Halloween costumes. By using an ethnographic approach we can see how something as apparently simple as clothing can reveal a wealth of subcultural values. Though fans are more enthusiastic in their media consumption and easier to identify, that does not always mean it is easy to get in touch with them. In traditional ethnography, the researcher can simply move into a village (though even that is not always as simple as it may sound) and then interact continually with his/her subjects. But studying subcultures within one's own community requires a different approach. Researchers working within modern industrialized societies cannot simply live with their subjects. Instead, they must seek out members of the subculture wherever they may congregate, befriend them, and ask their permission to study them. Many universities also require ethnographic projects to be approved by a human subjects review board before research can begin in order to ensure the rights and safety of both the researcher and the proposed subjects.

Gaining access to a subculture can sometimes be a long and arduous process of being introduced to the right people, passing tests of legitimacy, and becoming familiar enough to the group that they may eventually accept you. For many traditional anthropologists, the high point of their fieldwork experience is when a member of the village symbolically adopts them, or when they are asked to undertake a ritual to become part of the tribe. Similarly, researchers working with contemporary subcultures may invest years before being fully accepted and trusted by their subjects. Even after strong contacts have been made within a subculture, ethnographic research in modern industrialized societies can be very labor intensive. Janice Radway has argued that a fundamental challenge for ethnographic studies of media reception is the problem of dispersed audiences and nomadic subjects.[9] Groups such as comic book fans can be difficult to pin down. Ethnographers of popular culture often must conduct their research whenever and wherever they can. Gatherings like conventions can be eminently useful, but they are too brief to allow a sustained period of observation. Media and subcultural ethnographers often spend months or even years establishing contacts and/or chasing around the city trying to gather information about the subjects.

It is likely that the long process of being accepted by members of a subculture and the onerous leg-work involved in data collection are two of the reasons that most scholars who use an ethnographic approach to fandom were themselves fans before they began to study the phenomenon. I, for one, have been a life-long comic book fan and was as likely as many of my students to wear a superhero T-shirt to class everyday (and I suspect every contributor to this book was also a comics fan long before they became academics). This is not as unusual as it may sound. After all, every Shakespearean scholar started out as a fan of the Bard, and every marine biologist was initially just a fish enthusiast. Still, it is important to point out one's own affiliation when doing ethnographic research because the data never speaks for itself. The ethnographer is always an intermediary between the research subjects and the reader, and his or her presence should be recognized because it affects how the data is interpreted and presented.

PROCESS

As a point of clarification, I want to emphasize that I do not believe most of the work typically classified as subcultural or media reception "ethnographies" (my own included[10]) are really ethnographies in the strictest anthropological sense of the term. Researchers studying goths, punks, bikers, Trekkers, ringers, cos-players, or any other subgroup found within our own larger national or regional cultures may use qualitative ethnographic methods, but that is very different from the day-in, day-out experience that traditional anthropology relies on. Still, by using ethnographic methods like participant observation and extensive interviews, researchers can move beyond the imposition of their own cultural assumptions about the "meaning" of something (like a TV series or a piece of clothing) and begin to understand what the deeper significances are for the people who consume or experience that aspect of popular culture.

The first step for any ethnographer is to provide some context for readers by identifying the subjects involved, the methods used for gathering data, and the relevant time frame of the research. The data for this chapter is drawn primarily from research conducted during the fall of 2008 and the spring of 2009. Some of the material is supplemented by my earlier ethnographic study of Milestone Media comic book fans, and some follow-up interviews that occurred in the mid-2000s. The primary subject group consisted of 28 individuals (20 males, 8 females) who self-identified as serious comic book superhero fans. All of the subjects were in their late teens or early twenties and described themselves as economically middle-class. The research was conducted in and around northwest Ohio, though many of the subjects were originally from different parts of North America. Seven of the subjects were students of mine, while the other 21 were individuals I met through two local comic book stores, either by introducing myself or after being referred to a specific fan by employees of the store (cultural gatekeepers are an essential asset for ethnographers, whether they are comic shop owners or tribal elders). The primary method used was informal interviewing. Rather than a formal interview, which all too often implies an unequal relationship in favor of the interviewer—who controls the subject, the tempo, and the language used—I consider my interactions with these fans to be more akin to conversations. In this case conversations were much more effective because the age difference between most of the subjects and myself (I am in my early forties) would seem even more distancing in a formal setting. I wanted to avoid the fans' perception that I was an authority (a university professor) with some sort of judgmental agenda. Instead of trying to "get at" certain perceptions I was developing through direct questions, I found conversing about a shared interest to be much more conducive in a collaborative sense. Here I have taken a cue from Lindlof and Grodin, who discussed the practical advantages of the collaborative, unstructured style of interviewing as especially effective when faced with the difficulties of studying a dispersed audience and a system of media use (e.g., reading) that cannot be observed directly.[11] Moreover, conversation based on affiliation seemed to encourage the reader's enthusiasm because it is the way fans speak with each other, and it also avoids any misperceptions that the researcher may be simply a judgmental outsider.

In the case of this project, finding the subjects was relatively easy. Whenever I saw a fan wearing a superhero T-shirt at a comic book store, at a convention, or even in the classroom I simply identified myself, explained the project and engaged them in conversation about their clothing. All of the subjects were eager to talk about their fashion statement. "This is my favorite Batman shirt," exclaimed Steve, a 17-year-old high-school student, "I have about five more at home but I love that he looks really bad-ass on this one!" All of the other respondents were just as enthusiastic. For example, Kevin, a 35-year-old salesperson declared: "My superhero shirts are just about all I wear when I'm not at work. They are kind of my trademark." And Julie, a 20-year-old college student, excitedly claimed: "I love all my superhero shirts! Not a lot of women are into comics so this kind of sets me apart from the crowd." What quickly became apparent was that all of the people I spoke with were not embarrassed by wearing shirts that others may associate with childhood heroes. Rather, the respondents were proud to wear their favorite heroes on their chests and to detail the extent and the type of their superhero shirt collections. All of the subjects claimed to have at least five superhero shirts, and several owned over 30. Three of the 28 subjects claimed that they were familiar with the characters primarily through recent Hollywood films and television programs; the remaining 25 identified themselves as serious comic book fans. Interestingly, only four of the participants said they simply purchased any superhero shirt they thought looked good; the rest had very specific types of superhero shirts. The most common type of collection (over 50 percent) was devoted to favorite characters (e.g., only Batman, Spider-Man, or Wonder Woman shirts); others owned shirts with characters from specific publishers (e.g., only Marvel, DC, or Top Cow); and two of the individuals would only wear shirts they had made or altered themselves. The visible pleasure all of these fans took in wearing super-hero shirts, and the seriousness with which they collected them, helps to reveal several key subcultural principles. The most obvious revelation is that the shirts allow people to publicly declare themselves as members of comics fandom. Or, as Josh, a 20-year-old college student remarked: "My shirts let everyone know I'm a proud comic book aficionado. I'm a super-geek!"

SAMPLE ANALYSIS

As a marker of cultural status, or subcultural belonging, what we wear has always been an important tool. In all cultures, clothing is a primary means by which we understand other individuals and is a symbol by which we convey our own sense of identity. Think about how often we in Western culture characterize someone's economic, racial, or professional status by the type of clothing they wear. In a similar manner, we identify people as part of a subculture by the way they are dressed. Goths wear black exclusively, bikers wear jeans and leathers, skateboarders wear baggy clothes, and so on. Comic book fans wearing superhero T-shirts is a very literal way to mark themselves as part of a fan subculture. In his seminal study of British youth, *Subculture: The Meaning of Style*, Dick Hebdige emphasized the symbolic importance that clothing carried as a means to declare group affiliation and as a form of resistance to dominant cultural standards.[12] Hebdige described how groups such as punks, mods, and teddies used radical clothing styles to set themselves apart from the general populace and to convey their ideological frustration with the political and economic conditions they found themselves in during a period of British decline. Though not as explicitly political in motivation as the radical styles of punk, many of the individuals I interviewed stressed the importance of their shirts as a way to mark themselves as non-conformists. "I kind of like that most people look down on comics fans," said Mike, a mid-twenties medical student

> cause most people are idiots. Comics fans tend to be smarter—at least I like to think so—and embracing the fact that you are a comic book nerd by something as simple as wearing a shirt is a way to say "screw you" to all the people who are dressed exactly alike with clothing from Abercrombie and Guess.

Likewise, Luke, a high-school senior, claimed

> I want everyone to know that I'm into comics even if they are not "cool." I'm not going to be brainwashed by MTV and magazine ads that tell me what I'm supposed to look like to be accepted. I'm into comics and they're fun, so I take a lot of pride in being different from most of the kids I go to school with.

For these two, and for most of the other subjects, wearing superhero T-shirts is a way to distance oneself from the perceived conformity of our larger commercial society. They see themselves as above, or beyond, merely accepting the media-imposed cultural standards of "cool" clothing. In Hebdige's terms, they demonstrate a degree of resistance to cultural conformity.

In addition to marking someone as a member of comics fandom, the respondents also perceived their own T-shirt collections, and those of others, as an indicator of how serious and knowledgeable a fan someone is. "I have a pretty awesome collection of shirts," declared John, a 24-year-old police officer.

> Some are really old, some are foreign, some are limited editions. I'm really proud of them because they let everyone else—at cons or the comic shop—know that I'm a hard-core fan. I know my shit when it comes to superheroes and some of the younger customers who have seen me around will ask me what books they should be reading and what I think about certain storylines.

Likewise, when I approached a teenage boy going through the clothing racks at Monarch Comics in Toledo and asked if he was looking for anything specific, he said:

> Yeah, I want the same shirt that the guy behind the counter is wearing. My friends and I come in here every Wednesday and he always has a different cool shirt on. He must have hundreds of them. I wish I had a tenth of the collection he does. Must be nice to have the inside track and get first dibs on the best comics and shirts … and to have an unlimited supply of comics to read.

Comments like these were repeated over and over again. Julie claimed to be the envy of her friends because she had "the most kick-ass Wonder Woman and Batgirl shirts." Casey was described by two companions as knowing "the most about Iron Man, and he has the T-shirts to prove it."

This tendency to equate certain shirts with prestige suggests that the quality and quantity of each fan's T-shirt collection is indicative of what is referred to as "cultural capital" within the subculture. The idea of cultural capital (or cultural economy) was initially proposed by the French ethnographer Pierre Bourdieu in his study of upper-class Parisian society.[13] Bourdieu noted that within group dynamics a hierarchy emerges based on the members' perceived relative status, a ranking based in the Parisian case on an individual's accumulation of both economic capital (material wealth) and cultural capital (knowledge, experience, expertise). Cultural Studies scholar John Fiske extrapolated from Bourdieu's concept to argue that a type of shadow cultural economy exists for fan communities in that, regardless of someone's economic or social status within the larger culture, individuals in the subculture can accumulate a great deal of status (subcultural capital) if they are seen as especially knowledgeable about topics or can demonstrate an advanced level of commitment to the subject.[14] In this sense, the wearing of superhero T-shirts amounts not just to being part of comics fandom, but to declaring oneself, and being perceived by others, as a serious fan or a type of expert. In other words, the shirts indicate a possession of subcultural capital of a higher level than that obtained by more casual fans.

The two subjects who only wore self-made T-shirts may at first glance seem to be an anomaly in this era where superhero T-shirts are readily available in every comics store, Wal-Mart, and Target. "I refuse to wear any of the mass produced, boring T-shirts that you can find in every grocery store," argued Susan, a bartender in her early thirties.

> If I'm given a shirt by someone for my birthday or Christmas I always cut it up and make something new out of it. I keep the image of the character but I turn the shirt into a dress, or rip it and rearrange it onto another shirt.

When I first spoke with Susan she was wearing one of her favorite creations, a long-sleeved shirt with images of Harley Quinn and Black Widow stitched together so they appeared to be holding hands. "I really like this one because it is clearly one of a kind," she explained. "Since they are from different companies, it is impossible to find a shirt with the two of them together unless you make it yourself." On another shirt Susan had sewn an image of Batgirl onto a picture of a Segway scooter so that it looked like she was happily riding it off to some adventure. Sean, the other do-it-yourself shirt maker was a 26-year-old freelance designer who specialized in making iron-on transfers. "I like messing around in Photoshop after I've scanned an image I like of Wolverine or Daredevil or whoever," said Sean, "then once I've finished cropping it and adjusting colors I print it out on special paper and iron it on to a cheap T-shirt." Both Susan and Sean prided themselves on wearing only unique shirts and both recounted stories of other comics fans enviously asking where they had gotten them.

This practice of creating one's own clothing rather than simply buying it off the rack has a long tradition in subcultures. While it may be an anomaly among comics fans, making one's own superhero T-shirts can be understood as similar to what Hebdige described as the art of "bricolage" practiced by punks.[15] *Bricolage* is a French term Hebdige used to characterize the way punks would put together and wear unrelated items (e.g., safety pins, tampons, Boy Scout patches) in order to convey new and unsettling meanings to their clothing. More precisely, these do-it-yourself T-shirt makers are an example of what Henry Jenkins calls "textual poaching," a particularly interesting activity among fan groups.[16] Jenkins argues that fan activities such as filking (singing folk songs about television characters), making fan art (drawings, paintings, or photo manipulations of popular characters), or creating slash fiction (original stories or videos that place familiar characters in novel, often homoerotic, situations) are modern examples of poaching, the historical act of illegally hunting game from royal preserves. Contemporary textual poaching can be understood as fans appropriating corporately owned characters from their official texts and adapting them to create works that speak to fans' desires and fantasies that would never be sanctioned by those who hold the legal rights. Most textual poaching may be harmless fun, but some, such as explicitly homosexual depictions of Batman and Robin, can have serious legal ramifications when corporations like DC Comics, and its parent company Time Warner, have a vested interest in preserving Batman and Robin's wholesome and safely heterosexual image. Yet textual poaching, even when as seemingly benign as putting Harley Quinn (a DC property) and Black Widow (a Marvel property) together on a shirt, is evidence that fans do not simply make-do with the mass-produced narratives they consume. Rather, fans and even casual consumers actively use and re-imagine texts to fulfill their own needs.

The final point I'd like to make about the importance of superhero T-shirts for their wearers is that in addition to marking membership and relative standing within a fan community, all of the respondents appeared to have a personal connection with the characters they wore. This connection is most apparent when the individuals focused on collecting specific characters. As Steve explained, he only wore Batman shirts because

> Batman is my favorite superhero. Not just because he is cool but because he has no superpowers. He is just a normal guy—OK, a normal really rich guy—but he is the best hero because he is the smartest and works really hard to be true to his ideals.

Likewise, Rick, a 28-year-old graduate student, said he always wears Spider-Man shirts because "he doesn't really fit in with other supes. He has all these amazing powers and is super strong but he is unlike any other superheroes.... He sees the ridiculousness of the whole concept and is always funny." Others, like Jenna, a 24-year-old who describes herself as a modest feminist, concentrates on female superheroes because:

> Comics are such a guy thing, a pile of over-the-top muscles and testosterone. It's hard to be a feminist comic fan sometimes and so I latch on to the few female heroes who are more than just their sex appeal. That's why I have so many Wonder Woman and Supergirl and Batgirl shirts. I like a lot of the male centered books, but when I'm among other fans I want them to know that I care the most about superheroines.

Each of these fans, and most of the others I spoke with, use superhero T-shirts as a way to identify themselves as fans of specific characters because those heroes embody certain ideals (intelligence, humor, feminism) that the wearer values.

By collecting and wearing shirts of heroes who embody specific characteristics, the fans are symbolically creating a link between themselves and those characteristics. The shirts act as a bridge between what anthropologist Grant McCracken calls the "real" and the "ideal."[17] In other words, all cultures and all individuals constantly negotiate the precarious balance between our real world and our communal or personal ideals. The way things are is seldom the way we desire them to be. For a culture struggling with the reality of racism, the ideal may be a future where skin color is irrelevant. For an individual faced with real economic difficulties, the ideal may be dreams of winning the lottery. For individual comic book fans, like many of the ones in this study, the reality may be a boring job, long hours of school, being a bit socially awkward among peers, or experiencing sexism or racism or any other undesirable social ostracization. In contrast to their mundane reality, these fans embrace an ideal represented by certain characters. The ideal intelligence of a Batman, strength of a Superman, humor of a Spider-Man, female power of a Wonder Woman, and so on. As Stuart, a 26-year-old mechanic, insightfully put it:

> I wear these shirts because I identify with Wolverine. I think I'm like him in a lot of ways. Not the killing stuff ... but I am straight forward and don't take a lot of crap. I have a sense of humor, but can be really serious and focused when I need to be. Wolverine is kind of how I ideally see myself—without any of the spandex though.

Something as simple as a T-shirt can make abstract ideals feel concrete. As McCracken argues:

> Goods help the individual contemplate the possession of an emotional condition, a social circumstance, even an entire style of life, by somehow concretizing these things in themselves. They become a bridge to displaced meaning and an idealized version of life as it should be lived.[18]

The function of superhero T-shirts as a link or bridge between the real and the ideal may not be a factor for all the collectors; some may do it just because it is fun or stylish, but the passion almost all of the subjects demonstrated about their shirts suggests a very deep and personal meaning.

There is nothing in comic books themselves that could help explain to the non-fans in my class why so many of their classmates routinely wore superhero T-shirts. Nor could different methodological approaches to the text reveal any great insights into the passion of the fans. Yet, by utilizing an ethnographic approach, speaking with and observing real people, we can begin to understand that something as simple as wearing certain T-shirts can be loaded with personal and subcultural meanings. Clothing can represent membership in a fan community, it can symbolize an expertise about the subject, it can be used as a way to resist cultural conformity or as a means to re-work the official meanings of the characters. The shirts can even act as a bridge between our mundane selves and our idealized self-perceptions. As a methodological approach, ethnography is a lot of work, but the insights we can gain from talking with real people and considering how they see and use things like T-shirts is well worth it.

NOTES

1. Clifford Geertz, *The Interpretation of Culture* (New York: Basic Books, 1973).
2. See, for example, James Clifford and George E. Marcuse, *Writing Culture: The Poetics and Politics of Ethnography* (Berkley: University of California Press, 1986); James Clifford, *The Predicament of Culture: Twentieth-Century Ethnography, Literature and Art* (Cambridge, MA: University of Harvard Press, 1988); and Paul Atkinson, *The Ethnographic Imagination: Textual Constructions of Reality* (London: Routledge Press, 1990).
3. For a review of the influence of CCCS scholarship, see Patrick Bratlinger, *Crusoe's Footprints: Cultural Studies in Britain and America* (New York: Routledge, 1990).
4. See, for example, Theodor Adorno and Max Horkheimer, "The Culture Industry: Enlightenment as Mass Deception" reprinted in James Curran, Michael Gurevitch, and Janet Woolacott, eds., *Mass Communication and Society* (London: Edward Arnold Press, 1977).
5. Janice Radway, *Reading the Romance: Women, Patriarchy and Popular Literature* (New York: Verso, 1987).
6. Henry Jenkins, *Textual Poachers: Television Fans and Participatory Culture* (New York: Routledge, 1992).
7. Julie D'Acci, *Defining Women: Television and the Case of Cagney and Lacey* (Chapel Hill: University of North Carolina Press, 1994).
8. For a historical overview of Subcultural Studies, see Ken Gelder and Sarah Thornton, eds., *The Subcultures Reader* (New York: Routledge, 1997); for introductions to the field of Fan Studies, see Lisa A. Lewis, ed., *The Adoring Audience* (New York: Routledge, 1992) or Matt Hills, *Fan Cultures* (New York: Routledge, 2002).
9. Janice Radway, "Reception Study: Ethnography and the Problem of Dispersed Audiences and Nomadic Subjects," *Cultural Studies* 2 (3) (1988): 359–376.
10. Jeffrey A. Brown, *Black Superheroes: Milestone Comics and Their Fans* (Jackson, MS: University Press of Mississippi, 2001).
11. Thomas R. Lindlof and Debra Grodin, "When Media Use Can't Be Observed: Some Problems and Tactics of Collaborative Audience Research," *Journal of Communication* 40 (4) (1990): 8–28.
12. Dick Hebdige, *Subculture: The Meaning of Style* (London: Methuen Press, 1979).
13. Pierre Bourdieu, *Distinction: A Socila Critique of the Judgment of Taste,* (Cambridge, MA: Harvard University Press, 1984).
14. John Fiske, "The Cultural Economy of Fandom," in *The Adoring Audience,* ed. Lisa A. Lewis (New York: Routledge, 1992), 30–49.
15. Hebdige, *Subculture.*
16. Jenkins, *Textual Poachers.*
17. Grant McCracken, *Culture and Consumption* (Bloomington, IN: Indiana University Press, 1990).
18. Ibid., 110.

SELECTED BIBLIOGRAPHY

Adorno, Theodor and Max Horkheimer. "The Culture Industry: Enlightenment as Mass Deception." In *Mass Communication and Society*, edited by James Curran, Michael Gurevitch, and Janet Woolacott, 349–383. London: Edward Arnold Press, 1977.

Atkinson, Paul. *The Ethnographic Imagination: Textual Constructions of Reality.* Routledge: London, 1990.

Bourdieu, Pierre. *Distinction: A Social Critique of the Judgment of Taste.* Cambridge, MA: Harvard University Press, 1984.

Bratlinger, Patrick. *Crusoe's Footprints: Cultural Studies in Britain and America.* New York: Routledge, 1990.

Brown, Jeffrey A. *Black Superheroes: Milestone Comics and their Fans.* Jackson, MS: University Press of Mississippi, 2001.

Clifford, James and George E. Marcuse. *Writing Culture: The Poetics and Politics of Ethnography.* Berkeley: University of California Press, 1986.

Clifford, James. *The Predicament of Culture: Twentieth-Century Ethnography, Literature and Art,* Cambridge, MA: University of Harvard Press, 1988.

D'Acci, Julie. *Defining Women: Television and the Case of Cagney and Lacey.* Chapel Hill: University of North Carolina Press, 1994.

Fiske, John. "The Cultural Economy of Fandom." In *The Adoring Audience,* edited by Lisa A. Lewis, 30–49. New York: Routledge, 1992.

Geertz, Clifford. *The Interpretation of Culture.* New York: Basic Books, 1973.

Gelder, Ken and Sarah Thornton, eds. *The Subcultures Reader.* New York: Routledge, 1997.

Hebdige, Dick. *Subculture: The Meaning of Style.* London: Metheun Press, 1979.

Hills, Matt. *Fan Cultures.* New York: Routledge, 2002.

Jenkins, Henry. *Textual Poachers: Television Fans and Participatory Culture.* New York: Routledge Press, 1992.

Lewis, Lisa A., ed. *The Adoring Audience.* New York: Routledge, 1992.

Lindlof, Thomas R. and Debra Grodin. "When Media Use Can't Be Observed: Some Problems and Tactics of Collaborative Audience Research." *Journal of Communication* 40 (4) (1990): 8–28.

McCracken, Grant. *Culture and Consumption.* Bloomington: Indiana University Press, 1990.

Radway, Janice. *Reading the Romance: Women, Patriarchy and Popular Literature.* New York: Verso, 1987.

Radway, Janice. "Reception Study: Ethnography and the Problem of Dispersed Audiences and Nomadic Subjects." *Cultural Studies* 2 (3) (1988): 359–376.

21

CRITICAL ETHNOGRAPHY

The Comics Shop As Cultural Clubhouse

Brian Swafford

Nestled between a coffee shop and a Middle Eastern restaurant is a non-descript door that marks the portal into the local comic shop. Having been in my fair share of comic shops, the sights and sounds were familiar enough. Along the wall next to the door are the racks of new comics on display. The latest issues all greet an entrant into the shop. While these comics represent an industry that earns billions of dollars annually, there are still some ... troubling ... items. In particular, the heroines that share the covers with the heroes have a particular look: tall, with narrow waists, curvy hips, and ample bust lines.

The cover art and representations of women may be designed to appeal to a particular male audience, yet they also serve as a deterrent to "unwelcome" entrance by outsiders, in this case women. Looking around the shop, the four patrons playing a tabletop game, the two employees behind the counter, and the three other patrons leafing through the wares of the shop are all male. As I stand there, taking in the scene, the entrance bell clangs and a man, with a woman in tow, enters the shop looking for his latest comics. As she hides behind his arm from the other patrons, I overhear her ask why she had to come inside.

"I'll just be a minute. It's okay."

"I don't belong in here. Why do you always drag me in here?"

"Whatever. I've got 'em. We can go."

In a typical trip to the local comic shop, an avid reader will likely scan the new releases for interesting titles, ask for pulls (reserved items), and purchase the desired comics before leaving the shop for the week. Yet the preceding story takes a step back from the routine to explore how the comics themselves and the community members enact practices that ostracize others. In this case, the female visitor to the shop said she didn't belong and hid from view. This is a brief example of the type of work done through critical ethnography. Critical ethnography is defined as a qualitative research approach concerned with relations and power inequities between individuals and the sociopolitical framework, transformation of these relations, and attention to the research process as a form of action.[1] The researcher will go to a locale and observe the behaviors of community members before attempting to explain how the community practices entrench certain power relationships.

In this chapter, critical ethnography will be utilized to examine one local comic book shop to see how the practices of the patrons craft a particular culture within the shop. Unlike other methods that focus more on an analysis of some text, critical ethnography is more focused on the process of observation with an eye toward uncovering how the everyday practices of people perpetuate and reinforce greater societal power relationships and standards. As such, there needs to be a greater focus on how a researcher will observe a setting and then report the findings. This chapter explains how the commonplace practices that are often taken for granted can reveal a great deal about the underlying assumptions of the way the world works. Before getting into the key points about fieldwork and writing the analysis, certain fundamental assumptions of critical ethnography must be considered.

UNDERLYING ASSUMPTIONS

Ethnographic research emerged out of anthropological studies that asked researchers to go out into the field, live in a location, and observe and report the behaviors of the indigenous people. The focus of this conventional ethnography has been on cultural descriptions and analysis, with meaning coming through the interpretations of the researcher.[2] In many ways the ethnographer's goal is to "make the familiar strange, the exotic quotidian."[3] In other words, the ethnography observes the everyday experiences of a particular location and then attempts to provide meaning for the behaviors that were observed. While the critical ethnographer may utilize many of the techniques and practices of the traditional ethnographer, critical theory moves to the forefront of the analysis.[4] Dwight Conquergood claims that critical theory "is committed to unveiling the political stakes that anchor cultural practices."[5] Critical ethnography is a way of challenging conventional narratives of cultural inquiry through a more reflective style of thinking about relationships between society, knowledge, and social power structures.[6] In his musings about critical ethnography, Jim Thomas claims that critical ethnography should not be thought of as theory, but rather as a perspective. Critical ethnography provides value premises which lead to particular questions and establish a means of challenging the powerful forces of society.[7]

The first assumption of critical ethnography is that behaviors can only be observed by being there, in the field. Good ethnographic work requires a researcher to go out into the field to observe behaviors. George Marcus says that an ethnographer should focus on a strategically selected locale that will provide greater insight into the happenings of a particular community.[8] Ethnography has been called an embodied practice because it relies on the researcher taking careful notes about observable behaviors.[9] Before any analysis can occur, a researcher must go into the field and observe until behaviors become repetitive.

The second assumption is that critical engagement emerges through dialogue with community members in the field. Unlike traditional ethnography that focuses on observations, the critical ethnographer seeks to engage in dialogue with the members of the locale.[10] The reliance on dialogue is important for a few reasons. Initially, it breaks down the barrier between the observer and the observed. Through the use of critical theory, scholars began questioning the usefulness of findings that came only from observation without any attempt to find out how the community members might explain their behaviors.[11] Additionally, dialogue challenges the subjectivity of the researcher by raising questions about representations, bias, and subjectivity.[12] When engaging in dialogue, it is very difficult to ignore the lived experiences of the community members.

The third assumption is that power relationships are expressed through our lived experiences. Disparities based on sex, gender, ethnicity, socio-economic, and sexual orientation are all around us. The critical ethnographer is charged with seeking to uncover how the everyday practices of the selected locale maintain and reinforce hegemonic and oppressive forces.[13] A great deal of research has been done to explore how language choices and important cultural artifacts have been used to oppress the feminine.[14] By unmasking the hidden power structures that maintain the oppressive practices of the community, the critical ethnographer can then begin providing a means of working toward social change.

The fourth assumption is that the critical ethnographer must engage in reflexivity. Reflexivity is the practice of critically engaging with the fieldnotes and observations to ensure that what is being written up is an accurate reflection of the community practices.[15] With so much of ethnography being tied up in the writing, it is important for the critical ethnographer to take into account biases and personal viewpoints that creep into the analysis. As the author of the text, the critical ethnographer has a great deal of power to shape the discussion of the community practices. Yet we all know of the wise words of Ben Parker: "With great power comes great responsibility." Making sure to support claims through the observations from the field are vital to this process.

PROCESS

With an understanding of the underlying assumptions of critical ethnography, a greater discussion of the process of investigation can commence. The next section will explore major ideas that help guide the fieldwork done by the researcher in the selected locale.

Field Practices

It should be clear that critical ethnography is a *process* of investigation. Perhaps the easiest way to think of doing critical ethnography is to divide up the process into two major procedures that make good ethnography. The field practices, or the going into a particular locale and observing behaviors and entering into dialogue with community members, mark the first stage of critical ethnography.[16] Without being there in the field to observe and converse with the community members, it is impossible to make any substantive claims about community practices.[17] Then comes the writing phase, where the investigator will write up the observations and findings, making sure to utilize critical theory or theories that are most relevant to the study as a lens to view those findings.

Prior to going out into the field, it is important to do some background research and planning.[18] Before selecting a locale, a researcher must first think about the questions and topics that will guide the research. For example, Matthew Pustz was interested in comic book culture.[19] Pustz claimed that comic book fans were different than the ordinary American and the most important site for the comic fans was the comic book store. As such, he selected two comic book shops in his area for his investigation. In addition to thinking about the locale, it may also be helpful to find an insider in the community to serve as a guide to help negotiate entrance into what could be a closed community. A researcher could accidentally offend community members through inappropriate behaviors, comments, or questions, which is why an informant can smooth this process and prevent these mis-steps.[20]

An informant or insider from the community not only can provide background information on the group being studied, but can also make introductions that will facilitate the ethnographic dialogue that is key to this type of study. Unlike traditional anthropological studies where the researcher keeps a distance from the observed community, critical ethnography invites the researcher to participate in the community being studied.[21] This participation came about after what has been dubbed the "Crisis of Representation."[22] One of the major criticisms of traditional ethnography is that the study author speaks for the community members but may never have had any direct interactions with those community members. By being an active participant, the researcher is able to both ask questions about community practices and behaviors, as well as provide a more informed voice for the community.

Being in the field and participating in the community are very important, but it is also vital that researchers take detailed fieldnotes of their observations and interactions.[23] With fieldwork often lasting for extended periods of time, the fieldnotes are the only way to ensure that the thoughts of the researcher will be available from the first moment in the field to the last. While in the field, it is important to review and edit the fieldnotes once away from the locale and keep a separate copy in a safe location.

In any ethnographic work, the fieldwork is vital to understanding what is going on in the selected locale. It is the responsibility of the researcher to provide sufficient detail for a reader to understand what community life is like in the designated locale. Upon completing the fieldwork, the researcher must then turn the fieldnotes into a document that readers will use to gain insight into the community. The next section explores the writing-up process of critical ethnography that converts the observations and conversations into a final product.

Writing It Up

Upon leaving the field, the next phase of the critical ethnographic process is the writing up of the findings. There are multiple levels of this phase where the researcher must provide the stories of the community members as evidence for the claims being made. Initially, the researcher must analyze the fieldnotes and observations to uncover themes and power relationships.[24] Critical investigations are often concerned with representations of social structures as seen through the eyes of a disadvantaged group.[25] The critical ethnography will focus on how existing power structures are used to oppress groups and promote the hegemonic powers of others. Feminist scholars have examined the practices and structures that oppress women, as an example. The fieldnotes should help to reveal the community practices that demonstrate the taken-for-granted social hierarchies. It is through this analysis that the researcher can begin to formulate ideas about the critical theories that would best inform the findings. For example, if the fieldnotes revealed that the community objectified women through the portrayals of women in stories and representations, a feminist lens would help reveal the ramifications of these practices.

Reflexivity is a key component of critical ethnography. Through the writing process, it is important for the researcher to account for the reactions, feelings, and reflections that the researcher may have that could taint the findings.[26] New experiences, personal feelings, and inherent biases are all possible. A good researcher does not simply ignore those feelings. Instead, the researcher should begin asking questions about why those reactions, reflections, and feelings are coming up. Through careful self-examination, the researcher can provide more insight into how entrenched certain ideas have become within the community being studied.

After drafting the findings, the researcher should take them back to the community and ask if the report accurately represents community life. In the appendix of his book *Sidewalk*, Mitchell Duneier points readers to the fact that he started over after having completed a manuscript about his fieldwork when his study's primary participant pointed out that Duneier was focusing on the wrong issues.[27] While this may have been a frustration for Duneier, it does point out an important need to go back and check with community members about the accuracy of statements and the representations of community practice. The ethnographer does not want to write up "incorrect" findings. However, it is important to remember that not all feedback is valuable, since some community members will wish to portray themselves in a more favorable light.

Having discussed the underlying assumptions, field practices, and the writing-up process of critical ethnography, it is now time to turn to a piece of sample analysis. The next section will outline an actual ethnographic investigation. This sample will walk readers through the project rationale, highlight some of the fieldwork, and provide a brief analysis of the findings.

THE SELECTED LOCALE FOR SAMPLE ANALYSIS

For the comic book reader, there may be no more important locale than the local comic book shop. The local comic book shop, in general, is the place where readers can pick up new comic releases, find missing back issues, purchase comic paraphernalia, and even hang out with other comic readers and patrons. These shops become safe havens for fans to gather and participate in comic fan culture. Patrons of the comic shop are free to interact with other fans and be open in their fandom while in the shop. However, once the fan leaves the shop, that fan must hide, or at least minimize, his/her fandom in public. Thus, the local comic shops serve as a cultural clubhouse. This sample analysis utilizes the metaphor of the comic shop as a cultural clubhouse. To understand the clubhouse metaphor, I have employed ethnographic methods of participant observation at the local comic shop in a Midwestern college town over the span of several months. At the local comic shop, I had the opportunity to talk with patrons, read suggested comics, and become part of this local cultural enclave. Through the stories and actions of fans, as well as the physical space of the comic shop, I argue that the clubhouse metaphor is both appropriate and enacted through the practices of the fans.

SAMPLE ANALYSIS

There is just something special about the local comic book shop. Yet few have taken the time to explore the comic shop as an important cultural locale for the comic book fan community. In his investigation, Pustz visited his local comic shop in Ames, Iowa to see how that particular store created a "safe space" for comic fans that might shield those patrons from the views of the greater society.[28] For me, the comic shop was a bit different. From the outside, it was hard to tell what occupied the space until you were standing in front of the store. The marquee for the store was a wood board, painted dark blue and covered with drawings of several comic characters. An entrance to the store was just off to the side of the display window, which featured a few posters of major comic sagas. Putting all of this together, the comic shop exterior blended into the surrounding shops.

Whatever the exterior did to discourage entrance to the random passers-by, the interior was warm and inviting. In the middle of the store were two brand-new couches made of supple brown leather. Behind the couches, bookshelves covered one wall, and the shelves were filled with graphic novels. The tops of the bookshelves featured a mix of toy figures, some open, some in the box. This mix of toys satisfied both the collector and the little kid inside me. As I perused the graphic novel section, I found several comics I wanted to add to my collection. Since I was there to observe the interactions at the comic shop, I decided to sit down with a stack of graphic novels and begin reading.

Setting the Scene: A Brief Review of Literature

The expression of fan culture is "not meant for mass consumption," but intended to demonstrate "a high level of textual literacy within the fan group."[29] In the world of comics, the comic books "convey" the image that will illicit a response from the reader. The power of comics allows the reader to better conceptualize events on the page and how those events might be mirrored in real-world occurances.[30] When fan groups come together around an idea, they work to produce mutual meanings.[31] The creation of mutual meanings by fans stimulates the production of norms and rituals that are hallmarks of fan cultures. Comic fan culture emerges from the interactions of the fans with their beloved comics and the fans with each other, frequently occurring at the local shop.[32] As Pustz notes, it is in the comic shop that the fans can be their "true" selves.[33]

Doing Fieldwork: Discussion of Research Practices

Ethnographic research requires an investigator to become deeply immersed in the field for a sufficient time period to gain a detailed understanding of how members of a community interpret their culture.[34] The data presented in this study were collected through participant observation during fall of 2008 at a local comic shop in a small Midwestern college town, covering 30 hours of fieldwork. My investigation led me to observe interactions between store employees and store patrons. I paid particular attention to the layout of the shop to determine the cultural significance of the displayed paraphernalia. I chose to take mental notes while inside the shop and then quickly return to my office to jot down my fieldnotes. I decided not to "interview" the shop patrons because I was afraid that the sight of my notebook and the thought of my questions might prevent the honest dialogue that was possible through my own membership in the greater "club" of comic fans. Yet I did talk with shop patrons, as well as listening in on their conversations while I was visiting the shop. In my observation of comic fans, I found that the stories of the comic shop evoke the metaphor of the clubhouse, a sacred space for members only that is characterized by a unique type of talk and unique expectations of behavior.

Making Observations: The Clubhouse Metaphor

After spending so much time immersed in the comic fan community, both as a researcher and a fan, I realized that the comic shop served as an important cultural site for community membership. Fans who regularly visited their local comic shop called it "an extension of home," and a place "where we could be with those like us" and "not worry about how everybody else sees us." For shop patrons, the comic shop is a safe space, free of judgment and welcoming of the fan community—in essence, a clubhouse.

The comic book shop represents an important cultural landmark for the comic fan community. The notion of the clubhouse is fitting because it implies that creation of many American boys: A fort or stronghold that kept members safe from the outside world and outsiders at a distance. The comic book shop has been thought of as a location that is like home to the fans, but dark and daunting to the outsider. The clubhouse metaphor has four parts: a designated meeting space (fort); a secret code (passwords); a gender division ("no girls allowed"); and a member-based leadership ("no adults either").

The Fort: Meeting Place for Club Members

Initially, the clubhouse metaphor is based around a physical location for club members to gather. When kids build a clubhouse, it is typically some unused space that has been resurrected as a communal space. Treehouses and forts are commonplace for these secret clubs. The comic shop is no different.

Even though the brick façade of the shop blends in nicely with the rest of the downtown area, the inside is another matter entirely. When you walk through the front door, you come face-to-face with the new-release wall, filled with the latest issues of comics, and the overstock bins, boxes filled with older issues of comics. Directly in front of you is the cash register and service desk. There are display cases surrounding the register area, showing toys and comics of value. One of the most interesting things about the service desk is the pull files. Regular patrons can have certain comic titles set aside by the staff. Then, at their own convenience, the customers can stop in and pick up these titles without having to hunt through the new issues. While the outside of the shop is not necessarily inviting, the interior is a place where community members are rewarded for their patronage through special services like the pull lists.

To the left of the cash register is the lounge area. The couches and coffee table invite patrons to sit, read comics, talk with other patrons, and otherwise relax in the store. Having visited the lounge on several occasions, I can tell you that the couches make great places to sit and read comics.

Behind the lounge and the cash register is the gaming area, where five folding tables have been set up to allow players to engage in games of *Magic: The Gathering* at any time. On every occasion I was in the store, at least one of the tables was being used to play. When not being used to play card games, the tables are also used as study areas. On one visit, a young woman sat at the back corner, working on a laptop. At the other end of that table, a man was eating his takeout Chinese food and reading an article. The dual use of the space as a study area and a gaming arena was fascinating. Yet there is no better example of the duality of group membership than the young man who was sitting on the couch reading a comic with his backpack within arm's reach. As he packed up his comics to leave the store, he also put the Greek tragedy that was hidden beneath his comic back in his bag.

The comic shop is used as a place for comic fan community members to frequent. While comic fandom is a component for seamless entry, the space is used as a commercial site, a lounge, a gaming hang-out, and a study hall. The uses of the clubhouse fit the needs of the club members.

Password, Please: The Talk of the Comic Fan Community

Often, the clubhouse is not secret per se. Community members can see the space marked off by the club. However, to gain access to the clubhouse, individuals must prove their membership. The easiest example of this is to speak the language of the club, or to know the secret code words. To fit in, community members must be able to talk the talk of the group.

In a comic shop, a clear way to identify community members from non-community members is to ask them about comics. For example, my visits to the local comic shop coincided with the release of the graphic novels chronicling the death of Captain America. As I was reading my copy, Jay, a visitor to the store, tapped me on the shoulder and asked about the book.

> "Is that the one where Captain America dies?"
> "Yeah."
> "How do you feel about it? I'm a bit conflicted. I never really cared for Cap before, but now that he's gone, I miss him. And Bucky just can't fill Cap's boots."
> "For sure. I liked it better when Cap only had a shield. Bucky carrying a gun just isn't the same."

For those who are fans of Captain America, the terminology used in this exchange is commonplace. "Cap" is short for Captain America and is used by readers as a sign of familiarity with the character. In the story arc, Captain America's one-time side-kick, Bucky, has grown up and assumed the mantle of Captain America. Those fans that are familiar with the saga still refer to Steve Rogers as Captain America and Bucky as the side-kick.

The talk of the fan communities create an inclusive–exclusive dynamic, with in-group members being privy to the talk of the community. To outsiders, the talk is jargon heavy and nearly incomprehensible. The talk of the fans at the comic shop demonstrates a unique form of secret code meant for group members only. While the sign on the comic shop window says "Open," the talk of the shop says "Members Only."

No Girls Allowed: A Gendered Division at the Comic Shop

Thinking back to those secret clubs children would form, gender was one of the lines demarcating the ability to become a member of the group. For boys, they were very vocal in their feelings toward female membership. Most depictions of the boyhood fort or clubhouse had the "No Girls Allowed" sign visibly displayed for all to see. Moving this metaphor into the realm of comic shops, there is a similar sentiment through the practices of the community members.

Walking into the comic book shop, you are greeted by a wall of newly released comics on one side of the room and comic character posters on the other. Jeffery Brown notes that most comic buyers are male.[35] The resulting comics do prominently include women, yet the women that appear in the comic book pages are drawn with heaving bust lines and impossibly narrow waists. Much like the criticism of the Barbie doll for creating an impossible image of womanhood, comics regularly feature women as sex symbols for the male fantasy.[36]

While times may be changing, the comic shop is still a boys' club. Looking back at the story of the couple coming into the shop that opened this chapter, it is easy to feel the woman's nervousness at being in the comic shop. She said that she didn't "belong in here" and she didn't want to come into the shop. Her words gave voice to the sentiment that the shop was really a space for the predominantly male readers of the comics. Yet her body language was even more telling than her words. She was dragged into the shop by her boyfriend as if to say she would rather wait on the street than enter the shop. When he finally stopped pulling her along, she positioned herself so that his body could serve as a shield between her and the rest of the shop patrons. She did not want to see the shop and clearly did not wish to be seen by those in the shop. Factoring this example with there being so few other women entering the shop and the idea of a boys' clubhouse is not a stretch of the imagination. Both the comics themselves and the patronage of the shop make this a "boys-only" zone, symbolically saying "no girls allowed."

No "Adults" Either: Employees as Community Members

Perhaps the hallmark of the childhood clubhouse is that there are no outsiders involved in the clubhouse. There are no teachers or parents to oversee what goes on. Instead, it is just the children together as club members. Looking at the comic shop, the employees are unlike traditional employees. They are likely to be mistaken for patrons unless you pay close attention, thus demonstrating the lack of traditional authority figures, or adults, to go with this metaphor.

When I entered the shop, an employee behind the counter was talking with three customers about a recent story arc in the Marvel Ultimates universe. As they were talking, a second employee came out of the back storage room with boxes of new comics and began stocking the displays. Once the conversations were completed, the only ones left in the shop were the two employees, a group of four gamers playing *Magic*, and me. As I browsed the graphic novels, the first employee told the second employee to "sit down and take a break. There's nobody here." This was a bit of a shocker to hear, since I was standing within ten feet of the register. And the gamers were loudly discussing each other's gameplay. Yet the second employee thought nothing of it, sitting down on the couch with a couple of comics. He immediately began reading his chosen comics.

If I hadn't seen the employee unpacking boxes earlier, I would have assumed that he was just another patron. The employees do not wear uniforms. The two that were working this day were wearing comfortable clothing. Subsequent visits to the comic shop revealed more of this laid-back work environment for the employees. The comic shop implicitly promoted a work environment where the employees served a dual role as employee and as patron. In the role of employee, they maintained the store, displayed merchandise, answered questions, and filled orders. Yet the more interesting role would be that of patron. The employees played the games other patrons played. They read comics during their shifts. And they lounged on the couches as any other patron might. In fact, there were times where it was difficult to tell who was working at the store and who was just hanging out.

Unlike more traditional organizations, the fan community of the comic shop is self-organized insofar as the employees are also patrons. Their workplace is their play space and their play space is their workplace. Thus, the notion of self-governance or group-member leadership is attained.

Leaving the Shop: Concluding Thoughts

There is perhaps no more important location for the comic book fan than the local comic shop. With so many outsiders still considering comics to be for kids, comic fans have tried to gather together in places that foster, not hinder, fan community development. As the focal point of this effort, the comic shop has become a cultural clubhouse, providing safety and security for the comic fans. These safe havens allow group members to talk about, read, and enjoy comics. While the clubhouse metaphor may have issues with gender and access, for group members, it is a celebrated space of both commerce and community.

Critical ethnography is a process of observation where a researcher will go into the field, study the everyday practices of community members, and analyze how those practices maintain societal power relationships. To conduct this type of research, it is assumed that the researcher will go into the field, engage in dialogue with the community members, explore how the power relationships are expressed, and reflexively consider the accuracy of the observations. Since critical ethnography involves fieldwork, it is important to find the key location for the group being studied. I have argued that the comic shop is one such location for comic fans. Upon completion of the fieldwork, the next step is writing up the findings, paying particular attention to the stories of community members. It is our stories that shed light on what we find important and valuable in the groups with which we are associated. Through careful consideration, we can peel back the layers of the fan culture in order to understand how the relationships in and among group members establish and maintain power. The critical ethnographer will uncover the power disparity and offer comment about how the power relationships are maintained or could be challenged.

NOTES

1. Colleen Varcoe, "Abuse Obscured: An Ethnographic Account of Emergency Nursing in Relation to Violence Against Women," *Canadian Journal of Nursing Research* 32 (4) (2001): 98.
2. Jim Thomas, *Doing Critical Ethnography* (Newbury Park: Sage, 1993), 3–4.
3. James Clifford, "Introduction: Partial Truths," in *Writing Culture: The Poetics and Politics of Ethnography*, ed. J. Clifford and G.E. Marcus (Berkeley: University of California Press, 1986), 2.
4. Dwight Conquergood, "Rethinking Ethnography: Toward a Critical Cultural Politics," *Communication Monographs* 58 (1) (1991): 179.
5. Ibid., 179.
6. Jim Thomas, "Musing on Critical Ethnography, Meanings, and Symbolic Violence," in *Expressions of Ethnography: Novel Approaches to Qualitative Methods*, ed. R.P. Clair (New York: State University of New York Press, 2003), 45.
7. Ibid., 46.
8. George E. Marcus, "Contemporary Problems in Ethnography in the Modern World System," in *Writing Culture: The Poetics and Politics of Ethnography* ed. J. Clifford and G.E. Marcus (Berkeley: University of California Press, 1986), 172.
9. Conquergood, "Rethinking Ethnography," 180.
10. D. Soyini Madison, *Critical Ethnography: Methods, Ethics, and Performance* (Thousand Oaks, CA: Sage, 2005), 8.
11. Conquergood, "Rethinking Ethnography," 179.
12. Madison, *Critical Ethnography*, 9.
13. Thomas, *Doing Critical Ethnography*, 4.
14. There are perhaps too many examples of feminist ethnography to name, but some books that provide a wealth of voices include Kamala Visweswaran's *Fictions of Feminist Ethnography* (Minneapolis: University of Minnesota Press, 1994); Ruth Behar and Deborah A. Gordon, eds. *Women: Writing Culture* (Albany:

State University of New York Press, 1995); and Sherna Berger Gluck and Daphne Patai, eds., *Women's Words: The Feminist Practice of Oral History* (New York: Routledge, 1991).

15. Conquergood, "Rethinking Ethnography," 191.
16. John Van Maanen, *Tales of the Field: On Writing Ethnography* (Chicago: University of Chicago Press, 1988), 14.
17. It should be noted here that any study involving human participants will require some form of institutional approval, normally in the form of Institutional Review Board (IRB) approval. IRB approval ensures that you do no harm to your participants and that your research is based in sound scholarship and field practices. The actual IRB process will vary from institution to institution, so be sure to contact your IRB personnel prior to going into the field.
18. Thomas, *Doing Critical Ethnography*, 34.
19. Matthew Pustz, *Comic Book Culture: Fanboys and True Believers* (Jackson, MS: University Press of Mississippi, 1999), ix.
20. Harry F. Wolcott, *The Art of Fieldwork* (2nd ed.) (Walnut Creek, CA: AltaMira Press, 2005): 80.
21. Conquergood, "Rethinking Ethnography," 191.
22. Clifford, "Introduction," 8.
23. Thomas, *Doing Critical Ethnography*, 39.
24. Ibid., 43.
25. Van Maanen, *Tales of the Field*, 128.
26. Wolcott, *The Art of Fieldwork*, 87.
27. Mitchell Duneier, *Sidewalk* (New York: Farrar, Straus, and Giroux, 1999), 333.
28. Pustz, *Comic Book Culture*, 3.
29. Amber Davisson and Paul Booth, "Reconceptualizing the Communication and Agency in Fan Activity: A Proposal for a Projected Interactivity Model for Fan Studies," *Texas Speech Communication Journal* 32 (1) (1997): 36.
30. Scott McCloud, *Understanding Comics: The Invisible Art* (New York: HarperPerennial, 1993), 9.
31. Christine Scondari, "Resistance Re-examined: Gender, Fan Practices, and Science Fiction Television," *Popular Communication* 1 (2) (2003): 111.
32. Jeffrey A. Brown, "Comic Book Fandom and Cultural Capital," *Journal of Popular Culture* 30 (4) (1997): 13.
33. Pustz, *Comic Book Culture*, 6.
34. Nick Trujillo, "Interpreting (the Work and the Talk of) Baseball: Perspectives on Ballpark Culture," *Western Journal of Communication* 56 (4) (1992): 352.
35. Brown, "Comic Book Fandom and Cultural Capital," 16.
36. Pustz, *Comic Book Culture*, 8.

SELECTED BIBLIOGRAPHY

Brown, Jeffrey A. "Comic Book Fandom and Cultural Capital." *Journal of Popular Culture* 30 (4) (1997): 13–31.

Clifford, James. "Introduction: Partial Truths." In *Writing Culture: The Poetics and Politics of Ethnography*, edited by James Clifford and George E. Marcus, 1–26. Berkeley: University of California Press, 1986.

Conquergood, Dwight. "Rethinking Ethnography: Toward a Critical Cultural Politics." *Communication Monographs* 58 (1) (1991): 180–194.

Davisson, Amber and Paul Booth. "Reconceptualizing the Communication and Agency in Fan Activity: A Proposal for a Projected Interactivity Model for Fan Studies." *Texas Speech Communication Journal* 32 (1) (1997): 33–43.

Duneier, Mitchell. *Sidewalk*. New York: Farrar, Straus, and Giroux, 1999.

Madison, D. Soyini. *Critical Ethnography: Methods, Ethics, and Performance*. Thousand Oaks, CA: Sage, 2005.

Marcus, George E. "Contemporary Problems in Ethnography in the Modern World System." In *Writing Culture: The Poetics and Politics of Ethnography*, edited by James Clifford and George E. Marcus, 165–193. Berkeley: University of California Press, 1986.

McCloud, Scott. *Understanding Comics: The Invisible Art*. New York: HarperPerennial, 1993.

Pustz, Matthew. *Comic Book Culture: Fanboys and True Believers*. Jackson, MS: University Press of Mississippi, 1999.

Scondari, Christine. "Resistance Re-examined: Gender, Fan Practices, and Science Fiction Television." *Popular Communication* 1 (2) (2003): 111–130.

Thomas, Jim. *Doing Critical Ethnography*. Newbury Park: Sage, 1993.

Thomas, Jim. "Musing on Critical Ethnography, Meaning, and Symbolic Violence." In *Expressions of Ethnography: Novel Approaches to Qualitative Methods*, edited by R.P. Clair, 45–54. New York: State University of New York Press, 2003.

Trujillo, Nick. "Interpreting (the Work and the Talk of) Baseball: Perspectives on Ballpark Culture." *Western Journal of Communication* 56 (4) (1992): 350–371.

Van Maanen, John. *Tales of the Field: On Writing Ethnography.* Chicago: University of Chicago Press, 1988.

Varcoe, Colleen. "Abuse Obscured: An Ethnographic Account of Emergency Nursing in Relation to Violence Against Women." *Canadian Journal of Nursing Research* 32 (4) (2001): 95–115.

Wolcott, Harry F. *The Art of Fieldwork* (2nd edn.). Walnut Creak, CA: AltaMira Press, 2005.

INDEX

Page numbers in **bold** denote figures.

CPSIA information can be obtained
at www.ICGtesting.com
Printed in the USA
FFOW01n0941031214
9193FF